FRENCH ROOTS IN THE ILLINOIS COUNTRY

FRENCH ROOTS IN THE ILLINOIS COUNTRY

The Mississippi Frontier in Colonial Times

Carl J. Ekberg

University of Illinois Press
Urbana and Chicago

Publication of this book was supported by a grant from Illinois State University.

This book is printed on acid-free paper.

Library of Congress Cataloging-in-Publication Data
Ekberg, Carl J.
French roots in the Illinois country : the Mississippi frontier in
colonial times / Carl J. Ekberg.
p.   cm.
Includes bibliographical references and index.
ISBN 0-252-02364-1 (alk. paper)
1. Illinois—History—To 1778.
2. Illinois—History—1778–1865.
3. Mississippi River Valley—History—To 1803.
4. French Americans—Illinois—History.
5. Land settlement—Illinois—History.
I. Title.
F544.E38   1998
977.3'03—dc21   97-486ᴦ
CIP

For Gloria, Andrew, and Hannah

Contents

Maps and Plans

Illustrations

Acknowledgments

David Buisseret, formerly of the Newberry Library and now at the University of Texas, Arlington, first suggested that I write about the land and the people of the Illinois Country. He was confident that one could start with the system of land usage in the region and proceed to re-create the colonial culture from the ground up. David's encouragement led to the writing of this book, as did Herbert H. Rowen's insistence that I read Marc Bloch's classic study of rural France when I studied under Rowen at Rutgers University.

The staffs at many archives have helped me to find obscure documents and maps pertaining to my research. These depositories include the Service Historique de la Marine at the Château de Vincennes; the Archives Nationales d'Outre Mer in Aix-en-Province; the Canadian National Archives in Ottawa; the Chicago Historical Society; the Huntington Library in San Marino, California; the Louisiana State Museum in New Orleans; and the Missouri Historical Society in St. Louis. Particular individuals stand out for their willingness to spend time helping me to find relevant books and manuscripts. I wish especially to thank Jeanette Basler, county clerk in Ste. Genevieve and custodian of the archives there; Norman Brown of the Missouri Land Surveys, Rolla; Richard Day of the University of Vincennes, Indiana; John Hoffman of the Illinois Historical Survey in Urbana; Tom Krasean at the Indiana Historical Society in Indianapolis, who also bought me lunch and introduced me to the Indiana State Archives; Alfred Lemmon of the Historic New Orleans Collection; Bill Meneray of the Tulane University Archives; Sally K. Reeves, director of the New Orleans Notarial Archives; Wayne C. Temple and the late Lowell Volkel of the Illinois State Archives, Springfield; and Joan Winters of the Milner Library at Illinois State University.

I also wish to express my gratitude to persons who expended valuable time and effort to provide me with copies of documents that related directly to my research. U.S. Appeals Court judge Morris S. Arnold of Little Rock, the master of Arkansas colonial history, shared rare documents and maps pertaining to Arkansas Post. Mary Antoine de Julio, the reigning authority on early Prairie du Chien, Wisconsin, tracked down obscure documents in the Crawford County Courthouse. William D. Reeves of New Orleans, a connoisseur of early parish records in Louisiana, provided copies of documents from Pointe Coupée that I never would have discovered on my own.

Many experts in different fields have read all or parts of this book in various stages of its completion, and each has contributed to it in different ways: David Buisseret, William E. Foley of Central Missouri State University, Cornelius J. Jaenen of the University of Ottawa, Robert McColley of the University of Illinois, Anton J. Pregaldin of St. Louis, master genealogist of the Illinois Country, and William D. Walters of Illinois State University. Elizabeth Perkins of Centre College provided some useful criticisms of my conclusions about American frontier violence. Various members of the Society for French Colonial Studies and the Center for French Colonial History have listened to my presentations on topics included in this study and have offered invaluable suggestions.

Christine and Daniel Beveraggi in Paris, Ann and Rod Johnson in St. Louis, and Bernie and Vion Schram in Ste. Genevieve offered me the hospitality of their homes while I pursued research in neighboring archives; and they did this with good humor while being quite mystified about the significance of my work.

Paul T. Schollaert and Robert D. Young, Illinois State University's dean of the College of Arts and Sciences and acting dean of the Graduate School, respectively, supported my work with summer research grants and helped to provide the subvention necessary to produce this book in its present form. John Freed, chair of the Department of History at Illinois State University, also provided funds to assist this publication; moreover, as a medievalist, John was always confident that my research on open-field agriculture in colonial Illinois was worthwhile, and he offered consistent encouragement. Bruce Bethell, copyeditor at the University of Illinois Press, made innumerable stylistic improvements in the text, for which I thank him. I am also grateful to Hannah Ekberg, Richard Urban, and Cherie Valentine, who provided invaluable help in compiling the index.

Portions of chapter 6 previously appeared as "The Flour Trade in French Colonial Louisiana," *Louisiana History* 37 (Summer 1996): 261–82; portions of the conclusion appeared as "Agriculture, Mentalités, and Violence on the American Frontier," *Illinois Historical Journal* 88 (Summer 1995): 101–16. I am grateful to the Louisiana Historical Association and the Illinois Historical Society for granting permission to use these materials.

Abbreviations of Source Collections

AAE   Archives des Affaires Étrangères. Paris, France.

AGI   Archivo de Indias. Seville, Spain.

ANC   Archives Nationales, Coloniales. Paris, France.

ASP, PL   *American State Papers, Public Lands.* 9 vols. Washington, D.C.: U.S. Government Printing Office, 1832–61.

BN   Bibliothèque Nationale. Paris, France.

CP   Clarence W. Alvord, ed. *The Critical Period, 1763–1765.* Collections of the Illinois State Historical Library, vol. 10. Springfield: Illinois State Historical Library, 1915.

CR   Clarence W. Alvord, ed. *Cahokia Records, 1778–1790.* Collections of the Illinois State Historical Library, vol. 2. Springfield: Illinois State Historical Library, 1907.

HMLO   Loudoun Collection, Huntington Library Manuscripts. San Marino, California.

IHS   Indiana Historical Society Archives, Indiana Historical Society. Indianapolis, Indiana.

ISA   Illinois State Archives. Springfield, Illinois.

ISL   Indiana State Library. Indianapolis, Indiana.

JR   Reuben G. Thwaites, ed. *The Jesuit Relations and Allied Documents.* 43 vols. Cleveland: Burrows Brothers, 1896–1904.

KM   Kaskaskia Manuscripts. Randolph County Courthouse. Chester, Illinois.

KR   Clarence W. Alvord, ed. *Kaskaskia Records, 1778–1790.* Collections of the Illinois State Historical Library, vol. 5. Springfield: Illinois State Historical Library, 1915.

MHS   Missouri Historical Society Archives. Missouri Historical Society. St. Louis, Missouri.

NR   Clarence W. Alvord and Clarence E. Carter, eds. *The New Regime,*
            1765–1767. Collections of the Illinois State Historical Library, vol.
            11. Springfield: Illinois State Historical Library, 1916.
PC   Papeles Procedentes de Cuba, in AGI.
SGA   Ste. Genevieve Archives. Microfilm in MHS.
SHA   Service Historique de l'Armée. Château de Vincennes, France.
SMV   Lawrence Kinnaird, ed. *Spain in the Mississippi Valley, 1765–1794.*
            American Historical Association Report for 1945. 4 vols. Wash-
            ington, D.C.: U.S. Government Printing Office, 1946.
SRM   Louis Houck, ed. *The Spanish Regime in Missouri: A Collection of*
            Documents and Papers relating to Upper Louisiana. 2 vols. Chicago:
            R. R. Donnelly and Sons, 1909.
TP   Clarence W. Alvord and Clarence E. Carter, eds. *Trade and Poli-*
            tics, 1767–1769. Collections of the Illinois State Historical Library,
            vol. 16. Springfield: Illinois State Historical Library, 1921.
VOC   Margaret K. Brown and Lawrie C. Dean, eds. *The Village of*
            Chartres in Colonial Illinois, 1720–1765. New Orleans: Polyanthos
            Press, 1977.

FRENCH ROOTS IN THE ILLINOIS COUNTRY

Eastern North America in the Eighteenth Century

In the settlement of America we have to observe how European life entered the continent, and how America modified and developed that life and reacted on Europe. Our early history is the study of European germs developing in an American environment.
—Frederick Jackson Turner

INTRODUCTION

The Illinois Country was a loosely defined region of the middle Mississippi Valley, parts of which were claimed at various times during the eighteenth century by France, Great Britain, Spain, and the United States. This study is devoted largely to *French* colonial history, however, for the practices and attitudes analyzed herein derived overwhelmingly from France—as well as from the geography and climate of the region itself. At the end of the French regime in North America (1763), the Illinois Country boasted the largest concentration of French subjects outside the St. Lawrence Valley to the north and the New Orleans area to the south. Ironically, a recent thousand-page tome on the history of French colonization, written by a distinguished French authority on the subject, contains no discussion of the Illinois Country.[1] Gregory H. Nobles's new volume, *American Frontiers: Cultural Encounters and the Continental Conquest,* despite its title, uses the Illinois Country in an old way, merely as a stage for the exploits of George Rogers Clark during the American Revolution.[2]

The Illinois Country is best known through Clarence W. Alvord's classic study *The Illinois Country, 1673–1818,*[3] which was the first volume in the official centennial history of the state of Illinois. Alvord readily acknowledged that the colonial Illinois Country bore "little resemblance to the present state,"[4] but because his task was to celebrate the state's centennial, he confined his study largely to the region delineated by modern state boundaries. For example, the eastern portion of present-day Missouri, which in the eighteenth century was an integral part of the Illinois Country, appears only tangentially in Alvord's study. But the mighty river that today separates Illinois from Missouri was in colonial times a geographical feature that united rather than divided, and the French Creole communities on the two sides of the Mississippi were bonded by the river, as well as by shared blood, language, religion, and customs. This study, which is not circumscribed by modern political boundaries, subsumes the Illinois Country on both sides of the river as a single, cohesive entity. Between 1700 and 1750 this region of the middle Mississippi Valley underwent a metamorphosis greater than any it had seen since the end of the Pleistocene era. The natural landscape of the Mississippi's floodplain was transformed into an array of villages, agricultural fields, and pasturelands. This study is not about voyageurs and the fur trade, as important as those topics are.[5] St. Charles and Peoria, for example, whose economies were based almost entirely on the fur trade, are not dealt with. Rather, I have focused on the habitants, their families, and their slaves—how these groups settled the land, worked the fields, and marketed their agricultural products.

The pattern of land usage, settlement, and agriculture that developed in the eighteenth-century Illinois Country was unique for French colonial America and descended from traditional rural practices in northern France. Land usage was basically tripartite, consisting of compact villages, open-field plowlands, and communal pasturing areas. The elongated strips of farmland in the Illinois Country, which superficially resembled the familiar ribbon farms in the St. Lawrence River valley, in fact served very different purposes. French Canadian ribbon farms were independent, multipurpose plots, each containing residence, kitchen garden, outbuildings, grain fields, orchard, and woodlot. Agricultural strips in the Illinois Country, on the other hand, were always plowlands, which were clustered together in a system of open-field agriculture; they did not contain residences or outbuildings. This configuration of land usage in colonial Illinois was unique for eighteenth-century North America and had important ramifications for the organization of Creole society in the Mississippi Valley and for the *mentalités*[6] of the region's inhabitants.

Land usage and agriculture in colonial Illinois bore striking resemblances to traditional patterns in France, but agricultural labor had different bases in the two regions. African slaves were introduced to the Illinois Country via the Mississippi River soon after the founding of New Orleans in 1718, and before long they constituted a significant portion of the labor force. By the mid-eighteenth century black slaves composed one-third of the population in colonial Illinois, which was a larger percentage than in the American South on the eve of the Civil War. What little is known about African American slavery in the Illinois Country indicates that the institution there was quite unlike that in the better-known American South. This study will examine how black slaves in colonial Illinois were governed by French colonial legal codes and regional practices and how slaves and habitants together worked the first extensive grain fields of the American Midwest.

After the founding of New Orleans, administrative jurisdictions were juggled in French North America, and the Illinois Country was formally incorporated into the colony of Louisiana. Political power flowed from Europe to New Orleans and then to the Illinois Country, which for French administrators was often synonymous with Upper Louisiana. In addition to serving as the capital of Louisiana, New Orleans functioned as the colony's commercial metropole. New Orleans is today the great entrepôt for the American grain trade, but the commercial connection between the grain fields of the Midwest and this seaport began in the 1720s under the French regime in Louisiana. The significance of the colonial flour trade down the Mississippi to New Orleans has been remarked before,[7] but this topic receives its first detailed examination in the following study.

The unique patterns of settlement, land usage, and agriculture that developed in the Illinois Country during the early eighteenth century had important consequences for the culture and *mentalités* of the Creole inhabitants of the region. Authorities on communal agriculture have often discussed how such a system impacted societal mores and mental structures,[8] although this has never been attempted for the Illinois Country. This impact is more easily studied because French Creole society in the Mississippi Valley, which had developed in near isolation for more than a half-century, was confronted by a massive influx of Anglo-Americans toward the end of the eighteenth century. Americans occupied the land differently, practiced agriculture differently, and thought differently, and the abrupt juxtaposition of their society to the French Creole society that preceded it in the Illinois Country casts their profound differences into sharp relief. This study concludes with an examination of the radically different *mentalités*—French Creole and Anglo-American—that confronted each other in the Illinois Country at the close of the colonial era.

A final explanatory note: although by the mid-eighteenth century many Illinois habitants had some component of Indian blood coursing in their veins, this study does not deal specifically with American Indians, with the métis population as a unique cultural entity, or with race relations in general. Fine studies already exist on these topics.[9]

All the farms in Canada stand separate from one another, so that each farmer has his possessions entirely separate from those of his neighbor.
—Peter Kalm, *Travels in North America*

1 French Longlots in North America

FRENCH CANADA

French Canadian families lived separately, as Peter Kalm, a Swedish (born an ethnic Finn) traveler and diarist, observed; each family settled independently on its own elongated parcel of land.[1] The distinctive longlots of the St. Lawrence River valley eventually cast their progeny across much of the continent, and today longlots of French Canadian extraction are features of North American geography that may be seen from Quebec to Texas and from Illinois to Ontario.[2] Scholars have thoroughly studied longlots in some regions where they occur, such as the St. Lawrence Valley; in other areas—Illinois, for example—they are little known.[3] The purpose of this introductory chapter is to provide a context for examining settlement patterns in the Illinois Country by presenting an overview of French longlots throughout North America. Terry G. Jordan, a cultural geographer, studied longlots in early Texas and published his findings in one of the rare works devoted to this cadastral feature within the United States.[4] Jordan loosely defined a longlot as any rectangular parcel of land whose depth was at least three times its width.[5] My study embraces a wide assortment of longlots from many regions of North America that were influenced by French surveying practices during the seventeenth and eighteenth centuries, but I define a longlot more restrictively than Jordan did, setting the minimum width-to-length ratio at 1:10.

The longlot as a basis for rural or village settlement patterns is ancient, perhaps dating back as far as Mesopotamian civilization, but the historical antecedents to longlots in the Illinois Country stem from medieval Europe. Rectilinear longlots associated with distinct geographical features, either natural or artificial—streams, dikes, canals, forests, or roadways—developed in many regions of Europe during the Middle Ages. Linear settlements, consisting of rows of longlots, were common in the German-speaking world and have been much studied by German scholars.[6] German nomenclature is therefore often applied to linear villages composed of longlots: *Straßendörfer* ("street villages"), *Waldhufendörfer* ("forest longlot villages"), *Flußhufendörfer* (riverain villages), and so forth, according to the geographical features toward which the villages were oriented. This settlement pattern also occurred in various areas of northern France, where it is known variously as *en arête de poisson* (herringbone), *village-route* (street-village), or *hameau-allongé* (string town). Agriculturists ordinarily built their homes at the front of these longlots facing the local artery of transportation, and the arable lands, orchards, woodlots, and so forth stretched out behind the residential plot. This type of land usage created linear, or string-town, settlements, where neighbors lived within hailing distance of each other but not in compact, nucleated villages; this pattern was neither substantially dispersed nor tightly grouped. A well-known document from twelfth-century lower Germany specifies longlots 720 rods long and 30 rods wide, which meant that neighbors lived roughly 500 feet apart.[7] French settlers in various regions of North America created similar herringbone assemblages of longlots, an excellent example being early nineteenth-century settlement along the Fox River near the head of Green Bay.[8]

A totally distinct variety of longlot developed across the northern European plain in early medieval times. Long, narrow parcels known as furlong fields in English, *champs allongés* in French, and *Langstreifenfluren* in German evolved as features of arable cultivation. These agricultural longlots and the longlots of the string-town communities had different origins, for the former developed as products of the tillage practiced on them rather than as features of a settlement or cadastral pattern. In some places in Europe these two distinct varieties of longlot existed side by side in the same community, with one variety serving as residential plots and the other as plowlands.[9] In his classic study of French rural life, Marc Bloch described the agricultural longlots that he studied in northern France: "Each of them extended in the

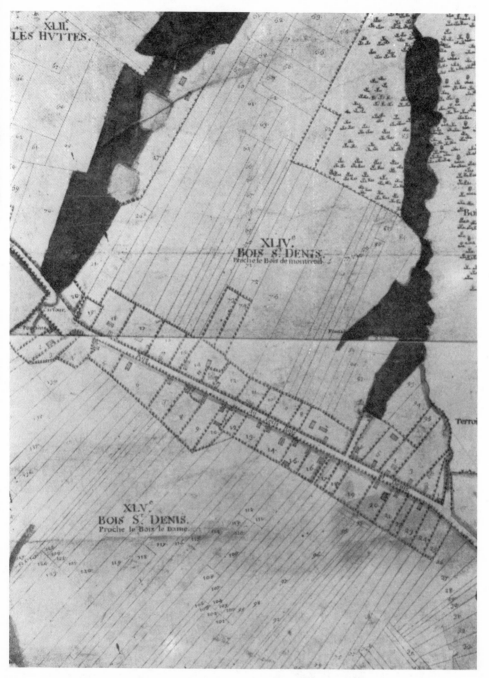

Herringbone (*en arête de poisson*) settlement pattern from medieval France. Notice the distinction between the residential plots and the agricultural fields. Reproduced from Marc Bloch, *Les Caractères originaux de l'histoire rurale de France,* plate 1.

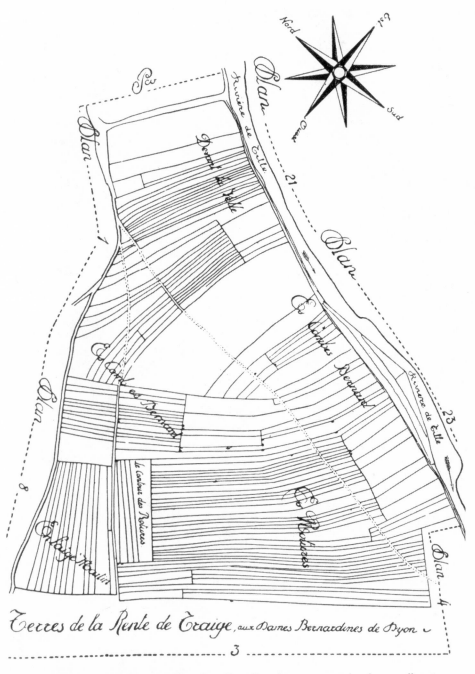

Plowlands, medieval France. These bundles of longlots represent the *champs allongés* of open-field agriculture. Reproduced from Marc Bloch, *Les Caractères originaux de l'histoire rurale de France,* plate 6.

same direction as the furrows. Their widths, which were perpendicular to this axis, were narrow, however, being in many cases only one-twentieth of the lengths. Sometimes the furrows extended for a hundred meters or more."[10]

Longlots defined by the agriculture practiced on them were usually devoted to cereal-grain production and were not cluttered with dwellings or outbuildings. Individually owned parcels were grouped in clusters—*faisceaux* or *quartiers* in France and furlongs in England (*furlong* was used for both linear and superficial measurements)—which in turn were assembled in one field. With no fencing between the strips, these agricultural longlots were part of a system of open-field agriculture that I discuss in this study. It has been observed that there is a curious, superficial resemblance between the "ribbon-like farms" of settlement longlots in New France and "the 'stripes' of an English manor of the thirteenth century."[11] The essential point here is that agricultural longlots, with their characteristic plow "stripes," had no *intrinsic* relationship to the multipurpose cadastral longlots that are the principal topic of this chapter.

NEW FRANCE

The best-known longlots in North America are those that extended back from banks of the St. Lawrence River between Quebec City and Montreal. Running from the river's edge back into the hinterland, those Canadian longlots are eye-catching when represented on a map and have become the most familiar aspect of human geography for New France. A typical French Canadian longlot along the St. Lawrence River contained the following, proceeding roughly from front to back: residence, barn, barnyard, arable fields, pasture, and woodlot.[12]

A little-known fact, however, is that French longlots of some variety appeared everywhere in North America where there was the least bit of French influence, from the St. Lawrence Valley westward to Michilimackinac and to the Detroit region, where longlots proliferated up and down the Detroit River and all its tributaries. They then appeared further westward at Green Bay and Prairie du Chien (now in Wisconsin) and all the way to the Red River of the north; vestiges of longlots are easily discernible on modern plat maps of the city of Winnipeg. Longlots of French derivation then extended southward to the Illinois Country (including St. Louis) and to Lower Louisiana, where they were first laid off along the Mississippi and then continued along the banks of smaller rivers and bayous. These Louisiana longlots were distinctly depicted on French maps as early as the 1720s, shortly after the founding of New Orleans. Finally, in the opinion of Terry Jordan, longlots of French ex-

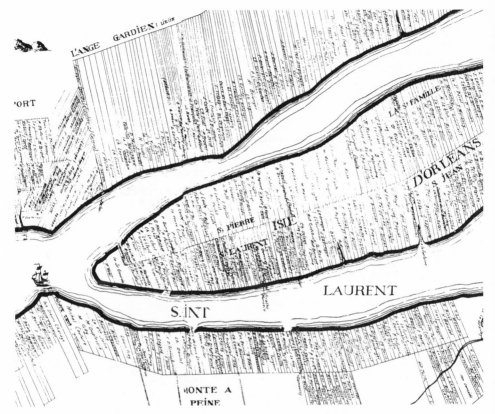

The familiar longlots of the St. Lawrence Valley from 1709. Each longlot comprised an independent ribbon farm. Original located in the Ministère des Terres et Forêts de Québec.

traction were conveyed by some circuitous route all the way to Texas, where they became remarkably widespread, given the sporadic and tangential nature of the French presence in that region.[13]

Familiar only to colonial specialists are the longlots that characterized a number of New England settlements, including the thoroughly studied towns of Sudbury and Rowley, Massachusetts.[14] At Rowley, for which we have a detailed map from the early nineteenth century, one section of the town developed in the classic style of a linear settlement extending along a roadway, that is, a *Straßendorf*.[15] Long rectilinear lots faced the road, with residences pushed up toward the front and the agricultural fields laid out behind; the residential portions of the longlots were clearly delineated on the map. The pattern at Rowley was curiously like that of Louisiana except that the geographical feature of orientation was a road instead of a river or bayou. This similarity may have stemmed in part from some common European ancestor, from recollections among both French and English colonists about how things had been done in the Old World, but there is no evidence that French Canadian strip farms were modeled after those in New England.[16]

Max Derruau, a cultural geographer, argued that longlots established at Beauport in the mid-1630s were the first such in the St. Lawrence Valley and that the cadastral pattern there derived directly from real estate contracts drafted in le Perche, a small French province tucked in between Normandy to the north and Maine to the south.[17] The settlement pattern in le Perche, Derruau maintained, consisted of a mixture of *Straßendörfer* and *Waldhu‐ fendörfer*. That is, longlots extended between an arterial roadway and the edge of a forest, and they provided the model for the first rectilinear longlots in the St. Lawrence Valley, although in Canada a river served in place of a road‐ way. The noted French Canadian historian Marcel Trudel took Derruau to task for arguing that the first Canadian longlots originated only in 1637 and that they derived from *villages-rues* models in le Perche. Trudel pointed out that longlots laid out perpendicular to the St. Lawrence River first appeared on the outskirts of Quebec City in 1635 and that there is no evidence that this configuration derived from cultural baggage carried to the St. Lawrence Valley from Europe.[18] It does not seem unreasonable to assume, however, that an‐ cient European cadastral patterns played some role in the development of longlots along the St. Lawrence River, even if the first of these did not derive specifically from models in le Perche, as Derruau maintained.

Derruau did not deny that the particular geography of the St. Lawrence Valley had a direct bearing on the settlement pattern that emerged near Que‐ bec City by the mid-seventeenth century—namely, that long, narrow plots facing the river were a practical manner of apportioning property in the St. Lawrence Valley. Richard C. Harris, also a cultural geographer, adduced five purely environmental reasons for the location and shape of Canadian longlots:[19] (1) access for the largest number of habitants to the main artery of transportation, the river; (2) residence on one's own land, yet convenient prox‐ imity to one's neighbors on either side; (3) ease of surveying long lines per‐ pendicular to the St. Lawrence; (4) access to the river for fishing, for fish were an important source of protein to early French Canadians; and (5) a useful variety of soil and flora types, for the course of each longlot, running back into the hinterland from the river, was likely to encompass diverse terrains.

All scholars of early seigneurialism in the St. Lawrence Valley remark on the case of Robert Giffard, to whom in 1634 the Company of New France conveyed a seigneury at Beauport, just outside Quebec.[20] Giffard was one of

the first seigneurs to subdivide his concession, and in 1637 he conveyed to
Noël Langlois a rectilinear plot of 300 square arpents facing the St. Lawrence
near Beauport. The arpent was an ancient French unit of measure equaling
approximately 192 English feet as a linear unit and 0.85 acre as a superficial
unit. It was ubiquitous wherever the French surveyed in North America
during the Old Regime. In the quasi-manorial system of seventeenth-century Canada, Robert Giffard was the seigneur and Noël Langlois the *roturier*
or *censitaire*. The first term derived from the fact that Langlois's parcel of land
was granted *en roture,* meaning that the land was held in neither seigneurial
nor freehold tenure. *Roture* became the standard appellation for the French
Canadian longlots that composed the ribbon farms of the St. Lawrence River
valley. Similarly, because Langlois was obligated to pay Giffard the French
manorial quitrent called the *cens,* Langlois was a censitaire, as Giffard was a
seigneur. Langlois's roture near Beauport was a rectilinear parcel with a
width-to-length ratio of nearly 1:30.[21] Sizes and width-to-length ratios of
Canadian rotures varied a great deal, although Harris proposed that a ratio
of approximately 1:10 was more or less standard.[22]

As the population of New France grew, the cadastral pattern along the
banks of the St. Lawrence River expanded and became more complex. A second row of rotures was added inland behind the original one, which faced
immediately on the St. Lawrence. This second rank, which lacked river frontage, was rather odd because several of the salient practical reasons for creating longlots applied only to those located on river banks. This strongly suggests that by the time the second row was platted off, long-standing cultural
traditions as well as practical considerations were coming into play. Furthermore, tributaries of the St. Lawrence—the Puante, St. François, du Loup,
Richelieu, and so forth—became secondary axes for longlot rotures, as did
other rivers such as the St. John. Greer described one Théophile Allaire's ribbon farm in the parish of St. Ours on the lower Richelieu, which occupied
two arpents facing the river and ran back into the hinterland thirty arpents.[23]
It therefore constituted a typical small French Canadian longlot roture, having a width-to-length ratio of 1:15 and consisting of sixty square arpents.

The smallest units of rural real estate in the St. Lawrence Valley were the
longlot rotures, which were grouped together into larger entities called *rangs*
or *côtes.* Trudel explained the nomenclature this way: *côte,* which was in common usage before *rang* was ever used, at first pertained to settlements along
the banks (i.e., côtes) of the St. Lawrence River, but it soon became a more
generalized term that, depending the circumstances, could mean a rang, any
particular area of settlement, or a seigneury. *Rang,* which began to be used
only after 1663 but became more popular as time went on, was more specific,

meaning either a cluster of adjacent rotures or a line of habitations.[24] A seigneurial map drawn in 1702 shows clearly the assemblages of longlots that composed the various côtes in the Montreal area.[25] At first glance these côtes and their clusters of longlots might be mistaken for the clusters of champs allongés that constituted the quartiers of plowlands in the traditional open-field agriculture of northern France. That mistaken identity, however, would lead to profound confusions about settlement patterns and land usage, for the longlots near Montreal were not plowlands but rather multipurpose plots of settlement—each containing residence, kitchen garden, woodlot, orchard, arable fields, and so forth. Whether a rang of rotures that constituted a French Canadian côte was located immediately on the bank of the St. Lawrence River or back in the hinterland, each longlot roture was occupied by one French Canadian habitant and his family, each longlot (or sometimes several contiguous plots) thus constituting an independent and more-or-less self-sufficient farmstead (*habitation*).

During the seventeenth century, settlement in New France remained decidedly dispersed. This dispersed pattern persisted despite the government's earnest efforts to sponsor village development. Intendant Jean Talon, for example, promoted the three curious star-shaped villages just north of Quebec City.[26] But neither Canadian seigneurs nor censitaires welcomed the government's efforts to promote village life. Deffontaines remarked that "French Canada was not favorably disposed to nucleated settlements,"[27] and Harris went so far as to say that French Canadian habitants in the St. Lawrence Valley had a positive "aversion" to village life, which they viewed as a threat to their ferociously independent spirits.[28]

It is now commonplace to note that the French Canadian settlement pattern in the St. Lawrence Valley was dispersed, "un type extensif de peuplement,"[29] and that Canadian habitants were rugged individualists. Less easy to resolve is the chicken-and-egg question, whether the settlement pattern created individualists or individualists created the settlement pattern. Hamelin, for example, commented that the distance between neighbors and the fact that the habitants were individual owner-exploiters of their rotures "explains the individualist spirit of the habitants."[30] This analysis from the bottom up suggests that the individualism of Canadian habitants was rooted in their settlement pattern and style of agriculture. Louise Dechêne agreed with this materialistic construction, commenting that Canadian "habitants did not group their houses in villages because it would have been too time-consuming to get to their fields, to make hay, to cut wood, and to tend to their animals morning and evening."[31] On the other hand, Hamelin also analyzed from the top down, arguing that the dispersed settlement pattern of the St. Lawrence Valley was a consequence of "individualistic aspirations" and represented a revolt against Old World strictures imposed on French peasants by nuclear villages and the regime of open-field agriculture.[32] Without attempting to resolve the tricky question of cause and effect, it may be noted that a kind of geographical-cultural truism prevails—individualism and dispersed settlements tend to go hand in hand, whereas compact villages and communal agriculture limit individual choices and promote cooperative efforts. I will revisit this issue with regard to the Illinois Country in the conclusion.

UPPER CANADA: DETROIT

Now located in the American Midwest, during the French colonial regime Detroit and its environs were part of Upper Canada (*pays d'en haut*). Founded by the Canadian adventurer and administrator Antoine de Lamothe Cadillac in 1701, Detroit, like Michilimackinac, was a major center of the western fur trade during the first half of the eighteenth century. Unlike Michilimackinac, however, Detroit became more than a mere trading place, military outpost, and mission center. Such places were occupied largely by transients or temporary residents, whereas Detroit had a sizable community of habitants, permanently settled agriculturists. After the War of the Austrian Succession (1740–48), the governor general of New France, Roland-Michel de La Galissonière, took strong steps to develop an agricultural community at Detroit.[33] When the British occupied Detroit, Lieutenant Governor Henry Hamilton wrote that "the soil is so good that great crops are raised by careless & very ignorant farmers, Wheat, Indian Corn, Barley, Oats, Pease, Buck Wheat yield a great increase."[34] Hamilton sneered at what he saw as French ignorance, but his observations make it clear that French habitants found the soil and climate at Detroit suitable for arable agriculture.

Early in the eighteenth century, Canadian habitants began to carve farm sites out of the forest on both banks of the Detroit River and along the shores of Lake St. Clair, and these farmsteads took the form of longlots with their long axes oriented perpendicular to the waterways. Doubtless this settlement pattern was modeled after that in the St. Lawrence River valley. In 1707 Cadillac conveyed the first recorded land grant near Detroit to François Delorme. The concession consisted of a tract of land with two arpents of river frontage running twenty arpents deep, that is, a longlot with a typically Canadian ratio of 1:10.[35] The grant was also characteristically Canadian in that it was hedged in with many seigneurial obligations associated with concessions in the St. Lawrence Valley. Because there was no local seigneur at Detroit, the French crown itself served as seigneur for Delorme's grant, and he

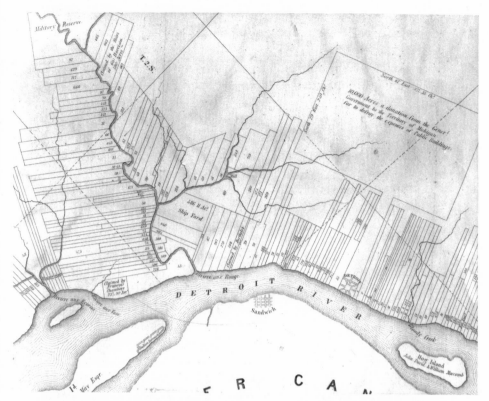

French longlots in the Detroit region as shown on a U.S. General Land Office map. This settlement pattern replicates that from the St. Lawrence Valley. Map reproduced courtesy of the Burton Historical Collection of the Detroit Public Library.

was in principle obligated to pay a quitrent of fifteen livres per year in perpetuity. This bastard manorialism was brought to the Detroit region from the St. Lawrence Valley, but it is impossible to determine the system's strength in a place as remote as Detroit. As late as 1784 the British commandant at Detroit was ordered to collect manorial dues from the local French habitants,[36] but it is doubtful that such a collection ever occurred.

Land claims published in the American State Papers indicate that French concessions near Detroit were usually forty arpents deep (Delorme's twenty-arpent-deep parcel notwithstanding) and varied from two to five arpents wide.[37] Many habitants, however, increased their holdings by obtaining second, or "rear," grants from the French commandants at Detroit.[38] These contiguous and equal-sized parcels immediately behind the original concessions doubled their size, making them eighty arpents deep. This was easily done at Detroit, where no natural geographical rear boundary such as a bluffline existed. Aaron Greely, a surveyor working for the U.S. surveyor general's office, conducted the first modern survey of longlots in the greater Detroit region in 1808. Enormous difficulties, and frequent legal disputes, arose in trying to accommodate the old French claims to modern, more-or-less scientific surveys. In any case, Greely's surveys, and also the somewhat later surveys conducted by the U.S. General Land Office (hereafter GLO), present a remarkable view of the French longlot pattern in the Detroit region. Longlots were a pervasive feature in this region, facing not only the Detroit River, Lake St. Clair, and the St. Clair River but also lesser streams such as the River Rouge and the River Raisin.[39] Modern images taken from satellites[40] show vestiges of the French longlots especially well on the east side of the Detroit River, where urban development has been less destructive of the old landscape than on the west side.

The significant issue here is that longlots in the Detroit region were multipurpose parcels. That is, they were integrated farmsteads with dwelling houses toward the waterfront and then kitchen gardens, outbuildings, orchards, plowlands, and woodlots stretching out behind. As in the St. Lawrence Valley, settlement was not nucleated but dispersed in a string-town configuration that would have placed neighbors just within hailing distance—dispersed but not totally isolated and unfriendly. Bela Hubbard recounted from his early days in Michigan, "I have heard old habitants say they could shout to each other from their doorsteps."[41] A recent study of the early River Raisin community persuasively argues that the settlement pattern there was modeled after those that existed along the Detroit and the St. Lawrence Rivers. Longlots fronted on the river, were surveyed in arpents, averaged three arpents in width, and had width-to-length ratios ranging from 1:10 to 1:20, and each parcel contained an independent family farm consisting of residence, outbuildings, orchard, garden, meadow, and plowlands.[42]

In 1782, toward the end of the American Revolution, the British commandant at Detroit, Major Arent De Peyster, ordered a detailed census of the region. This census reveals a broadly based agricultural community that produced cereal grains, potatoes, and livestock and that even contained a significant number of slaves, who apparently served as agricultural laborers.[43] The dispersed settlement pattern at Detroit persisted, however: no agricultural villages developed, and arable lands were never bound together into a regime of open-field agriculture. This meant that settlement and agriculture at Detroit remained closer to the patterns in the St. Lawrence Valley than to those in the Illinois Country, where open-field agriculture and compact villages obtained throughout.

UPPER CANADA: MICHILIMACKINAC

Riparian longlots appeared in scattered fashion in several areas near the Straits of Mackinac, but they dominated settlement only in an area on the north side of the straits, on the peninsula at St. Ignace.[44] GLO surveyor John Mullett surveyed the longlots at St. Ignace in 1828, and his plat reveals unmistakably the French Canadian settlement pattern there.[45] Fort de Buade and the Mission of St. Ignace had been built north of the straits before the end of the seventeenth century, but these sites were utterly abandoned by the turn of the eighteenth century,[46] and the longlots at St. Ignace were created much later—by French Canadians, to be sure, but after the United States had acquired the region. All seventeen claims filed with the GLO from St. Ignace pertain to longlots a full eighty arpents deep and generally three or four arpents wide.[47] At Detroit longlots eighty arpents deep were the result of doubling the concessions by extending them back into the hinterland after the original grants had specified the standard forty arpents. At St. Ignace, on the other hand, the two steps were apparently telescoped into one, suggesting that the eighty-arpent pattern employed at St. Ignace was borrowed from Detroit. Moreover, the width of Pointe St. Ignace lent itself to ribbon farms that ran across the peninsula approximately eighty arpents. At Detroit and St. Ignace, as in the St. Lawrence Valley, the longlots were multipurpose, serving as locations for dispersed farmsteads, outbuildings, arable fields, and so forth.

UPPER CANADA: GREEN BAY

The first European to visit Green Bay was probably Jean Nicolet, who journeyed westward from the St. Lawrence Valley in 1634–35 seeking a route to the Orient. This body of water leading southwest from Lake Michigan enticed early French explorers, for rumors abounded about the "Great River" (the Mississippi) to the west, and hope persisted about discovering a northwest passage across North America to the "Grande Mer de l'Ouest." Various French explorers, including Jacques Marquette and Louis Jolliet, were therefore impelled to investigate Green Bay and its largest affluent, the Fox River, before they explored the lower end of Lake Michigan and the portage at "Checagou" that gave access to the upper Illinois River.

The French called the Winnebago Indians "les Puants," the stinky ones, and because Winnebagos lived along the western shore of Lake Michigan, the French early on (at least as early as the Marquette-Jolliet expedition in 1673) began to call Green Bay "la Baye des Puants." This unsavory name—quite at odds with the fresh, wholesome resonance of "Green Bay"—remained the

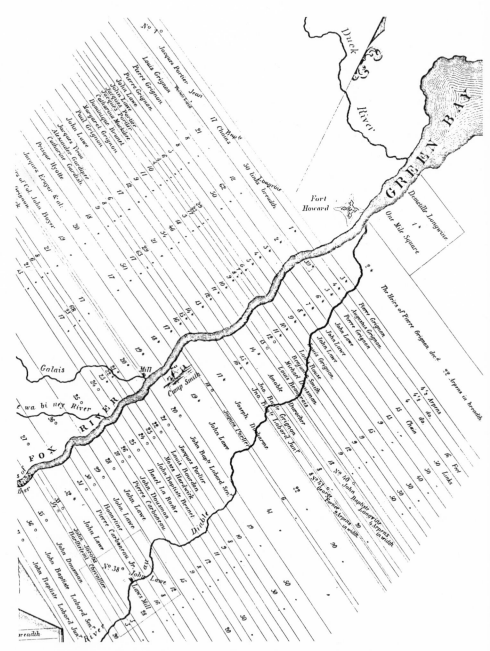

Herringbone pattern of longlots in the Green Bay region. These parcels, fronting on the Fox River, represent a replication of the settlement pattern from the St. Lawrence Valley. General Land Office map, from *ASP, PL.*

standard French appellation for almost 150 years and was still in use at the
end of the French regime in North America; Bowen and Gibson's English
map of North America published in London in 1763 still labeled the area
"Puans Bay."[48] Jonathan Carver, however, who traveled extensively through
the Midwest during the late 1760s, routinely referred to "Green Bay" as early
as 1766.[49] French Canadians seem to have taken the more agreeable name
from the English and soon used the French version, "la Baye Verte."

For the entire duration of the French political regime in North America
(i.e., up to 1763), it is impossible to discern a distinct settlement pattern—
other than that of a wooden palisaded fort with a scattering of rude dwellings surrounding it—at Green Bay. The place served as a fur-trading entrepôt, as a small military outpost, and occasionally as a mission center, but
there is no early evidence of any permanent agricultural community. The
hivernants who wintered there while engaged in the western fur trade do
not seem to have crossed the threshold and become habitants who remained year around to sow and harvest crops on the alluvial soil of the
lower Fox River valley.

Charles de Langlade, the famous métis partisan warrior, moved to
Green Bay in 1763, and during the following two decades a number of other
mixed-blood families from Canada settled there.[50] Growth during this
period was slow, however, and by 1785 there were only seven families and
fifty-six residents. After the turn of the nineteenth century, the population
at the head of the bay spurted up, and in 1820 Henry Schoolcraft reported
"sixty dwelling houses and one hundred inhabitants."[51] Both Schoolcraft
and a modern authority on the subject, Jacqueline Peterson, agree that this
community was composed overwhelmingly of métis residents.[52] Kerry A.
Trask has recently observed, with an appropriately depictive turn of phrase,
that "the settlement itself was more a rambling neighborhood sprawling
along the Fox River than a compact village nestled in a wilderness clearing."[53] Trask also quotes a Yankee schoolteacher who in 1822 described
Green Bay as being composed of mixed bloods who occupied the shores
of the Fox River and "divided it off into little strips stretching back from
the banks to the fringes of the forest."[54] Clearly the residences of the métis
community at Green Bay were not clustered together in a nuclear village
in any meaningful sense of the term.

Early U.S. land claims at Green Bay bring us back to French colonial riparian longlots. An 1821 settlement plan of Green Bay clearly displays these
longlots with their dimensions, despite the plan's disclaimer that it was "Not
founded on Actual Survey." The names attached to these lots reveal that

most claimants, though not all, were of French Canadian extraction. The fact that widths of these properties were given sometimes in French arpents and sometimes in English chains (one chain equals sixty-six English feet) strongly suggests that the lots were laid out in a transitional period, circa 1800, when the residents were largely French Canadians but the government was either British or American. Green Bay land claims submitted to the U.S. land commissioners in 1823 corroborate this, for the claimants often argued that they had been cultivating the land on the longlots since 1805.[55] Widths of the longlots at Green Bay, whether reckoned in arpents or chains, varied a good deal. The depths, on the other hand, were shown as indeterminate on the 1821 plan, and many claimants simply did not mention depth. Those that did, however, claimed eighty arpents of depth, which then became the dimension consistently employed by the U.S. land commissioners. The depth of the longlots at Green Bay, as at St. Ignace, almost certainly derived from the model at Detroit, which long antedated Green Bay as an agricultural settlement. Ebenezer Childs, an early Anglo-American resident of Wisconsin, noted that French longlots at Green Bay "were very narrow on the river, running back three miles."[56] Without knowing the mathematical relationship between English miles and French arpents, Childs presented an accurate estimate, for three miles is roughly equivalent to eighty linear arpents.

French Canadians, mostly métis, initiated agriculture at Green Bay circa 1795, when they began to utilize, in common, a large tract of land situated at the head of Green Bay.[57] This commons was rather vaguely defined, both as to extent and to usage. It contained "two square miles, more or less," was not enclosed with a fence, and was used by the members of the local métis community for anything they wished, from pasturage to pumpkin raising. U.S. land commissioners understood this and in 1823 referred to this land as "a tract of land as meadows in common," which did not lay within their jurisdiction.[58] The settlers at Green Bay had certainly not, as has been suggested, "marked off common fields" to practice open-field arable cultivation;[59] sharing a commons in conjunction with individually occupied ribbon farms was a well-established practice in the St. Lawrence Valley.[60] From the head of Green Bay, French Canadians moved up the Fox River, creating, without the assistance of any surveyor, a spread of ribbon farmsteads. Nothing even remotely approaching a nuclear village was present at Green Bay, for the habitants there lived in a dispersed, strung-out pattern, seldom even within hailing distance of their closest neighbors. This settlement pattern resembled that of the St. Lawrence Valley, the Detroit region, or the faraway lower Mississippi Valley more than it did the nucleated agricultural villages of metropolitan France or the Illinois Country, and it was not adapted to any sort of common or open-field agriculture. As land claims reveal, however, unlike in the St. Lawrence Valley, which was more densely populated, single owners at Green Bay often held multiple longlot parcels. Pierre Grignon, for example, claimed five strips, two facing the Fox River from the south and three facing the river from the north.

The fur trade was for decades the raison d'être of Green Bay. Agricultural pursuits in the area—above and beyond kitchen gardening—did not begin until well after the end of French sovereignty in 1763. Indeed, three decades later, in 1793, Robert Dickson, a Scots trader, wrote critically that "there have long been settled some Canadians who sow but little grain, they have about 100 head of Horned Cattle and a number of Horses which run wild in the woods most part of the year. Altho' every one on his Road to the Mississippi [from Canada] passes La Baye and would mostly wish to purchase Corn, Flour, Butter, or fresh Provisions, Yet such is the indolence of the People settled there that we pay half a Dollar for a quart of milk."[61] The Scotsman with an entrepreneurial temperament could not imagine why the métis at Green Bay did not practice commercial agriculture and attributed this failure to a deficiency in character—the métis were naturally lazy. Although the residents at Green Bay did not cultivate for a market economy, they certainly were tilling the soil in a limited fashion for their own sustenance.

According to an early American settler, Joseph Arndt, plowing at Green Bay, as in every other French settlement in North America, was done with heavy wheeled plows drawn by oxen. Arndt said that the women (i.e., métis and Indian women) performed most of the agricultural labor, raising maize, wheat, potatoes, peas, and other "Indian crops." Although Arndt described arable agriculture at Green Bay in which plows and oxen were used to raise wheat and maize, his depiction suggests little more than subsistence agriculture. As late as 1822 settlers at Green Bay were described as "retired French voyageurs and half-breed French and Menomonee" who had "taken up the whole shore of the river . . . and divided it off into little strips"[62] that stretched from the river back to the forest. For these métis, as Jacqueline Peterson has remarked, settling down "generally meant fishing and tinkering in their gardens and orchards . . . [;] they only pretended to cultivate the soil."[63] Until well into the nineteenth century, Green Bay continued to be fundamentally a trading community, with the younger métis men engaged principally in the fur trade, while the women and the older men raised foodstuffs for their families. The community at Green Bay was thus radically different from those of the Illinois Country, where sedentary habitants had practiced commercial agriculture since the early eighteenth century.

LOUISIANA

Louisiane, the land of Louis (i.e., King Louis XIV), became a place name in French colonial North America in April 1682. At that time René-Robert Cavelier de La Salle arrived at the mouth of the Mississippi River and grandiosely claimed the entire watershed of the river plus the adjacent coastline of the Gulf of Mexico for his royal master. By 1700 the French had founded outposts at Biloxi, Dauphin Island, and Mobile Bay. In the spring of 1708 the governor of Louisiana, Jean-Baptiste Le Moyne de Bienville, who wished to develop a local food supply, conveyed agricultural land grants to five aspiring planters. These grants were located south of Lake Pontchartrain along Bayou St. Jean, near where New Orleans would be founded a decade later. Measured off in traditional French arpents, each of these concessions consisted of a longlot, four arpents wide and thirty-six arpents deep, and each of them fronted on the bayou.[64] Given Bienville's familiarity with the cadastral pattern of his native St. Lawrence Valley, where longlots faced the river with width-to-depth ratios of approximately 1:10, it seems likely that the longlots at Bayou St. Jean derived directly from the Canadian pattern.

In 1716, two years before the founding of New Orleans, the government of Louis XV, under the regency of Philippe, duc d'Orléans, promulgated what became the most influential land ordinance in colonial Louisiana.[65] This edict, which emanated from the royal Conseil d'État, bemoaned the fact that provincial officials had granted large concessions that could not be cultivated and that this practice was contrary to the healthy and productive development of the colony of Louisiana. Furthermore, it gave the colony's governor and his associate, the commissaire-ordonnateur, the right to reunite to the royal domain all conceded lands that were not being put to productive use. Lastly, the edict decreed that henceforth all real estate conveyed by the crown in Louisiana should be "in the proportion of two to four arpents front by forty to sixty in depth."

This brief edict had momentous consequences for the human geography and the history of the Mississippi Valley. The specifications of the edict, dictating plots of "two to four arpents front," implied that the rectangular parcels of real estate envisioned were to face a distinct geographical entity—a canal, a river, a roadway, a bayou, a bluffline, or the ocean itself—that provided a well-defined linear front. The front mentioned in the edict was very likely a reference to river frontage, and the governing council in France was foreseeing colonial growth northward up the major rivers that flowed into the Gulf of Mexico, including the Mobile and the Mississippi. In French Canadian parlance the riverfront edge of the rotures was called "le fronteau."[66]

The French American empire was emphatically a riverain empire, and the configuration of New France along the St. Lawrence provided a virtually irresistible model for settlement up a major river.[67] Indeed, given that long rectilinear lots had been de rigueur in the St. Lawrence Valley for some seventy-five years when the 1716 edict was promulgated and that this peculiar Canadian system was well known, it is likely that the edict was intended to replicate, mutatis mutandis, the Canadian pattern in Louisiana. The system had proved to be practical in the St. Lawrence Valley and might be just as functional in the Mississippi Valley. A map of the lower valley, which was drafted anonymously shortly after the founding of New Orleans, clearly depicts longlot concessions facing the river both below and above the new provincial capital. Interestingly, this source also shows longlots north of New Orleans oriented perpendicular to Bayou St. Jean rather than to the Mississippi. In September 1725 the Superior Council in New Orleans reported back to France that "arpenteurs" were busy surveying lots located between Bayou St. Jean and New Orleans and that soon they would return to the river and continue their work along both banks.[68] Although Louisiana did not have the St. Lawrence Valley's seigneuries or seigneurs, the cadastral pattern of longlots measured off in arpents, facing a major waterway (and some minor waterways), was remarkably similar.

In Louisiana nomenclature the longlot is often called the "arpent lot" or the "arpent system," for the obvious reason that all surveys throughout the colonial period (Spanish as well as French) employed the French arpent as the basic unit of measure.[69] This terminology is rather confusing, however, for although longlots in French North America were almost always surveyed in arpents, not all property surveyed in arpents was laid out in longlots. As I show in the following chapter, residential plots in some parts of the Illinois Country were routinely laid out in square, rather than elongated, plots, which usually measured one arpent or twenty-five toises (one toise equaling 6.4 English feet) per side.[70] Therefore, when discussing elongated rectilinear parcels of real estate in French North America, the preferred usage is *longlot*, understanding that virtually all longlots of French origin discussed in this study were originally surveyed in arpents.

Justly famous as an important part of the landscape of the lower Mississippi Valley, the Louisiana longlot has generated interesting debate. All scholars trace the origins of the longlot back at least as far as medieval Europe, and everyone agrees that the longlot became widespread, was admirably suited to the terrain of the lower Mississippi Valley, and has had enormous influence in shaping the human geography of that region. Nevertheless, the French Canadian ancestry of the lower Mississippi Valley riverain longlots

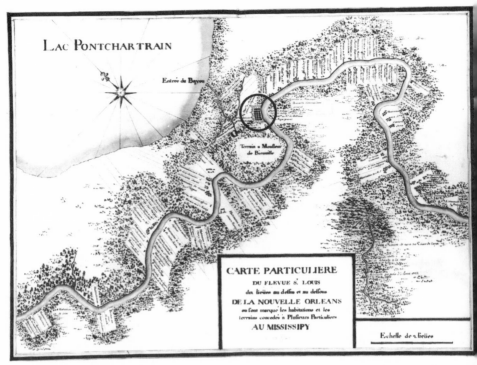

Longlots fronting the Mississippi near New Orleans (circled), ca. 1723. These parcels represent individual plantations, creating a cadastral pattern similar to that of the St. Lawrence Valley. Map reproduced courtesy of the Edward E. Ayer Collection, The Newberry Library, Chicago.

has never been fully explored. This is curious, for it is hard to imagine that the members of the Regency Conseil d'État who drafted the consequential edict of October 1716 did not have the basic cadastral gestalt of the St. Lawrence Valley in mind when they wrote that edict. In any event, three facts strongly suggest that early Louisiana longlots did derive from those in the St. Lawrence Valley: longlots had existed in New France for more than a half-century before the Louisiana edict of 1716 was drafted; they were well-known features that had been extensively mapped prior to 1716; and the dimensions of Canadian longlots and those specified in the edict were roughly the same.

Two students of Louisiana cadastral systems and settlement patterns, William B. Knipmeyer and John Whitling Hall, have briefly discussed the Louisiana longlot in terms of the eternal environment versus culture dichotomy. That is, did the Louisiana longlot emerge from a unique physical setting, or was it imposed on the landscape by the cultural baggage that the French carried with them when they arrived there? Knipmeyer argued that "the system was not devised to suit the particular topographic conditions, even though a system resembling it would probably have been invented if none had existed."[71] Hall, taking some issue with this statement, remarked, "The fact remains that the arpent system is uniquely adapted to an equitable division of alluvial lands in Louisiana."[72] More recently Glenn R. Conrad has taken a similar position, remarking that "for reasons of transportation and communication, the colonial concessions [of Louisiana] were located primarily along the banks of navigable streams. Therefore, common sense had dictated that for every landowner to have completely free access to his property each privately owned tract of land would have to front on a river or bayou."[73] Even more recently Edward T. Price has concluded that "no completely satisfactory explanation has been offered for the special association between French settlement and riparian longlots in North America."[74] True enough, but it does seem apparent that riverain longlots in French Louisiana resulted from both a particular environment and a specific transmitted culture; the cultural baggage carried to Louisiana from Canada worked eminently well there, for the former colony, like the latter, developed along a major river and its tributaries.

ARKANSAS POST

Within the greater Mississippi River watershed beyond the confines of the New Orleans region, numerous longlots were created that owed their existence to French surveying practices in Louisiana. Beyond the confines of the Illinois Country proper,[75] which I discuss in detail in the following chapter, the best examples are Arkansas Post, located on the Arkansas River some distance upstream from its mouth, and various manifestations in Texas.

Arkansas Post struggled to survive at various locations on the Arkansas River, dating all the way back to 1686, as Morris S. Arnold has explained in his *Unequal Laws unto a Savage Race*.[76] The only location for which we have an accurate eighteenth-century plan, however, is the site that the French called Écores Rouges. Located on the north bank of the Arkansas River about thirty-six miles from the Mississippi, this site was first occupied by the French between 1749 and 1756. At the latter date the establishment was returned to a location further down the Arkansas River, a site that was more convenient because closer to the Mississippi but that was also more vulnerable to flooding. In March 1779, during the Spanish regime in Louisiana but under the auspices of a commandant of French Creole extraction, Balthazar de Villiers, Arkansas Post was removed to its former location at Écores Rouges. At this time, Villiers drafted a plan of the proposed settlement, *Établissement du Poste des*

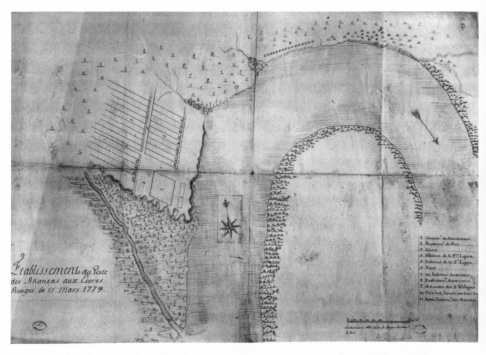

Longlots, both residential and agricultural, at Arkansas Post. Open-field agriculture was not practiced at Arkansas Post. Original in the Archivo General de Indias, Seville. Photograph courtesy of U.S. Judge Morris S. Arnold.

Arkansas aux Écores Rouges de 17 mars 1779, which contains a good view of two types of French longlot from the colonial Mississippi Valley.

Villiers explained to the governor general in New Orleans that all the longlots in his new settlement were to be twenty toises wide (about 128 English feet), and the scale on his plan shows that at least one row of longlots was to be 106 toises (about 678 feet) deep.[77] Why Villiers chose to use toises rather than arpents as the basic unit of measure is not clear, but Arkansas Post may be the only location where toises rather than arpents were used for surveying longlots. In any case, the row of longlots at Arkansas Post that measured 106 toises deep faced the Arkansas River to one side and the main thoroughfare of the settlement to the other; it was, one may say, a *Straßendorf* settlement. Villiers explained that the lots in this front row were intended for the merchants, those "who hardly ever bother to make a crop." The longlots in the second row were intended for agriculturists, however, and although these lots were also twenty toises wide, Villiers's plan depicts them extending well back into the untamed hinterland behind the post.

All the longlots at Écores Rouges were multipurpose parcels of land. Each merchant in the front row had his residence on a parcel of real estate and also conducted his trade from the same site, and each habitant in the second row lived and practiced agriculture on one elongated, rectangular tract of land, French Canadian style. These two varieties of longlot were well-suited to the local riverain geography and the practical needs of Arkansas Post, which was both a commercial and agricultural settlement. At the same time, the longlots were a cultural derivation stemming back to Lower Louisiana, to French Canada, and ultimately to medieval European settlement patterns. Lastly, it is manifestly apparent that none of the longlots at Écores Rouges was part of a communal or open-field regime of agriculture.

TEXAS

As noted at the beginning of this chapter, Terry Jordan's study of longlots in Texas is the only detailed study ever devoted exclusively to these phenomena within the United States. Texas is far beyond the geographical focus of this study, but Jordan's work raises a number of important issues that bear on land usage and settlement patterns in the Illinois Country. Jordan dealt exclusively with settlement, or cadastral, longlots; he was not concerned with champs allongés, the longlot parcels that characterized open-field agriculture. After probing deeply into medieval European settlement patterns, Jordan concluded that the historical antecedents of longlots in Texas were French rather than Spanish: "The key to the Texan long-lots probably lies in France and the French North American colonies."[78] Jordan concurred with Max Derruau and Pierre Deffontaines, cited earlier in this chapter, that longlots from northwestern France provided the prototypes for the ribbon farms of the St. Lawrence Valley. Complete agreement therefore exists that the longlots of the St. Lawrence Valley did derive from Europe and were not simply a spontaneous and practical adaptation to the particular geography of the valley; this cadastral system, even though it was cultural baggage from Europe, did prove to be convenient in that New World environment.

Jordan then described how the settlement pattern of the St. Lawrence Valley leapfrogged across the face of North America from Canada to Detroit, to the various communities of the Illinois Country, to the lower Mississippi Valley, and finally to Texas itself. He found the riverain longlots ("Flußhufen") around New Orleans, Natchitoches, and Ste. Genevieve to be of key importance in the diffusion of this cadastral pattern to Texas. Nonetheless, if Jordan had dug as deeply into the configuration of the longlots of the Illinois Country as he did into those of medieval Europe, he would not have come to that conclusion, for longlots in the Illinois Country, and especially those at Ste. Genevieve, were very different from those in the St. Lawrence and lower Mississippi Valleys. Those in the latter two areas were self-contained ribbon farms, whereas those in the former were arable strips within compounds of open fields. That is, the longlots of the Illinois Country, although superficially resembling those of French Canada and Lower Louisiana, in fact represented vastly different approaches to land usage, settlement, and agriculture.[79] Clarence W. Alvord remarked briefly on these differences early in this century,[80] although widespread confusion still reigns concerning the distinction between longlots in French Canada and Louisiana and those in the Illinois Country.[81]

One of Jordan's most interesting revelations is that the longlots in the region of San Antonio—and only those—were idiosyncratic. "They differed from those of Europe and French America in several important respects. First, the farmsteads were not situated on them, but on plots in the nearby town, . . . Moreover, the pastureland remained communal and was not included in the long-lot holdings."[82] Jordan's reference to Europe evidently pertained to the *Hufendorf* settlements in which longlots with residences at the front composed linear settlements; he was not referring to plowlands made up of champs allongés, furlong fields. Indeed, Jordan's study of Texan longlots does not address their possible relationships to certain kinds of agriculture. One wonders, for example, whether the longlots he described at San Antonio, which contained no residences and no pastureland, may have been incorporated into some system of open-field grain cultivation. This seems most unlikely, but if that was the case, then settlement and agriculture in the San Antonio region under the Spanish regime resembled those of the Illinois Country during the colonial era, even though there was no apparent communication or direct cultural link between the two regions.

CONCLUSION

Longlots surveyed in French arpents by persons of French extraction eventually appeared in various regions of North America far removed from the valleys of the St. Lawrence and lower Mississippi Rivers: Texas, Detroit, Prairie du Chien, Winnipeg, and all the communities that made up the eighteenth-century Illinois Country—Cahokia, Kaskaskia, Chartres, Vincennes, Ste. Genevieve, St. Louis, and so forth. Moreover, in the Illinois Country the longlot was employed in a way that occurred nowhere else in French North America, for it became an integral part of a regime of open-field agriculture.[83] This distinctive use was evidently the result of thoroughly intertwined envi-

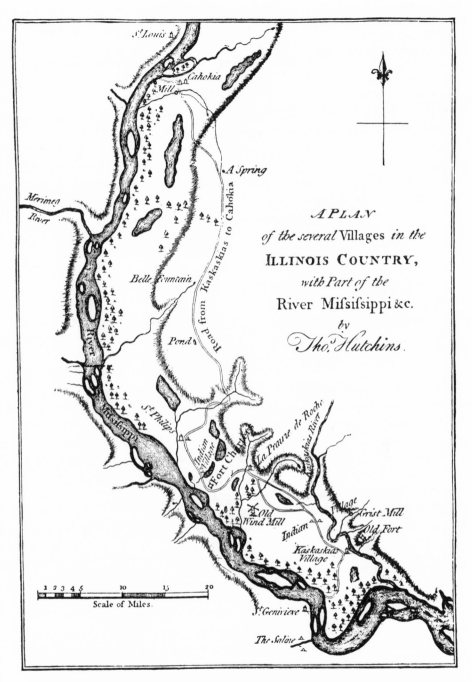

French villages in the Illinois Country. Notice the trunk road running from Cahokia to Kaskaskia. Map drawn by the British officer Captain Thomas Hutchins in 1771 and reproduced here from his *Topographical Descriptions*, 1778.

ronmental and cultural factors. The hospitable environment was the alluvial valley of a great river located in a temperate climate, whereas the transmitted culture descended from two places, French Canada and metropolitan France. From the first came the habit of establishing longlots, surveying them in arpents, and orienting their long axes perpendicular to a river; from the second came the traditional open-field agricultural practices of the northern European plain. In the following chapter I examine how longlots and open fields were integrated into the distinctive settlement pattern of the Illinois Country.

The French . . . had not, as we have, separate fields, nor did they reside on the cultivated land in general. They dwelt in villages, on lots of ground containing an arpent square, . . . which they inclosed with pickets of cedar or other durable wood.
—Judge Sidney Breese, *Early History of Illinois*

2 SETTLEMENTS IN THE ILLINOIS COUNTRY

Constantin-François Chasseboeuf, comte de Volney, was an eighteenth-century savant who traveled from Philadelphia to the American West in 1796; he was a friend and correspondent of another Enlightenment polymath, Thomas Jefferson. Volney had originally intended to travel to the far western edge of the United States, which in 1796 was the Mississippi River, but after he had reached Vincennes in the valley of the lower Wabash River, he returned eastward. As he explained to Jefferson in a letter written at Lexington, Kentucky, "I turned my back on the monotonous and immense prairie that extends from the Wabash, and even the White River, all the way to the Missouri, and now I am heading for Cincinnati."[1] With that one cavalier sentence, Volney dismissed the entire Illinois Country, and thereby the Frenchman destroyed his chance to see the most densely populated ethnic French region in the American Midwest. Jefferson could not admonish Volney for this mistake, for in 1796 the man who would within seven years acquire Louisiana for the United States was himself largely ignorant of the greater Mississippi River valley.

A half-century after Volney wrote disparagingly about the Illinois Country, Francis Parkman correctly described it as "a region which to our forefathers seemed remote and strange, as to us the mountain strongholds of the Apaches, or the wastes of farthest Oregon."[2] In colonial times the geographical limits of the Illinois Country were never precisely defined, and they varied with time, circumstances, and political perspectives. Before the names *Illinois* or *Ilinois* were ever applied to a geographical region, they were used to identify Lake Michigan, which a Jesuit map of 1671 labeled "Lac des Ilinois."[3] Whether the word was employed to identify a body of water or a geographical territory, early French explorers used it to designate the region associated with the Illinois Indian nation, roughly the northern two-thirds of the present state of Illinois, plus adjacent areas in Missouri, Iowa, and Wisconsin. The Minet map of 1685[4] depicts a large area southwest of Lake Michigan as "les Ilinois," and three years later Marco Coronelli designated a broad swath of territory between the Great Lakes and the Mississippi River "Paesi degl[i] Ilinois,"[5] the Italian equivalent of "Pays des Illinois," or the Illinois Country.

When in the early 1720s the French royal government and the Compagnie Royale des Indes established a civil government and a military presence in the upper Mississippi Valley, Illinois was defined in various ways. In May 1722 a royal ordinance creating a provincial council for Illinois defined the territory as including the valleys of the Arkansas and Wabash Rivers, the French settlements on both sides of the Mississippi "as far up as they go," and all the tributaries of the Mississippi.[6] The broadest definition of the Illinois Country therefore made it coterminous with French Upper Louisiana—that is, all French-claimed land south of the Great Lakes and north of the mouth of the Ohio River, including both sides of the Mississippi and the lower Missouri Valley.

Constant friction between Canada and Louisiana concerning trading rights led to a sharper and more restricted definition of the Illinois Country during the 1740s. In 1745 Governor General Vaudreuil[7] of Louisiana established the eastern and northern boundaries of the Illinois Country as follows: up the valley of the Wabash River to the mouth of the Vermillion (near present-day Danville, Illinois), thence northwest to Le Rocher (present-day Starved Rock State Park on the upper Illinois River), and thence westward to the confluence of the Rock and Mississippi Rivers (present-day Rock Island, Illinois).[8] These boundaries meant that Vincennes on the Wabash River and Peoria on the Illinois River were included within the Illinois Country. On the other hand, the Ouiatenon post on the upper Wabash, the portage at "Checagou," Prairie du Chien at the mouth of the Wisconsin River, Green Bay at the mouth of the Fox River, and Detroit were excluded from the territory defined by Vaudreuil.

By the end of the French regime (1763) and the founding of St. Louis (1764), the Illinois Country usually referred to the settlement area, on both sides of the Mississippi, running from St. Louis in the north to Kaskaskia in the south, including the communities of Cahokia, St. Philippe, the fort and village of Chartres, Prairie du Rocher, and Ste. Genevieve. During the Spanish colonial regime in Louisiana, traditional nomenclature continued to be employed. Lieutenant Governor Manuel Pérez referred to himself in 1789 as "commander in chief of the western part and districts of Illinois,"[9] and at the very end of the colonial era, Spanish administrators in Upper Louisiana continued to refer to their capital city as St. Louis of the "Ylinueses." This study focuses on the French-founded settlements along both banks of the Mississippi between St. Louis and Kaskaskia, which for convenience' sake shall be called the Illinois Country.[10] This relatively small section of the middle Mississippi Valley constituted a homogeneous cultural region, "a physical or cultural space defined by a set of behaviors and a mode of life associated with the particular group or groups occupying that space."[11] In the case of the Illinois Country, the occupying groups were the ethnic French and French Creoles (whose ancestry came from either French Canada or metropolitan France) along with their Indian associates and their African slaves; métis were soon present in significant numbers. The mixture of these groups created a culture that was unique for colonial North America.

By 1720 Cahokia (founded 1699) and Kaskaskia (founded 1703) were already undergoing slow transformations. Established as mission and fur-trading outposts, they were gradually evolving into agricultural communities with less transient populations. The two villages were composed increasingly of habitants, resident agriculturists who were often married to Indian women, especially in the early days.[12] Slaves, at first Indian and then both Indian and African, were used for agricultural labor. Land surveys, insofar as they were being done at all, were conducted in French arpents, both linear and superficial. The habitants, fur traders, and missionaries who inhabited the villages of the Illinois Country during the first two decades of the eighteenth century developed a distinctly tripartite pattern of land usage. Although not clearly conceptualized or articulated, a de facto configuration of villages, outlying clusters of arable fields, and separate commons for pasturage was emerging even before 1719 and became increasingly distinct as time went on.

For about two decades the Illinois Country survived in a kind of political and administrative limbo. The Seminarian priests at Cahokia and, more important, the Jesuit fathers at Kaskaskia provided some hierarchical structure for the region, but during the first two decades of the eighteenth century, the Illinois Country had no fort, no French troops, no colonial administrators, and no substantial governmental presence. All this changed dramatically between

1717 and 1719: New Orleans was founded, the Royal Indies Company was charged with developing the colony's economic resources, the Illinois Country officially became part of Louisiana, and a convoy of bateaux carried French troops and officials from New Orleans up the Mississippi to Kaskaskia. Together these events marked a turning point in the history of the Illinois Country, in the history of French North America, and in a sense, in the history of the American Midwest, for never before had the European colonizers of the New World made such a major investment in this region.[13]

The convoy that ascended the Mississippi River during the winter of 1718–19 (having left the newly founded outpost of New Orleans in December 1718) carried, in addition to a company of detached marines and a handful of lead miners, the three persons who would constitute the nucleus of the new provincial government in the Illinois Country: Pierre Dugué, sieur de Boisbriant, "first lieutenant of the king in the government of Louisiana and commandant in the Illinois"; Marc-Antoine de la Loëre des Ursins, commissioner of the Royal Indies Company; and Nicolas-Michel Chassin, *garde magasin* (storekeeper) of the company.[14] These three men would constitute the Provincial Council in the Illinois Country, the governing body that was in turn responsible to the Superior Council of Louisiana, which sat in New Orleans.[15] The Royal Indies Company, a royal chartered organization, governed Louisiana until 1731, when control of the entire colony reverted to the French crown.[16]

The convoy probably arrived in the Illinois Country in May 1719, and Boisbriant's first correspondence from the region emanated from Kaskaskia in July 1719. The new commandant and his company put up at Kaskaskia because it was the largest settlement in the Illinois Country and because there was as yet no military outpost of which to take command. Indeed, Boisbriant's first task was to reconnoiter the area on both sides of the Mississippi to select a fort site; the fort would play three distinct roles in the Illinois Country: military headquarters, governmental center, and local depot for the Royal Indies Company. By the summer of 1719, Boisbriant decided to erect this fort on the east side of the Mississippi, the side on which all French settlements in the Illinois Country were located at that early time, "six leagues by land and twelve by water" upriver from Kaskaskia. Probably Boisbriant selected this site because of its central location—between Cahokia to the north and Kaskaskia to the south and in the midst of various Illinois Indian settlements.[17]

The fort, which Boisbriant began in the spring or early summer of 1719, was located on the river side of the floodplain prairie that extended from the Mississippi several miles eastward to the bluffline. It was a wooden, palisaded structure, one arpent square, with two diagonally opposite corner bastions that commanded the four curtain walls. Boisbriant named this first fort in the region "Fort de Chartres" in honor of Louis, duc de Chartres, a son of Philippe d'Orléans, regent of France during the minority of Louis XV. Between 1719 and the end of the French regime in the Illinois Country (1763), the French built three discrete versions of Fort de Chartres in the same general vicinity.[18] Boisbriant's, the first of these forts, was not a very imposing structure, and it was occupied only briefly, but it did become the center of a new locus for settlement in the Illinois Country. Immediately outside the fort the village of Chartres developed; a bit to the north of the fort Boisbriant settled the Michigamea Indians on land reserved for them; a few miles to the north the lead miner Philippe Renaut (he signed his name thus) founded the community of St. Philippe in 1723; and a few miles to the southeast the village of Prairie du Rocher emerged during the early 1730s.

Commandant Boisbriant was a Canadian from the seigneurial class, a member of Governor General Bienville's political coterie, and "adored" by the habitants of the Illinois Country for his gracious manners.[19] The commandant was therefore in a good position to accomplish the variety of tasks with which he had been charged. His first priorities were to establish a French military presence in the area, create some semblance of government, and encourage the mining operations in which much hope and a substantial amount of money had been invested. Militia companies were created in each village, the Provincial Council began to function, and royal notaries recorded legal documents for the first time in the region. Philippe Renaut started to explore for mineral deposits of all kinds and began exploiting the rich lead mines that were already known to exist on the west side of the Mississippi, in what is now the lead belt of southeastern Missouri.[20]

LAND TENURE IN ILLINOIS

Cadastral practices and settlement patterns are difficult to determine during the earliest history of the Illinois Country (1699–1722), for civil records from that period do not exist. No royal notaries were present in the region, and no one served in lieu of them to draft legal instruments—land grants, real estate titles, property transfers, and so forth. When Boisbriant arrived in the Illinois Country, the habitants in the region were merely squatters on the land that they were cultivating. No officials had granted any land during the first two decades of the eighteenth century, unless the Jesuit fathers had taken it on themselves in an informal and unofficial way to regulate land tenure in some fashion, without, however, committing any records to paper. Boisbriant apparently did not begin tendering specific documents of conveyance for land grants in the Illinois Country until after he had been in the region for three full years, for the first such extant documents date from May 1722.

Boisbriant was in no rush to grant land, but almost immediately he began to impose some order and structure on land usage at Kaskaskia, doing so in the spring of 1719. In February 1727 the habitants of Kaskaskia wrote to the regional officials at Fort de Chartres, reporting: "It is nearly eight years since M. Boisbriant caused to be drawn the lines of the grand square of the prairie, which they [the habitants] now cultivate, and caused to be designated to each inhabitant his respective land. He then established a common for cattle, which completes the boundary of the land ceded at that time."[21] These words provide the first documented evidence of a longlot cadastral pattern at Kaskaskia, for later land records and maps demonstrate that the individual holdings within the "grand square of the prairie" were in fact ribbon strips of arable land, often two arpents wide, that stretched from the Mississippi River east to the line of the "grand square." Even though Boisbriant "caused to be designated to each inhabitant his respective land," it is a fair assumption that the basic morphology of arable parcels at Kaskaskia had existed in unofficial fashion before Boisbriant arrived in the Illinois County in 1719. That is, Boisbriant simply clarified, regularized, and affirmed a system of longlots that the habitants at Kaskaskia had already established before he took command of the region. Given that most of these early habitants in the Illinois Country had come from Canada, it was not unnatural that they should employ a system of longlots that superficially resembled the rangs of ribbon farms in the St. Lawrence River valley. The essential difference was that Canadian roturiers lived on their self-contained rotures, whereas in the Illinois Country the habitants lived within compact agricultural villages that stood removed from the arable fields.

Rather than draft individual patents in 1719, Boisbriant simply recorded the various land claims in a register while awaiting official deeds of title from the Royal Indies Company.[22] If it were available, this land register would be a source material of the highest value for reconstituting land-holding patterns in early Illinois. It does not seem to have survived, however, even though copies were probably sent to the Superior Council in New Orleans and to the directors of the Royal Indies Company in Paris. Nor were the promised warranty deeds ever forthcoming from the company, whose principal interest in the Illinois Country was quick profit from silver mines rather than long-term investment in agricultural land. The absence of consistent documentation for early land tenure created a nightmare for U.S. land commissioners in the early nineteenth century when they set about trying to verify the old French claims.

Louisiana in its entirety, including the Illinois Country, was conveyed by royal patent to the Compagnie d'Occident (Company of the West) in 1717. Early land concessions in Illinois were therefore made on behalf of this company, which was later absorbed into the Royal Indies Company.[23] Boisbriant began to convey real estate concessions on behalf of this company in May 1722 and continued these conveyances until he was recalled to Lower Louisiana in 1724. Sources concerning these earliest land grants in the Illinois Country are disparate and of varying quality and reliability—they include original documents, transcriptions, translations, mere epistolary references, and notations on early GLO plats. In any case, to understand the cadastral system and land usage in early Illinois, as well as its later evolution, the early concessions granted by Commandant Boisbriant must be examined.[24]

When Boisbriant arrived in the Illinois Country in the spring of 1719, he had a variety of precedents, models, and regulations regarding land tenure and land usage revolving in his mind: the Canadian model from the St. Lawrence Valley, with which he had grown up, consisting of seigneuries subdivided into longlot rotures that created the rang pattern; the royal edict for Louisiana of 1716, which called for longlots two to four arpents wide and forty to sixty arpents deep; and finally the ad hoc pattern that already existed in some areas of the Illinois Country when he arrived there. The sketchy extant documentation suggests that the Royal Indies Company's first land grant in the Illinois Country went to Boisbriant himself in September 1721. This concession consisted of a square tract of land, one league (approximately 2.76 miles) on each side, that faced the Mississippi from the east side of the river.[25] The large tract of land was located "about two leagues above the village of Kaskaskia" and included "two small facing islands" in the Mississippi, which reveals that Boisbriant's concession occupied the area where the village of Prairie du Rocher would later emerge.[26] The size, shape, and configuration of Boisbriant's concession would not have been out of place in the St. Lawrence Valley, which perhaps reflects Boisbriant's Canadian background. His father, Sidrac Michel de Boisbriant, had held at different times two Canadian seigneuries,[27] and Pierre Dugué may have requested the kind of concession with which he was familiar, or perhaps royal officials in France had simply chosen to employ a Canadian model in the Illinois Country.

Despite the fact that Boisbriant's concession had been granted "en franc alleu," in fee simple, rather than "en fief" or "en seigneurie," existing evidence suggests that this concession was conceived as a Canadian-style seigneury.[28] Some years after Boisbriant left the Illinois Country late in 1724, he conveyed his large concession to his sister's son, Jacques-Gaspard Piot de L'Angloiserie, sieur de Ste. Thérèse.[29] The Ignace-François Broutin map of 1734 shows the area where Prairie du Rocher would later develop as the "prérie de Ste. Thérèse."[30] Ste. Thérèse attempted to subdivide this concession into Canadian-style rotures, whose proprietors, technically roturiers, would owe him certain modest manorial rents. This was a logical and natural course of action for Ste. Thérèse, for he was familiar at first hand with the bastard manorial system of the St. Lawrence Valley; his father, Charles-Gaspard Piot de L'Angloiserie, had in marrying Boisbriant's sister received from his father-in-law a Canadian seigneury, L'Isle Ste. Thérèse, and had thereby also acquired "Ste. Thérèse" as part of his surname.[31] In February 1734 Ste. Thérèse conveyed without charge a parcel of land six arpents wide to Joseph Buchet in the "domaine du Rocher" with the stipulation that Ste. Thérèse reserved his seigneurial rights to the running water for the purpose of establishing gristmills. Although Buchet received the six arpents without immediate consideration, he was obliged annually to pay Ste. Thérèse one-half minot of wheat for each arpent of width of Buchet's tract and two capons for each two arpents of width.[32] Therefore Buchet's annual manorial dues theoretically amounted to three minots of wheat and six capons, and Buchet was in principle a Canadian-style censitaire. The policy of conveying rotures free of initial charge in return for annual manorial dues was stipulated in a royal edict promulgated by Louis XIV at Marly in 1711, which means that Ste. Thérèse's grant to Buchet in 1734 was in keeping with royal policy and Canadian practice at that time.[33] No evidence confirms, however, that Buchet, who had the rather elevated position of official storekeeper at Fort de Chartres, ever paid any of these manorial dues to Ste. Thérèse; likely he did not.

La Salle had brought seigneurialism de jure to the Illinois Country back in the 1680s. In 1683 Pierre Prudhomme was granted a concession on the upper Illinois River en fief and was given seigneurial privileges that included "right of dovecote, of wine press, of fortification, and of low justice."[34] Thus did the language of a decaying system of land tenure from France make its way to the Illinois frontier, where it must have seemed comically out of place.[35] Despite the high-flown language about seigneurial rights and manorial dues contained in Ste. Thérèse's donation of 1734, later evidence demonstrates that this bastard manorialism never matured in the Illinois Country. By means of an indenture drafted in New Orleans in 1737, Ste. Thérèse conveyed "to Augustin L'Anglois my domain of Prairie du Rocher, and I exact nothing from the settlers on the same prairie; they are all lords and masters."[36] Ste. Thérèse's language here betrays a certain uneasiness about the egalitarian quality of the Mississippi frontier. A seigneurial-manorial system carried from France to New France was eventually transplanted in attenuated form to the Illinois Country, where obviously it did not take strongly to root; by 1737 it had become so withered that it was for all intents and purposes moribund.

That this was to be, however, was not at all clear to Boisbriant when he sat down at his desk in the newly built Fort de Chartres in the spring of 1722 to begin drafting land grants. On May 10, 1722, Boisbriant and des Ursins granted at least twelve concessions in a single day, and it seems likely that most, perhaps all, of these were conveyed en roture; if so, then the grantees were at least in principle burdened with manorial dues just like the censitaires in French Canada. Although there is not a single original manuscript of any one of these conveyances, several verbatim transcriptions exist that are faithful to the originals right down to idiosyncratic spellings. Early Illinois governor and historian John Reynolds claimed that the oldest land grant in Illinois was that conveyed to Charles Danis on May 10, 1722.[37] Danis's concession was surely one of the oldest, and it is worth presenting in full:

> We, Pierre Dugué de Boisbriant, chevalier de l'ordre militaire de St. Louis, lieutenant of the king in the province of Louisiana, commandant in the Illinois, and Marc-Antoine de la Loëre des Ursins, principal secretary ["commis"] for the Royal Indies Company at the Illinois trading post.
>
> On the request of Charles Danis have granted him a piece of land ["terrain"] of five arpents on the bank of the Michigamea River [the Kaskaskia], which runs north and south, with Monsieur Philippe on one side and Monsieur Melique on the other, extending west to the Mississippi.
>
> Pursuant to our authority, the said piece of land has been accorded to Charles Danis en roture. While awaiting the formal concession that will be sent by the General Directors of the Royal Indies Company, he may work, clear, and sow the land. And we declare that the said conceded land will revert to the domain of the said company should the said Charles Danis fail to work on the land within one year and one day.
>
> At Fort de Chartres, May 10, 1722[38]

These early concessions, of which the preceding example is typical, are rich sources. The Royal Indies Company was in a sense functioning as seigneur in conceding agricultural lands in the Illinois Country en roture. Yet no manorial dues were apparently required of those habitants who received land en roture as long as the conveyance came directly from the company; at least there is no evidence that any such dues were ever collected. The homesteading provision, that the habitant had to begin working the land within a year and a day or forfeit it, was similar but not identical to the rule

in Canada, where censitaires were required to establish hearth and home
("tenir feu et lieu") on their rotures within one year or suffer them to be reunited to the seigneurial domain.[39]

On the other side of Danis's concession was the land of "Meleque," that is,
Pierre Melique, a lieutenant in the detached French marines who were garri-
soned at Fort de Chartres. He had arrived in the Illinois Country with
Boisbriant's convoy and was killed in 1726, along with seven of his men, by Fox
Indians along the Missouri River, where he was buried, a long way from his
native Amiens.[40] Melique's habitation was well-known in the early Illinois
Country and is depicted clearly on the 1734 Broutin map as the "Établissment
de feu M. Melique," the plantation of the late Monsieur Melique; the name long
survived the owner. No document reveals precisely when Melique received his
large concession near Kaskaskia, but it was apparently late in 1721 or early in
1722. Very likely Melique's grant came *after* Boisbriant had received his own
concession in September 1721. On the other hand, Melique's grant antedated
Danis's grant of May 1722, for the latter concession was located facing the
Kaskaskia River in relation to Melique's property.

Lieutenant Melique may have been a personal favorite of Boisbriant, or
perhaps he had inside influence with the Royal Indies Company and received preferential treatment from the overlords of Louisiana. His and
Boisbriant's concessions seem to precede everyone else's in the Illinois
Country. Even the storekeeper for the powerful company, Nicolas-Michel
Chassin, had to stand in line behind Melique. On July 1, 1722, Chassin wrote
from the Illinois Country:

> The concession of M. Melique, a lieutenant from Paris who wishes to marry
> my sister, is located one-half a league from the village of Kaskaskia. It con-
> tains fourteen arpents [approximately 2,700 English feet] facing the Little
> River [the Kaskaskia]. It runs back the entire distance to the Mississippi,
> which is about three-quarters of a league [approximately two miles].
>
> I am planning to have one of them [a concession] about half a league from
> Fort de Chartres, where I'll be living. It will be at least twenty facing arpents
> and a league or more deep. I hope to get this land ["terre"] in fee simple ["en
> franc alleu"] and with seigneurial title.[41]

Chassin employed here the defining phrase *en franc alleu* in conjunction with
land titles. Certainly a parcel of real estate so designated could not be burdened with any manorial dues or rents. But the way in which Chassin used
the phrase in his letter suggests that in the Illinois Country, where the phrases
en seigneurie and *en fief* were never employed, *en franc alleu* could at least on
some occasions convey seigneurial title; that is, high-ranking persons own-

ing land under this title had a right to subdivide the land into rotures and collect manorial rents from the habitants who lived on and cultivated the rotures.[42] Chassin's letter also implied that Melique's concession near Kaskaskia, which Chassin used as a model for his own, was held en franc alleu and had been conveyed with seigneurial rights.

Chassin apparently never received the twenty-arpent concession of which he wrote, but in 1722 he and one Legardeur Delisle did jointly receive a seventeen-arpent-wide tract of land that ran from the Mississippi to the bluffline just above where the village of Prairie du Rocher eventually emerged.[43] Two years later, in 1724, Delisle conveyed his 50 percent share to Chassin, making the latter sole owner of the tract.[44] By 1730, however, Chassin had either died or disappeared for good from the Illinois Country; his métis wife, Agnès Philippe, renounced their marital community of property in 1730,[45] and the 1732 census of the Illinois Country lists her as "widow Chassin."[46] The same year, 1732, Philippe Renaut—the lead miner, engineer, and entrepreneur on whose success so much had been wagered in the Illinois Country—surveyed this tract of land on behalf of the "Council of Illinois."[47] Renaut remarked that Chassin had kept for himself the upper eight facing arpents and conveyed to other individuals the nine lower facing arpents, those closest to the hamlet of Prairie du Rocher. With his death or disappearance, however, the whole of the seventeen facing arpents soon wound up in the hands of other habitants who were encumbered with no manorial dues of any sort. If at one time there had been a seigneury in the making at Chassin's large concession, by the early 1730s all vestiges of it had disappeared.

Land grants, cadastral records, and real estate transfers are nonexistent for Cahokia's early history, 1699–1722. In June 1722, however, Boisbriant and des Ursins, after proclaiming their titles of office, "first lieutenant of the king in the province of Louisiana and commandant in the Illinois," and "principal clerk of the Royal Indies Company," drafted a concession for a large tract of real estate at Cahokia.[48] They ceded to "Messieurs the missionaries of the Cahokias and Tamaroas" a parcel of land "quatre lieues en quarré," which meant a square with sides of four leagues each, making a total of sixteen square leagues, or approximately 122 square miles. As with the other early concessions in the Illinois Country, the grant at Cahokia was supposed to have been confirmed by the directors of the Royal Indies Company in Paris, for this company was officially suzerain (though not sovereign) of all Louisiana at that time. Although it is apparent that this confirmation never occurred, the concessions that Boisbriant issued on the spot in the Illinois Country were later taken to be perfectly valid under the civil law principle of prescription, by which proprietorship of land may be established by long possession and usage. The enormous tract of land that Boisbriant granted to the Seminarians at Cahokia was, both in size and shape, in keeping with many of the seigneuries in the St. Lawrence Valley; indeed, it was a good deal smaller than the gigantic concession that the Seminary of Foreign Missions held at Beaupré just east of Quebec City.[49] Boisbriant described the Seminarians' concession as beginning "a fourth of a league [approximately 0.7 miles] above Cahokia Creek, which is above the Indian village, and extending toward Fort de Chartres along the Mississippi." It ran inland from the Mississippi across the river's floodplain and onto the highlands beyond the bluffline. This was unusual, for most concessions in the Illinois Country were confined to the alluvial floodplains of the Mississippi and Kaskaskia Rivers.

Boisbriant granted this concession "en franc alleu," and he repeated this phrase in the document of concession, as if to emphasize it. Although this concession was not granted en seigneurie or en fief, and the document mentioned nothing about seigneurial rights or dues, in this case the phrase *en franc alleu* evidently meant that the concession at Cahokia was indeed of seigneurial status. When in 1735 Father-Superior Jean-Baptiste Mercier drafted a map of Cahokia and environs, he entitled his map "Plan de la Seigneurie et Établissement de la Mission des Tamarois." The seigneurial status of the concession at Cahokia gave the Seminarian priests there, who served as seigneurs, the right in principle to collect manorial dues such as the *cens* and *rentes* from the local habitants. The cens was a token payment theoretically levied on all land held en roture, whereas rentes were substantial land rents paid to the seigneur.[50] In 1735 Father Mercier described himself as seigneur at Cahokia, but he also acknowledged that no settler in the Illinois Country had yet paid any manorial dues.[51] Manorial dues in Canada remained intact both in principle and practice during the eighteenth century; the seigneurs of the St. Lawrence Valley retained their seigneurial rights and they exercised them to their own advantage.[52] Nevertheless, a seigneurial system that remained alive and active in Canada did not transplant well to the frontier soil of the Illinois Country, despite the fact that provincial administrators obviously had some intention of accomplishing this. Father Mercier, with a tinge of nostalgia for the good old ways, opined that manorial rents would be collected in the future, but he probably knew that he was simply indulging in wishful thinking. As time passed in the Illinois Country, medieval European land tenure practices did not evolve; rather, they disappeared altogether.

In 1717 the regent of France, the duc d'Orléans, created with the help of John Law, a Scottish financial wizard, the Royal Company of the West (or Indies). Law dreamed that the natural resources of Louisiana would generate immediate wealth for the company, its shareholders, and of course himself. When this did not occur, public confidence in the company plummeted, debts mounted, and the regent dismissed Law as minister of finance in 1720.[53] The company nonetheless persisted in its plan to exploit the mineral resources of Upper Louisiana. In keeping with this ambition, Boisbriant and des Ursins conveyed extensive land grants to Philippe Renaut, the mining entrepreneur, on June 14, 1723.[54] Renaut's four large land grants—one on the floodplain of the Mississippi River about ten miles north of Fort de Chartres, one on the headwaters of the Meramec River west of the Mississippi, one at Mine La Motte near the St. Francis River, and one on the Illinois River near Lake Peoria—had nothing whatever to do with traditional settlement patterns or with longlot cadastral configurations. These four tracts were chunky parcels, measured in leagues rather than arpents, and were rather more squarish than elongated in shape. Each was conveyed en franc alleu, and each was intended specifically to contribute in some fashion to Renaut's mining enterprises.[55]

Renaut and his lead-mining activities west of the Mississippi, interesting though they are, are largely beyond the scope of this study, although his concession at St. Philippe warrants some discussion. This tract measured one league along the Mississippi and ran two leagues deep into the hinterland.[56] This meant that it extended eastward over the bluffline onto high ground, although there is no evidence that this upper portion of the concession was ever exploited during the eighteenth century. Renaut's concession, like that of the Seminarians at Cahokia, was unusual for its size, shape, and geographical diversity. Renaut surveyed and subdivided much of this tract and granted the land in longlot parcels, generally two to four arpents wide, that ran across the bottomland from the Mississippi to the bluffline, a distance of several miles in that part of the river valley. U.S. land commissioners in the early nineteenth century stated that "Renaut conveyed away in small allotments to sundry individuals" his concession at St. Philippe.[57] Early land office plats suggest that Renaut granted land to at least twenty-five habitants,[58] and a smattering of later documentation suggests that he often conveyed these grants verbally, without taking the time and effort to have a notary draft formal conveyances. In 1743, for example, one Nicolas Noisé petitioned the authorities at Fort de Chartres (the commandant and the civil judge) for a written deed of concession for two tracts of land at St. Philippe that Philippe Renaut had granted verbally to Noisé years before. According to Noisé, Renaut had promised him a "regular title" but had never gotten around to providing it.[59]

Renaut's position as landlord was much like that of the Seminarian priests at Cahokia; in both cases massive concessions (by Illinois Country standards) were granted en franc alleu, and in both cases the original grantees conveyed agricultural strips to what were, at least in principle, subtenants burdened with certain manorial dues. Several notarial records from 1741 shed light on these complex and confusing issues. These documents pertain to real estate that Renaut sold to Nicolas Prévost *dit* Blondin on September 2, 1741,[60] and one of them states that "Bienville, Governor General of Louisiana and its dependencies and an interested principal of the Company [of the Indies]," had written a letter declaring that Renaut was to be "seigneur of the said concession of St. Philippe." Assuming that Bienville had indeed written such a letter (it is not extant), it was likely dispatched to Boisbriant at about the time (June 1723) that he had conveyed the St. Philippe concession to Renaut. Because of its rarity in colonial Illinois records, the word *seigneur* fairly leaps off the page, and even more remarkable is that both real estate transfers from Renaut to Blondin in 1741 baldly state that the sales were made "contingent upon the cens and seigneurial rights," in addition to the monetary value placed on the land.

What can be made of these curious documents, the only such known from the Illinois Country specifically to dignify someone with the title *seigneur*? First, they confirm that in some cases land held en franc alleu did include, at least in principle, some seigneurial rights.[61] Second, they reveal that during the early 1720s French Canadians of seigneurial class who were serving as government officials in Louisiana, including Bienville in New Orleans and Boisbriant at Fort de Chartres, were envisaging a land tenure system in the Illinois Country that would closely approximate that in the St. Lawrence Valley.[62] Third, the language of manorialism persisted in some Illinois notarial documents at least as late as 1741, despite the fact that no direct evidence exists that seigneurial dues were ever collected on *any* piece of land held en roture in the Illinois Country.

As pure speculation, one wonders to whom, and for that matter where, Renaut as a seigneur should have rendered the traditional *foi et hommage,* the fealty and homage that all seigneurs owed their overlords. In seventeenth-century Canada ceremonies of foi et hommage took place at the Château de St. Louis in Quebec, where Canadian seigneurs holding fiefs directly from the king came to swear fealty to a representative of the French crown.[63] If the Canadian seigneurial system was to be the model for French Illinois, and to some extent it was seen as such, Renaut, as well as one of the Seminarian priests from Cahokia, should have gone to New Orleans to render foi et hommage before Bienville, who was both governor general and a principal in the Royal Indies Company.[64] No evidence exists that such a ceremony ever unfolded in New Orleans; indeed, the mere suggestion of it seems slightly ludicrous.

In January 1725 the Provincial Council of Illinois—which since the recent departure of Boisbriant late in 1724 consisted of the new commandant at Fort de Chartres, Charles-Claude du Tisné, plus the original members of the council, des Ursins and Chassin—drafted a curious document, perhaps unique in the history of the Illinois Country.[65] It specified that the land at Fort de Chartres granted earlier to Étienne Hébert,[66] captain of the militia, was now being conveyed en franc alleu. Although the original concession from May 1724 does not spell it out, the obvious implication is that Hébert had at first held the land en roture. The change in designation for Hébert's concession was being done "in consideration of the services that Hébert has rendered the [Royal Indies] Company." The Héberts were a large and influential family in early Illinois,[67] and the Provincial Council may have deemed it unseemly for a captain of the militia to hold land en roture. In any case, the "en franc alleu" designation accorded Étienne Hébert in January 1725 explicitly exempted his land from the burden of manorial dues of any sort. It is conceivable but unlikely that the phrase *en franc alleu* was also intended to convey seigneurial status on Hébert's land. As noted previously, on some occasions the legal expression *en franc alleu* was associated with seigneurial rights and privileges, but it seems unlikely that Hébert's modest strip (probably only three arpents wide) was intended to become a seigneury in the manner of the St. Lawrence Valley, or even in the fashion of Renaut's concession at St. Philippe.

To sum up, the system of land tenure in the early Illinois Country was variegated and complex. For example, an interesting configuration appears if we take the Ignace-François Broutin map of the Illinois Country done in 1734 and superimpose on it the approximate boundaries of the *large* concessions that were conveyed by the Royal Indies Company during the early 1720s. These concessions, all conveyed en franc alleu with seigneurial rights implied, form a pattern that suggests an embryonic St. Lawrence Valley model was emerging in the Illinois Country during the early 1720s under the auspices of the Royal Indies Company, Governor General Bienville, and post commandant Boisbriant. It was, however, an embryo that did not mature; it failed to evolve because after 1723 no more large concessions that might be construed as seigneuries were granted and because manorial dues never became widespread or permanent. Although Father-Superior Mercier expressed the hope in 1735 that the Seminarian seigneury at Cahokia would soon collect manorial dues from the local habitants, this hope was never realized; although Nicolas Prévost *dit* Blondin was theoretically bound to pay Philippe Renaut manorial dues after he acquired land from him at St. Philippe in 1741, it seems unlikely that he ever made such payments. Many notarial documents from eighteenth-century French Illinois have been lost, and it is barely conceivable that their discovery would demonstrate a more profound and pervasive system of incipient manorialism and seigneurialism than is apparent from the now-extant records.

The early (apparently all from 1722) concessions that Boisbriant made on behalf of the Royal Indies Company that were specifically designated "en roture" never required that the grantees render manorial dues to the company, although the designation *en roture* surely implied that. Furthermore, there is no documentary evidence that the grantees were ever known as roturiers, who would be obliged to pay dues. When Boisbriant granted another series of concessions in May 1724, none of them contained the traditional, loaded phrase *en roture*. The nomenclature of manorial Canada—*seigneur, roturier, censitaire, cens et rentes, lods et ventes*—never took root in the Illinois Country. Within a short period of time, all property in the Illinois Country was de facto viewed as being held en franc alleu, with the owners neither obligated to pay dues nor conversely empowered to subdivide their land as seigneurs and collect dues. As Jacques-Gaspard Piot de Ste. Thérèse expressed it in 1737, the Illinois habitants were all "lords and masters" over their real estate, and he did not mean the phrase in a seigneurial sense.[68] In brief, land tenure in the Illinois Country was more modern than in French Canada and obviously more modern than in most of metropolitan France. The major qualification to this, which I explore in the next chapter, was that the proprietors of arable strips within the open-field complexes in the Illinois Country were not free to enclose them, thus separating their plowlands from those of their neighbors in order to practice individualistic agriculture.

SETTLEMENT PATTERN

When Boisbriant arrived in the Illinois Country in early 1719, he set out to affirm and extend a settlement pattern that was already emerging, at least in incipient form. During the first two decades of the eighteenth century, residential customs, especially in the region around Fort de Chartres, were mixed and complex; there were a handful of dispersed farmsteads, some straggling linear groupings, a few large plantations, and a number of budding nuclear villages. As time passed a less variegated pattern evolved in which there was a gravitation toward the villages, with fewer habitants living on dispersed farmsteads in the midst of their agricultural lands. This evolution toward nuclear, agricultural villages had profound and long-term consequences for agriculture, settlement, government, community life, and even the mental structures of the habitants of the Illinois Country.

A defining characteristic of the medieval longlots that composed linear settlements was that virtually all elements of life and livelihood were concentrated on one parcel of land. Residential plot, arable fields, pasture land, woodlot, and orchard were all encompassed on a single longlot. Residences were located in front, facing the feature of transportation that had originally dictated the orientation of the longlots. The longlots that developed in most areas of French colonization in North America—the St. Lawrence Valley, the Straits of Mackinac, Detroit, Green Bay, Prairie du Chien, the lower Mississippi Valley, and even Texas—were similar to medieval models and probably derived from them (though at some distance).

For complex reasons, land usage in the Illinois Country evolved in a different fashion. The Illinois pattern, which reached maturity by mid-eighteenth century, was distinctive because residential plots, plowlands, pastures, and woodlots were rigorously separated; nuclear villages, arable fields, and common lands made up the ubiquitous and indivisible triad of this pattern. Nineteenth-century Anglo-Americans were fascinated by this (to them) unfamiliar system, and comments about it appeared even in the popular press. In 1836, for example, James Hall wrote an article for a Quincy, Illinois, newspaper, the *Bounty Land Register*, entitled "Sketches of the West." In this piece Hall remarked about Kaskaskia that "the common field is a tract, composed of various grants . . . made to individual inhabitants in franc alleu (fee simple) and which from the first has been enclosed in one common fence, and subjected to certain regulations. We see here a custom peculiar to the French. There was attached to almost every village a common, belonging to the village, . . . which was left unenclosed; for pasturage and other purposes."[69] A half-century later Sidney Breese—lawyer, judge, and sometime historian—became one of the first professional authorities to note and comment on the idiosyncratic settlements of the French colonists in early Illinois: "The manner in which the settlers cultivated is peculiar, I believe, to the French, and deserves a passing notice. They had not, as we have, separate fields, nor did they reside on the cultivated land in general. They dwelt in villages, on lots of ground containing an arpent square, . . . which they inclosed with pickets of cedar or other durable wood."[70] The early Illinois settlement pattern, which both Hall and Breese believed was "peculiar to the French," is of course familiar to students of European medieval history in general, and was peculiar to the French only in the settlement of North America.

Medievalists have long debated the causes of the clustering of the western European population into nuclear villages, which was proceeding apace by the year 1000. Scholars have adduced various factors—increasing population density, changing technology, the development of the open-field system of cultivation, and the need for mutual defense—to explain this clustering. The great Marc Bloch, exaggerating to make a point, once remarked that an entire society may have evolved from a single technological device: "The wheeled plough ['charrue'] led to elongated plowlands, which in turn called for collective efforts; thus, a foretrain connected to a plowshare created an entire social structure."[71] Bloch has been gently chastised for placing too much emphasis on technology as a causal force when he associated plows, long furrows, collective labor, and nucleated villages.[72] More recently medievalists have tended to attribute population clustering to requirements for security rather than to communal agriculture and to place the initiative with the lords rather than the peasants.[73] That is, the impetus to create nuclear villages came from the top down rather than the bottom up and originated for reasons of safety rather than for agricultural organization. In any case, for medievalists the simply framed question of which came first, open-field agriculture or compact, nuclear villages, is still not without relevance.

For the Illinois Country, much closer to us in time and more fully documented than medieval Europe, this question is more easily answered: nuclear villages composed at first of missionaries, traders, voyageurs, and associated Indian groups developed at both Cahokia and Kaskaskia *before* any substantial agriculture was practiced in those areas. Furthermore, precisely as Genicot argues in the case of early medieval Europe, nuclear villages in the early Illinois Country were required for security. As Reynolds observed about the early French Illinois villages, "these settlements . . . [were] so weak and so far removed from any civilized communities, and amidst savage nations of Indians, that the inhabitants were forced to rely on each other for self-preservation."[74] This was patently the case in the 1720s, when predatory warriors of the Fox tribe preyed on French settlers who strayed from their villages.[75] In 1724 Boisbriant wrote from Kaskaskia to the directors of the Royal Indies Company that the "Foxes lie in wait around our French and Indian settlements every summer, or rather, almost all year long. This means that the habitants do not dare venture out except in groups."[76] A year later a resident of Kaskaskia, Tessier *dit* Lavigne, was "killed by a group of enemies only two steps from the village."[77] This kind of pressure from the Foxes surely discouraged Illinois habitants from living on dispersed farmsteads in the fashion of their French Canadian ancestors.

The Foxes were less threatening after they suffered a major defeat in 1730,[78] but dangers on the Illinois Country frontier diminished only slightly. During the last stages of King George's War (1744–48), Governor General Vaudreuil explained to the minister of marine, Comte Jean-Frédéric de Maurepas, that the commandant in the Illinois Country, the chevalier Charles de Bertet, had consolidated all the Illinois villages into one (presumably Kaskaskia) and surrounded it with "good palisades" because of fear of an attack from the Shawnees.[79] Vaudreuil wrote this from distant New Orleans, and there is no evidence from the Illinois Country that such a dramatic defensive consolidation was ever effected. In any event, Vaudreuil's sense of the situation in the Illinois Country underscores the need that was felt even in mid-eighteenth century to create compact, defensible villages in the region.

Jean-Jacques Macarty Mactigue,[80] a successor to de Bertet as commandant at Fort de Chartres, did not advocate consolidation of the Illinois villages, but he did have a defensive plan of his own. He wrote to Governor Vaudreuil, "It would be absolutely necessary . . . that you should give your orders that all the villages built and to be built should be aligned in sixty foot squares, so that the places may be walled as is done at Detroit and elsewhere in Canada as a protection against Indian raids."[81] Once again, no evidence exists that this plan was ever implemented. The geometrical planning and defensive perimeters that Macarty advocated never appeared in the Illinois Country, except at St. Louis under the colonial Spanish regime in anticipation of the British-Indian attack of 1780. Nonetheless, rather tightly nucleated villages persisted in the Illinois Country on both sides of the Mississippi throughout the eighteenth century.

Compact villages were therefore deemed necessary in the Illinois Country for security, but it is apparent that the development of a particular type of agriculture reinforced clustered settlements. Open-field tillage and the requirements of community defense together conspired to create a distinctive settlement pattern and a system of agriculture. As an early historian of Indiana succinctly put it: "Vincennes had somewhat the nature of a commune. This resulted partly from a general saving of labor and expense that could be effected by a community of interest in some things, and partly from the necessity of grouping the houses about the fort to prevent exposure to attack from hostiles."[82] The nuclear villages throughout the Illinois Country throve on the open-field agriculture that surrounded each of them. This system did not have to be invented afresh by the Illinois habitants who practiced it, for many of them were well versed in communal agricultural practices as they were still employed in many regions of metropolitan France. Moreover, the collective discipline and community regulations that communal agriculture required made the preexisting nuclear settlements ideal social and political units for governance. Georges Duby's remarks about medieval European villages, that the "small farmers . . . intermingled in the village enclave must have found themselves bound together by many ties into a community,"[83] are equally applicable to the habitants and the villages of the Illinois Country. This issue will be discussed more fully in the next chapter.

Within the compact villages of the Illinois Country, the residential plots (*terrains* or *emplacements*) were of different sizes and shapes; one need only glance at Captain Philip Pittman's plan of Kaskaskia from 1765 to observe that fact.[84] Nonetheless, there was a tendency for the "standard" plot to be roughly square, with each side measuring either one arpent (192 English feet) or twenty-five toises (160 English feet) and for the individual parcels to be grouped together in square blocks of four, each block measuring roughly 300 to 400 feet per side.[85] John Reynolds commented: "The French villages were laid out by common consent. . . . The blocks were about three hundred feet square, and each block contained four lots. The streets were rather narrow, but always at right angles."[86] Illinois habitants were in fact not as geometrically precise as Reynolds suggested. In May 1792 Vincennes became the first of the Illinois Country communities to be surveyed by a professional American surveyor, Samuel Baird. The unfortunate Mr. Baird, who had the tidy mind of a good surveyor, was distraught to discover an "extreme irregularity" in the layout of the village. Whereas the standard residential plot in Vincennes was supposed to be a square with each side measuring twenty-five toises (about six-tenths of an acre), Baird found that for some plots "no more than twenty could be given without altering the whole street." Baird rectified a bit here and chiseled a bit there and wound up drafting a reasonably coherent plat map, containing forty-three residential plots, of the old French village of Vincennes on the Wabash, which had become part of the United States of America in 1783.[87]

For substantial families, each of these large residential compounds included not only the residence itself but also various and sundry other buildings and features: a cow barn, a stable, a henhouse, an orchard, a vegetable garden, a bakeoven, a well, sometimes a slave quarters, and occasionally a freestanding kitchen. Henry Brackenridge described the Ste. Genevieve that he knew from the mid-1790s: "Although there is something like regularity of streets, and the houses are built in front of them, they do not adjoin, while the gardens, orchards, and stables, occupy a considerable extent of ground. Each house with its appurtences, has the appearance of one of our [i.e., Anglo-American] farm-yards. All kinds of cattle, cows, hogs, sheep, mingle with the passengers, in the streets."[88]

Nicolas de Finiels, a military engineer who lived in St. Louis in 1797–98, made a similar observation about the capital of Spanish Upper Louisiana, which although under Spanish sovereignty was still fundamentally a French Creole town: "St. Louis has never had a central market, and each resident must have a substantial garden in order to be able to lay in a supply of vegetables for the winter. He must have a poultry yard, a stable, a barn, and sheds in order to house his animals and to store his fodder and farm equipment. His residence in town is a microcosm of a farm."[89] The French Creole towns of the Illinois Country had a decidedly rural flavor about them. Fernand Braudel has remarked about early modern European villages that the "towns urbanized the countryside, but the countryside 'ruralized' the towns too. . . . In fact town and countryside never separate like oil and water."[90] Clearly the sounds, sights, and smells of Illinois towns were those of an agricultural countryside: cocks crowing, calves bawling, pigs squealing, urine sizzling, and manure steaming. Some of this rural flavor is still discernible at the restored Jean-Baptiste Vallé residence in Ste. Geneviève, Missouri, which occupies a parcel of ground still nearly one arpent square.

In his study of traditional French agriculture, Marc Bloch did not dwell on the structure of the rural villages. However, he did comment briefly about the residences of the peasants who worked outlying fields but who lived in villages rather than on dispersed farmsteads. He pointed out that the dwelling houses in these agricultural villages were surrounded by gardens and orchards and that a protective wall enclosed the entire complex of house and gardens. Indeed, he noted that *garden* (or *jardin*) was a German word that was synonymous with "close" or "enclosure." The enclosures that surrounded village residences were intended to protect houses and gardens from foraging livestock. "The fences indicated that the land inside the enclosure was not for grazing by the communal herd."[91] Precisely the same situation obtained in the villages of the Illinois Country.

John Brinckerhoff Jackson, a landscape historian, defined the meaning of gardens—that is, enclosures—in human experience over the centuries. He elaborated on Bloch's analysis (though he was apparently unaware of it) that the words *garden* and *enclosure* originally had identical meanings; he traced *garden* back to an Indo-European root, *gher,* that appears in many Indo-European–based words "for such apparently disparate things as farmyard, pasture, sown field, hedge," and so forth.[92] Jackson was interested in how the garden related to the dwelling house, which was "the focus of the enclosure," and how gardens might best be distinguished from grain-producing lands. Quite obviously the garden provided fruits and vegetables that supplemented a diet based largely on cereal grains; the garden was the horticultural branch of subsistence agriculture. At the social level, however, the garden was also a more private preserve. In an agricultural community based on open-field cultivation, the arable fields were subject to close community regulations. "The garden or enclosure was . . . long defined as a distinct family-centered, family-ruled territory, withdrawn or detached from the village community."[93] Furthermore, gardens were virtually extensions of houses and were ordinarily worked as such by the women in the household. The grain fields, on the other hand, were primarily the bailiwick of the men. Although Jackson was entirely ignorant of settlement and land usage in the Illinois Country, his observations are entirely applicable.

From the west side of the Mississippi, Henry Brackenridge, recalling his schooldays in Ste. Genevieve, described how residential property was subdivided and fenced: "The yard was enclosed with cedar pickets, eight or ten inches in diameter, and six feet high, placed upright, sharpened at the top, in the manner of a stockade fort. In front, the yard was narrow, but in the rear, quite spacious, and containing the barn and stables, the negro quarters, and all the necessary offices of a farm yard. Beyond this, there was a spacious garden enclosed with pickets, in the same manner with the yard."[94] The Vital Bauvais estate in colonial Ste. Genevieve was therefore a complex of dwelling house and various enclosures. Brackenridge's description affirms Jackson's analysis of the uses and the importance of domestic spaces, which the Bauvaises carefully delineated with the help of picket fences.

The former Jean-Baptiste Vallé property at Ste. Genevieve, previously mentioned, remains an enclosed village estate that retains much of the character that it had when Jean-Baptiste built the house circa 1793. The enclosed quality is important, for Creole families in the Illinois Country had a veritable passion for fencing their residential plots. This passion was a matter of taste, whose roots went back to medieval times, as well as of practicality. George Morgan, an Anglo-American merchant, noticed this while living in British Illinois in 1770. At the former Fort de Chartres—Fort Cavendish to the British—Morgan recorded a conversation with Colonel John Wilkins about the virtues of picket fencing: "I told him that I would Picket in my Lott. . . . He answered it was not worth while as no one would buy my Lott after the [British] Troops went home from here. I answered that the Pickets would always be an inducement for Some of the French to Purchase my House and Lott, *even if it was only for the sake of the Pickets.*"[95]

Pickets for residential fencing were usually of either oak or, preferably, the longer-lasting red cedar. In 1781 François Vallé of Ste. Genevieve ordered 1,243 cedar pickets for a fence. Reckoning each picket at between seven and eight inches in diameter, and assuming that they were set into the earth, picket-to-picket, two feet deep, these pickets would have enclosed a plot almost precisely one arpent square with a fence six feet high. The picket fences surrounding the major residences in all the towns and villages of the Illinois Country were a distinctive feature of the region's settlement customs, and the persistent demand for good pickets drove up the price of red cedar, which by the 1790s cost three times as much as oak.[96]

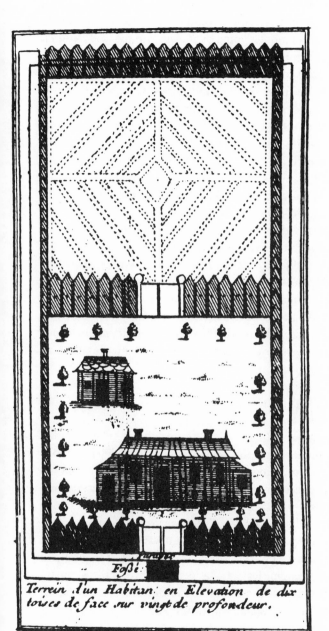

Terrein d'un Habitan: en Elevation de dix
toises de face sur vingt de profondeur.

A residential complex from colonial Louisiana. Notice the formal garden, the surrounding picket fence, and what are perhaps slave quarters behind the dwelling house. Reproduced from Jean-François Benjamin Dumont de Montigny's *Mémoires historique sur la Louisiane*, 1753.

The fundamental tripartite pattern of land usage throughout the Illinois Country—nuclear villages, open fields, and commons for pasture—evidently was based on rural European models going back deep into the Middle Ages. At the beginning of his authoritative work on rural life in medieval Europe, Georges Duby described this configuration: "What we might describe as three concentric zones formed the picture which the author of *Annales Cameracenses* preserved of his childhood village at the end of the twelfth century— the village enclosures, the *coutures,* that is the arable, and finally surrounding all, a broad uncultivated belt."[97] This pattern of land usage, which was central to European peasant life, did not descend to the Illinois Country from Canada, as did many of the early settlers who came to the region. For all intents and purposes, agricultural villages did not exist in seventeenth-century Canada, where the habitants preferred a dispersed form of settlement. Richard Harris has emphasized that to French Canadians the village meant "supervision by the seigneur, the curé, or even the intendant"[98] and that the Canadians opposed village life in order to have the liberty to engage clandestinely in the fur trade. Louise Dechêne argues that Canadian habitants did not cluster their houses in villages because of practical considerations relating to agricultural life.[99] Whatever motivated the French Canadians to maintain dispersed settlements, the habitants in the Illinois Country chose to create and inhabit nuclear villages despite the practical inconveniences this may have been entailed.

THE ILLINOIS COUNTRY: CAHOKIA

Cahokia was the first European settlement in the French Illinois Country with a claim to being a permanent village, and it now pretends to having had a continuous existence since its founding at the close of the seventeenth century. During the late 1690s, priests of two orders, the Society of Jesus (Jesuits) and the Seminary of Foreign Missions (Seminarians), became familiar figures along the middle reaches of the Mississippi River. These two groups competed, usually in a collegial fashion, for position as missionaries at various Indian villages. In 1699 three Seminarians—François Jolliet de Montigny, Jean-François Buisson de St. Cosme, and Antoine Davion—were dispatched by the Seminary of Foreign Missions of Quebec to found a mission in the heart of North America beyond the territory of the Illinois tribes. The latter provision was intended explicitly to avoid any complicating rivalry with the Jesuits, who, going back to Jacques Marquette, had already established a strong presence in the Illinois Country. Davion, Montigny, and St. Cosme did not adhere to the letter of their instructions when they founded the Mission of the Holy Family at

Cahokia, for the Indians who congregated there were indeed tribes of the large Illinois nation. In any event, the mission that was founded at Cahokia in 1699 still prospers, now as the Parish of the Holy Family.[100]

The mission was situated at an Indian village on the east side of the Mississippi, near the mouth of Cahokia Creek, and across the river from the site where a Jesuit mission was established in 1700, at the mouth of the River Des Peres. At that time, the village at Cahokia was composed of various groups of the Illinois nation, including the Cahokias, the Tamaroas, and a few Peorias. Additional Seminarian priests soon arrived, including Marc Bergier, vicar general of the bishop of Quebec, who was resident pastor at Cahokia from 1700 to 1707. Until Kaskaskia was established in 1703, however, a scattering of Jesuit priests also passed through Cahokia, visiting and assisting their competitors in the Mississippi Valley missionary field. Indeed, for the first several years of the mission's existence, it was not clear whether it would be controlled by Seminarians or Jesuits, and an episcopal commission was required to resolve the issue.[101]

For several reasons, Cahokia played a significant but secondary role in the history of the Illinois Country throughout most of the French colonial period. First, whatever their importance, the Seminarians could not generally compete with their brothers from the Society of Jesus who established themselves at Kaskaskia in 1703; the Seminarians did not possess the organizational structure, the weight of numbers, or the driving proselytizing ambition of the Jesuits. Second, Cahokia continued to be a bit removed from the largest concentration of population in the French Illinois Country, Kaskaskia, and from the military and administrative center of the region, Fort de Chartres. Cahokia and its satellite, Prairie du Pont, did undergo a surge of expansion late in the eighteenth century, however, after the French regime in Louisiana had collapsed and the American Revolution ended. The 1787 enumerations of males ("Recensement des habitants et de leurs enfans males") in the Illinois Country show Cahokia and Prairie du Pont with an aggregate population of 240 male residents and Kaskaskia with 191, the latter having suffered a major exodus of inhabitants during the chaotic 1780s.[102] As with all the early Illinois settlements, Cahokia's first years lie in a penumbra cast by scarce documentation. In 1720 the itinerant Jesuit Pierre-François de Charlevoix passed through the area and remarked: "We went to lay in a Village of the Caoquias, and Tamarouas: These are two Nations of Illinois, which are united, and who do not together make a very numerous Village."[103] Charlevoix did not even bother to mention the mission establishment or the parish of the Holy Family, which at that time were already being directed by Jean-Baptiste Mercier, long-time father-superior at Cahokia.

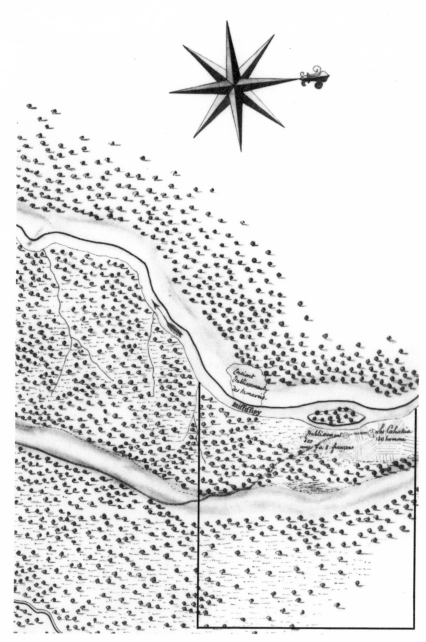

Detail of Ignace-François Broutin map of 1734 with the Seminarian seigneury at Cahokia delineated. Notice the French village, the Indian village, and the surrounding plowlands. Map reproduced from *Indian Villages of the Illinois Country,* ed. Sarah Jones Tucker, plate 22.

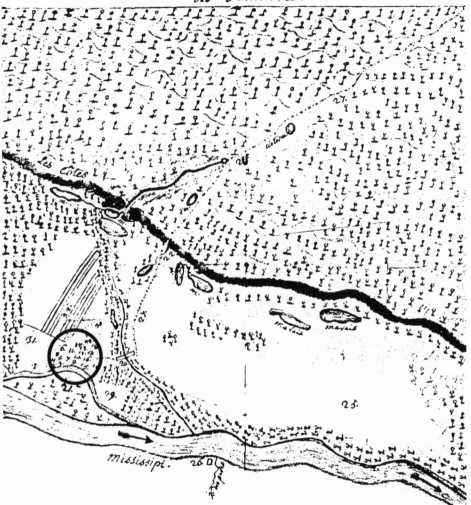

Settlement at Cahokia in 1735 as depicted by Jean-Baptiste Mercier. Notice the compact village (circled), the adjacent plowlands, and the bluffline. Photograph courtesy of the Illinois State Museum, Springfield.

Unique in the Illinois Country, the vast Seminarian concession encompassed all components of the Cahokia settlement: mission complex, French village, Indian village, military outpost, agricultural fields, pastures, barns, and other outbuildings. In the summer of 1723, an official of the Royal Indies Company compiled a census of the Illinois Country that listed at Cahokia seven habitants, one *volontaire* (day laborer), one married woman, and three children. Excluded from this earliest census of the community was the entire mission establishment; all transients, such as the voyageurs; and all slaves, of which there were probably some Indian and some African.[104] This 1723 census is only a rudimentary document, but it does reveal that Cahokia was in the process of becoming an agricultural community (witness the seven habitants). The census also demonstrates that of the three principal population loci in the Illinois Country at that time—Kaskaskia, Fort de Chartres, and Cahokia—Cahokia had the smallest population.

The 1732 census of the Illinois Country does not list the number of habitants at Cahokia,[105] but the small number of slaves and domestic animals enumerated reveals that this mission settlement was hanging on by its fingernails at that time. A more valuable document for gaining an understanding of Cahokia during the 1730s is an annotated plan done in 1735 by Father-Superior Jean-Baptiste Mercier. This document is in fact two discrete plans drafted on one 36-cm by 48-cm sheet, for the mission complex, depicted in small scale on the general plan, is shown in detail on a larger-scale inset.[106] The map encompasses the full sixteen square leagues that composed the entire concession granted by Boisbriant and des Ursins in 1722. Indeed, the 1735 map of Cahokia is the earliest map of the Illinois Country clearly to depict the threefold pattern of land usage that became de rigueur in the region. First there is the tightly nucleated village that contained the mission compound, the Church of the Holy Family, a minuscule fort, the commandant's house, the residences of the habitants and several merchants, a number of slave (both African and Indian) quarters, and a scattering of barns and stables. This nucleated village complex occupied a roughly pie-shaped parcel of land bordered on one side by the Rivière du Pont (a small tributary of the Mississippi), on another side by a small channel of the Mississippi, and on the third side by a fence line called "la clôture de la Commune." Therefore, in the case of early Cahokia, *commune,* a word that can mean many things in French, meant the village complex, the parish, or the community. In this instance the word was used not unlike it is in modern France, to mean the territory of the smallest administrative division.

Outside the village proper, the general plan distinctly depicts a cluster of arable fields, a compact grouping in which elongated strips are clearly delineated. These strips were obviously longlots of some sort, and Father Mercier's gloss on the map reveals that the widest of the strips, located in the center of the grouping and designated as "Domaine," was six arpents wide. This suggests that the strips belonging to the individual habitants were two to three arpents wide, more or less the usual widths for the Illinois Country. These strips were agricultural longlots (champs allongés) rather than cadastral longlots. That is, each strip specifically represented the plowlands of a habitant rather than the habitant's entire longlot parcel, for the complete parcels would have run all the way from the Mississippi to the bluffline. In all likelihood the cultivated strips were merely segments of larger cadastral longlots, and in the case of Cahokia, the arable strips were oriented the same way as the larger cadastral longlots. It was rare anywhere in the Illinois Country for an entire longlot to be devoted *exclusively* to arable cultivation, for marshes and clumps of woods often transected the alluvial bottomlands. Furthermore, the plowlines of the culti-vated strips were not necessarily oriented the same as the cadastral longlots, although at Cahokia in 1735 they were.

Father Mercier explained that on either side of the domaine, which re-mained the property of the mission, seven strips of land (three on one side and four on the other side of the domaine) had been granted to seven habi-tants. Therefore it is clear that Seminarian priests, who had received their vast tract of land en franc alleu, were exercising a seigneurial right to subdivide (perhaps more an obligation, for seigneurs in Canada were expected to at-tract settlers to their seigneuries), and the very name—"domaine"—for the land belonging to the mission affirmed the missionaries' position as sei-gneurs. The Seminary of Foreign Missions in fact held two seigneuries, Beaupré and Ile Jésus, in the St. Lawrence Valley.[107] Mercier also explained that the mission at Cahokia had unofficially conveyed to each of the seven habitants three additional facing arpents and that these longlots were to have the same orientation as the domaine, although there is no indication precisely where they lay in relation to it.

Interestingly, all the early strips were oriented so that the long sides were roughly perpendicular to the Mississippi River and to the bluffline. Father Mercier explained that the local habitants "absolutely insisted that their lands begin at the bank of the little river [Cahokia Creek], . . . and that they must be granted in depth to the bluffs, as they have been granted by all the concessioners or seigneurs to all the settlers of the Illinois."[108] The habit of orienting longlots perpendicular to a major waterway had surely been car-ried from the St. Lawrence Valley to the Mississippi Valley, where the habi-tants, most of the earliest of whom were transplanted Canadians, insisted on replicating a system with which they were familiar. The bluffline, located some fifty arpents back from the river, served as a convenient rear boundary for the cadastral longlots and thereby reinforced the pattern imported from the St. Lawrence Valley. This pattern must already have been in use, at least in some approximate fashion, when Boisbriant began to grant longlot concessions in 1722. The distinctive longlots at Cahokia—which stand out on early GLO maps, continue to govern the grid of city streets in East St. Louis, and are easily discernible in recent landsat photographs—thus date from early in the eighteenth century and are truly a vestige of French colonial culture in Illinois.

Examining the Cahokia agricultural strips within the context of the longlots in the St. Lawrence Valley or the lower Mississippi valley, however, one is struck by an obvious and critical difference: at Cahokia not a single one of the longlots has any structure of any kind shown on it—no residences, slave cabins, barns, or other agricultural outbuildings, although the plan is detailed enough to have shown such structures if they had existed. Indeed, the plan's detailed legend reveals that the resident agriculturists, the habitants, all lived within the compact French colonial village in individual residences with their barns located nearby. The longlots of the St. Lawrence Valley and those of Cahokia functioned very differently, but in both cases cultural habits of the French in North America are apparent: they had a strong inclination to measure off in arpents elongated, rectangular parcels of land with the long axes oriented at right angles to a large river.

South of Cahokia village, in a low-lying area of less fertile land across the Rivière du Pont, lay one area of the Cahokia commons. This was called the "Prairie des Buttes," prairie of the bluffs, for it lay between the Mississippi River and the bluffline. Other parts of the commons lay in other low-lying areas along the Mississippi: one was located on the Isle de la Ste. Famille, which was separated from the left riverbank by a slough; another was located between Cahokia Creek and the Mississippi. These areas were true commons, consisting of land that was not granted to any individual as owner or tenant; the commons was an area for pasturing livestock, gathering wood, and doubtless for hunting rabbits, squirrels, and prairie chickens.

In comparing French Cahokia with French Canada—for the priests, habitants, and fur traders who lived there came from Canada—one is somewhat puzzled by land usage at the former. Longlots were present to be sure, but longlots that were so different from those in the St. Lawrence Valley that the two sorts are difficult to compare. Indeed, one may more easily compare Cahokia as depicted on the 1735 map and a thirteenth-century French manorial village: the father-superior of the mission served as the local seigneur; the habitants served as the agricultural laborers; a nucleated village centered on the parish church was clearly present; a bundle of plowlands stood outside the village proper; and less fertile land was devoted to a commons for pasturage. This comparison should not be carried too far, however, for if one probes into the economic and social details of the community, the differences between Cahokia and a medieval French manor loom large. Habitants at Cahokia had more freedom and mobility than French peasants—even free peasants; the agricultural fields at Cahokia were puny relative to the village; and slaves, both African and Indian, were used in Cahokia. The comparison between the French villages in the Illinois Country and traditional French villages is nevertheless not so far-fetched as to be frivolous.

The mission complex at Cahokia could translate easily enough into a medieval abbey that had become the nucleus for a village: the Seminarians owned the "domaine" and the local gristmill and parceled out the remaining agricultural land to habitants, who at least in principle owed them manorial dues. A second glance at the 1735 map, however, brings one sharply back to eighteenth-century North America. Just beyond the French village at Cahokia was the Cahokia Indian village, and inside the French village were the quarters of the resident African and Indian slaves, some owned by the missionaries and some by the habitants. Moreover, collection of manorial dues, which Father Mercier had hoped would soon begin, never came to pass. Cahokia was North American sure enough, but land usage in the community—compact village, unfenced plowlands, and commons—meant that it more closely resembled a community from medieval France than any settlement in Canada or Lower Louisiana.

PRAIRIE DU PONT

Flowing diagonally across the Mississippi's floodplain near Cahokia was a small stream that entered the river a mile or so below the village. A wooden bridge spanned this stream toward its lower end, giving the Cahokia habitants easier access to the prairie on the far side. As Father Mercier explained in a letter to Louisiana governor general Vaudreuil, "We have built a bridge of timbers over a little river at least half a league from here for easy communication between the two prairies."[109] The far prairie, which made up part of the original Cahokia commons, was called "la prairie du pont" because of the bridge (*pont*) that gave the villagers access to it. As time went on, a small village grew up on this prairie, and although it was at first merely a dependency of Cahokia, it eventually assumed an identity of its own. The new village was named, appropriately enough, Prairie du Pont (now inelegantly transmogrified to "Dupo"). Along with this identity came the ubiquitous tripartite land usage pattern of the Illinois Country. How was it that this particular system, so common in certain portions of France but unknown anywhere else in the French colonial world, developed in the Illinois Country?

John Reynolds, early Illinois governor and historian, described this settlement pattern at Prairie du Pont without inquiring into its origins or significance:

> The village of Prairie du Pont was settled by emigrants from the other French villages, in the year 1760, and was a prosperous settlement. They had their common field and commons, which was confirmed to them by the government of the United States. This village is situated about one mile south of Cahokia, and extended south from the creek of the same name, for some distance. It is a kind of suburb to Cahokia. The arpent lands of this common field extended from the bluff to the Mississippi, with a few exceptions, and were three or four miles in width. It is stated that this village, in the year 1765, contained fourteen families.[110]

Reynolds perpetuated some confusion in this passage by not clearly differentiating "common field" (i.e., arable land) from "common" (i.e., pasture), but in any case he adduced 1760 as the year of Prairie du Pont's founding. In another passage Reynolds stated that the settlement at Prairie du Pont dated from "about 1754."[111] Even apart from the semantic issue of precisely what constitutes a village, the early history of the village at Prairie du Pont is obscure. Nonetheless, a brief examination of Prairie du Pont's origins demonstrates the importance of the agricultural village in the Illinois Country.

Prairie du Pont's early history centers on Antoine Girardin,[112] who acquired a substantial amount of land in and around Cahokia during the mid-1760s. The Seminarian priests, who had been established at Cahokia since 1699, departed with the disappearance of French sovereignty in the Illinois Country, and in 1763 their properties were sold off.[113] Girardin rose to become the area's most prominent citizen, serving variously as judge, commandant at Cahokia, and commandant of Prairie du Pont. Despite his preeminence (perhaps because of it), he was not always popular with the local habitants. In April 1780 the embryonic American court at Cahokia, which George Rogers Clark had created after his conquest of British Illinois,[114] received a complaint presented by "Les habitant[s] Des Cahos" against Antoine Girardin "on account of the land, which he is conceding, and the injury, which that does the village; and they demand that M. Girardin be forbidden to continue, since he has no right to form a village and to concede lands, which have been reserved for this village."[115] As American commandant in the area, Girardin was apparently carving up portions of the Cahokia commons and ceding them to individual owners in the fledgling village of Prairie du Pont. Although the court concurred with the complaints of the habitants in 1780, Girardin triumphed in the long run, for arable land was increasingly dear at Prairie du Pont. In June 1783 the Cahokia court ordered that a census be taken of all citizens, that arable strips be distributed within a common fence, and that an area be designated as commons for pasturage. Although the clerk of the court, François Saucier, had some difficulty spelling *sitoyen,* this word was now beginning to be used as a synonym for *habitant* in that portion of the Illinois Country governed by the American Republic—but not on the monarchial Spanish side of the Mississippi.[116]

The case of the Cahokia habitants versus Girardin reveals that the creation of a new hamlet in the Illinois Country was an event of some consequence, for associated with an agricultural village were the important communal issues of commons, common arable fields, fencing, and mutual obligations for maintaining a regime of open-field agriculture. The appearance of a new village cut right to the heart of community life for the habitants of the Illinois Country. By 1783 an American court was overseeing the development of a pattern of land usage and settlement that had been passed down to the Mississippi frontier from traditional practices in rural France. These issues arose in 1786 when a group of Cahokia habitants, including Antoine Girardin, complained that the prairie at Prairie du Pont, which "has belonged for all time to the habitants both for cultivation and as a commons for their animals," was being seized on the basis of a concession granted by Father Pierre Gibault to one of Clark's officers back in 1779. The complaining habitants pleaded their case in a memorial sent directly to the U.S. Continental Congress. They apparently received no immediate redress to their grievance but were eventually vindicated when U.S. land commissioners judged that the 1779 concession was invalid and that the commons at Prairie du Pont should remain intact.[117]

Prairie du Pont represents a type of satellite agricultural hamlet that developed in various locations in the Illinois Country. As Prairie du Pont lay outside Cahokia, so Prairie du Rocher and St. Philippe lay outside Chartres, New Bourbon lay outside Ste. Genevieve, and Carondelet and St. Ferdinand lay outside St. Louis. These satellite hamlets were always smaller than their parent villages. They sprang up because a growing population needed residential space and because they were necessary to bring local habitants closer to their plowlands. As arable fields spread up and down both sides of the Mississippi River, the original nuclear agglomerations became too distant from some of the plowlands. The habitants chose not to erect dispersed farmsteads, which would have been scattered across the entire floodplain of the

Mississippi, but instead founded additional agricultural villages, which brought their residences within striking distance of their individual arable strips within the open-field compounds.

The U.S. Congress in 1791 recognized the French way of life in the Illinois Country by officially conveying the commons to the inhabitants of Cahokia and Prairie du Pont, and in 1809 U.S. land commissioners clearly articulated the divisions of land usage at these communities by recognizing the following categories: "Commons, Common Field, and Town Lots." Remarkably the commissioners said of the common field that "the original boundaries of this tract have been found by the present surveyor; and there seems to be no dispute between the individuals claiming here about their titles or their boundaries."[118]

THE ILLINOIS COUNTRY: KASKASKIA

Kaskaskia was located at the southern terminus of the trunk roadway that connected all the French communities on the east bank of the Mississippi River. This artery ran from Cahokia across the alluvial bottomland and onto the bluffs, descended to pass through St. Philippe (several miles north of Chartres), passed by the fort itself, continued down through Prairie du Rocher (located on the lowlands just under the rocky bluffs), hugged the bluffline all the way down to the Kaskaskia River, turned down along the northwest bank of the river, passed through the Kaskaskia Indian village, and finally terminated in Kaskaskia, metropole of the Illinois Country, although not its seat of government.[119]

The Jesuit establishment at Kaskaskia was larger (i.e., it consistently had more resident priests and more slaves) than the Seminarian mission at Cahokia, and the Jesuits held substantial amounts of real estate, both in the village and in the arable compound.[120] Kaskaskia as a whole was never subsumed as part of a Jesuit concession, however, nor did the Jesuits hold a seigneury in the Illinois Country (they held eight in the St. Lawrence Valley);[121] this was true from the time of the community's founding in 1703 to 1763, when the Jesuit order was suppressed.[122] The Jesuits therefore never effected in the Illinois Country what they accomplished in their well-known Paraguayan colony, where land, governance, and mission were the exclusive domain of the Society of Jesus, a veritable theocracy.[123] Kaskaskia's development was both remarkably different and remarkably similar to Cahokia's. It was different because the geography of the area along the Kaskaskia River was quite unlike that at Cahokia and because the Jesuits at Kaskaskia never had, as the Seminarians did at Cahokia, a seigneurial grant encompassing the entire community;[124] it was similar because both these early French Illinois communities were anchored by Roman Catholic mission complexes and because they both developed the same pattern of land usage—village, plowlands, and commons.

An early amateur historian of Illinois, J. Nick Perrin, described this pattern succinctly and accurately:

> The early French settlers settled in villages. Around their houses they enclosed a lot of ground which they used for garden and stable purposes. Their farms extended from the villages out over the adjacent prairie or bottom lands and were narrow strips which extended from the villages to the river or creek on the one side and the bluffs on the other. The inhabitants thus lived in communities which afforded mutual protection while at home and also while working in their fields. These farms were known as the "Common Fields." In addition to this there was a "Common" which furnished them in common with pasturage and fuel.[125]

Perrin knew enough about the system he was describing not to confuse common fields with true commons, and he understood clearly the different uses to which the two distinct areas were put. The only thing he failed to do was explain *why* the farms of arable land were called the common fields. In any case, the configuration described so well by Perrin already existed in incipient form when Boisbriant arrived in the Illinois Country in 1719, and he reinforced it by designating commons areas for pasturing cattle.[126] The commons at Kaskaskia was apparently the first such tract officially allocated for that purpose, and Boisbriant's act did much to affirm and perpetuate the existing pattern of land usage. The informality of the pattern prior to this act is made apparent by the fact that several of the local habitants were cultivating land in the area designated as commons. Rather than simply expel them, Boisbriant gave them the option of fencing off their plowlands in the commons to protect their crops. If they exercised this option, it must have been only briefly, for the commons at Kaskaskia was soon devoted exclusively to pasturage.

The land that Commandant Boisbriant designated for the principal commons consisted of three contiguous areas: the land immediately surrounding the village, a strip along the lower left bank of the Kaskaskia River, and the lower end of the peninsula that separated the Kaskaskia from the Mississippi River. This low-lying peninsula was marshy and partly wooded and was sometimes referred to as "la pointe de bois."[127] This was the largest of the commons tracts at Kaskaskia and comprised some 7,000 to 8,000 acres (this varied with the caprices of the Mississippi); it was separated from the arable

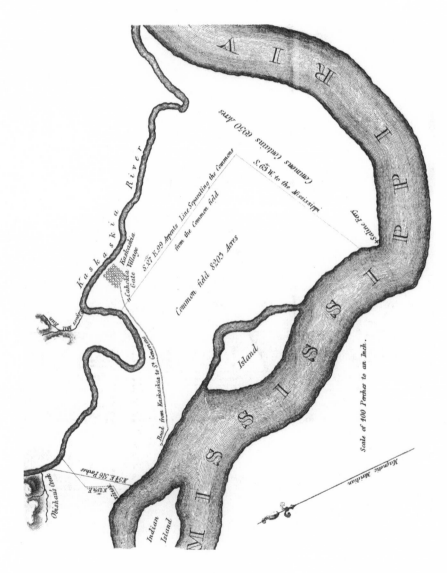

Kaskaskia region in the early nineteenth century. Notice the tripartite pattern of land usage—commons, the common fields, and the compact village. U.S. General Land Office map, from *ASP, PL.*

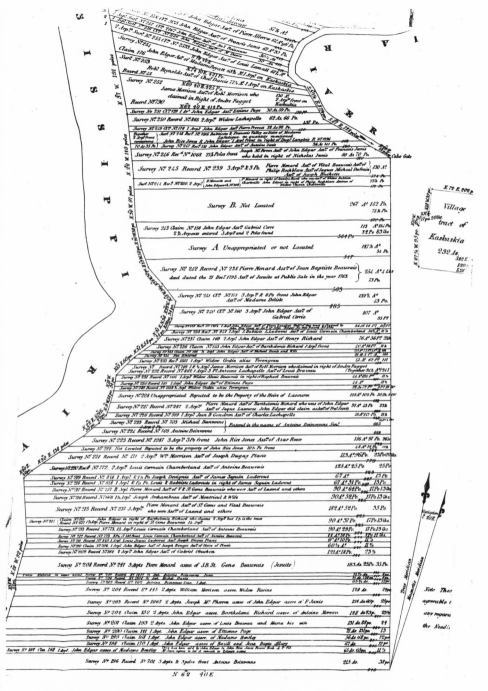

The open-field complex at Kaskaskia. During the colonial era no fencing existed between the individual strips. Similar compounds of plowlands existed at every French village in the Illinois Country. U.S. General Land Office map, from *ASP, PL.*

Compact village of Kaskaskia in 1766. Notice the parish church (D), the commandant's residence (C), the Jesuit mission complex (B), and the irregular street plan.
Map reproduced from Philip Pittman, *The Present State of the European Settlements
on the Mississippi River.*

compound by two straight lines, la Grande Ligne and la Petite Ligne. The first
of these ran roughly south from the bank of the Kaskaskia River, passing
several hundred yards to the west of the village; the second and shorter line
ran roughly east from the bank of the Mississippi. The two lines met several
miles south of the village to form what was intended to be a perfect right-
angle corner, the "Grand Carré" or "Trait Quarré," as it was called.

Clearly delineated on the GLO maps of the early nineteenth century, these
two boundary lines played a central role in the life of Kaskaskia for nearly
two hundred years; they were the two axes on which the entire agricultural
system of the region was based. After all the plowland west of the Grande

Ligne and north of the Petite Ligne had been conceded, two different commandants in the Illinois Country, de Bertet and Macarty, considered moving the Petite Ligne southward, which would have enlarged the compound of arable strips. The local habitants opposed this, however, and it was never done.[128] The venerable Grande and Petite Lignes were immutable and remained precisely where Boisbriant had laid them down in 1719. When "Old" Kaskaskia was destroyed by the Mississippi River in the late nineteenth century, the grid for "New" Kaskaskia was laid out precisely inside the right-angle corner of the Grand Carré.

The Kaskaskia commons designated by Boisbriant was used for several decades without any provincial authorization. Finally, on June 16, 1743, the habitants sent a petition to Governor General Pierre de Rigaud de Vaudreuil and Commissaire-ordonnateur Edmé-Gatien Salmon in New Orleans regarding the commons ("la commune") at Kaskaskia. The response from New Orleans, dated August 14, 1743, is an essential document for understanding land usage and settlement at mid-eighteenth-century Kaskaskia.[129] Although Vaudreuil and Salmon were not familiar at first hand with the configuration of agricultural lands and fences at Kaskaskia, it is apparent that they had received detailed information from the Illinois Country, including a map. Their response to the citizens of Kaskaskia provided for the first time in black and white both a conceptual and a practical framework within which the pattern of land usage in the Illinois Country continued to evolve.

Vaudreuil and Salmon began their response by noting that the petition they had received from Kaskaskia was in effect a request to render official the existence of a commons ("une commune") that had already existed for "a long time." This commons for pasturing livestock was located on the pointe de bois. Vaudreuil and Salmon saw no problem in accomplishing this "by virtue of the authority conveyed to us by His Majesty [Louis XV]." Following this preamble, Vaudreuil and Salmon declared that the commons would begin just below the concession belonging to a habitant named Cavallier. That is, in descending the alluvial peninsula between the Kaskaskia and Mississippi Rivers, Cavallier's elongated strip of plowland would be the last such strip to remain in possession of an individual.[130] Further down the point all land would be in the public domain, that is, commons for pasturage. A roadway, "le chemin du trait quarré," would be maintained for passage through the arable field into the commons, and fences along it would be maintained by those habitants whose fields were contiguous to it. Furthermore, fences between the village plot and the arable fields would have to be built and maintained by the community at large. The 1743 edict spelled out the conditions concerning wood gathering on the commons, a vital issue given the prodigious quantities of wood consumed for building and fuel in the Illinois Country. All persons having access to the commons for pasture (presumably this would mean all habitants who owned arable strips) also had a right to harvest trees *for their own use* either for building purposes or firewood, the main point being that the commons could not be exploited for commercial purposes.

The decree of Vaudreuil and Salmon clarifies the pattern of land usage that was becoming increasing dominant in the Illinois Country. The village plot of Kaskaskia, the strips of plowlands, and the commons all appear as discrete entities in the document. That Vaudreuil and Salmon, neither of whom had ever set foot in the Illinois Country, could so clearly conceptualize this unusual (for French North America) pattern suggests that these two colonial administrators were familiar with traditional French agricultural villages. Although land usage in Illinois was very different from that in the environs of New Orleans, it was remarkably similar to that in rural metropolitan France.

The earliest map of the Illinois Country detailed enough to be useful in analyzing settlement was drafted by Bernard Diron d'Artaguiette in Paris in 1732.[131] This map depicts the Illinois Country as Diron knew it when he was an officer in the French marines stationed at Fort de Chartres during the 1720s.[132] This map is the first to show *two* Kaskaskia villages, one French and the other Indian. As one of the series of events that transformed the Illinois Country during 1719–20—the arrival of soldiers and administrators from New Orleans, the building of the first Fort de Chartres, and the establishment of Kaskaskia as a parish—the Indian village of Kaskaskia was removed from the French village of the same name. Commandant Boisbriant—in consultation with the Jesuit missionaries, who had served as de facto governors at Kaskaskia between 1703 and 1719—made the decision to relocate the remains of the Kaskaskia tribe about one and a half leagues up the Kaskaskia River from the French village.[133] Precisely why this was done is not known, but probably the intent was to protect the Indians from the debaucheries of the randy voyageurs who congregated in French Kaskaskia at that time. The habit of maintaining discrete but proximate French and Indian villages was characteristic of all three major nuclei of French settlement on the east side of the Mississippi in the Illinois Country—Kaskaskia, Cahokia, and Fort de Chartres; this was also true of Vincennes on the Wabash, where a village of Piankashaws lay just outside of town, and of Ste. Geneviève, close to which a group of Peorias settled toward the end of the eighteenth century. In any event, both Kaskaskias were located on the northwest bank of the Kaskaskia River on the alluvial plain separating that river from the Mississippi.

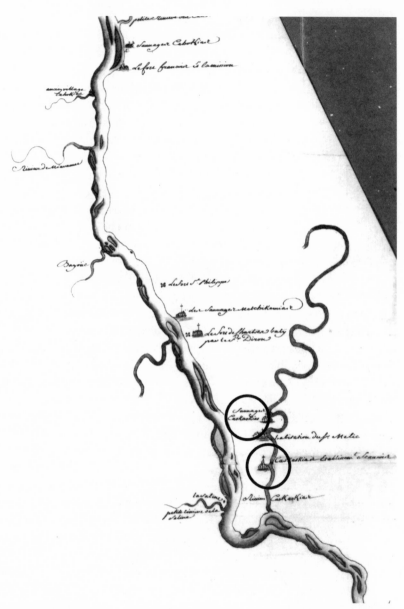

Diron d'Artaguiette map of Illinois Country of 1732. Notice the two "Caskaskias" (circled), one French and one Indian, with the "habitation du Sr. Melic" located between them. Reproduced courtesy of the Archives du Service Historique de la Marine, Château de Vincennes.

The d'Artaguiette map is an abstracted portrayal of the settlements in the Illinois Country and does not depict details of land usage surrounding the villages. The first map to attempt this was drafted in 1734 by Ignace-François Broutin, a French military engineer and cartographer stationed in New Orleans. Although there is no evidence that Broutin ever visited the Illinois Country, his map demonstrates that he had access to substantial quantities of data about the region. The title of his map, "Carte d'une partie des Illinois," contains the honest disclaimer of a careful engineer, "pour idée seullement." Broutin was too modest, for his map is remarkably accurate in many ways.[134] He showed, for example, the infrequent exceptions to the prevailing residential settlement pattern of nuclear villages. These were the "habitations" or "établissements" (plantations) strung out along the roadway that ran between Kaskaskia and Fort de Chartres. Pierre Melique, lieutenant in the French marines, Jacques-Gaspard Piot de Ste. Thérèse, nephew of Boisbriant, and Charles-Claude du Tisné, twice commandant at Fort de Chartres, were all members of the early power elite in the Illinois Country who owned these plantations.

While his residence was at the fort, Melique's habitation was closer to Kaskaskia than to Chartres, lying just downstream from the Kaskaskia Indian village. It is not possible to determine the exact layout of the arable fields at Melique's plantation; probably they were strips much like those owned by the habitants who lived in the village. The Louisiana census of 1726 indicates that Melique owned one black slave, who presumably worked as an agricultural laborer on his plantation.[135] For the most part, however, Melique's plantation was managed and worked by a tenant sharecropper, one Joseph Gardon, and early notarial records reveal some details of their business arrangements.[136] After Melique was killed by Indians in 1726, his plantation was sliced up into smaller longlots to serve as plowlands for other habitants; the early GLO surveys show no vestiges of Melique's seventeen-arpent tract.[137] In any event, habitations such as Melique's, perhaps modeled after those in Lower Louisiana, were unusual features; they were not typical of land usage or settlement in the Illinois Country at any time during the eighteenth century. Rather, throughout the colonial period nuclear villages remained the rule.

From the very beginning, Kaskaskia was a distinctly nucleated community; that is, almost everyone—missionary priests, traders, and agriculturists—lived in a rather compact village (two villages after the Indian village was separated from the French village, ca. 1719) rather than scattered about in isolated homesteads. The French village never had a master plan such as the waffle-iron grid that governed the development of New Orleans. Natalia Belting commented that the early village was not a planned settlement but

"like Topsy jes' growed."[138] Although Kaskaskia's growth was organic and irregular, some sort of crude measurements and surveys were obviously done.
Residential plots sizes varied in size and shape—625 square toises (i.e., twenty-
five toises per side), one square arpent, two square arpents, occasionally rectangular plots of one by two arpents. In any case, most of the residential parcels in Kaskaskia were roughly square or rectangular, and the streets were
oriented more or less east and west or north and south. If the early habitants
lacked a theodolite for turning crisp right angles, they at least had a good
compass; and if they sometimes lacked a surveyor's chain for measuring distances accurately, they at least used a measured (and perhaps even crudely
calibrated) length of rope for determining arpents.[139]

Captain Philip Pittman's remarkable 1766 plan of Kaskaskia shows an
irregular grid centered on the parish church and including the large Jesuit
missionary compound.[140] Irregular or not, Kaskaskia was indisputably a
nucleated village with no evidence on Pittman's map of outlying farmsteads
or plantations. Indeed, all structures shown on this map are located within
a 1,500-foot radius of the village center. Other sources (i.e., the Kaskaskia
Manuscripts) suggest that there may have been a *few* outlying farmsteads, but
Pittman did not deem them significant enough to depict on his plan.

Pittman did not portray the arable fields, but fairly large expanses of land
both north and south of the village are labeled "Common." These areas were
almost certainly the true commons—used for pasturage, wood gathering, and
so forth—and not common-field plowlands. Using Pittman's plan in conjunction with the GLO map of the Kaskaskia area from 1808, the entire eighteenth-century settlement pattern becomes clear. The GLO map depicts the
nucleated village as a discrete entity, freestanding in the midst of unlabeled
terrain.[141] This unlabeled land would correspond to the areas designated as
common land on Pittman's plan. Then, a bit further west and the main subject of the Land Office surveys, lay the large expanse of arable strips, running
westerly all the way to the east bank of the Mississippi River. Juxtaposing the
two maps, Pittman's from 1766 and the GLO's from 1809, provides a good
perspective on land usage and community customs at French colonial
Kaskaskia: nuclear village, commons, and open-field arable strips. As in the
case of Cahokia, early nineteenth-century U.S. land commissioners clearly
understood local land usage: "Common, Common Field, and Town Lots."
These commissioners described the nature of the common field by remarking that "this tract . . . is composed of the various grants, in severalty, to the
inhabitants of the village, and, from the first, has been enclosed by one common fence."[142] Thus the land commissioners manifestly understood that it
was the fence, and not the field itself, that was held in common.

THE ILLINOIS COUNTRY: FORT DE CHARTRES

Marines detached from the French royal navy built a series of forts de Chartres in the same general vicinity during the French regime in the Illinois Country.[143] As noted previously, Boisbriant directed the erection of the first of these in 1719. This fort became the nucleus for the village of Chartres, which in turn served as the nucleus for the parish of Ste. Anne.[144] Of the various villages in the French Illinois Country, only Chartres was founded specifically by government initiative; the others simply evolved into identifiable communities that began with fortuitous coalescenses of voyageurs, missionaries, habitants, and their American Indian associates. Marcel Giraud has correctly observed that Chartres, with its soldiers and officials, had no rival as the "administrative center of the Illinois country."[145] Moreover, at Cahokia and Kaskaskia parish and village precisely coincided, whereas the parish of Ste. Anne included not only the village of Chartres but also the smaller outlying settlements of St. Philippe and Prairie du Rocher. As in traditional European society, the parish was the fundamental unit of social and governmental organization in the Illinois Country.[146] Chartres contained the parish church, while the two outlying communities were served by mission chapels. With the coming of British troops to Fort de Chartres in 1765 and the ensuing demise of the village of Chartres, the parochial headquarters was transferred to the existing outlying mission of St. Joseph at Prairie du Rocher, which name the parish retains to this day.

Local officials from the fort (Boisbriant and des Ursins) conveyed the first official grants for agricultural land near Fort de Chartres in 1724, although some habitants had surely staked out and cultivated select plowlands before that date. The complete text of one of these follows, for virtually every phrase reveals something about early surveying, settlement, and agriculture in the Illinois Country:

> The Provincial Council, upon the request of Hébert the younger to grant him a piece of land ["terrain"] to settle on, we, by virtue of the power granted us by the Royal Indies Company have granted to the said Hébert three arpents of land ["terre"] by fifty in depth, the front running S.W. ¼ S. and the depth N.E. ¼ N., bounding on the one side to Jacques Catherine and on the other to Bellegrade, to be located on the line the Council shall think proper, which shall be specified to one side, and on condition that he shall settle, dwell on the said land ["terrain"] and improve it, and in default of doing this, it shall be reunited to the domain of said Company after a year and a day. At Fort de Chartres, 2 May 1724.[147]

Although the granting authorities, Boisbriant and des Ursins, did not specifically adduce the royal land edict of 1716, it is apparent that they had it in mind (perhaps even a copy in hand) when they drafted this land grant; Boisbriant, after all, was already an officer in Louisiana when the edict was promulgated.[148] The homesteading provision, that the concession would revert to the Royal Indies Company (as surrogate for the crown) if the grantee did not settle on and improve the land, was introduced to Louisiana real estate law by this edict. Furthermore, the size and proportions of Hébert's parcel, three by fifty arpents, fitted well within the edict's guidelines of two to four arpents frontage by forty to sixty arpents in depth. A nice coincidence occurred in that the dimensions specified in the edict suited remarkably well the geographical configuration of the region surrounding Fort de Chartres, for the alluvial bottomland stretched back fifty to sixty arpents (approximately two miles) from the Mississippi's bank to the bluffline. This must have been coincidence, for it is virtually inconceivable that the authors of the 1716 edict possessed a detailed knowledge of the Illinois Country's geography and tailored the edict to fit it. In any case, the edict and the geography of the Illinois Country worked serendipitously to reinforce and perpetuate certain modes of cadastral patterns and land usage.

The orientation of Hébert the younger's grant,[149] roughly northeast as determined by compass, remained consistent for the Fort de Chartres area throughout the colonial period. When in the early nineteenth century U.S. surveyors finally surveyed and platted these early French claims, the long sides of the rectangular parcels near Fort de Chartres were assigned magnetic headings of N 25½ degrees E.[150] Furthermore, the American surveyors adhered rigorously to the fifty-arpent lengths for the longlots that constituted the French claims.

The same day that Boisbriant and des Ursins granted Hébert the younger his tract of land, they granted at least two similar tracts, one to Jacques Catherine measuring one by fifty arpents,[151] and one to François Cerré of two by fifty arpents.[152] The magnetic orientations of these tracts were the same as Hébert's, and in fact Catherine's parcel and Hébert's were adjacent. There is not sufficient information to explain the differing widths of these three tracts—one, two, and three arpents—but possible explanations include differing requests by the grantees, various family sizes, variation in the quality of the respective tracts of land, or different degrees of political influence.

In all three of these conveyances Boisbriant and des Ursins used the operative word *terre.* That is to say, the land being conveyed was in fact intended principally for agriculture. On the other hand, the grants also contain the term for residential plot, *terrain,* and make it clear that the grantees were intending to live on the same parcel of land that they cultivated. Therefore, in each of these three particular cases, a classic variety of longlot was being established: a rectilinear parcel of land, with a high width-to-length ratio and with residential and plowlands contiguous.

The terms of these three concessions suggest that at that early stage of development in the Fort de Chartres area, a distinct, nucleated community had not yet emerged. We have no way of knowing precisely where on their longlots Hébert, Catherine, and Cerré built or were intending to build their residences. Supposing that they built their residences close to the front of their parcels, that is, close to the riverfront, these habitants were living in a strung-out, linear pattern with the proximity of neighbors depending on the breadth of the respective longlots. This configuration would have been similar to the one that had developed earlier in the St. Lawrence Valley and that was concurrently emerging in the lower Mississippi Valley near New Orleans. The fact that Jacques Catherine's land was bounded on one side by the "commons of Fort de Chartres" reveals that these ribbon farmsteads in the early Illinois Country were not remote and widely dispersed but were relatively close to one another and to the fort. This linear settlement pattern was rare in the Illinois Country and occurred with any regularity only at Chartres, and even there only at the earliest stages of the community's development.

Just how these longlots near Fort de Chartres were surveyed and set off with monuments is revealed in a document from 1733:

> In the year 1733 on the 18th of May, I clerk in the Illinois was ordered by Monsieur [Louis] de St. Ange, commandant in this province, to proceed with Monsieur Buchet, agent for the king's affairs in Illinois, and Monsieur Belline Fabert, inhabitant, to Fort de Chartres at the request of Madame [Nicolas] Chassin, for the purpose of establishing the necessary boundaries that separate the agricultural land ["terre"] of Sieur de Lessart from the domaine of the said Madame Chassin, in accordance with the alignments and measurements of the survey that Monsieur Regnault had accomplished the day before in the presence of Monsieur the Commandant. . . . We set three monuments along the long alignment. The middle one, which is located on the edge of the road to Ka [Kaskaskia] is a piece of mulberry arising out of the ground about one foot. There is a stone buried beneath it with a piece of lead bearing an engraved cross underneath it. The second [monument], on the bluff end, is also a piece of mulberry with a stone like the first, but without any lead. The third, on the Mississippi end, is simply a stone. In the future, these monuments will prevent any disputes that could arise between the said Sieur de Lessart and the said Madame Chassin.[153]

The Madame Chassin who initiated the survey was Agnès Philippe, the mixed-blood daughter of Michel Philippe, a French Canadian, and Marie Rouensa, daughter of a Kaskaskia Indian chief. In 1722 she had married Nicolas Chassin, the storekeeper at Fort de Chartres, but he never returned to the Illinois Country after a trip to Lower Louisiana in 1729.[154] At the time of 1733 survey, Agnès Philippe Chassin was therefore functioning as the head of her family, and since her husband was presumed dead, she had all the rights of widowhood under the Coutume de Paris, the law that governed inheritance practices throughout French colonial America.[155] As I mentioned previously, Chassin had become half-owner of a large land grant—seventeen facing arpents—in 1722, shortly before his marriage to Agnès Philippe. Madame Chassin's property, which was the subject of the 1733 survey, may well have been a portion of that seventeen-arpent tract. "Monsieur Regnault," who conducted the survey, was surely none other than Philippe Renaut, the lead miner who had in 1723 founded the community of St. Philippe several miles north of Fort de Chartres. Renaut was apparently serving as the omnibus engineer in the Illinois Country at that time, conducting land surveys as well as mining lead. Finally, the reference to "the road to Ka" reveals roughly where Madame Chassin's real estate was situated. That is, it was located along the trunk route of the Illinois Country that ran from Cahokia in the north to Kaskaskia in the south, and it lay somewhere along that road just south of Fort de Chartres, between the fort and Kaskaskia, near where Prairie du Rocher later developed.

Numerous land records from the 1720s and 1730s reveal that habitants in the vicinity of Fort de Chartres were building residences on their agricultural land "in the prairie," as contemporary records described the situation. In July 1724, for example, Charles Gossiaux and his wife, Jeanne Bienvenu, sold a house and its dependencies, "situated in the prairie," to François Robert *dit* Bellerose, a soldier from Fort de Chartres.[156] A year later Antoine François Pelle *dit* La Plume contracted with the carpenter Jacques-Joseph Catherine to build a house on La Plume's land "in the prairie" near the fort.[157] If the house was being erected at the front (riverfront) of his longlot, La Plume's land and residence were helping to compose a loosely linear community in the style of the St. Lawrence Valley.

In May 1724 Nicolas Buffreau de Bellegrade, a royal notary at Fort de Chartres, compiled an estate inventory.[158] Pierre Etevenard *dit* Beausoleil had fallen victim to marauding Fox braves, and in accordance with the Coutume de Paris, a complete inventory of all property, real and personal, that had constituted the community of Pierre and his widow, Marie Maurice Médard, was made at Marie's request. The Beausoleil inventory includes two tracts of real estate: first, a two-arpent-wide tract running from the Mississippi to the bluffs (i.e., about fifty arpents), and second, a dwelling house situated on a two-arpent-square parcel of land. This parcel was located so close to the river that the house was in danger of being "carried off by the current." Although the records are not sufficiently complete to determine the precise situation in this case, it appears that these two parcels of land were contiguous or, more exactly, that the two-arpent residential plot made up the front portion of the fifty-arpent-deep longlot. If this was the case, then again we see a longlot configuration similar to those in the St. Lawrence Valley.

The first clear dissociation of agricultural land from residential property in the Fort de Chartres area appears in a real estate transaction of May 1725.[159] St. Pierre *dit* La Verdure sold to Jean-Baptiste Turpin a longlot measuring two by fifty arpents located "in the prairie of Fort de Chartres." In addition, La Verdure sold Turpin a square residential lot measuring twenty-five toises per side. French colonists in the Illinois Country used both toises and arpents to measure residential lots; agricultural parcels, however, were measured exclusively in arpents. A lot twenty-five toises per side was about 30 percent smaller than one square arpent, but why arpents were used to measure some residential lots and toises for others is not clear. It is apparent that the residential lot that La Verdure was selling in 1725 was not simply the front portion of his agricultural longlot, for the one parcel was measured in arpents, and the other in toises. Moreover, the adjacent property owners as named in the warranty deed, which was the usual method employed in the Illinois Country to identify a piece of property, were different for the two parcels. These disparate facts lead to the conclusion that La Verdure was selling an agricultural longlot in the prairie of Fort de Chartres and a residential lot in the new village of Chartres.

As the population of the Illinois Country grew and settlement expanded, three discrete parishes emerged—the Holy Family at Cahokia, founded by Seminarians from Quebec; the Immaculate Conception at Kaskaskia, founded by Jesuits; and Ste. Anne at Fort de Chartres, which was usually served by Recollet priests. These three parishes represented distinct concentrations of population, and the last of these to develop was at Fort de Chartres. It is not clear precisely when a scattering of habitants settled down to farm in the area where the fort was built; almost certainly it was before Boisbriant began to erect the first fort in 1719. In any event, no documentation exists concerning the first settlers in the area, for systematic record keeping did not begin until Boisbriant and his complement of soldiers and administrators (including a royal notary) arrived from New Orleans.

Early maps and civil records regarding the community at Chartres indicate that settlement in that region was more diffuse than at either Cahokia or Kaskaskia. It is difficult to discern a definite and consistent configuration of settlement at Chartres circa 1725, but it seems that some habitants lived in a fledgling village near the fort; that others lived toward the front of their long agricultural plots, in a kind of strung-out, linear pattern; and that some lived on dispersed farmsteads "in the prairie," as it was said. Down the trunk road toward Kaskaskia, at La Grande Prairie, was the plantation of "Jean-Baptiste Lalande le jeune," whose father was a habitant in Kaskaskia. The son was doing well on his own at Grande Prairie, owning six African slaves, five Indian slaves, and operating what was then probably the only windmill in the Illinois Country.[160]

At Chartres, as at Cahokia and Kaskaskia, there was an Illinois Indian village, some distance removed from the French settlements. The Michegamea village lay just up the Mississippi from the fort and is clearly shown on the 1732 d'Artaguiette map. A league or so beyond the Michegamea village was another minor locus of population, the settlement of St. Philippe, founded by the lead miner Philippe Renaut and named after his patron saint. The village of St. Philippe, which was served spiritually by a mission chapel from Ste. Anne at Fort de Chartres, Notre Dame de la Visitation, was the nucleus of the massive concession, two square leagues (approx. 15.2 square miles), that Boisbriant had granted Renaut in June 1723 as a logistical base for his lead-mining operations on the west side of the Mississippi.

The Broutin map of 1734 reveals that the entire settlement of the Illinois Country from Cahokia in the north to Kaskaskia in the south was located on the floodplain of the Mississippi and Kaskaskia Rivers. No villages or habitations existed above the bluffline, which Broutin clearly delineated, although the roadway from Fort de Chartres north to Cahokia ran along the top of the bluffs for part of the distance.[161] Broutin labeled St. Philippe the "village de Mr. Renaud" (i.e., Renaut), and his placement of the plantation of Jacques-Gaspard Piot, sieur de Ste. Thérèse, labeled "prérie du Mr. Ste. Thérèse," reveals that this embryo shortly became the agricultural hamlet of Prairie du Rocher. Indeed, as early as 1732 the official census of that year listed one Gossiaux, who lived with his wife, his child, and his black slave, as a habitant at "prairie de Roche."[162] This is the earliest record to contain that name, which suggests that a new nuclear settlement was emerging in that area during the early 1730s. This new village would soon have its own compound of arable strips and its own commons for pasture, completing the classic configuration of land usage that prevailed throughout the Illinois Country.

As in medieval Europe, the poorer lands in the Illinois Country were devoted to commons, and the better lands were parceled out into arable strips. At Fort de Chartres the commons area was along the low-lying land close to the Mississippi, and within this area were located the first Fort de Chartres with its glacis, the embryonic village of Chartres, and the pastureland for the local habitants. By definition the commons did not support arable agriculture well. This combination of commons and arable strips was similar to that at Kaskaskia, although at the latter there was no fort and the compact village had evolved to maturity at an earlier date. At St. Philippe an area along a creek just under the bluffs was devoted to commons, as well as a substantial tract of woodland above the bluffs, for Renaut's large concession extended inland well beyond the bluffline.

The process of rigorously separating pastureland from arable, an essential step in the development of any open-field system of agriculture, is more difficult to follow at Chartres than at Kaskaskia or Cahokia. This may be because land usage was, at least at first, less sharply defined at Chartres than at the other communities. More likely, however, it is because the disruptions brought about by the French and Indian War were more severe at Chartres than at any other community in the Illinois Country: the village of Chartres disappeared shortly after 1765, the parish of Ste. Anne was supplanted by the parish of St. Joseph at Prairie du Rocher, and large numbers of notarial documents from Chartres were lost. In 1804 one Joseph Taillon, an old man who had once been a tailor at Chartres, testified in St. Louis that "the archives of the said place [Chartres] were destroyed and abandoned to the hands of all persons who wished to rummage through them."[163] Old man Taillon was perhaps overstating the case, but the documentation from Chartres is sparser than that from Kaskaskia and Cahokia.[164]

The earliest civil records from Chartres contain a request made in 1723 for enclosing pigs in the area around the fort and the village.[165] The request was made by the habitants to the provincial council, which was composed of officers from Fort de Chartres and local representatives of the Royal Indies Company. Boisbriant, builder of and commandant at the first fort, held the position of greatest authority in the council, and the council reacted to the request by issuing a decree that required all livestock, not only pigs, to be fenced in. These 1723 documents do not contain precise dates, but very likely they originated in the spring of that year. For more than a century in the Illinois Country—under French, Spanish, British, and American regimes—control over livestock during the spring planting season was an urgent issue for all the agricultural land in the Mississippi Valley between the mouth of the Missouri River and the mouth of the Kaskaskia River. This in turn dictates that most documentation regarding agricultural regulations originated during the spring months.

During the early 1720s, the settlement at Chartres was just emerging as a distinct community to become, after Cahokia and Kaskaskia, the third nucleus of settlement in the Illinois Country. No corpus of regulations, local or provincial, existed to deal with the vital issue of protecting arable fields from errant livestock, and no ad hoc system had evolved by which the fields were protected with a fence of their own. At that early stage of Chartres's development, the critical mass of population required to build a great common fence around the arable fields was not available. Moreover, the community cohesiveness required to frame and enforce the rather complex regulations for building and maintaining such a fence probably did not yet exist. Consequently, the arable lands were not enclosed with a common fence during Chartres's earliest years; rather, domestic livestock was fenced in, confined to a common pastureland (along the bank of the Mississippi River) so that the animals would not have access to the plowlands from sowing time until harvest.

Nevertheless, the habitants of Chartres did eventually undertake the massive task of fencing the entire compound of arable strips with a common fence. Comments by early U.S. land commissioners[166] together with the early GLO plat maps of the region present a rather clear picture of the mature open-field complex at Chartres and its relationship to other areas of land usage. Probably at the same time that Boisbriant definitively separated the arable fields from the commons pasture at Kaskaskia with the Grande Ligne and the Petite Ligne, he also ordered this done at Chartres in a slightly different fashion. A single straight line about three miles long (later reckoned as N 64½ degrees W) was laid out, separating the arable fields from the commons. This baseline, which ran from the Coulée de Nau down to the upper line of the Prairie du Rocher common fields, served as the front line for the longlots in what became the arable compound at Chartres. The open field at Chartres was therefore defined by this baseline on the southwest, the Ste. Philippe common fields on the northwest, the bluffline to the northeast, and the Prairie du Rocher common fields to the southeast. Although the longlot concessions within this compound technically ran back only fifty arpents *toward* the bluffline, de facto they went all the way *to* the bluffline. This meant that the front boundary of the longlots (the baseline) required a picket fence but the rear did not. As in the other compounds of open fields in the Illinois Country, the longlots within the compound at Fort de Chartres were devoted largely but not exclusively to arable cultivation. That is, significant portions of these longlot concessions were virtually always occupied by coppices, ponds, and marshes. The extent of the wasteland within the plowlands varied to some degree on the weather each year, as it still does on the alluvial bottomlands near Prairie du Rocher.

At neighboring Prairie du Rocher a patch of swampy land near the village, "Marais Gossiaux," at first constituted a customary lowland commons, but over time it proved to be inadequate for the needs of the community. In the spring of 1743 the habitants of Prairie du Rocher addressed a petition to the commandant of Fort de Chartres, the Chevalier de Bertet, and his *écrivain principal*, François-Auguste de la Loëre Flaucourt, asking for additional common pastureland.[167] De Bertet and Flaucourt accommodated the citizens of the village by conveying to them one square league of commons on the hills above the village. Although not unique, this assumption of land above the bluffline was unusual in the Illinois Country, where agricultural activities were generally confined to the floodplain of the Mississippi and Kaskaskia Rivers. The large upland Prairie du Rocher commons (one square league equaling 7.6 square miles) remained public domain until well into the nineteenth century, a cadastral artifact of a by-gone pattern of land usage. In 1809 U.S. land commissioners opined that the upland commons at Prairie du Rocher was "of little value, except as it may afford wood and pasturage for the inhabitants of the village."[168] The practical-minded land commissioners were oblivious to the splendid panoramic view of the Mississippi Valley that may be enjoyed from the bluff above Prairie du Rocher.

THE ILLINOIS COUNTRY: VINCENNES

Colonel George Croghan visited "Post Vincent" in 1765 and described the inhabitants as a "parcel of Renegadoes from Canada and are much worse than Indians."[169] Croghan was clear and unequivocal in his pronouncements about the town, but historically Vincennes has always been rather ambiguous. Given that it lay on the east bank of the Wabash (Ouabache in French colonial parlance) River, should Vincennes be included as part of the Illinois Country? Did this outpost, founded in the early 1730s by Sieur François-Marie Bissot de Vincennes,[170] fall within the colonial jurisdiction of Canada or Louisiana? In his classic study *The Illinois Country, 1673–1818*, Clarence W. Alvord gave Vincennes but short shrift. Alvord's book was of course written as part of the centennial history of the state of Illinois, and Vincennes, lying in the state of Indiana, did not fit within the appropriate modern political boundaries to be included in a history of Illinois.

French administrative correspondence dealing with the Wabash Valley, however, demonstrates that Vincennes fell within the bailiwick of Louisiana's governor general in New Orleans, whereas the outpost at Ouiatenon (near present-day Lafayette, Indiana), a hundred-odd miles further up the Wabash River, came under the jurisdiction of the Canadian governor in Quebec City.[171] When Jean-Jacques Macarty was dispatched up the Mississippi from New Orleans in the autumn of 1751 to assume command of the Illinois Country, he was specifically instructed to consider Vincennes within his jurisdiction.[172] Charles-Philippe Aubry, the last French governor of Louisiana, remarked that "the Fort of Vincennes is the last Post in the Department of Louisiana."[173] As part of French Upper Louisiana, Vincennes rightly may be considered part of the Illinois Country. George Rogers Clark's campaign into the Illinois Country during 1778–79 was not complete without seizing Vincennes, and after Clark's conquest the state of Virginia considered Kaskaskia and "Saint Vincents" as part of the same territory. When the U.S. Congress began to deal with the sticky issue of old French land claims in the far west, it treated the claims at Vincennes as though that post were part of the Illinois Country.[174]

The French Canadian settlers who founded and lived at Vincennes were unaware that the center of the lower Wabash River would eventually form a political boundary between the states of Indiana and Illinois. Habitants at Vincennes used whatever land suited them for whatever purposes on both sides of the river, and the river, rather than serving as a dividing line, was the geographical feature that bound the community together. As it turned out, it suited the inhabitants of Vincennes to build their fort and develop their village on the east side of the Wabash while utilizing land on both sides of the river for various agricultural pursuits, including grain production and animal husbandry.

Vincennes was the only French colonial community outside the Mississippi Valley at which land usage evolved into village, commons, and compounds of arable strips. This pattern developed over time and was surely not the basis for the community at the time of its founding in the 1730s, when Vincennes was a fur-trading and military outpost, inhabited more by transients than habitants. French colonial authorities in Louisiana first thought of Vincennes as an outpost to block the access of British traders to the Indian tribes of the Wabash Valley. Descendants of the original settlers viewed their forefathers as having come "to establish themselves in trade and commerce with the natives possessing and inhabiting the country on the Wabash and adjacent waters."[175] Over time, however, Vincennes did evolve into an agricultural settlement not dissimilar to Kaskaskia and Cahokia, its older siblings to the west. Like the latter two, Vincennes also had an associated, but discrete, Indian settlement, the Piankashaw village.[176] Throughout the eighteenth century numerous family ties bound Vincennes and the French communities in the Mississippi Valley together, and there was continuous social and commercial intercourse between Vincennes and the other villages. Persons such as the Reverend Pierre Gibault and the surgeon Jean-Baptiste Laffond moved with perfect ease between the communities of the Mississippi and Wabash Valleys. The parishioners and patients in one were much the same as those in any one of the others.[177] The parallel patterns of land usage that evolved at Vincennes and Kaskaskia were not merely coincidental or fortuitous; they were based on similar geography, similar climate, similar needs, and the same cultural baggage that had been transmitted down the centuries and over the ocean from medieval France.

On his journey through what was then the western part of the United States in 1796, the comte de Volney visited the settlement of Vincennes on the Wabash River. He commented that "maize, tobacco, wheat, barley, squashes, and even cotton, grow in the fields around the village, which contains about fifty houses, whose cheerful white relieves the eye, after the tedious dusk and green of the woods."[178] The village that Volney was so pleased to see at Vincennes was a compact, nuclear village located immediately on the east bank of the Wabash River. The nuclear configuration of Vincennes originated in its function as a trading outpost and was doubtless reinforced by the community's role as a defensive outpost—defensive against Indians, English, or Americans, depending on the occasion. As the village evolved into an agricultural settlement with meadows and plowlands, the nuclear structure persisted.

Samuel Baird, the GLO surveyor who drew a plat map of Vincennes in 1792 containing forty-three residential lots, remarked: "It is with regret I am obliged to present one so extremely irregular. But it is not within my power to make it more regular without deranging almost all the possessions."[179] Baird's plat, as well as French notarial records of real estate transactions,[180] make it abundantly clear that residential lots in early Vincennes were exceedingly irregular. Obviously they had not been surveyed but had been roughly measured or paced off—sometimes in arpents, sometimes in toises, and sometimes in no discernible known unit of measure. Furthermore, many carelessly documented concessions had been destroyed or lost over time, and on one occasion a "royal notary ran off with all the public papers in his possession."[181] In any event, the pattern of land usage at Vincennes, which developed early in the village's history, included long arable strips, measured in arpents, that fronted on the Wabash River. Gentilcore has observed about Vincennes that "following the French Canadian custom, the farm lots were

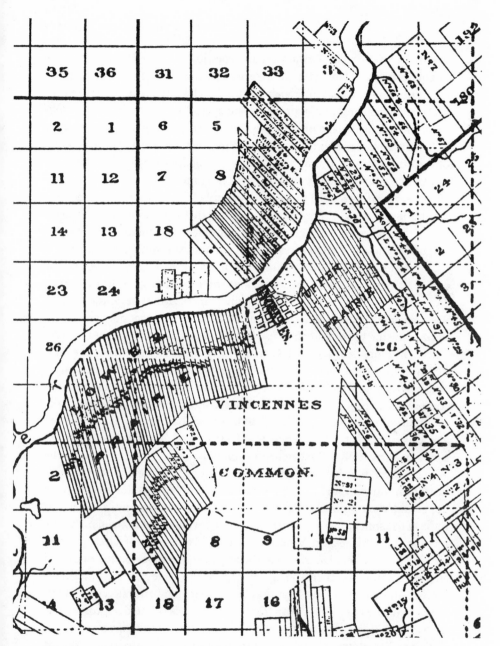

Vincennes region showing the jarring dissimiliarty between French colonial and American cadastral patterns. East of the Wabash River notice the village, the open-field plowlands ("Upper Prairie" and "Lower Prairie"), and the "Vincennes Common." West of the river are multipurpose longlots, where open-field agriculture was not practiced. Map reproduced from *The Vincennes Donation Tract in the States of Indiana and Illinois.*

aligned in rows."[182] This is true as far as it goes, but he missed the fundamental difference between land usage at Vincennes (and all the other Illinois Country communities) and that in French Canada.[183] The difference was that in the Illinois Country residential property and agricultural property were *totally* dissociated. The pattern of land usage at Vincennes proper was alien to the St. Lawrence Valley and to Lower Louisiana, but it was very similar to that of the other French communities in the middle Mississippi Valley and not unlike that of traditional village patterns in France.

The pattern at colonial Vincennes is complicated, however, by the fact that in addition to the clusters of arable longlots that lay immediately contiguous to the village, another group of longlots faced the village from the west side of the Wabash. These parcels were of less uniform width than the longlots on the east side of the river, for many of them were more than two arpents wide. Furthermore, structures of various sorts, including residences, barns, and fences, were located on the west-bank parcels, and these classic longlots were never enclosed with a common fence for agricultural purposes.[184] Indeed, it seems likely that the west-bank ribbon farms at Vincennes were fenced off individually, French Canadian style. Therefore, Vincennes exhibited two distinct varieties of Franco-American longlot: first, the exclusively arable variety, in which bundles of generally two-arpent-wide lots were encompassed within one common fence as a cluster of plowlands; second, the multipurpose variety that included residences, outbuildings, and fields, which also existed along the St. Lawrence, at Detroit, and along the lower Mississippi. Front portions of multipurpose longlots, facing Vincennes across the Wabash River, may be seen on a bird's-eye lithograph done in 1857. This illustration shows as well the large expanses of arable lands that made up the upper and lower prairies at Vincennes. Vincennes was the only case in which these two distinct functional varieties of longlot coexisted in the same settlement area. In this respect, Vincennes is a perfect example of a dual pattern, looking to the Canadian model in the St. Lawrence Valley on the one hand and to the French settlements in the Mississippi Valley on the other. This mixed pattern at Vincennes may have been mere happenstance, or perhaps it was a consequence of location, for Vincennes was situated approximately midway between Detroit to the north and Kaskaskia to the west.

When British troops arrived at Vincennes in 1779, attempting to thwart George Rogers Clark's invasion of Illinois, the commander, Henry Hamilton, noted in his journal that "their fields of corn [i.e., grain] are not enclosed, all their cattle being pennd in one common enclosure of about 2000 Acres in extent."[185] Hamilton's remark reveals that at Vincennes fields were protected from browsing cattle by fencing in the common pastureland rather than fencing around the compound of arable strips. In 1790 Winthrop Sargent—secretary to General Arthur St. Clair, recently appointed governor of the Northwest Territory—wrote to President George Washington from Vincennes and remarked that the habitants of Vincennes had fenced in their commons about 1760 to "confine their cattle within its boundaries, and keep them out of their wheat fields: for, contrary to the usage of farmers generally, the cattle are enclosed, and the cultivated lands are left at large."[186] This produced the desired objective of protecting the grain fields from errant livestock; it was simply an alternative fashion of accomplishing the same thing.

The commons at Vincennes lay south of the village and east of the "Lower Prairie" compound of plowlands. Estimates concerning the size of this commons varied considerably over time. In 1779 Henry Hamilton described the Vincennes commons as containing about 2,000 acres, but in 1790 the public overseers of "the common fence" at Vincennes certified that the commons was 3½ miles long and 2½ miles wide and that it contained about 5,460 acres.[187] When the inhabitants of Vincennes petitioned the U.S. government for confirmation of their commons in 1790, they claimed that it contained "about two thousand four hundred acres of good, and three thousand acres of sunken lands."[188] The government accepted something very close to this figure (5,400 acres) and conveyed the land to the inhabitants of Vincennes by federal statute in 1791.[189] After Hamilton's sojourn at Vincennes in 1779, the commons was probably expanded substantially, and in any case his figure of 2,000 acres was merely a crude estimate. When Samuel Baird surveyed the Vincennes commons in the early 1790s, he commented, "I have not followed exactly the present fence as it is now very different from what it was a few years since; in some places there is a part of the ancient common without the present survey and in some others some taken in that never has been under fence."[190] The shrinkage of the commons in the nineteenth century was the result of parcels being surveyed and granted to individual proprietors, which eventually happened to each of the commons in all the former French colonial communities in the American Midwest.

The commons at Vincennes required a massive circumferential fence to confine the livestock and protect the grain fields. This was far and away the largest and most important structure in the community, for everyone's subsistence depended on it. One estimate reckoned this fence as "about two miles in depth and eight miles in front."[191] In 1807 the French-Swiss immigrant to Vincennes Jean Badollet wrote to his friend Albert Gallatin, Thomas Jefferson's secretary of the treasury, that the "devastation of the timber of the United States land round this place [Vincennes] is a matter of serious consideration. This town being situated in a prairie, every inclosure in it, & the fences of the vast fields in the prairie are, made of timber growing on the public lands on the river above this place."[192] European immigrants were often taken aback by the cavalier extravagance with which New World settlers consumed their forests, attacking them with fire and ax with no thought for the future. Pierre-Charles Delassus de Luzières, a French aristocratic émigré who settled near Ste. Genevieve in the early 1790s, commented in much the same vein as Badollet.[193]

THE ILLINOIS COUNTRY: STE. GENEVIEVE

Fully to appreciate the unique pattern of land usage in the Illinois Country, one must pass to the west side of the Mississippi, for there, at Ste. Genevieve and St. Louis, the system evolved into its most elaborated and complete form. The fact that this development occurred under the Spanish colonial regime in Upper Louisiana is of little or no significance, for the pattern was quintessentially French. Indeed, the punctilious legal habits and record keeping of Spanish bureaucrats meant that the earlier French pattern from the east side of the Mississippi became most densely documented in Spanish Illinois at Ste. Genevieve and St. Louis.

During the first half of the eighteenth century, settlement in the Illinois Country was confined exclusively to the eastern side of the Mississippi, from Cahokia in the north to Kaskaskia in the south; no permanent community of any sort existed on the west side of the Mississippi River in this entire region. There was no urgent need to extend the line of French settlement across the river, and for decades the French seem to have considered the trans-Mississippian West more or less an Indian domain. They crossed the Mississippi to extract two vital minerals, lead and salt, but they did not plow the land or put down village roots. Ste. Genevieve, named after the patron saint of Paris, was the first of the Illinois Country settlements established west of the Mississippi. Founded about 1750, or conceivably a few years earlier, Ste. Genevieve began as a kind of agricultural satellite of Kaskaskia. The first generation of habitants in Ste. Genevieve came mostly from Kaskaskia, and for the first decade of its existence the new community had no parish church; the Jesuit fathers from Kaskaskia simply maintained a mission chapel there and recorded the births, marriages, and burials in the Kaskaskia parish registers. A ferry across the Mississippi and a short road across the tongue of land between the Kaskaskia and Mississippi Rivers kept the two communities in constant and intimate connect.

Ste. Genevieve offers the student of French colonialism in the middle Mississippi Valley a richer combination of physical remains and documents than does any other community. A number of the distinctive vertical-log houses have been preserved; vestiges of the arpent-square residential plots are still to be seen; a vast swath of alluvial bottomland remains the nucleus of the local agricultural economy; and large quantities of source documents—notarial, administrative, and sacramental—are accessible.[194] Unlike Kaskaskia, early Ste. Genevieve was located directly on the bank of the Mississippi River. With the exception of several small Mississippian Indian mounds, there was little to break up the surrounding topography, consisting of alluvial bottomlands that ran back to a rather sharply defined line of hills or bluffs. The alluvial plain was called the "plaine basse" or the "pointe basse"; the hills were called simply "les côtes." Nicolas de Finiels commented that the view from these hills was "one of the most picturesque in the entire Illinois Country."[195] This view, which encompasses in a single glance all the salient geographical features of the area— Mississippi River, alluvial floodplain, and distinct blufflines—has changed little since the eighteenth century.

Documentation from the early 1750s, when the Old Town of Ste. Genevieve was beginning to emerge as a distinct community, is exceedingly thin. During the first half of 1752, however, two successive commandants at Fort de Chartres, Jean-Baptiste Benoist de St. Claire and Jean-Baptiste Macarty, issued a series of land grants at Ste. Genevieve, which at the time fell within their jurisdiction.[196] These concessions—granted to François Rivard, Toussaint Héneaux, Joseph Lamy, Jean-Baptiste Lasource *fils*, and Dominique Thaumure—shed a good deal of light on the process of settlement at early Ste. Genevieve. Each of the grantees was given three arpents of agricultural land plus an emplacement in the village for his residence. These grants were contingent on two things, however: (1) Each grantee had to maintain hearth and home in Ste. Genevieve for a minimum of one year or suffer forfeit of the land. (2) Each had to agree to provide some logs for the chapel that was planned for the new village. The homesteading provision was in accord with the Regency Edict of 1716 and with a royal ordinance proclaimed by Louis XV in 1743, both of which specified that if concessions were not put to productive use, they would be reunited to the royal domain.[197] The proposed church was initially to be a mission chapel of Kaskaskia's parish of the Immaculate Conception, for Ste. Genevieve was not elevated to canonical parish status until 1759.

During its earliest days, Ste. Genevieve exhibited a settlement pattern more distended than those of its sibling communities on the east side of the Mississippi River. The village was strung out for some distance along the west bank of the Mississippi River, although the residences were clustered closely enough to constitute a nuclear village. The earliest property transactions identify residential plots (emplacements or terrains) on the basis of contiguous neighboring plots. When Nicolas Albin sold a lot to Joseph Tassin in 1753, Louis Normand *dit* Labrière, André Vignon, and some member of the increasingly important Vallé family each owned one of three adjacent lots. Along the fourth side ran a street, which may have lain parallel to the Mississippi River.[198]

The land grants that Benoist de St. Claire conveyed at Ste. Genevieve in early 1752 specify that the emplacements of the grantees were to be designated by "Monsieur Saucier." This was the French military engineer François Saucier, who had been dispatched from New Orleans to design the new Fort de Chartres, which was to be a defensive keystone of the French empire in North American. The fact that a trained engineer was to locate the residential plots in the new village suggests that these parcels of real estate were to be carefully platted. Yet there is no solid evidence that Saucier ever conducted the surveys required for such exact platting. The earliest land surveys at Ste. Genevieve are for agricultural land,[199] and none exists for residential property. Moreover, several early transactions for town lots specify that they had not been surveyed.[200] At Ste. Genevieve, as at all the villages of the Illinois Country, with the exception of St. Louis, town development was highly informal.[201] All that can be said with some sureness is that town lots in the Old Town of Ste. Genevieve, as in most of the other villages of the Illinois Country, tended to be *approximately* square with each side measuring *approximately* one arpent or twenty-five toises. To go beyond that is to impose too much modernity on a society that was not fastidious about measurements in either time or space. Early nineteenth-century surveys of the New Town of Ste. Genevieve reveal that the residential lots in the new village were intended to be one square arpent, although they were evidently not surveyed by a qualified engineer using precision instruments.[202]

Ste. Genevieve first appeared as an independent settlement on the 1752 census of the Illinois Country.[203] This document, composed by the commandant at Fort de Chartres, Major Jean-Jacques Macarty, is neither complete nor entirely accurate. It is nevertheless an indispensable source for understanding the Illinois Country at mid-eighteenth century, and it provides substantial information about the early habitants at Ste. Genevieve and their agricultural land. Eight households contained a total population of twenty-three souls: men and women, adults and children, white and black, free and slave. In other words, it was a small but representative cross-section of the Illinois Country in general. The agricultural land owned by each head-of-household was recorded: two arpents, three arpents, or as many as four arpents, the largest amount of land being owned by the local militia captain, André Deguire *dit* La Rose. Macarty did not specify whether these arpents were linear or superficial, but likely they were *facing* arpents. That is, each habitant's holding was given in the number of arpents his land stretched along the bank of the Mississippi, and it was understood that each tract of land extended from the riverbank back to the bluffline, a distance of forty to fifty arpents, as later surveys would demonstrate. Therefore the topography and cadastral system at the Old Town of Ste. Genevieve more closely resembled the area at Chartres than at Kaskaskia; longlots two to four arpents wide, perpendicular to the Mississippi River, and running back to the bluffline.

After the Peace of Paris (1763) and the arrival of British troops on the east side of the Mississippi in 1765, both Ste. Genevieve and St. Louis experienced rapid expansion. The Spanish side of the river was usually more hospitable for the habitants of the Illinois Country than was the British side, and immigrants flocked to Ste. Genevieve and to St. Louis. As late as 1768, the latter was referred to as "Poste St. Louis sur la partie française en la province de la Louisiane."[204] In 1766 François Lalumandière *dit* Lafleur of Kaskaskia requested a concession of land at Ste. Genevieve in order "to take refuge in my fatherland" and because Kaskaskia had been "ceded to the enemies of the religion [i.e., Roman Catholicism] and the fatherland."[205] Lalumandière was probably not sure precisely who controlled the west side of the Mississippi, France or Spain, but in any case Ste. Genevieve was preferable to British-held Kaskaskia; Spain after all had a Bourbon monarch, just as France did, and Spaniards were Roman Catholics, as Lalumandière himself was.

With the exuberant growth of the late 1760s, the settlement pattern at Ste. Genevieve became both more complex and more distinctly nucleated. Residential lots developed along both sides of Grande Rue (Main Street), which paralleled the west bank of the Mississippi, and minor cross streets were cut roughly at right angles to Main Street. At the same time, the village retained some of its string-town configuration. In the mid-1760s the British officer Captain Philip Pittman described Ste. Genevieve as a string town that was a mile long and contained seventy families.[206] F. Terry Norris's recent study of Old Town Ste. Genevieve presents a detailed analysis of how this settlement, which was linear yet sufficiently compact to qualify as nuclear, developed before being abandoned in the late 1780s, following a period of severe floods.[207]

At some point (it is impossible to determine precisely when) the habitants of Ste. Genevieve began to construct a tremendous edifice. This structure was the enormous palisaded fence that eventually surrounded the entire body of arable land at Ste. Genevieve to protect the grain fields from foraging livestock. According to one eighteenth-century witness, these open fields encompassed over 7,000 acres, all under one fence.[208] This fence, maintained by all habitants who held arable strips within the enclosure, was a vital structure in the community, for the very survival of the community depended on its existence and upkeep. How agriculture in this vast open field, the Grand Champ, was regulated will be examined in the following chapter.

The growth of a more tightly nucleated village at Ste. Genevieve and the establishment of the great communal fence accompanied the development of a generally accepted area of commons. The commons was less clearly delineated at Ste. Genevieve than at any of the other communities in the Illinois Country. No government edict, such as those that officially established the Kaskaskia and Prairie du Rocher commons in 1743, was ever promulgated for Ste. Genevieve, and no map or plan ever designated a commons for the town. GLO surveyors always distinguished the "common fields" from the "commons" when describing land usage at the old French communities on the east side of the Mississippi, but for Ste. Genevieve they did not do so. The Ste. Genevieve commons evolved ad hoc as the community grew during the 1760s, and it was defined simply by a process of elimination: de facto, all land in the region that was neither part of the compact village nor included within the Grand Champ was by definition commons. As in the communities on the east side of the Mississippi, this commons constituted land that was less well suited for tillage and was available to everyone in the community for pasturage, wood gathering, and so forth.

A series of severe floods during the 1780s, especially that of 1785, impelled the townspeople to relocate their village to higher ground several miles from the original town site.[209] This move was not effected en masse but was nevertheless largely accomplished by 1793, by which time the commandant and the parish priest had moved to the new location. At about the same time, an aristocratic émigré from the French Revolution, Pierre-Charles Delassus de Luzières, founded the nearby settlement of Nouvelle Bourbon. This community was located several miles south of the emerging New Town of Ste. Genevieve and was situated high on the bluffs overlooking the floodplain of the Mississippi and the remains of the Old Town. By the early 1790s, therefore, three communities existed in close proximity to one another: the remains of the Old Town of Ste. Genevieve, New Ste. Genevieve, and New Bourbon. Habitants from all three villages were members of the same parish, and each of them owned plowlands in the Grand Champ, which contained the great majority of the grain fields in the region.

In 1792 the local priest, the abbé Paul de St. Pierre, described his parish as consisting of three villages:

The first is Old Ste. Genevieve, sad remains of the [flood] waters, which consists of a propped up church, an old rectory, and miserable quarters for the soldiers. . . . The second is Mont Généreux [soon to become New Bourbon], which village of twenty houses is very well situated for agriculture and is located only half a league from New Ste. Genevieve. . . . The third is therefore New Ste. Genevieve. It is located twelve arpents [about 4,306 feet] from the Mississippi along a small river [Gabouri Creek] that is navigable for a good half of the year.[210]

The plan reproduced here, which depicts the Ste. Genevieve region in 1793, was sketched by Delassus de Luzières, and in May he wrote to the Spanish governor general of Louisiana, Hector de Carondelet, and explicated the plan.[211] This plan—the only known one drafted in colonial Ste. Genevieve—identifies the Old Town as "Ste. Geneviève," New Bourbon to be as "Mont Généreux," and the New Town of Ste. Genevieve as "Petites Côtes."[212] The plan has a primitive, folksy quality to it—there is no scale, and relief is shown only by a few hatch marks—yet the cartographer was able to rise to the conceptual level of abstracting the three communities: Ste. Geneviève, Petites Côtes, and Mont Généreux. Moreover, the parallel dotted lines that show property divisions in the big common field were drawn to represent individual arable strips as *precisely* two arpents wide.[213] This is consistent with what we know about the dimensions of many of the agricultural parcels in colonial times. De Luzières saw fit to identify only one individual habitation, that of John Dodge, an Anglo-American who had moved to the area in the late 1780s after having developed a gangster's reputation on the east side of the Mississippi. He continued to be an outsider on the west side of the river, choosing to live in an isolated residence rather than in one of the local villages. Recently granted agricultural land, which lay outside of the confines of the great common fence, is labeled "Nouvelles concessions."

The plan does not include the settlement at the salt springs, "La Saline," but does show two "chemins," one along the Mississippi and one atop the bluffs, both of which led downriver to the Saline. The Saline had existed since time out of mind for the sake of extracting salt from the saline springs that arose on the banks of the Rivière de la Saline. A permanent settlement of Creole habitants had never been situated there, but during the 1790s the Saline had become a locus of settlement for Anglo-American immigrants from the east side of the Mississippi River.[214]

When the Old Town of Ste. Genevieve was abandoned in favor of the New Town, the dissociation of plowlands and residential plots became total. No habitant in the New Town could sit with his wife on the rear gallery of their

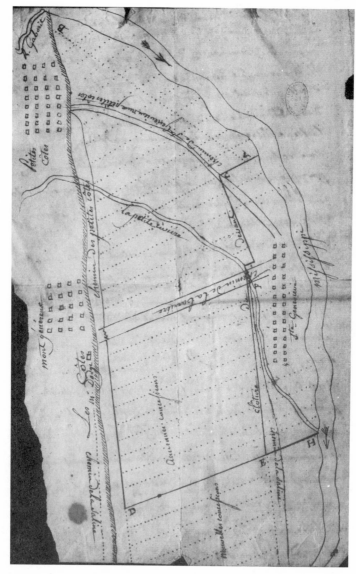

The Grand Champ at Ste. Genevieve. The parallel lines (two arpents apart) separate individual habitants' plowlands. The Old Town of Ste. Genevieve is designated "Ste. Geneviève," the New Town, "Petites Côtes," and New Bourbon–to–be, "Mont Généreux." Map drawn by Delassus de Luzières in 1793 and reproduced courtesy of the Archivo General de Indias, Seville.

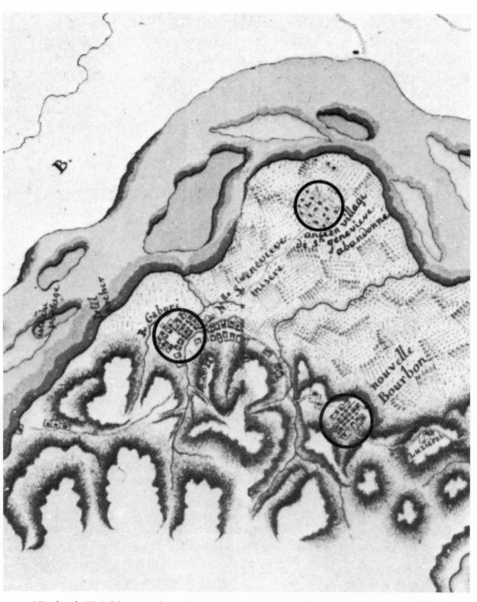

Nicolas de Finiels's map of Ste. Genevieve region, 1797. The circled entities are, from top to bottom, the abandoned Old Town of Ste. Genevieve, the New Town of Ste. Genevieve, and New Bourbon. Reproduced courtesy of the Archives du Service Historique de la Marine, Château de Vincennes.

residence and watch, as he once had, his fields in the Grand Champ turn from
gray to green to golden as the plowing, planting, and growing seasons progressed from April through August. Despite this dramatic change in the settlement at Ste. Genevieve that was wrought by the move from Old Town to New
Town, a larger and more important pattern persisted; the threefold structure
of the agricultural community—nuclear village of habitants, fenced compound
of arable strips, and commons for pasturage—was not effectively altered.

THE ILLINOIS COUNTRY: ST. LOUIS

St. Louis was markedly different from the other villages that made up the
heart of the Illinois Country. It was different because it was founded on what
was de jure Spanish territory, because it was established specifically as a fur-
trading outpost, because it was a fortified town, and because it became the
capital of Upper Louisiana. Although St. Louis was founded to serve as an
outpost for the trading activities of Maxent, Laclède, and Company,[215] the
community soon acquired a pattern of settlement and land usage that was
of long standing in the Illinois Country. Frederic L. Billon, a nineteenth-century St. Louisan who had a passionate interest in his city's history, described
how land was utilized at the colonial settlement:

> Land immediately adjoining the village on the northwest, being the most
> suitable, was set aside for cultivation, and conceded in strips of one arpent
> in front by forty in depth, and each applicant allotted one or more, accord-
> ing to his ability to cultivate it. This was called the common-field lots. . . . The
> land lying southwest of the village[,] being well watered with numerous
> springs and well covered with timber, was set aside for the village commons,
> in which the cattle and stock of the inhabitants were kept for safety and con-
> venience.[216]

The common fields eventually became known as the "St. Louis Common
Fields," which by the end of the colonial era was but one of the five complexes
of plowlands surrounding St. Louis. In any case, in this succinct description
of early St. Louis, Billon accurately portrayed the fundamental tripartite
pattern of land usage that was the iron rule of the Illinois Country.[217] Billon
also made it clear that the common fields at St. Louis were not in fact held
in common. The compounds of unfenced arable strips might better be called
open fields, for in the language of the early GLO surveyors, the real estate
within these compounds had been "granted and confirmed in small tracts
[i.e., strips] to sundry individuals."[218]

When in 1859 the city of St. Louis was preparing to sell most of the last vestiges of the once extensive St. Louis Commons, the editors of the city's principal newspaper, the *Missouri Republican,* remarked, "A brief history of these lands, at this time, therefore, may not be out of place, and we propose to make out an account as brief as consistent with its accuracy and proper connections."[219] What followed was an excellent description of land usage that had characterized colonial St. Louis and its immediate environs. The journalist began by relating the development of the various compounds of arable fields that surrounded St. Louis to the south, the west, and the north. The strips within the compounds had been granted by French and Spanish authorities generally to the "heads of families" and were as a rule one arpent wide by forty arpents deep. Although the article referred to the "Common Fields," the journalist made it clear that it was the fencing surrounding the compounds, and not plowlands themselves, that was the object of communal effort. This system, according to the *Missouri Republican,* was adopted to keep the cultivators in close proximity to one another in case of attack by hostile Indians and because a commonly maintained fence "effected a great saving of time, trouble, and expense to the individual owners." The journalist may be excused for failing to observe that similar configurations had existed in French agriculture for at least a millennium. That is, in addition to the general practical advantages that such a system may have offered at early St. Louis, it had also descended from specific practices of European communal agriculture.

The *Missouri Republican* went on to describe the *true* commons, which was defined as containing 4,510½ French arpents, or 3,837 English acres. This real estate was an integral part of the community but, unlike the arable compounds, had not been subdivided and granted to individual proprietors during colonial times:

> The successive French and Spanish Lieutenant Governors allowed and recognized . . . to the inhabitants at large, the body of land called the "St. Louis Common," lying South and South-west of the village, whence the villagers procured their supply of fuel, and etc. Like the Fields, the Common was surrounded by an enclosure, and stringent laws existed, . . . for the maintenance of the fences and for the general management of both Common and Common Fields. Thus a decree of Governor François Cruzat, of 22d September 1782, apprises us that the guardianship of the fences was entrusted to one Commission of inhabitants.

The commons located at all the French colonial communities on both sides of the Mississippi were used by the inhabitants for gathering firewood,

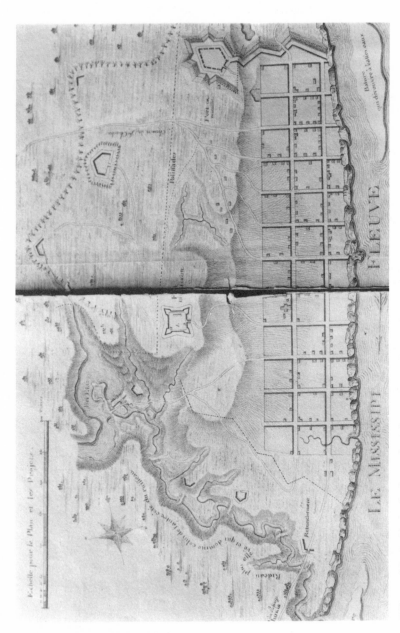

Village of St. Louis in the late colonial era. Notice the regularity of the street plan, unusual for a village in the Illinois Country. The rudimentary fortifications shown here were never completed. Inset from Charles Warin's 1796 map, reproduced from Georges-Victor Collot's *Journey in North America*.

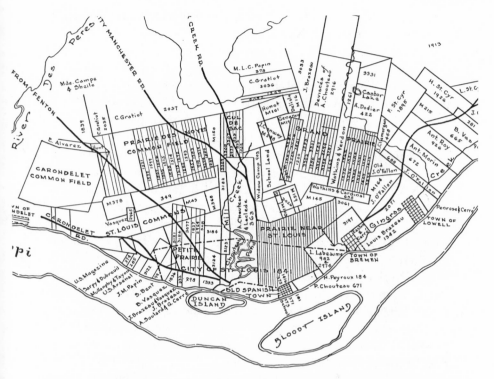

St. Louis region from the *Hutawa Atlas* of 1848. The colonial settlement pattern of compact village ("Old Spanish Town"), clusters of plowlands, and commons is clearly discernible. The various grids that compose the modern street plan of St. Louis all derive their orientations from the colonial longlots shown here.

which, given the voracious appetites of the residential fireplaces, became increasing scarce and precious toward the end of the colonial era.[220] Nonetheless, the most important use of the commons was for pasturing livestock, for the arable fields were closed off to animals during the sowing, growing, and harvesting seasons (from April through October).

As for the village itself, St. Louis was the most rigorously planned community in the Illinois Country. As an old man, Auguste Chouteau recounted how he had surveyed and platted the town in the year of its founding, 1764, and thenceforth the village had remarkably straight streets, right-angle intersections, and rectangular residential blocks.[221] The blocks ordinarily measured 240 by 300 French feet and were usually subdivided into four residential plots, either terrains or emplacements, each measuring 120 by 150 French feet.[222] St. Louis was the only community in the Illinois Country in which residential properties were measured with some care, and the configuration of residential property was quite unlike that used in any other community in the region, on either side of the Mississippi. In the other villages—from Cahokia to Chartres to Kaskaskia to Ste. Genevieve—town lots were roughly measured or paced off in square arpents or toises, not carefully chained off in pieds.

Auguste Chouteau was only fourteen or fifteen when he platted the early village, however, and doubtless it was Auguste's older associate, Pierre de Laclède Liguest, who conceived the rational, geometric plan for his settlement.[223] Laclède's plan was not based on any French Canadian or Creole Illinoisan tradition of urban planning. Rather, his model was almost certainly New Orleans, which had been laid out by the French military engineers Adrien de Pauger and Louis-Pierre Le Blond de la Tour during the early 1720s and with which Laclède was familiar from firsthand observation.[224] Pauger and de la Tour had themselves followed the model of urban planning with which they were familiar from the French port cities of Lorient, Rochefort, and Brest.[225] These fastidious engineers worked within the *esprit géométrique* of the time, laying out a waffle-iron grid facing the Mississippi River, at the center of which were the parish church and the Place d'Armes.[226] Laclède planned St. Louis in much the same fashion, and the plan of Upper Louisiana's capital was in fact a smaller version of Lower Louisiana's capital.[227] This provided an agreeable symmetry of urban planning, linking via the axis of the Mississippi River the capitals of Upper and Lower Louisiana.

St. Louis was the only fortified town ever to defend Upper Louisiana. Cahokia, Chartres, Kaskaskia, and Ste. Genevieve, at one time or another, each had a fort located either inside or close to a compact village. During the late 1740s, moreover, some thought was given to erecting a defensive palisade around the village of Kaskaskia to protect the townspeople from hostile Indians.[228] This was never undertaken, however, and although rudimentary Fort Kaskaskia overlooked the village from atop the bluffs, Kaskaskia never had a defensive perimeter.[229] Laclède did not in fact plan St. Louis as a fortified outpost in 1764. Rather, it was fear provoked by the Anglo-Indian attack of 1780 that prompted the building of the first palisade around the town.[230] During the 1790s the Spanish government hired two professional military engineers, Louis Vandenbemden and Nicolas de Finiels, to oversee construction of sturdier fortifications at St. Louis, but the task was not yet completed at the time of the Louisiana Purchase.[231]

Colonial St. Louis was first and foremost a trading outpost and administrative center, but subsistence agriculture was also practiced there from the town's earliest days. By the time of the Louisiana Purchase, the town was surrounded by five complexes of arable fields, which were subdivided into individual longlots measured off in arpents. This pattern was not planned or imposed by Laclède, Chouteau, or any government authorities in St. Louis but instead evolved out of local traditions of settlement and agriculture, which went back at least a half-century to the development of Cahokia and Kaskaskia. That is to say, habitants, most of whom were already second- or third-generation Illinoisans, created these arpent longlots in a pattern with which they were already familiar.[232]

At St. Louis, town, open fields, and commons were all encompassed within what eventually became Township 45 North, Range 7 East (of the fifth prime meridian), of the grid that the U.S. Land Ordinance of 1785 created. The configuration of lands at colonial St. Louis could not mesh neatly with the waffle-iron grid of townships laid in one-mile square sections, for the pattern at St. Louis had developed well before the west bank of the Mississippi became U.S. territory. The township grid system simply had to accommodate itself to a radically different cadastral system that had evolved with French colonial land use practices. The tidy geometrical grid of Enlightenment topographic planning that the Continental Congress proposed with the Land Ordinance of 1785 served no better in the Illinois Country than it did on the eastern seaboard, with its crazy-quilt pattern of metes and bounds.

Smaller communities lying outside St. Louis—Carondelet just to the south, St. Ferdinand or Florissant to the northwest, Portage des Sioux on the peninsula between the Missouri and Mississippi Rivers, and St. Charles several leagues up the Missouri—developed land usage patterns and agricultural practices much like St. Louis's. Compact, nucleated villages, compounds of arable strips, and true commons are shown on the early GLO maps for each of these settlement areas. Carondelet is best documented, and there the compound of arable strips ran northward and met the St. Louis Commons and Prairie des Noyers Common Fields along their southern extremities. At St. Ferdinand the strips of plowland ran perpendicular to the Missouri River (rather than the Mississippi), and the commons lay further back, in the direction of St. Louis. Modern landsat images clearly show the old orientation of the plowlands at St. Ferdinand, just north of St. Louis's present-day Lambert Airport.[233] To accommodate an agricultural economy, the town of Florissant was not located on the bank of the river but rather was more conveniently situated inland, on the borderline between plowlands and commons. The manifestly tripartite pattern of land usage at these outlying settlements, all of which date from the late eighteenth century, no doubt derived directly from Cahokia and Kaskaskia, the oldest of the colonial communities on the eastern side of the Mississippi.

UPPER CANADA: PRAIRIE DU CHIEN

Prairie du Chien possesses the most picturesque place-name of any French-founded community in the upper Mississippi Valley. It is not entirely clear whether this name derived from the prairie dogs that inhabited the alluvial plain of the Mississippi or from the name—"Chien" (i.e., "Dog")—of a Fox Indian chief whose band had at one time occupied the area. Henry R. Schoolcraft, Stephen H. Long, and James H. Lockwood accepted the latter derivation.[234] On the other hand, in 1766 Jonathan Carver used the plural version, "Prairie des Chiens"; seven years later Peter Pond invented an English equivalent, "Planes of the Dogs";[235] and in 1780 John Long called the place "Dogs' Field."[236] Therefore, when Nicolas Boilvin, the francophone U.S. Indian agent at Prairie du Chien in the early nineteenth century, used the name "Prairie des chiens,"[237] it seems likely that he was immortalizing the local prairie dogs. In any event, Prairie du Chien was the last Franco-American community to develop the distinctive pattern of land usage that characterized all the communities within the Illinois Country, and it was the only settlement outside of the region to do so.[238]

Prairie du Chien, located immediately on the east bank of the Mississippi just above the mouth of the Wisconsin River, was north of what was usually considered Louisiana in colonial times; this region was more commonly thought of as part of western Upper Canada. Marquette and Jolliet passed near Prairie du Chien's future site in 1673, but they apparently did not stop over there as they glided out of the Wisconsin River, turned their canoes south, and headed down the Mississippi on their historic voyage.[239] The Nicolas Bellin map of 1755, "Partie Occidentale de la Nouvelle France ou Canada," shows a fort at this location that the cartographer labeled "Ancien Fort François de S. Nicolas."[240] This was a reference to an outpost that supposedly had been erected at the mouth of the Wisconsin River in 1683 by Nicolas Perrot, a renowned voyageur who was active in the western Great Lakes at that time.[241] It is difficult to imagine, however, that any vestiges of Perrot's outpost (if he did in fact build one) were left by 1755. Bellin likely included this site on his map because, as a French royal cartographer working on the eve of the French and Indian War, he wished to help establish French claims to as many far-flung places in North America as possible.

Given its location, with convenient water routes in all directions, Prairie du Chien was no doubt used by French Canadian fur traders as a rendezvous point before it became a minor military outpost. Unlike most other settlements on the French Canadian frontier, however, Prairie du Chien never served as a missionary center. By the time of its founding, the Jesuits, who were the most tenacious of the French frontier missionaries, were already on the defensive, and the proselytizing energy of the French Catholic Reformation had run its course.

Tradition has it that a group of French Canadian *coureurs de bois* fleeing the Indian wars on the upper Mississippi established a trading post at the mouth of the Wisconsin River in 1737.[242] This would have been merely a temporary settlement, however, and Peter L. Scanlan argued persuasively that the first non-Indian inhabitants, the French Canadian Cardinals, settled at Prairie du Chien in 1754.[243] Scanlan's argument is corroborated by a document suggesting that a French military outpost was established at Prairie du Chien in 1755,[244] when both the French and British were positioning themselves for the impending war for empire in North America. Indeed, this was the year that Franco-British rivalry in North America led to the virtual massacre of General Edward Braddock's command near the Forks of the Ohio. In 1820 an American land agent, Isaac Lee, speculated that the "Old French Fort" that he showed on his map of Prairie du Chien[245] "was probably calculated for defence against musketry and small arms only. None can recollect the time of the erection of this fort; it was far beyond the memory of the oldest."[246] In any case, the French fort at Prairie du Chien was likely built during the 1750s, when the French were preparing for war and when the great stone Fort de Chartres was being built further down the Mississippi between Kaskaskia and Cahokia.

A French presence, probably both commercial and military, surely existed at Prairie du Chien by the mid-1750s, although the settlement first acquired major significance as a trading center after the French and Indian War, when the land on which it was situated had become British territory. Although Prairie du Chien was under British sovereignty after 1763, French Canadians (often métis) developed it as a trading post and stamped the community with their character. In 1780 John Long remarked that Prairie du Chien was "a town of considerable note, built after the Indian manner," by which he perhaps meant that buildings were erected helter-skelter, with no rational street plan.[247] After Prairie du Chien became U.S. territory in 1783, the trading outpost was still controlled by French Canadians working for financial agents (increasingly British) located in Montreal. According to the terms of Jay's Treaty (1795), Britain was to abandon all its outposts in the Northwest Territory (Michilimackinac, Detroit, Green Bay, Prairie du Chien, Grand Portage) by 1796, but these terms were not punctiliously observed, and these outposts continued to be dominated by British subjects (mostly French Canadian métis) right down to the end of the War of 1812.[248] In 1811 Boilvin wrote to Secretary of the Interior William Eustis in Washington, D.C., warning, "Great danger, both to individuals and the Government, is to be apprehended from the Canadian traders, who endeavor to incite the Indians against us."[249]

Despite the preponderance of French Canadians in the population, from 1801 until 1812 Prairie du Chien lay de jure within St. Clair County, which was part first of Indiana Territory (to 1809) and then of Illinois Territory (after 1809). During that period real estate transactions and other civil proceedings from Prairie du Chien were often recorded in Cahokia, which was the seat of St. Clair County. In 1811, for example, Henry Munro Fisher of Prairie du Chien offered property in and near Prairie du Chien as collateral on a loan from George Gillespie, a merchant from Montreal.[250] This property included a one-acre lot in the main village of Prairie du Chien and a two-hundred-acre agricultural tract in the "prairie" behind the village. This transaction was drafted and notarized in Michilimackinac on August 22, 1811, and recorded in Cahokia on December 31, 1811. Fisher's loan probably pertained to investments in the fur trade, and the range of the places involved in the transaction—Michilimackinac, Montreal, Prairie du Chien, and Cahokia—reveals something about the complexities and the vast distances attendant on this trade in the early nineteenth century.

Prairie du Chien was structured on a cadastral pattern of longlots, as was every other French settlement in the upper Mississippi Valley. Indeed, for Prairie du Chien it is more accurate to speak of *patterns* of longlots, for at Prairie du Chien there were two distinct varieties of French longlot, one for residential properties and one for agricultural lands.[251] The earliest detailed map of Prairie du Chien and environs was drafted in 1820 by Isaac Lee, who was justice of the peace and U.S. land agent. Honestly acknowledging on the map that it was "not taken from actual survey," Lee produced a much tidied-up construct that is nevertheless a useful historical document. In addition to showing the locations of Fort Crawford (built during the War of 1812) and the "Old French Fort," Lee's map depicts a unique type of settlement. The principal residential center was located, along with Fort Crawford, on a tract of land fronting directly on the Mississippi that was sometimes separated from the main bank of the river by a low-lying former channel of the Mississippi; directly eastward, on the main bank of the river, was another residential cluster; and third, north along the main bank, above the "Old Catholic Burying Ground," was another locus of residential development. Up and down the Mississippi, to the east of all residential areas, lay the agricultural fields, which ran across the alluvial bottomland from the Mississippi and the village parcels to the bluffline. The bluffline distinctly delineated a floodplain roughly 2,000 feet wide in the south and 650 feet in the north.

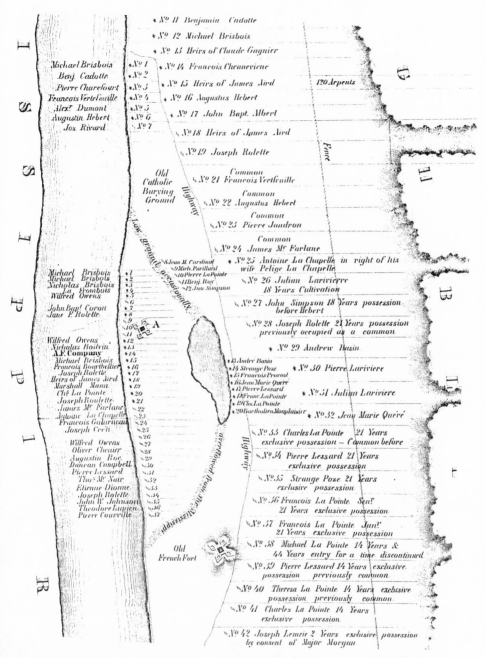

Prairie du Chien in 1820. Notice the multiple longlots (both residential and agricultural), the extended village, the "Old French Fort," and the newer American fort. Map done by U.S. land agent Isaac Lee, *ASP, PL.*

In 1828 the U.S. government settled the outstanding land claims in Prairie du Chien, and Lucius Lyon of the surveyor general's office conducted a detailed survey of the entire village. The resulting map was much more accurately drawn than the 1820 map, and exact measurements were given for the various parcels of real estate.[252] Both maps show an interesting variety of longlots, all related in some way to patterns from other settlements in French North America, yet unique in their overall configuration. Farthest west, on land that became an island during high waters, was located the "Main Village," as Lyon called it. Longlots in this area were rectangles with width-to-length ratios ranging from approximately 1:10 to 1:20, the long sides running perpendicular to the Mississippi River. These lots contained four to seven acres of land and constituted small village estates. In addition to dwelling houses, such lots doubtless also contained barns, stables, pigpens, chicken coops, orchards, and kitchen gardens, but they were not large enough to accommodate arable fields devoted to the production of cereal grains. For example, in May 1809 Indian agent Boilvin purchased three town lots in Prairie du Chien enclosed with a cedar-post fence, a house, and other buildings.[253] Some of the most important members of the community, including Boilvin, lived in the Main Village. Moreover, the American Fur Company had its headquarters in this village, situated virtually under the walls of Fort Crawford.

The agricultural lands of Prairie du Chien lay on the mainland proper, running from the high bluffs westward either to the bank of the Mississippi or to the swampy area that lay between the island of the Main Village and the riverbank. Lucius Lyon called these "Land Lots" to distinguish them from the village lots. In the depositions that the U.S. land commissioners took to verify ownership, these lots are called "Farm lots."[254] These agricultural parcels were also longlots with their long axes running perpendicular to the Mississippi, but they were of much larger scale than those in the Main Village, with width-to-length ratios varying between 1:5 and 1:10 and areas ranging between 32 and 281 square acres. Many habitants who lived in the Main Village owned one or more of these "land lots." Prairie du Chien therefore contained two distinct varieties of longlots, one residential and one agricultural, oriented basically the same way but of rather different width-to-length ratios, very different sizes, and totally different uses.

The settlement at Prairie du Chien contained not only the Main Village but also two additional clusters of residences, St. Friol Village and the Upper Village. Near the bank of the Mississippi, at the western end of the agricultural longlots, ran the principal roadway of the region. The residential clusters developed at two locations along that roadway. In these villages, both located on the mainland, the residential lots were less elongated than in the Main Village and obviously had been carved out of the agricultural fields. Some, though not all, of the habitants who lived on residential plots in these villages owned contiguous plowlands that stretched from their residential property back to the bluffline. Such cases provided Prairie du Chien with a residential-agricultural longlot pattern that was similar to parts of medieval Germany and also of Rowley, Massachusetts, in early colonial times.[255] In general, however, the close association of residential plot with agricultural plot had broken down (if it had ever consistently existed), and the settlement pattern that emerged consisted of a nuclear residential community with three loci of concentration in conjunction with distinct agricultural outlots.

One of U.S. land agent Isaac Lee's deponents in 1820 was Dennis Courtois, who had been a resident of Prairie du Chien since the early 1790s. He remarked that the agricultural lands there were held "alternately in common, and improved in detached parts as each should please, and this by common consent of the villagers."[256] Likely these words are Isaac Lee's translation of what Courtois told him in Mississippi Valley French patois, and it is of some importance to try to discern more precisely what Courtois meant by "alternately in common, and improved in detached parts." Lee's 1820 abstracted map of Prairie du Chien depicts a very long fence line extending approximately up the middle of the prairie and lying parallel to the Mississippi on the west and the bluffline on the east. This fence line cut the long agricultural lots on the prairie into two parts, and Lee noted on the west side of some of these lots, toward the river, that they were "Common." How this long fence line functioned within the agricultural system at Prairie du Chien is clarified by the field notes that surveyor Lucius Lyon took in 1828. In discussing the fourth farm lot, Lyon commented that "the back part near the bluff is cultivated, and the remainder lies in common—Soil 2nd rate."[257] Therefore the agricultural pattern on the prairie at Prairie du Chien apparently was based on having the long farm lots divided on the basis of two discrete functions: the portions located nearest the bluff (Courtois's "detached parts"), which had the best soil, were devoted to arable tillage, whereas the portions located to the west of the fence line, with less good soil, were used for common pasturage. The latter area, although generally referred to as a "commons," was in fact slashed across by the invisible property lines of the individual owners. This explains the peculiar ambiguity of Lee's abstracted map, on which he labeled portions of the farm lots at Prairie du Chien "Common" at the same time that he designated each proprieter by name. In his notes Lee further explained that the "whole extent of the prairie on which is situated the village of Prairie des Chiens, excepting so much of it as is fenced and in the exclusive possession of individuals, is claimed by the villagers and inhabitants of that settlement as a common."[258]

Two maps and several related documents from the 1820s therefore reveal that early land usage at Prairie du Chien consisted of several varieties of French colonial longlots that served both residential and agricultural purposes. Furthermore, these sources indicate that the pattern of land usage was fundamentally tripartite, consisting of nucleated village (complicated by several nuclei), arable plowlands, and common pasture land.[259] Prairie du Chien, at the western end of the Wisconsin and Fox Rivers corridor, developed settlement and agriculture patterns much like the French Creole communities lower down the Mississippi—Cahokia, Kaskaskia, Ste. Genevieve, and so forth. Green Bay, on the other hand, at the eastern end of the corridor, was modeled after the St. Lawrence Valley and exhibited autonomous ribbon farms with no communal agriculture.

CONCLUSION

The various communities of the Illinois Country on both sides of the Mississippi were founded at different times: Cahokia and Kaskaskia at the turn of the eighteenth century; Vincennes, Ste. Genevieve, and St. Louis between 1730 and 1764; and Carondelet, St. Ferdinand, and Prairie du Chien at the end of the century. They were founded in different locations with different environments: Kaskaskia on the alluvial floodplain of the Kaskaskia River, Ste. Genevieve on the west bank of the Mississippi, St. Louis on a plateau west of the Mississippi, Vincennes on the east bank of the Wabash, and Prairie du Chien far to the north. They were founded for different reasons: Cahokia as a mission center, Vincennes as a military outpost, Ste. Genevieve as an agricultural community, and St. Louis and Prairie du Chien as entrepôts for the fur trade. It is an arresting fact that despite these substantial differences of time, place, and original purpose, all these communities developed the same basic pattern of land usage, the iron triad of settlement in the Illinois Country: nuclear village, compound of arable fields, pasture commons. This pattern of culturally imposed geography, with its profound economic, social, and psychological ramifications, became the most significant defining feature of the Illinois Country on both sides of the Mississippi River.

This configuration was not brought to the Illinois Country from French Canada or from Lower Louisiana, and it was not imposed by fiat of the royal government, although government ordinances recognized and affirmed it. It was a system that undoubtedly originated and evolved partly in response to local needs and local geography. Nonetheless, the remarkable similarity between the pattern of land usage in the Illinois Country and that which had obtained for centuries in northern France suggests that the French colonists of the region possessed a mental template for a system that was part of the cultural baggage they had carried with them from the Old World. The pattern in the Illinois Country evolved in the communities on the east side of the Mississippi during the first three decades of the eighteenth century and had become dominant by circa 1730. The next half-century was the classic phase of this pattern, and there were few exceptions to it. That is, virtually all habitants in the region lived in nuclear villages, participated in open-field arable agriculture, and utilized common zones for pasturing their livestock. Freestanding habitations that existed outside of this system—Antoine Bienvenu's at Prairie du Rocher or Joseph Buchet's at St. Philippe—were extraordinary phenomena.

Beginning in the mid-1780s, however, the old system began to break down. Many newcomers to the Illinois Country developed rural estates beyond the confines of the old compact villages. These newcomers included Anglo-Americans, such as John Dodge and Elias Kent Kane, but also men such as Pierre Ménard, a French Canadian, and Charles Gratiot, a French Swiss. Ménard's residence survived the Mississippi's destruction of Old Kaskaskia because it was located outside town on higher ground, and Gratiot's one-league square plantation west of St. Louis was a well-known landmark by the end of the eighteenth century. Finiels's manuscript map of the Illinois Country drawn in 1798 accurately portrays the scattering of outlying habitations on both sides of the Mississippi. This gradual erosion of the nuclear village settlement pattern did not immediately entail destruction of the entire traditional system of land usage. Open-field agriculture continued on well into the nineteenth century at some communities, but by 1800 American-style dispersed farmsteads were proliferating as the wave of the future for rural life in Illinois.

Furthermore, toward the end of the eighteenth century, "outlots" began to appear in numbers. The fact that the Creoles of the Illinois Country never had a specific term for outlots is good evidence for the relative rarity of this phenomenon during most of the colonial period. To be sure, some habitants who lived within the traditional nuclear villages had always owned outlying parcels of land that were neither village lots nor arable strips within the open-field compounds. These plots probably served as areas with specialized uses, as commercial orchards or feedlots for livestock. But the size and number of these parcels increased dramatically during the 1790s. This increase is readily apparent in the area surrounding Ste. Genevieve, where influential persons— members of the Vallé, Bauvais, and Lachance families, as well as the parish priest, Jacques Maxwell—received sizable outlying concessions from Spanish colonial authorities. When Theodore Hunt recorded the land claims in the St. Louis and Ste. Genevieve regions for the U.S. government in 1825, the vast majority of the parcels he investigated fell either within one of the villages proper or within one of the compounds of arable strips that lay outside each village. Nevertheless, Hunt also included some claims for what he identified as "outlots." For example, the heirs of Vital St. Gemme Bauvais claimed a large outlot (480 square arpents) that lay south of Ste. Genevieve near New Bourbon.[260] The traditional tripartite configuration of land usage still dominated the landscape of the inhabited portion of the Illinois Country at the time of the Louisiana Purchase, but clear signs were already present that the Old World style of village agriculture was doomed to extinction in a region that was rapidly becoming Americanized in its economic and social structures.

You may behold at one and the same time a hundred plows going, under one inclosure, which belongs to the French [at Vincennes] who cultivate in Common.
—Jonathan Jennings

3 OPEN-FIELD AGRICULTURE

THE OPEN-FIELD SYSTEM

The preceding chapter discussed the tripartite pattern of land usage that evolved at French settlements in the Illinois Country after the eighteenth century began. This chapter focuses on one component of the triad, the open-field system of cereal-grain cultivation that developed in the early eighteenth century and continued to influence agriculture in certain regions of Illinois and Missouri until the end of the nineteenth century. Both French and English colonists brought systems of open-field agriculture to the New World, but the colonial histories of their respective systems are remarkably different. English colonial open-field agriculture was established on the eastern seaboard of North America early in the seventeenth century, but for all intents and purposes it had disappeared by the end of that century.[1] French colonial open-field agriculture developed in full-blown form *only* in the upper Mississippi River valley,[2] was just barely emerging at the turn of the eighteenth century, and reached full maturity at a time when the open fields of New England were long since forgotten.

Open-field agriculture in France has received little scholarly attention since Marc Bloch published his seminal study on French rural history in 1931. When in 1960 Pierre Goubert commented briefly on open-field agriculture in Beauvais, his only historiographical reference point was Bloch's work, and he wrote that "the question of fences must be taken up again."[3] Some French localities have been studied during the last thirty-five years,[4] but recently open fields have received considerably more attention in Great Britain than in France.[5] An interesting reflection of this British scholarship is the French neologism *l'openfields,* now commonly employed in French publications as an appropriated word, without italics.[6] In any case, European scholarship on open-field systems is useful background for studying agriculture in the Illinois Country, for there is no doubt that Old World models informed communal cultivation in the New World.

Recent scholars of common-field agriculture do not entirely agree in defining its requisite components. Joan Thirsk adduced "four essential elements" of the system: open arable fields divided into individually occupied strips, common pasturing on the stubble and fallow fields, common use of nonarable pasture and wasteland, and communal regulation of the agricultural system.[7] J. Z. Titlow and Richard Hoffman maintain that Thirsk's third essential element, common pasture on nonarable lands, was not essential because a common-field system could function effectively without it.[8] Interesting though this discussion may be, it is irrelevant for the Illinois Country, because common pasturage on wasteland was omnipresent in the region; every French Creole community on both sides of the Mississippi had a recognized commons for pasturage.

Pierre de Saint-Jacob has recently compressed the entire discussion of traditional European agriculture and land usage by explaining that "commons and collective rights are the essential components of the [village] community."[9] Saint-Jacob also justified his own research by remarking that "a modest contribution to the deep history of the village community, whose neglect is astonishing in a country [France] where so much work has been done on agriculture, seems rather useful."[10] With regard to the Illinois Country, it may be speculated that nuclear villages were an essential component of the open-field regime, for they existed at every Illinois community that had open arable fields. Indeed, although Thirsk did not mention nuclear villages as an essential element in her original article on common fields, in a later piece she commented that "wherever people lived in villages or hamlets, that is, in close proximity to one another, they were liable to create a field system. In short, field systems could be, and usually were, as numerous as nucleated settlements."[11] Hoffman agreed by noting that "common-field agriculture was closely associated with a nucleated settlement pattern."[12] And in his recent *Géographie historique de la France,* Xavier de Planhol treats open-field agriculture and nuclear villages ("villages groupés") as concomitant components of an integrated settlement pattern.[13] For further discussion in another forum, it may be useful to suggest that nuclear villages were in fact a fundamental element of the common-field system, whether in eighteenth-century Illinois or in medieval and early modern Europe. In any case, every feature of the common-field system as Thirsk and Hoffman have recently defined it (and as Marc Bloch defined it several generations ago) was present in the eighteenth-century Illinois Country, even though no manors or seigneurs as such ever existed there.

Common-field agriculture in the Illinois Country emerged rather quickly following the establishment of nuclear villages in the region, and to some extent this system of agriculture derived from the compact settlement pattern. That is, if the French colonial cultivators in the middle Mississippi Valley were first compelled to live in compact villages for reasons of security, common-field agriculture was a convenient method of exploiting the soil of the bottomlands surrounding the villages. John Reynolds approached the origins of the common fields in Illinois from another perspective, remarking that the French colonial cadastral system of long, narrow strips made fencing of individual parcels impractical. Therefore, surveying habits (which Reynolds did not know originated in French Canada) governed fencing patterns that in turn governed agricultural practices.[14] This argument contains a grain of truth, although in many regions of North America (most obviously throughout St. Lawrence River valley), French American habitants lived on ribbon farms without practicing common-field agriculture. In any case, the institution of common-field agriculture in the Illinois Country, which was markedly similar to traditional rural practices on much of the northern European plain, was evidently based on cultural baggage that came from France, not from French Canada, even though many Illinois habitants had Canadian roots.

The preceding chapter suggested that confusion in distinguishing commons from common fields has been a persistent problem when studying land usage and agriculture in the Illinois Country. Logan Esarey's comprehensive history of Indiana published in 1915 completely confused the two when discussing agriculture at eighteenth-century Vincennes: "The villagers laid off an ample commons of 5,000 acres which they enclosed with pickets. On this commons each villager had one or more strips for cultivation."[15] These remarks represent a total misapprehension of land usage in a system of open-field cultivation, but problems with imprecise nomenclature led to confusion about commons and common fields even in colonial times. Two French officials at Fort de Chartres, Buissonière and Flaucourt, issued a decree for the Illinois Country in March 1737 in which they used *commune* to refer to the arable fields taken as a whole.[16] Several months later Captain Le Blanc, commandant in Kaskaskia, called the compound of arable strips at Kaskaskia the "Commune Générale."[17] The land in each of the Illinois Country communities that was surveyed into strips that were grouped together into a single arable complex did not, and does not, lend itself to easy classification or precise nomenclature. During the spring sowing, summer growing, and autumn harvest seasons they were more or less freehold property, although the owners could not erect any fences on them. After the harvest, when the livestock of every habitant had free range over them, the arable strips became communal land for pasturing.

French officials in New Orleans—either because as outsiders they did not get caught up in local and confusing terminology, or because they were veteran writers of provincial decrees and therefore wrote with more precision— used less confusing language than Buissonière and Flaucourt. In a 1743 decree pertaining to Kaskaskia, Governor General Vaudreuil and Commissaire-ordinateur Salmon called the commons "la Commune," and they referred to the complex of arable strips simply as "les terres concédées," plowlands conceded by grant.[18] This language makes their decree a noticeably clear and useful document for helping to decipher the agricultural system in the colonial Illinois Country.

In the early nineteenth century, the American board of land commissioners at Kaskaskia understood perfectly well the sense of the phrase "les terres concédées." They described the common field of Cahokia and Prairie du Pont in 1809 thus: "This tract . . . is composed of the various grants or allotments made to the several inhabitants of these villages and from the first have been enclosed by one common fence."[19] The arable strips in the Illinois Country were indeed surveyed, although not always very precisely, and granted to individual proprietors. The phrase "from the first" is not altogether accurate but merely reflects the fact that the American land commissioners did not know the full history of the large compounds of arable strips in the Illinois Country. *Open-field* and *common-field* will be used as synonymous expressions throughout the remainder of this study, although it was the fence surrounding the arable fields in each community that more appropriately may be said to have been held in common.

John Reynolds, whose curiosity was piqued by the old French system of common-field agriculture, succinctly described the system of communal fencing that he had seen functioning in early nineteenth-century Illinois:

"The custom among the inhabitants of the Illinois villages, in regard to making and keeping in repair, the fence of this common field was, that each proprietor of land should make and keep in repair the fence passing over his land. . . . This system was based on the principle that each land proprietor should make the fence in proportion to his land."[20] Reynolds was describing the practice by which each habitant was responsible for the fence lines along the short ends of his particular ribbon strip, while the long, lateral fences were maintained in common. In essence, each community in the Illinois Country had but one extended agricultural fence, the one surrounding the compound of arable fields. In contrast, French Canada displayed a multiplicity of small fences, with every habitant fencing in his own land and also fencing off the various fields and meadows within his particular roture. Peter Kalm observed about the St. Lawrence Valley, "There was a superabundance of fences around here, since every farm was isolated and the fields divided into small pastures."[21]

A cultural geographer has recently remarked that "it is primary in all sedentary societies to organize the land for individual ownership or communal management."[22] The remainder of this chapter will examine how the habitants and the government in the Illinois Country provided for the communal use and management of agricultural land in the region.

L'ABANDON

Communal pasturing of livestock in areas designated specifically for that purpose was practiced in northern Europe for nearly a thousand years before the French settled in North America. In the St. Lawrence River valley during the seventeenth century, seigneurs often set aside commons on which their habitants could pasture livestock, although the seigneurs also reserved the right to repossess this land if they saw fit.[23] The ubiquitous common pastures in the Illinois Country were therefore well within older French and French Canadian traditions. Commons for pasturage were always carved out of lands that were marshy, rocky, or wooded and were therefore not well suited for plowing. The existence of these commons did not directly impinge on the issue of arable farming except where fencing was required to separate plowlands from pastures.

In regions of the great northern European plain, however, another practice existed in which animal husbandry and grain production became fully intertwined. This was the practice of converting the arable fields into common pasture once the crops had been harvested. Called by a variety of names—*vaine pâture, droit de parcours, paissance collective*—in metropolitan France and usually *l'abandon* in the French Illinois Country, common grazing on the stubblefields was an integral part of open-field agriculture wherever it was practiced.[24] Vaine pâture served two practical purposes. It provided additional pasturage (i.e., in addition to the commons) for livestock, and in turn the nitrogen-rich droppings of the animals provided a modicum of natural fertilizer for the arable fields. Moreover, it placed sharp limits on individual property rights. Indeed, where the system was fully developed and enforced, it meant that proprietorship of arable land was reduced to the right of tillage, that plowmen never in fact owned anything more than the right to cultivate their arable strips from sowing time until harvest. A seventeenth-century French jurist went so far as to proclaim that once the crops were harvested, "the plowlands, by a sort of law of nations, belong to everyone, rich and poor alike." Bloch's research suggested that this was not precisely true in practice, for pasturing on the stubblefields was regulated to benefit the larger and wealthier landowners.[25] There is no evidence that such regulation occurred in the Illinois Country.

In metropolitan France, where two- and three-field crop rotation was practiced and where both spring and winter grains were sown, vaine pâture functioned in this fashion: after the grain had been harvested in the fields where biennial rotation was practiced (the two-field system), the fields would lie fallow for an extended period—more than a year if a rotation was being made from spring-sown grain to winter wheat, and ten months or so if the rotation was reversed. In the regions of triennial rotation (the three-field system), the system was somewhat different. After the harvest, fields that had contained winter wheat would not be sown again until spring planting time, whereas those that had contained the spring-sown grain would lie fallow for more than a year. During these periods the fields were open to communal grazing.[26] The Illinois Country was of course quite different, for crop rotation of either the biennial or triennial variety was *never* practiced there. The rich alluvial bottomlands of the Mississippi, Wabash, and Missouri Rivers were, like the lower Nile Valley in Egypt, periodically rejuvenated by spring floods, and the French habitants never rotated crops.

Vaine pâture was less important in French North America than in metropolitan France for the obvious reason that everywhere in America there was more spare land available for pasture. That is, pasturing on arable lands once the harvest was in was less urgent in America than in Europe, where grazing land was always at a premium. Nonetheless, the practice of vaine pâture had a powerful hold on the French peasant mentality, and the practice was carried to North America by French colonists, many of whom had peasant origins. Uncharacteristically placing the idea before the practice, Marc Bloch went so far as to say that vaine pâture arose "first of all from an idea or way of thinking"[27] rather than from practical necessities imposed by material conditions. Bloch's thesis in this case is perhaps affirmed by Louise Dechêne, who explained that in the agricultural areas surrounding seventeenth-century Montreal, the habitants, "rather curiously, superimposed on their system of individual exploitation a practice of seasonal paissance collective which could only have provoked many problems."[28] Collective grazing on the stubble of grain fields is a bit hard to conceptualize within a context of doggedly individualistic agriculture, and as Dechêne's last phrase indicates, vaine pâture must have been fraught with difficulties in French Canada. In any case, collective grazing in the St. Lawrence Valley "was limited to the vicinity of Montreal except in the earliest years of New France. In the Lower Richelieu [Valley], enclosure was always the rule and the only departures from 'agrarian individualism' were the common pastures and meadows established by the seigneurs."[29] It is apparent that the practice of l'abandon in the Illinois Country was a rural custom whose ancestry was distinctly more French than French Canadian.

Common pasturing of livestock on the stubble following the harvest was an issue that was integrally intertwined with the kind of cereal grains that were sown in the open fields of the Illinois Country. In France both *blé de printemps* (spring wheat) and *blé d'hiver* (winter wheat) were sown, depending on the area, but in general winter wheat was the more popular variety in regions dominated by open-field agriculture.[30] Indeed, the only grain-sowing illustration among the several agricultural scenes depicted in Jean duc de Berry's early fifteenth-century illuminated manuscript, "Très Riches Heures," is for the month of October,[31] and October is the traditional month for sowing winter wheat in temperate climates. French Canadians, however, seldom sowed winter wheat because the rigorous climate of the St. Lawrence River valley was not well suited for it.[32] Louise Dechêne remarks that in the Montreal region, the "dominant cereal grain was [spring] wheat, a northern variety that ripened rapidly and had been selected for the colony for that reason."[33] Rather curiously, there is some evidence from the mid-eighteenth century that French settlers at Detroit were planting winter wheat,[34] but the varieties of cereal grains at Detroit had no bearing on the issue of vaine pâture, because the habitants there did not practice open-field agriculture; their fields were cultivated as individual family enterprises, French Canadian style. According to a little-known epistoler, one Monsieur Lallemant, the Illinois habitants followed in the footsteps of their Canadian cousins by planting spring wheat. Lallemant wrote from Kaskaskia on April 5, 1721, that "people sow here from the month of March until April 26, and they harvest from July until August 15."[35]

Commandant Pierre Dugué de Boisbriant, who had issued the first ordinances for agricultural fencing in Illinois,[36] discussed wheat production in a letter he wrote from Fort de Chartres in 1724: "Wheat was being sown at the beginning of March. But I noticed that it was not in the ground long enough to be properly nourished and that it was not cold enough here to prevent the wheat from wintering in the ground. Thus I made the first attempt at sowing wheat in the autumn, which worked so well that the habitants decided to plant all of their wheat in the autumn."[37] Winter wheat and the practice of l'abandon would have been difficult to reconcile in the Illinois Country, for the latter required that arable fields be abandoned to foraging livestock each autumn. Indeed, substantial evidence indicates that the long-term tendency was quite the reverse of that suggested by Boisbriant—namely, that over time spring wheat became more popular than winter wheat. John Reynolds commented on vaine pâture as he had seen it used by the old French agriculturists in early nineteenth-century Illinois: "They sow spring wheat, as their common fields were occupied by the cattle all winter." Reynolds was confidant about these issues, for he reiterated them in three discrete publications.[38] He noted that the French Creole farmers with whom he was familiar planted spring wheat because "spring wheat made good, dark bread, which many preferred to the bread made of fall wheat."[39]

Henry Marie Brackenridge, who lived in Ste. Genevieve on the west side of the Mississippi during the 1790s and had many opportunities to observe French Creole cultivators at work, remarked that "their agricultural labors commence in the month of April, when the inhabitants, with their slaves, are seen going and returning, each morning and evening, for eight or ten days, with their ploughs, carts, horses, and so forth." (Incidentally, this passage succinctly portrays the nuclear village as a concomitant of open-field agriculture, with the habitants tramping out to their arable fields each morning and returning to their residences in town each evening.) Brackenridge further remarked that spring wheat was a customary planting in the Grand Champ at Ste. Genevieve and explained this custom by noting that "in the rich alluvia, it is thought, that wheat sowed in the spring is best; it does not grow so rank, and is less apt to lodge or mildew."[40] Perhaps even though the Illinois climate was entirely suitable for winter wheat, the undrained alluvial soils of the river bottoms were not. Lieutenant Governor Zénon Trudeau remarked in 1794 about the habitants of Upper Louisiana that they "have the habit of sowing their grains in the spring rather than in the autumn. This gives them a double harvest of infinitely superior grain which should not be mixed with any other grains which blackens and spoils their flour."[41] Even today, with modern drainage systems and new hybrid varieties of wheat, most winter wheat in Illinois and Missouri is sown on drier, lighter upland soils.

AGRICULTURAL REGULATIONS

The interwoven issues of grain production and vaine pâture, or l'abandon, may be seen in early Illinois ordinances dealing with agricultural fencing. After the French crown assumed direct control of Louisiana in 1731 (replacing the Royal Indies Company), a system of colonial government developed in which the Illinois Country had royal officials that paralleled, but at a lower level, those in New Orleans. In the metropole of the colony were located the governor general and the commissaire-ordonnateur, the first a military position and the second a civil post. In the Illinois Country their counterparts were the commandant at Fort de Chartres and the écrivain principal, who was often referred to as the "subdelegate" of the commissaire-ordonnateur in New Orleans. During the late 1730s, the commandant at the fort was Alphonse de la Buissonière, and the écrivain principal was François-Auguste de la Loëre Flaucourt. These two men issued a series of decrees that illuminate the agricultural system and settlement pattern at Kaskaskia in some of its details and complexities. These decrees also reveal how provincial government policy was implemented at the local level.

On March 8, 1737, shortly before the start of the spring planting season, Buissonière and Flaucourt issued a decree concerning communal grazing on the arable fields in the Illinois Country. This decree is the earliest solid evidence that the habitants of the region were employing the medieval practice of vaine pâture.[42] They began by declaring that it was imperative to establish a definite time for releasing the cattle onto the stubble fields, "in order to protect the fruits of the earth." They then bemoaned the fact that the habitants had as yet adhered to no regulation concerning release of the cattle, that some selfish habitants harvested their grain and then neglected to maintain their share of the fences around the arable fields, and that this selfishness was doing much damage to the unharvested crops of others. Then came two corrective regulations: (1) Henceforth no cattle would be released onto the stubble of the arable lands until All Saint's Day, and each habitant's portion of the fences had to be maintained up to that date. (2) All livestock had to be withdrawn from the arable fields no later than April 1 of each year so that the fields might be prepared for spring sowing. The fine for contravening either regulation was a substantial 100 livres, for violators could disrupt agriculture for the entire community.[43]

The process by which this decree was disseminated throughout the region is of some interest. From Fort de Chartres a copy was dispatched to "Monsieur Le Blanc, captain of a company of detached marines and commandant in the village of Kaskaskia." Le Blanc in turn gave it to Jean-Baptiste Bertlot *dit* Barrois, the royal clerk and notary in Kaskaskia, who had it copied and distributed. Finally, the curé of the parish of the Immaculate Conception of Kaskaskia, the Jesuit Father Tartarin, was expected to assist the civil arm by "reading, broadcasting, and posting" the decree. In practice this meant that the good father would announce it after mass and then post it on the door of the parish church, which served as the community bulletin board. In this way the hierarchies of the Bourbon royal government and the Roman Catholic Church functioned in unison to govern French medieval agricultural practices in the Illinois Country—an exotic process in America's heartland.

Two weeks after the promulgation of this decree came an emendation in response to the "pleas of the habitants from Kaskaskia."[44] The deadline of April 1 was too early to give them time properly to prepare the fences around the arable fields. At Fort de Chartres the representatives of Louis XV's government in the Illinois Country, Buissonière and Flaucourt, softened their stance and gave the habitants two additional weeks; the fences would not have to be suitable to keep livestock out of the arable fields until April 15 of each year. In 1737, therefore, April 15 was selected as the most popular target date for completing agricultural fencing in the Illinois Country. From then until well into the nineteenth century—under French, Spanish, British, and American regimes—agriculturists of French ancestry who worked the Mississippi bottomlands in all the Illinois communities from St. Louis to Kaskaskia spent the last two weeks of March and the first two weeks of April working their fence lines surrounding the arable tracts.

In May 1737, two months after the original edict that established the policy of l'abandon, appeared another executive order pertaining to grazing.[45] This is an unusual document among Illinois Country sources because it originated with the Kaskaskia village commandant, Captain Le Blanc; governmental orders emanating directly from a local commandant in the Illinois Country during the French regime are exceedingly rare documents. Le Blanc, a royal marine, began his order by declaring that it was being issued on behalf of the king (Louis XV), the commandant (Le Blanc himself), and the officers of the militia at Kaskaskia. In presenting the order with this preamble, Le Blanc adduced the hierarchy of command, the king and himself, but gave it local cachet by bringing in the local militia officers, who would have been the most respected citizens of Kaskaskia. In any case, the substance of Le Blanc's order addressed the fact that some habitants of Kaskaskia continued to permit livestock to enter the sacred enclosure of the "Commune Générale" even after the grain had been sown. Le Blanc's order gave them five days to remove the marauding animals, after which guilty owners would be liable to a fine of fifty livres over and above the one hundred livres specified in the earlier edict of Buissonière and Flaucourt. Trespassing livestock were also to be seized and sold at public auction. Once again the church was brought in to buttress civil authority, for Father Tartarin was to read this edict at the high mass while standing beside the altar that held the gospel in the parish church of Kaskaskia.

All the documentation from 1737 strongly suggests that, contrary to what Boisbriant had written back in 1724, habitants of the Illinois Country were increasingly sowing spring wheat and practicing communal grazing on the stubblefields. Given that the various decrees and ordinances of 1737 all emanated from regional and local authorities, it may be deduced that the regulations represented the view of a substantial majority of the local habitants. That is, there is no evidence that the agricultural regulations of 1737 came down to the Illinois Country from higher authorities in New Orleans or at Versailles. Rather they represented an attempt by local authorities to remedy local problems in a region of mixed agricultural, producing both cereal grains and livestock, where the cultivators lived in agricultural villages and owned adjacent arable strips that composed open-field complexes.

Rather oddly, the system of land usage, including spring sowing of both wheat and maize and l'abandon after the harvest, that seemed to be increasingly entrenched in both practice and law in the Illinois Country during the 1730s was intruded on by outsiders in 1743. In that year the habitants at Kaskaskia petitioned Governor General Vaudreuil and Commissaire-ordonnateur Salmon to give official sanction to the existence of the Kaskaskia commons, the communal pasturing area located on the peninsular lowlands between the Kaskaskia and Mississippi Rivers. In their rather curious response, Vaudreuil and Salmon agreed to the habitants' request concerning the commons but then proceeded to present a new regulation regarding communal grazing on the stubble.[46] This regulation stated that to allow some habitants to plant winter wheat ("semences d'automne"), there would henceforth be no communal pasturing of livestock on the arable fields after the fall harvest; individuals could, however, oversee their own grazing animals on their own strips of arable land. This brief regulation, which proposed to abolish l'abandon, cut right to the heart of the communal system that had been institutionalized in the series of local ordinances promulgated in 1737 and was of course at odds with the traditional French practice of vaine pâture. The best explanation for this seemingly eccentric edict is that Vaudreuil and Salmon, as conscientious civil servants, were participating in the eighteenth-century movement toward more individualistic agriculture, in which governments were discouraging communal practices; they were attempting to impose modernity on the Illinois Country from their administrative offices in New Orleans.[47]

After this flurry of documentation from the 1730s and early 1740s, we find few surviving sources concerning agricultural fencing and l'abandon at Kaskaskia. Almost certainly April 15 remained the irrevocable and inflexible date for removing livestock from the arable fields, and no one released livestock again onto the arable until all growers had completed harvesting their wheat and maize; no one challenged the local authorities' power to regulate the agricultural system, a power that both descended from the king and ascended from consensus among the habitants. The relative absence of extant documents concerning these fundamental issues is in part simply because to the fact that many records from the French Illinois Country have not survived. Nonetheless, this absence is also due to the fact that these issues were so fundamental, so intimately connected to the survival of the community, and so generally agreed on by all parties involved that decrees, orders, and ordinances were superfluous. Spring sowing of cereal grains and communal grazing on the stubble fields after harvest had been woven into the fabric of the Illinois Country as customary laws. John Reynolds observed that the "early French had many customs in relation to the common fields that were just and equitable. There was a time fixed, that all should have their crops gathered. After that the fence was not attended to; and the same in the spring, to repair the fence and keep the stock out of the field."[48]

Open-field agriculture, authorities on the subject agree, requires detailed regulation to function well: sowing times, harvest times, crop rotation (where practiced), communal fencing, and common pasturing—all these issues must be regulated with some precision and determination. Nevertheless, documentation regarding the rules of open-field agriculture in traditional European society tends to be fragmentary and sporadic. Georges Duby remarks that "documents are extremely uncommunicative on this point."[49] In response to the question "Who made the rules?" Marc Bloch answered that "basically, they were not 'made.' They were customary; the group simply received them from tradition."[50] Richard C. Hoffman pointedly raised one of the issues that made community rules necessary: "The advent of grazing on open-field arable land created the problem to which communal regulation of agricultural manage-

ment was a response."[51] But Hoffman did not initiate a search to find the
systematic communal regulations of which he wrote. Joan Thirsk, however,
writing specifically about traditional English agricultural practices, insisted
that "our knowledge of field systems . . . derives largely from . . . bylaws, and
some analysis of their content is essential." This comment is entirely applicable to the study of open-field agriculture in the Illinois Country, for extant community regulations are the best sources for understanding the system of agriculture practiced there. Thirsk continued by noting that for
England, "unfortunately, it is rarely possible to find a set of bylaws for a village that is complete for any one period or year."[52] Fortunately for this study,
complete sets of communal regulations pertaining to open-field agriculture
are available from several communities in the Illinois Country.

The earliest fencing regulations in the Illinois Country, those from
Kaskaskia during the 1720s and 1730s, were decrees of regional and local governmental officials, the provincial authorities at Fort de Chartres and the
town commandant at Kaskaskia. These regulations were intended to serve
the interests of the local cultivators, and they could hardly have been effective without their general agreement. Nonetheless, there is no evidence from
the early history of the Illinois Country that assemblies of habitants were
required to approve fencing laws. Over time this changed, and by the end of
the eighteenth century such assemblies became de rigueur in the French Creole communities on both sides of the Mississippi. That is, the governing of
agricultural practices in the Illinois Country seems to have become increasingly democratized as time went by. This process of democratization *may* in
some fashion have been associated with a certain democratic spirit that was
spreading in the Western world at the end of the eighteenth century, the age
of the democratic revolution, as it has been called.[53] A more certain influence,
however, was an old-fashioned consensual process that had been functioning in metropolitan French villages for centuries. Ironically, this village democracy had its greatest impact in the Illinois Country after the French regime in North American had ended.

VILLAGE ASSEMBLIES

In 1893 a French lawyer, Henri Babeau, published his doctoral thesis, *Les
Assemblées générales des communautés d'habitants en France du XIIIe siècle à
la Révolution*, which was submitted to the Faculty of Law at the University
of Paris.[54] Babeau's thesis still stands as the best study of village governance
in Old Regime France, and much of it applies as well to village life in the Illinois Country.[55] Using extant notarial records as his basic source materials,

Babeau painted a portrait of a grass-roots rural society that was highly democratized for dealing with local issues.

In societies where village and parish usually coincided (which was generally true in both France and French North America), Babeau concluded, assemblies probably originated for the purpose of electing the *marguilliers*
(church wardens) who composed the *fabrique* (vestry) of the parish, and Marc
Bloch was later inclined to agree.[56] From this religious function, however, assemblies expanded their deliberative functions into virtually every area of village life. Babeau emphasized that no written statute ever specifically circumscribed their powers,[57] and at the highest level, village assemblies participated
in sending representatives to the Estates General. At the lowest level, within the
respective communities, local assemblies were "sovereign" and dealt with everything pertaining to the common interest of the villagers: supervision of livestock, roads, pastureland, woods, and so forth.[58] The relevant issue here is that
there was a strong tradition in French rural society for local assemblies to be
centrally involved in regulating community agriculture.[59]

Assemblées des habitants, or village assemblies, probably met throughout
French North America as well as in metropolitan France, although no one
has studied village assemblies in the French colonies. Church wardens, for
example, were selected by assemblies in Canadian parishes, as were syndics
(*syndic* was a word of ancient origin that had long been used for municipal
and corporate affairs in France), for dealing with community issues such as
local roads and bridges.[60] This was apparently true throughout colonial Louisiana as well. At Pointe Coupée an assembly of habitants met in 1778 to draft
and sign (many with their marks) a petition to the local commandant requesting that a common pasture be created for their livestock.[61] Assemblies
of habitants also met in the Illinois Country on both sides of the Mississippi.[62]
Indeed, documentation on local assemblies in French North America is perhaps most abundant from the Illinois Country, for this was the only region
where open-field agriculture, which required much local regulation, was
practiced. The fact of the matter is that most of the extant documentation
involving assemblies of habitants from the eighteenth-century Illinois Country pertains to these assemblies as agencies of agricultural regulation.

Village assemblies, whether they met in fifteenth-century France or eighteenth-century Illinois, always elected syndics to function as local officials for
all secular matters. Rétif de la Bretonne described the selection and function
of syndics in his native village of Sacy in lower Burgundy: "The assemblies
named the syndics, whose functions rather resembled those of consuls under the Romans—collectors of the *taille* [basic tax], guardians of the agricultural land to protect the crops, the vines, and the common pasture."[63] The

taille was never collected in the Illinois Country, but the syndics there were heavily involved with agricultural issues. The number of syndics varied considerably from community to community. In 1785 there was one at Cahokia and another one at neighboring Prairie du Pont,[64] whereas at Ste. Genevieve in 1778 there were no fewer than eight.[65]

If local assemblies had substantial powers of governance in French rural communities, the authority to convene such assemblies was an important issue. According to Babeau, in France up through the sixteenth century it was usual for the local seigneur or his representative to convene village assemblies, although in some regions like Auvergne habitants met of their own volition. Once again Babeau claimed that the system changed during the early modern period as seigneurial powers atrophied and that by the eighteenth century authorization by the seigneur was the exception rather than the rule. Instead, syndics convened the assemblies, over which they then presided.[66] Babeau perhaps exaggerated the autonomy of village assemblies, and Marc Bloch, who briefly discussed village assemblies, argued that local seigneurs retained substantial authority.[67] Rétif de la Bretonne pointed out that in his village "the seigneur's man was automatically president of the assemblies,"[68] and Rétif was the only literate eighteenth-century Frenchman to describe the intricacies of village governance.

In French Canada assemblies of habitants met "usually, if not as a rule, at the behest of the intendant or his deputy."[69] For the Illinois Country during the French regime proper (i.e., up to 1763), there exists no documentation to determine much about community assemblies or who convened them. Such assemblies surely existed, for the presence of local officials such as church wardens and syndics presupposes the existence of local elective assemblies; in the language of Old Regime France, marguilliers and syndics were by definition elected officials. However, given that the earliest fencing laws (those of the 1720s and 1730s) seem to have been simply decrees of the commandant at Fort de Chartres, it is likely that the authority to convene assemblies of habitants remained in the hands of the military officers in the Illinois Country—either the commandant at the fort or his subordinates in the various villages. This was also the case on the west side of the Mississippi under the Spanish regime, where village assemblies were convened by the commandant before the habitants could exercise their franchise and proceed to elect syndics.[70] On the American side of the river, the first complete set of community fencing regulations was approved by an assembly of habitants at Cahokia in 1785,[71] although the assembly was apparently convoked at the initiative of the commandant (by then an American official), Antoine Girardin.[72] A Northwest Territory law of 1799, however, specifically gave the habitants of the Illinois Country permission to meet on their own volition to regulate their open-field agricultural regime.[73]

Babeau began his study by employing an English expression—"self-government"—to identify the system he was studying; no phrase in the French language is so succinct and galvanic. Nonetheless, Babeau then referred to a classic French literary source to flesh out the definition for the local deliberative assemblies that interested him. Rétif de la Bretonne described his home parish as "having communal land, and therefore was governed just like a large family; everything was decided by majority voice ["pluralité des voix"] in assemblies that took place on the public square on Sundays and holidays after Mass was over and that were convened by the big bell."[74] Babeau elaborated on this by commenting that the public square in front of parish churches, the *parvis*, was often used for secular as well as religious functions, which was true in French North America as well. Everything from village assemblies to auction sales took place in front of the parish churches in the Illinois Country.

Composition of French village assemblies that Babeau studied varied somewhat over time and from place to place. The best generalization is that the assemblies were intended as forums in which all land-owning families should be represented, and the head of each such family was therefore by definition a voting representative.[75] This was likely the case in the Illinois Country as well, although there is fragmentary evidence of an oligarchic flavor to village assemblies. When Commandant Louis St. Ange de Bellerive was preparing to depart Vincennes in 1764, he advised the captain of the militia to resolve all local issues by convening "an assembly of the most notable of the habitants, in which things could be settled by *pluralité des suffrages*."[76] It has recently been argued that St. Ange's language here indicates that government in French colonial Vincennes was "neither autocratic nor democratic but oligarchic,"[77] which may be true. On the other hand, if Vincennes was governed like the other villages in the Illinois Country, all owners of agricultural land had a right to participate in village assemblies. This means that political participation at the local level was as open in the Illinois Country as in any of the British colonies at the time.

Marc Bloch insisted on tempering the democratic nature of village assemblies, noting that from the thirteenth century onward majority will in French communities was binding *only* if the majority included some of the wealthier members of the village.[78] In a similar vein, Babeau adduced a formula he encountered in notarial documents that spoke of the "majority and the soundest part ["plus saine partie"] of the habitants" of the community. For assemblies of habitants in the Illinois Country, the standard French phrase "pluralité des voix" was usually employed,[79] and there is no specific evidence that a majority voice, when it was called for, necessarily had to contain some members of the local power elite; however, that may well have been true in practice. Another manner of tempering the democratic quality of village assemblies was, as St. Ange advocated at Vincennes, to invite only "the most notable" of the habitants and then permit the majority to prevail.

Babeau became fascinated by what would now be called "the gender issue" and spent several pages examining what place women may have had in traditional community assemblies in France.[80] He concluded that in most regions widows, as heads of families, were usually admitted as voting representatives, especially in the earliest centuries for which he had documentation—the fourteenth, fifteenth, and sixteenth.[81] However, beginning about 1700 women's presence in the assemblies became increasingly rare, and during the course of the eighteenth century it became "exceptional." Babeau did not attempt to explain why this occurred, and obviously it is beyond the scope of this study to do so. Despite the fact that widows in colonial Illinois had a good deal of authority concerning family finances, they only rarely participated in village assemblies. At Cahokia in 1785, for example, agricultural regulations were determined specifically by "tous messieurs les habitants,"[82] although it is impossible to know whether women were pointedly excluded at Cahokia or merely chose to absent themselves. At Ste. Genevieve three years later, widow La Croix affixed her mark to a document that laid down agricultural fencing rules for the community.[83] Nevertheless, there were other widows in town who, although they were also heads of households, did not attend the assembly where widow La Croix joined the local menfolk in casting her vote of approval. Whether the general absence of women from assemblies of habitants in the Illinois Country was a reflection of what was occurring in France at that time or whether it was due to local factors cannot be determined.

Assemblies of habitants met in all Illinois Country villages during the eighteenth century and into the nineteenth century. The composition of each of these assemblies, and the procedures that governed their deliberations, were profoundly affected by the tradition of communal governance described by Babeau. Moreover, all the regulations and laws—local ordinances; territorial and state laws in Indiana, Illinois, and Missouri; and U.S. statutes—that dealt with open-field agriculture as it was practiced in the Illinois Country were influenced by the system that Babeau delineated. In a curious appendix to his thesis, Babeau made a grand conjectural leap (unusual in a doctoral thesis in jurisprudence) and commented that "it is proper to note that there was some French influence in the creation of American municipal government. One should not forget that part of the United States was

colonized by France. The colonists . . . must have taken with them a system
of local government with which they were familiar from the communities
of habitants in old France."[84] In this passage Babeau was reaching far beyond
both his sources and his knowledge of American history, for he apparently
knew nothing about the region of French colonization in North America
where the traditions of the village assembly from Old Regime France had in
fact exercised the most influence—namely, the Illinois Country. Had Babeau
known about the processes by which community regulations were established
and enforced in the Illinois Country, he could have added an additional dimension to his doctoral thesis. The best sources concerning the management
of communal agriculture by village assemblies in the Illinois Country come
from Ste. Genevieve and Cahokia.

STE. GENEVIEVE

Marc Bloch described the singular aspect of the open fields that dominated
the rural landscape of northern France. "The most striking thing about the
plowlands is their unfettered expanse."[85] John Reynolds remarked on precisely the same vistas created by the old-fashioned French agriculture outside of Kaskaskia: "I have seen the marks of the plow for twenty or thirty
continuous miles above Kaskaskia, in the bottom, where the land would
permit, and in an extensive range of country around the villages of Cahokia
and Prairie du Pont."[86] The Grand Champ at Ste. Genevieve constituted a
similar sweep of plowlands on the west side of the Mississippi. In 1807 a visitor
from New York State, Christian Schultz, claimed that the Grand Champ at
Ste. Genevieve "contain[ed] fifteen thousand acres of natural meadow, rich
and level as the planter could wish."[87] Henry Brackenridge, who knew the
town better than Schultz did, estimated that the common fence at Ste.
Genevieve enclosed 7,000 acres of open fields that were unbroken by any
internal fences,[88] and early nineteenth-century GLO plats of the "Big Common Field of Sainte Genevieve" reveal that Brackenridge's estimate was more
accurate than Schultz's.[89] In any case, the Grand Champ at Ste. Genevieve was
one of the largest compounds of arable fields in the Illinois Country, and,
for that matter, in North America. The great plowland achieved full maturity during the second half of the eighteenth century, and it continued to be
cultivated as a single open-field entity until the early twentieth century.

The vast, unbroken plowlands at Ste. Genevieve generated confusion
among early Anglo-American settlers about the nature of land tenure in the
Grand Champ. Having arrived to take command of Upper Louisiana for the
U.S. government in 1804, Captain Amos Stoddard observed: "On the Missis-

sippi are some extensive bottoms, the soil of which is prolific. Some of them are nearly three miles in breadth. The extensive one between the Mississippi, and Ste. Genevieve and New Bourbon, and *claimed as the property of these villages, . . .* is under good cultivation."[90] Stoddard's perception was wrong in this instance, for the Grand Champ was most certainly *not* village property. The strips of arable land inside the great fence at Ste. Genevieve were parcels of land granted to individuals, as they were in all the communities of the Illinois Country. These terres had always been bought and sold by individual property owners, although they were opened to common pasturage after the fall harvest was brought in.

It is noteworthy that the earliest known document to mention Ste. Genevieve by name is the record of a 1751 survey of one of the arable strips within the Grand Champ. Antoine Héneaux was the owner of this longlot, and he appears as one of the residents of Ste. Genevieve on the 1752 census of the Illinois Country. Héneaux was one of the first landowners in the new community west of the Mississippi, and more than a year before the census was taken he had had his property there surveyed by Bertlot *dit* Barrois, the notary-surveyor from Fort de Chartres. The record of this survey reveals so much about the cadastral system of early Ste. Genevieve that it must be given in full:

> I, Barrois de Bertlot, appointed surveyor at the request of the habitants of the Illinois, affirm to all those that it may concern, that this day, April 27, 1751, I betook myself at the express request of Sieur Antoine Héneaux, habitant residing at Ste. Genevieve, to land ["terre"] situated on the west-south-west bank of the Mississippi that belongs to him. On one side of him is land belonging to Sieur Desrousselles and on the other side land belonging to Sieur Ossant. On one end the land abuts the Mississippi and on the other the hills. It contains two facing arpents, with each arpent measuring ten perches of eighteen feet each, Paris measures. I established three boundaries and marked them each with two stone monuments, two along the side with Sieur Desrousselles, and one along the side with Sieur Ossant. These alignments run west-south-west and east-north-east, that of the crossing face runs north-north-west and south-south-east. I have done all of this at the wish of Sieur Héneaux, which I will verify if need be. Done and passed at Kaskaskia on the date given above. Witnessed by Barrois.[91]

This was undoubtedly one of the first surveys done of an arable strip at Ste. Genevieve, and it became a model for many of the longlots within the Grand Champ at Ste. Genevieve—a plot two arpents wide, running between the Mississippi River and the line of hills to the west, and set off with stone monuments.

Christian Schultz observed the traditional agriculture still being practiced on the Grand Champ early in the nineteenth century:

> The manner of using and improving their respective lots is regulated by law and custom; so that any person who permits his lot to lie idle, or who gets his crops in before his neighbors, cannot derive any profit or advantage from turning in his cattle, as this is only done on a certain day appointed, when the gates are thrown open, and the whole prairie [i.e., the Grand Champ] becomes a rich and well-foddered common for the cattle of the whole community. This custom is likewise observed at most of the French settlements in this country. They appear to have borrowed it from the Indians, who, in order to save the labour of fencing, always cultivate their maize in one common field.[92]

Schultz, from New York, obviously had no familiarity with traditional European open-field agriculture, and such communal cultivation had long since disappeared from the eastern seaboard regions of America. Therefore Schultz was obliged to attribute the unusual Creole agricultural practices at Ste. Genevieve to Indian influence. This attribution, although interesting, is almost certainly incorrect, for the Creoles in the Illinois Country were simply practicing communal agriculture as their ancestors in France had done it for centuries before the arrival of Europeans in North America.

The ungovernable Mississippi River was especially errant during the 1770s. Early in the decade the river swung eastward and undermined the riverside bastions at Fort de Chartres; later in the decade it swung westward and threatened the integrity of the community complex at Ste. Genevieve. On January 7, 1778, thirty-six habitants, nineteen of whom were able to sign their names, presented a petition to the Spanish lieutenant governor of Upper Louisiana, Don Francisco Cruzat. The petition first explained that the Mississippi River had recently eaten away some of its west bank, and homesites ("établissements") in one section of the village of Ste. Genevieve had had to be abandoned. The thirty-six habitants were therefore requesting that the section of the great fence ("clôture") that ran between the west side of the village and the arable fields be set back to create additional space for the village. In effect, this was asking that some arable land be sacrificed to provide more residential property in the Old Town of Ste. Genevieve.[93] This petition demonstrates the extent to which the great fence surrounding the Grand Champ at Ste. Genevieve had by 1778 become a fundamental part of the community. The mere thought of tinkering with the location of the fence required a formal petition to the commandant of Upper Louisiana, for no authority at the local level dared to adjudicate so important an issue.

Attached to the petition came an endorsement from François Vallé *père*, special lieutenant and civil judge at Ste. Genevieve. Vallé, head of a French Canadian family that had moved from Kaskaskia to Ste. Genevieve in the late 1750s, was one of the wealthiest and most respected persons in the village, and for that matter in all of Upper Louisiana. The Spanish-appointed military commandant, Don Sylvio de Cartabona, technically held rank over Vallé in the chain of command in Upper Louisiana, but in certain ways he had less authority in the village than Vallé, especially in civil matters. Cartabona represented the Spanish government in the village of Ste. Genevieve; Vallé represented the village of Ste. Genevieve to the Spanish government. In any case, Vallé's endorsement of the habitants' petition claimed that land was being "daily carried away by the Mississippi" but also expressed the concern that there was perhaps too little time to take corrective action before spring planting season arrived.

Cruzat's response, which came to Ste. Genevieve from the lieutenant governor's office (i.e., his residence) in St. Louis, reveals a good deal about the Spanish colonial administration of Upper Louisiana. Agreeing with Vallé that it was too late to solve the problem in 1778, Cruzat declared that a new fence line at Ste. Genevieve should be in place by March of 1779. More interesting, however, is Cruzat's judgment about the appropriate method for determining the location of the new fence. The astute lieutenant governor correctly perceived that the location of the line was a fundamental issue to the entire community. Therefore, he declared that the line would be "determined and established by a general assembly of the habitants with a majority of voices" deciding the issue. The habitants were all those citizens of Ste. Genevieve who owned arable land within the Grand Champ. Concerning the most serious issue in the community of Ste. Genevieve, agricultural fencing, the hierarchy of royal Spanish administration in Upper Louisiana proclaimed, "Let the people decide." Or at least the Spanish authorities were adhering to a well-known dictum of the Roman civil law, "quod omnes tangit similiter tangit, ab omnibus comprobetur,"[94] what impinges on all must be approved by all. While a democratic revolution of one sort was transpiring on the east coast of North America, another kind of democracy was already functioning in Spanish Ste. Genevieve. This variety of grass-roots democracy persisted throughout the entire colonial regime in Upper Louisiana, on both sides of the Mississippi and under French, Spanish, British, and American governments. The background to this consensual system was of course the ancient French tradition of village assemblies.

After receiving Cruzat's response, government and habitants in Ste. Genevieve set to work. On April 15 (a key date in the Illinois Country since official rules on fencing had originated back in 1737), all the habitants in Ste. Genevieve were invited to Cartabona's residence. For these purposes this modest vertical-log structure was called grandiloquently "la chambre du gouvernment." This practice of convening village assemblies at the local commandant's residence was consistent in Spanish Ste. Genevieve and St. Louis and was rather different from medieval European practice, where such assemblies were generally held at the parish church.[95] In any case, the assembly of habitants at Ste. Genevieve in 1778 elected eight syndics to draft a comprehensive list of regulations pertaining exclusively to agricultural fencing. Five of the syndics could sign their names, and three scrawled their marks, but all were highly respected members of the community.[96]

"Vested with public authority" (a curious turn of phrase in a royal colonial regime), the eight syndics drafted eighteen regulations, agreed to them among themselves, and promulgated them in the presence of Don Sylvio de Cartabona on May 9, 1778. This document's significance derives not from its having created a system but rather from its having codified in detail a system that had been evolving for a half-century. Although added to and amended, the regulations established in 1778 remained the basic code for agricultural practice in Ste. Genevieve until well into the nineteenth century. Furthermore, they represent the earliest detailed elaboration of a mode of agricultural life that had characterized the Illinois Country since the 1720s.

Ste. Genevieve Agricultural Regulations, 1778

1. On New Year's Day of each year an assembly of habitants will appoint one syndic and six arbiters whose task will be to inspect the fences surrounding the arable fields.

2. The fences around the arable must be "perfected" each year by April 15 in preparation for inspection. The first Sunday following April 15 the fences will be "received" by the syndic and arbiters.

3. The fences will not be "received" unless they are constructed so as to keep animals, especially swine, out of the arable fields where they will damage the crops.

4. When it appears to the syndic that some area of the fencing is not in good repair it is his responsibility to inform the owner of that particular stretch of fence in order that the owner can rectify the situation. If, "out of willfulness or for some other reason," the owner refuses this task, the syndic will hire someone else to complete it at the owner's expense.

5. If, despite these precautions, livestock penetrate into the arable fields and damage the crops sown there, the cost of the damages will be paid by those

persons whose fence is defective. If, however, the syndic and arbiters had approved the fencing on their last tour of inspection, the owners of the fence will not be held liable and the persons who incurred damage to their crops must accept the loss without further recourse.

6. If during the last inspection the syndic and arbiters discover stray livestock in the arable fields, who are there without knowledge of their owners, no one is liable unless it is clear that the animals entered the fields through defective fencing. In which case the owner of the defective fence must pay damages as estimated by the six arbiters.

7. Should the gatekeeper through negligence permit livestock to pass into the fields he will be held responsible and obliged to pay for the damages.

8. After the fences are "received" by the syndic and arbiters no one will be permitted to pass through under penalty of paying a ten-livre fine for the first offense, and for the second offense, twenty-four livres plus twenty-four hours in jail.

9. Should "evil persons" breach the fence for any reason they will be subject, over and above paying for damages, to a fine of fifty livres plus fifteen days in prison.

10. Should anyone discover someone entering the fields in countervention of the preceding clause they will immediately inform Monsieur le Commandant and if possible conduct the malefactor to jail. Should someone, however, either through misguided indulgence or personal interest refuse to do this they will then be deemed an accomplice to the crime and be subject to the same fine and jail sentence.

11. The owner of each section of fence must place his mark on the fence or he would face a fine of fifteen livres.

12. Should anyone take someone else's horse without his permission into the fields he will be subject to a twenty-five livre fine plus twenty-four hours in jail.

13. Should any tethered livestock in the fields break their tether and then be seized the person who captures them will receive a reward of five livres per head, and the owners of the land upon which they are captured will receive payment, as estimated by the arbiters, for the damages.

14. Should anyone remove the tether of any animal tethered in the fields he will pay a fifteen-livre fine plus paying damages as estimated by the arbiters.

15. No one is permitted to tether any animal on someone else's field without his permission. Should this occur the landowner may seize the animals, receive five livres per head from their owner, and have a right to claim damages.

16. Should any *slave* violate any of these regulations his owner must pay the fines and the slave will be whipped.

17. Each habitant may maintain a gate to his lands provided he secures it with a good lock or with a padlock.

18. All fines will be paid to one (chosen by Monsieur le Commandant) of the two village syndics selected each year for policing and maintaining the village. The fines will be used for public works in the community.

These eighteen clauses represent the most detailed and comprehensive set of open-field regulations for any community in the history of North America. Perhaps most remarkably they show a large degree of grass-roots democracy in village governance at Ste. Genevieve. A syndic and six arbiters were elected specifically for dealing with the fences, and two other syndics were elected for handling villages affairs in general. Monsieur le Commandant seemed to be less an authoritarian governor than a facilitator for the assembly of habitants, in which resided true sovereignty, at least for agricultural matters. This was in keeping with traditional practices of village life that Babeau described in his study of general assemblies. The well-oiled electoral machinery of colonial Ste. Genevieve (and St. Louis as well) renders risible Stephen E. Ambrose's Anglocentric pronouncement in *Undaunted Courage* that the first election "ever held" in North America west of the Mississippi occurred in August 1804 when the men of the Lewis and Clark expedition elected Patrick Gass sergeant.[97]

CAHOKIA

Antoine Girardin was a preeminent citizen of the Cahokia area in the period immediately following the American Revolution. He served repeatedly on the American court for the Cahokia District and also as commandant of both Cahokia and Prairie du Pont, which was the younger community situated just south of Cahokia.[98] As commandant at Cahokia, he drafted in early August 1785 a lengthy set of regulations regarding agricultural fencing at Cahokia.[99] The main thrust of these regulations pertained to a perennial issue in a region of mixed agriculture—protection of the cereal-grain crops from foraging livestock.

Girardin began by bemoaning the fact that as commandant and citizen, he had observed that for several years the fences surrounding the arable fields had not been maintained well enough to prevent the crops from being "devoured" by the livestock. Then followed nine regulations, which were all agreed to ("aprouvé") by the assembly of habitants at Cahokia. Unique for any fencing laws from any of the communities in the Illinois Country, the Cahokia regulations of 1785 specifically associated the right to pasture on the commons with ownership of plowland within the compound of arable fields. Association of pasturing rights on the commons with ownership of plowland within the open fields had been customary in Europe and New England.[100] Bloch commented about traditional France that "most often, . . . commons belonged to a village or hamlet and were an annex to the arable lands."[101] This was generally a less important issue in the Illinois Country, because there was more unclaimed land available for pasturage. In any case, at Cahokia after 1785 those "volontaires" (landless men) who wished to pasture their livestock on the commons were to be assessed a fee for the privilege. The assembly of habitants selected two syndics of fencing, one for Cahokia and one for Prairie du Pont, for one syndic alone "would not be able to oversee so long an extent of fence." These men were authorized to have dilapidated fencing repaired at the expense of delinquent property owners.

It is not apparent from this important source document whether the two syndics at Cahokia and Prairie du Pont were named ("il en sera nommé deux") by the commandant (Girardin in this case) or by the assembly of habitants. As previously quoted, Rétif de la Bretonne described syndics being chosen by assemblies in lower Burgundy, and fencing regulations from the west side of the Mississippi (at St. Louis and Ste. Genevieve) make it pointedly clear that the syndics in those communities were selected by the habitants themselves.[102] Presumably they were at Cahokia and Prairie du Pont as well. If Girardin had this power of appointment, however, we encounter the curious situation in which American Illinois was *less* democratic than Spanish Illinois. Girardin concluded these regulations with an editorial note that it was not "just that the industrious inhabitants should put forth all the efforts for the preservation of the grain, while the others remain inert and cause annually the destruction of the grain by their negligence and laziness."[103]

Susan Reynolds, in her recent study *Kingdoms and Communities*, remarks about medieval communities that "information about decision making is sparse,"[104] and Georges Duby noted that "in truth, we do not know them [village assemblies] very well for lack of documentary sources."[105] Interestingly, we have substantial information about decision making in some of the French Creole villages of the Illinois Country, and it does not seem inconceivable that knowledge of the open-field agriculture practiced in colonial Illinois could be relevant for medieval studies. As noted previously, important community business—auctions, announcements, estate sales, and elections—in the Illinois Country was often conducted in front of the parish church on Sunday after mass. On Sunday, August 7, 1785, the day following the habitants' approval of Girardin's regulations, the same habitants at Cahokia assembled in front of the parish church after mass and "approved by common voice" penalties and fines enumerated in a document that became an addendum to the regulations that had been approved the day before. Landless volontaires were to pay fifteen livres for the right to use the commons pasture; intentional breaching of the communal fence surrounding the arable incurred a fine of twenty livres, unintentional breaching of the fence incurred a fine of ten livres, and so forth. As was to be expected, the harshest penalty was reserved for errant pigs found in the grain fields, for they were to be killed forthwith and the owners not indemnified.[106]

The vast majority of the forty-odd habitants who agreed to these regulations and fines could not sign their names but rather affixed their marks. This collected mass of marks dramatically shows how a group of illiterate French Creoles engaged in a communal and fundamentally democratic process to regulate the basis of their lives. These kinds of assemblies of agriculturists had been meeting for centuries in western Europe (and probably elsewhere in Europe and the world). Georges Duby reproduced a not dissimilar set of agricultural regulations promulgated in 1315 at Folgara in northern Italy, although open-field agriculture was not practiced there. The preface to these Italian regulations from Folgara could just as well have been drafted in medieval France or in one of the French colonial communities in the Illinois Country: "In the communal place, in the general assembly of the men of Folgara, these rules have been laid down which must be observed by all."[107]

In January 1808 an assembly of villagers from Cahokia agreed to a new set of fencing regulations for their open fields.[108] These regulations from the American territorial period provide some significant contrasts and comparisons with regulations, such as those from Ste. Geneviève, that were drafted under colonial regimes. A Northwest Territory law of 1799 specifically sanctioned the village assembly at Cahokia,[109] but the initiative to convene the assembly came from the grass-roots level, from the villagers themselves. In contrast, assemblies of habitants that met under colonial regimes (either French or Spanish) were always convened by the commandant, the local representative of monarchical authority. Colonial regulations were very detailed and specific, running to nineteen clauses that defined standards, infractions, penalties, and so forth. The Cahokia regulations from 1808 contained a mere six clauses (after one was voided), suggesting that under American law, cultivators had more latitude to handle problems themselves in an ad hoc, consensual fashion; they did not require the rigid code of a monarchial regime. On the other hand, the Cahokia regulations reveal how deeply embedded

French habits and practices were in the Illinois Country, even after the region had been U.S. territory for thirty-five years. First, the very notion of convening a general village assembly to regulate agriculture hearkened back to French medieval practices. Second, the Cahokia villagers drafted their regulations in French, the last such laws in the United States to be so drafted. Third, they continued to build according to French specifications, erecting a fence that was five feet high, "French measure." A mere ten years before Illinois became a state, a significant percentage of its population still spoke the French language, thought in French terms, and practiced French communal agriculture.

CONCLUSION

The only region in French colonial America where arable agriculture was dominated by a regime of open-field cultivation was the middle Mississippi watershed, including Prairie du Chien as the northern-most example and Vincennes to the east on the Wabash River. Indeed, after the speedy demise of open-field agriculture in mid-seventeenth-century New England, this region was the only region anywhere in North America where such agriculture was practiced.[110] Open-field agriculture flourished in the Illinois Country for a variety of reasons: compact villages were necessary for protection against Indian attacks, and a settlement pattern of nuclear villages was ideal for open-field agriculture; the soils and climate of the Illinois Country were beyond comparison for cereal-grain production, and open-field agriculture is well-suited for such agriculture; and finally, the French and French Canadian habitants who settled the region early in the eighteenth century brought with them knowledge of open-field agriculture as part of their Old World cultural baggage, and this knowledge included familiarity with governance through village assemblies. These various factors interacted in a fashion that produced an economy and a society that were unique in colonial North America. The next chapter will examine the variety of laborers who tilled the open, arable fields of the Illinois Country.

Agricultural labors commence in the month of April, when the
inhabitants, with their slaves, are seen going and returning, each
morning and evening.
—Henry Marie Brackenridge, *Views of Louisiana*

4 HABITANTS, SLAVES, AND ENGAGÉS

Black men, white men, and red men all labored in the arable
fields of the Illinois Country from 1720 until after the turn of the nineteenth
century. They labored in the principal meaning of the French verb *labourer,*
that is, they worked the land with their plows. These men represented various degrees of free and bonded labor: landowning habitants and *cultivateurs;*
landless white laborers, or volontaires; and *journaliers,* or day laborers;
engagés, or indentured servants; and African, and likely Indian, slaves that
belonged to local habitants and to the Roman Catholic priests. All categories of these men built the fences, plowed the land, sowed the crops, took in
the harvests, and threshed the grain that sustained the unique agricultural
system of the Illinois Country.

As suggested by the words used for them, the persons who cultivated the
plowlands and grain fields of the French Illinois Country were overwhelmingly males. In his study of three rural parishes in Quebec, Allan Greer emphasized that agricultural labor in French Canada was primarily a family
affair.[1] That is, the usual socioeconomic unit in the St. Lawrence River valley in the eighteenth century was the nuclear family consisting of the habi-

tant, his wife, and their children; all members of this unit cooperated in exploiting the land of their family-owned-and-operated ribbon farm. Greer made no attempt, however, to examine the *division* of agricultural labor by gender on eighteenth-century farmsteads in the St. Lawrence Valley. Peter Kalm, the Swedish botanist, observed that during the haymaking season in the St. Lawrence Valley, "the men mow and the women rake."[2] The early fifteenth-century illuminated manuscript for the month of June from the "Très Riches Heures du Jean duc de Berry" also shows women raking hay in the fields of the Abbey of St. Germain, just outside the walls of medieval Paris.[3] It therefore seems apparent that in the traditional agricultural societies of France and French Canada, women were deemed perfectly suitable for haymaking. On the other hand, women engaged less often in mowing the grain fields with scythes and binding the freshly cut grain into sheaves; this heavier work was left largely to the men. Because haymaking was seldom practiced in colonial Illinois, one may deduce that women seldom engaged in agricultural labor.

On his excursion through the Champagne country in the early spring of 1787, Thomas Jefferson remarked: "I observe women and children carrying heavy burthens, and labouring with the hough. This is an unequivocal indication of extreme poverty. Men, in a civilised country, never expose their wives and children to labour above their force or sex, as long as their own labour can protect them from it."[4] Illinois habitants and their families did not live in extreme poverty, and there is no evidence that their wives, or the daughters, engaged in agricultural labor, although they perhaps had to pitch in and work alongside their menfolk when extraordinary conditions demanded it.

Finiels described the women of the Illinois Country villages as dedicated horticulturalists but made no mention of them working in the arable fields: "The women tend the poultry yards and the gardens. Interested in maintaining the latter, their delicate hands do not shrink from cultivating it themselves. They can be pardoned their elaborate evening toilette when they've spent the entire morning in the garden. . . . Decadence has not yet crept in when garden work is allied with the refinements of the toilette."[5] Finiels's Rousseauesque romanticism in this description does not diminish the accuracy of his observation. Women in the Illinois Country worked with their hands in the soil of their kitchen gardens, but they had not lost their French sense of feminine refinement, and they did not ordinarily work in the grain fields alongside their menfolk, their engagés, and their slaves.

Men who owned a longlot parcel or two of agricultural land and who maintained hearth and home in one of the nuclear villages associated with

The month of June from Jean de Berry's fifteenth-century *Très Riches Heures* shows women raking hay outside Paris. Original illuminated manuscript by the Limbourg brothers located in the Château de Chantilly.

a neighboring compound of arable fields performed most of the agricultural labor in the Illinois Country. These men were known by a variety of names, but most often simply as "habitants." In Old Regime France *habitant* usually meant "inhabitant,"[6] but in seventeenth-century Canada this word became useful to distinguish relatively sedentary agricultural settlers from more transient types such as voyageurs, even though the latter may have been residents of some parish in the St. Lawrence Valley. Voyageurs, who often wintered over at western outposts to engage in the fur trade, were sometimes called "hivernants," or "winter-overers." Habitants and hivernants therefore were two distinct varieties of colonists in French Canada.

Early documents from the Illinois Country reveal that *habitant* was being used in that region in the same sense—resident-farmer—that it was used in Canada.[7] During the 1720s, the first decade for which there are extant civil records from the Illinois Country, the word was used most frequently at Kaskaskia, which was the most solidly agricultural village of the various settlements in the area. Chartres, fort and village, for example, in addition to being an agricultural community, also served political, administrative, military, and commercial purposes, and there the royal notaries were less inclined to make use of the appellation *habitant*. As agriculture surrounding the fort and village continued to develop, however, this usage increased at Chartres as well.[8] The detailed map done of Cahokia by the Seminarian missionary priest Jean-Baptiste Mercier shows a consistent and purposeful use of *habitant*. Mercier obviously reserved the term for the seven resident-farmers of Cahokia and did not apply it to the other inhabitants of the community—priests, Indians, African slaves, soldiers, or merchants.

Habitants in each community made up the backbone of the local militia companies, served as elected church wardens, and composed the plenary assemblies that drafted and enforced local ordinances pertaining to agricultural fencing and so forth. The vast majority of these men worked their land with their own hands. Perhaps men of the highest economic and social status in each community—the Bienvenus in Kaskaskia, the Barbeaus in Prairie du Rocher, the Vallés in Ste. Genevieve, the Chouteaus in St. Louis—left the tilling of their agricultural lands to engagés, overseers, and slaves, but in general the habitants were out there in the grain fields working shoulder to shoulder with their slaves. When Henry Brackenridge observed agricultural laborers in colonial Ste. Genevieve toward the end of the eighteenth century, he witnessed habitants and their slaves trudging back and forth from the village to the Grand Champ together.[9]

The earliest colonial censuses of the Illinois Country—1726, 1732, 1752, all of which were done under the French regime—do not categorize persons according to occupation, with the exceptions of soldiers and missionary priests; therefore the word *habitant* does not appear in these documents.[10] The militia roster for Ste. Genevieve in 1779, which was then a Spanish possession but was still overwhelmingly francophone, was the first systematic listing by occupation of all the adult males in any one of the villages in the colonial Illinois Country. Forty-seven men out of a total listing of 175 were identified as "habitants." This made habitants second only to voyageurs, of which there were sixty-four, as the largest occupational category in Ste. Genevieve in 1779. A scattering of men were listed with double occupations: François Vallé, "civil judge and habitant"; Louis Bolduc, "habitant merchant"; François Coleman, "brewer habitant"; and Joseph St. Aubin, "blacksmith habitant." Once again we see that *habitant* was specifically used to designate resident-farmer and that some of the men of most wealth and highest status in the Ste. Genevieve of 1779—Charles Vallé, François Vallé *fils*, Jean-Baptiste Pratte, François Leclerc—were enumerated as "habitants."[11]

Similar militia muster rolls were composed for St. Louis, Ste. Genevieve's twin town, in 1779. St. Louis, the capital of Spanish Illinois, had two militia companies. Forty-six men in these two companies were listed as "habitants" out of a total of 217, making the proportion of habitants in St. Louis lower than in Ste. Genevieve.[12] The respective proportions of habitants for Ste. Genevieve and St. Louis reveal that the former was the more important agricultural community, whereas the latter was more important as a political, administrative, and commercial center. This information from the muster rolls of 1779 is consistent with other data regarding the twin towns of Spanish Illinois, including respective agricultural production.

On the other side of the Mississippi, at Cahokia and Kaskaskia, lists of habitants were drawn up in 1787 and sent to the Continental Congress in New York, which was beginning to take an interest in the new U.S. territories to the far west.[13] In keeping with the accepted definition of *habitant* at that time and place, these lists included only landowning resident-farmers and their male children. Although in the French inheritance practices that were still employed in the Illinois Country in 1787, female children were regarded as the absolute coequals of their brothers,[14] the female children at Cahokia and Kaskaskia were not going to become habitants; therefore they, like their mothers, were excluded from the incomplete censuses taken of these communities in 1787. Slaves and non-landholding transients, such as voyageurs, were of course also excluded from these enumerations.

The Spanish census done of St. Louis and Ste. Genevieve in 1787, "Padrón General de los Pueblos de Sn Luis y Sta Genoveva de Ilinueses," is a unique and curious document:[15] it is the only detailed enumeration ever done in colonial Illinois, on either side of the Mississippi, that provides, household by household, the names and occupations of all free persons, right down to the day laborers. As do all eighteenth-century censuses, this one contains many errors and has many omissions, but it is nevertheless an extremely valuable document.

Francisco Cruzat, the Spanish lieutenant governor in St. Louis, drafted the census using Spanish nomenclature. Rather than identifying the principal resident-farmers as "habitants," French Canadian style, Cruzat used the word *labrador,* the Spanish equivalent of the French *laboureur.* This word had long since come to mean something more than merely a common laborer. In traditional French rural life, according to Bloch, a laboureur was a tiller of the soil who owned draught animals, plow, and yoke or harnessing—not merely a plowman but a substantial villager, someone who had the wherewithal to own agricultural equipment.[16] Cruzat's term *labrador* on the 1787 census was yet another step removed from the English *laborer,* however. Many of the preeminent citizens of Ste. Genevieve and St. Louis—François Leclerc, Louis Bolduc, Jean-Baptiste Pratte, Charles Vallé, Joseph Brazeau, Charles Gratiot—were designated "labrador." Interestingly, even wealthy widows in both communities—Marie Thérèse Chouteau, Marie Lami, Anne Olivier, and Marie Louise La Croix—were listed as "labradora." It is apparent that on the 1787 census, *labrador* and *labradora* not only cannot be construed to mean "manual laborer" but cannot even be translated as "independent plowman." Cruzat meant to designate by these words persons of either sex who were heads of agricultural households. That is to say, Cruzat used the only word he could think of in Spanish that would be the equivalent of the French *habitant,* resident-farmer. In a certain sense Cruzat's Spanish words were even more precise, for the feminine form of *habitant, habitante,* was never used in the Illinois Country to designate a female head of an agricultural household. Nor was the obvious feminine of *laboureur, laboureuse,* ever used.

Additional complexity in the nomenclature for agriculturists in the Illinois Country appeared in 1797. Nouvelle Bourbon was an agricultural village established on the bluffs overlooking the Grand Champ just south Ste. Genevieve in the early 1790s. When the founding father of the town, the aristocratic refugee from the French Revolution Pierre-Charles Delassus de Luzières, drafted a census of the community in 1797, he employed the word *cultivateur* rather than *habitant* for describing the resident-farmers in New Bourbon.[17] This was obviously a French usage by a man who had only recently arrived in the Illinois Country. De Luzières honored no one in the New Bourbon of 1797 with a title that would have had higher status than *cultivateur,* with one exception—he designated himself as "Capitaine et commandant de ce poste." This was merely a statement of fact, and one wonders whether de Luzières would have found it beneath his dignity to be called a "cultivateur" himself. In any case, Bloch once again comes to our assistance by explaining that in traditional French rural society *laboureur* and *cultivateur* were for all intents and purposes synonymous.[18] Therefore, Delassus de Luzières, when he drafted the 1797 census of New Bourbon, was reaching for a word to describe independent agriculturists who would have been demeaned if they had been called "paysans." Indeed, given the fact that many of de Luzières's "cultivateurs" at New Bourbon owned black slaves, his designation *cultivateur* would translate as "planter" better than as "peasant."

Habitant, laboureur (in the Spanish, *labrador*), and *cultivateur* were therefore used as synonyms in the eighteenth-century Illinois Country, and they all meant "resident-farmer"—that is, an agriculturist of some property, means, and status. Virtually all these men were hands-on laborers, however, who went into the grain fields to plow, sow, and harvest alongside other types of agricultural laborers. Of the three synonymous words, *habitant* was overwhelmingly the most popular, and for this reason, as well as for convenience and consistency, this word will be employed throughout this study.

It is important to remark that the meaning of the word *habitant* as it evolved in the Illinois Country during the eighteenth century was somewhat different than the traditional meaning of *habitant* in the St. Lawrence Valley. Because of the existence of the seigneurial class in French Canada, *habitant* in that region came closer to meaning "peasant." When a seigneur in the St. Lawrence Valley spoke of "nos habitans," he was referring to his censitaires or peasants.[19] Greer, in his study *Peasant, Lord, and Merchant*, conspicuously defines the French Canadian habitant as a "peasant."[20] These French Canadian peasants were not precisely the same as peasants in metropolitan French, but in any case they were burdened with dues and obligations that affected them economically and that marked them socially as distinctly inferior to the Canadian seigneurs. For all intents and purposes, censitaires and peasants did not exist in Illinois Country, and the habitants of the region would have been incensed to have been called "peasants." This simple distinction in the definitions of the word *habitant* reveals a remarkable difference between French colonial society in the St. Lawrence Valley and that in the Illinois Country.

The primary workers in the arable fields of the colonial Illinois Country—on both sides of the Mississippi and throughout the eighteenth century—were the habitants themselves. As a French visitor, François Perrin du Lac, observed with some justification about Ste. Genevieve, "The habitants ['habitans'] are exclusively occupied with cultivation."[21] Of all the communities in the Illinois Country, Ste. Genevieve was the most thoroughly devoted to agriculture, and on the 1787 Spanish census Cruzat listed 66 percent of the heads of household in Ste. Genevieve as "labradors" (or "labradoras"), whereas in St. Louis only 41 percent were so designated.[22] But if Perrin was using the word *habitans* in the regional sense, and probably he was, his comment would have applied to all the communities in the Illinois Country. Indeed, Perrin's comment was a bit tautological, for by definition resident-farmers would have been occupied principally with agriculture.

AFRICAN SLAVES

C. Vann Woodward writing about white and black Southerners in the United States opined that "they have shaped each other's destiny, determined each other's isolation, shared and molded a common culture. It is, in fact, impossible to imagine the one without the other."[23] By mid-eighteenth century, when black slaves constituted one-third of the total population in the agricultural villages of the Illinois Country, Woodward's remarks were perhaps a fortiori true of that region.

When Cahokia and Kaskaskia were founded at the turn of the eighteenth century, there were no black slaves in the region. The first mention of the possibility of using African slaves as agricultural laborers in the Illinois Country dates from 1720. In October of that year, Pierre Dugué, sieur de Boisbriant, recently appointed commandant of the region, wrote from Kaskaskia that "a hundred Negroes would be marvelous for this settlement [the Illinois Country]."[24] Boisbriant went on to explain that black slaves could be used to clear land for agricultural purposes and that with an adequate supply of slave labor, Illinois would be able to furnish foodstuffs for much of Louisiana. The commandant never received the requested hundred slaves en masse, but numbers of black slaves were brought into the Illinois Country from Lower Louisiana for agricultural purposes during the early 1720s. When the Black Code for Louisiana was promulgated in 1724, the preamble explained the need for such a code by stating that the colony contained a large number of settlers "who use negro slaves for tilling the land."[25]

At the other end of the eighteenth century, Henry Brackenridge commented about the habitants at Ste. Genevieve that "their agricultural labors commence in the month of April, when the inhabitants, *with their slaves,* are seen going and returning each morning and evening, . . . with their plows, carts, horses, etc."[26] At the same time, Finiels, who resided in St. Louis, remarked that "when a habitant owns two or three [black slaves] to use in agriculture, he thinks he is in a position to undertake anything."[27] During the Anglo-Indian attack at St. Louis on May 26, 1780, the attackers found a number of habitants and black slaves planting maize together in the fields out-side of town. Some of these men, both free and slave, were killed and some were taken prisoner.[28] It is evident that beginning as early as circa 1720, black slaves worked as agricultural laborers in the Illinois Country, and that by the end of the colonial era they were being widely used on both sides of the Mississippi. Indeed, among the various kinds of workers, both hired and slave, that assisted the habitants of the Illinois Country, black slaves were the most commonly used and therefore the most important source of labor.

The remainder of my discussion about slavery as it pertained to agricul-ture in the Illinois Country will be confined to African slavery; Indian slav-ery will only appear tangentially. Interesting though the latter topic is, there were consistently fewer Indian slaves than black slaves,[29] and their numbers declined continuously; there is no firm evidence that Indian slaves were used as agricultural laborers; and furthermore, Indian slavery is a complex and distinct subject unto itself.

From the earliest days of Louisiana, French colonists had dreamed of acquiring a supply of slave labor. The heat and insects of the Gulf Coast were punishing for persons accustomed to the temperate climate of France, and the orphans, convicts, vagabonds, and prostitutes sent to populate Louisi-ana often died of disease and malnutrition.[30] The experience of the planta-tion owners on the Sugar Islands encouraged the settlers in Louisiana to look toward the west coast of Africa as a source for their labor supply. When French Canadian missionaries and fur traders established Cahokia and Kaskaskia, they did not bring African slaves with them from Canada.[31] The first black slaves to arrive in the Illinois Country were transported up the Mississippi from Lower Louisiana. By 1719, shortly after New Orleans was founded, sev-eral shiploads of Africans arrived in Louisiana under the auspices of the Company of the West, the royal chartered company that had assumed con-trol of the colony in 1717.[32] It seems likely that Jesuit missionaries at Kaskaskia were the first owners of black slaves in the Illinois Country. Slaves were in short supply and in great demand, and the Jesuits, with their substantial financial resources and powerful political connections, were in the best po-sition to purchase slaves and get them transported up the Mississippi. A document from 1720 describes the Jesuits as owning sixteen to eighteen slaves, "Negroes and savages."[33] Although it is impossible determine from this de-scription the precise number of black slaves in this grouping, the Society of Jesus in Kaskaskia was apparently the largest owner of slaves in the Illinois Country at that time.

In April 1721 Governor Jean-Baptiste le Moyne Bienville reported that three slaving ships had arrived in Biloxi from Angola, on the west coast of Africa.

These three slavers contained a cargo of 925 Africans, and although many were ill, Bienville was confident that a diet of maize (which Frenchmen themselves preferred not to eat) would soon restore the slaves to good health. We know that some of these new arrivals wound up in Illinois, for one month after the arrival of the slave ships, Bienville commented on the allocation of the newly arrived slaves: "The distribution has been made with great fairness. The colonists from Illinois who were in the lower colony have participated and are willing to testify to it. . . . Forty of these Negroes are reserved to row in the boats that will ascend [the Mississippi] to the Illinois Country."[34] From Bienville's report one cannot determine whether all forty of the black oarsmen had been allocated permanently to the settlers from the Illinois Country. However, given that these settlers had traveled all the way to Biloxi for the distribution of slaves, it seems likely that many of the blacks were destined to remain in Illinois. Bienville himself thought that African slaves would be useful in the upper Mississippi Valley grain-growing regions and commented that "wheat, rye, barley, and oats etc. will grow there more abundantly in proportion as the settlers have more slaves to cultivate the land."[35]

The black slavery practiced in the Illinois Country was originally a French brand of slavery. To understand this system of human bondage, it is necessary to comment on the famous Code Noir, the Black Code. This law code was first promulgated by the French crown for the West Indies in 1685[36] and was reissued, mutatis mutandis, for French Louisiana in 1724.[37] The Black Code defined the legal status of French black slaves: they were chattels that could be bought and sold like other personal property. The code also recognized slaves as human beings, however, for seventeenth-century Frenchmen were not interested in justifying slavery on racial grounds. The institution of human bondage was part and parcel of human society; it was normal and usual and therefore did not require rationalization. The Black Code is a dispassionate and tightly reasoned document—reasoned to serve not the blacks, or even their masters, but rather the interests of the absolute French state.[38]

The Louisiana Black Code contains fifty-five articles that make the following salient points: slaves were to be properly housed, clothed, and fed; slave children could not be sold away from their parents until they had arrived at puberty; masters could whip and bind their slaves, but the slaves could not be imprisoned, mutilated, or put to death without due process of the law; slaves could not be worked before sunrise or after sunset; old and infirm slaves had to be cared for; female slaves were not to be sexually exploited; slaves were to be baptized and schooled in the Christian (i.e., Roman Catholic) faith; slaves could not carry firearms or even "large sticks"; slaves were to be encouraged to marry with masters' consent but could not be compelled to marry against their will; interracial marriage and cohabitation were forbidden; and masters could not manumit slaves without government permission. Finally, the code provided slaves with the right to take their masters to court at no cost if they felt that their masters were abusing them in violation of other provisions. This last provision—if not the entire code— was surely an example of French lawmakers' excessive confidence in the ability of government to regulate human society. It is difficult to imagine a black slave in French Louisiana bringing suit against his master for inhumane treatment, as Article 20 of the Black Code authorized.[39]

Whether the Black Code was effective in regulating relations between French colonists and their black slaves is a serious question. Felix de Wimpffen, who visited St. Domingue in the eighteenth century, claimed that *no* article of the Black Code was enforced on that island of sugar plantations.[40] On the other hand, a recent scholar has concluded that on balance the code did help to mitigate the miseries of life for slaves in French Louisiana, even though it was not always enforced.[41] Indeed, there was virtually no governmental apparatus for its enforcement. For the distant and remote Illinois Country, there is even some question about the extent to which the provisions of the code were known, much less enforced. If an important measure of slave treatment is a willingness to baptize slave children, however, then the Illinois Country, where virtually every slave child was baptized, may have been the most humane slave society within the French colonial empire.[42]

In February 1751 Governor General Vaudreuil issued on behalf of the Superior Council of Louisiana and King Louis XV of France the "Règlement sur la police pour la province de la Louisiane."[43] Within the context of this title, the word *police* referred to everything concerned with the upkeep, cleanliness, and security of the public domain, but Vaudreuil's document dealt mostly with slavery. The thirty-first article referred "all other matters pertaining to Negroes to the Black Code, which has provided for all cases."[44] This was a rank overstatement, but Vaudreuil was merely being a good soldier within the royal colonial bureaucracy. In any case, the règlement of 1751 reflected Vaudreuil's ruminations about the way to strike a proper balance between severity and humanity in dealing with African American slaves. Surely not all French colonials in the Mississippi Valley meditated on this issue as Vaudreuil did, but the governor was experiencing some of the confusion of modern parents who seem to be losing control of their children and do not know whether to react by becoming more severe or more permissive. Vaudreuil manifestly believed that Louisiana colonists were losing their grip on their slaves, and his règlement represented an effort to clamp down on such nefarious activities as drinking of alcoholic beverages, circulating freely at night, frequenting of disreputable establishments (operated by freed Negroes), and reckless racing of horses. One can well imagine modern American parents drawing up a similar list concerning their children. Indeed, the règlement of 1751 was explicitly paternal in its wording. Article 19 admonished slave owners to discipline their Negroes "en bon père de famille," as a good father of the family.[45] Article 28 brings us back to the realities of eighteenth-century slaveholding society, however, for it prescribes "fifty lashes and branding of the fleur-de-lis on the buttocks for any Negro or other slave who is insolent, forgets he is a slave, and does not show appropriate submissiveness."[46] To what extent Vaudreuil's slave regulation of 1751 made its way up the Mississippi River to the Illinois Country remains unknown.

The patently paternal (not necessarily benevolent) attitude of the French colonists toward their black slaves was best expressed in the writings of Antoine Le Page du Pratz. Du Pratz was one of the many Netherlanders who took France as his adopted state during the Old Regime. In 1718, the year New Orleans was founded, Du Pratz sailed for French Louisiana to make his fortune. He was not successful in that ambition, and he returned to France in 1734, disenchanted with colonial adventures. Du Pratz did not lose interest in Louisiana, however, and during the 1750s he began to write about the colony in which he had once lived. The title of his *Histoire de la Louisiane*[47] was a bit of a misnomer, for large sections of this "history" contain practical advice for persons considering emigration to Louisiana. One section advises how the French colonist should manage his black slaves, and this section provides some rare information about what eighteenth-century Louisianans thought about their slaves.

Du Pratz's advice on managing slaves echoed much of the Code Noir on such matters as careful attendance to the slaves' physical and spiritual needs. Du Pratz's views were, however, less coldly bureaucratic and more personal and specific. For example, he was convinced that blacks had a different, stronger odor than Europeans and recommended that slave owners prudently locate their slave quarters in accordance with the prevailing winds so that the owners "be as little incommoded as possible with their natural smell."[48] Du Pratz based this advice on what he thought were physiological differences between blacks and whites rather than the generally poor sanitary conditions of slave quarters. In any case, he never continued on this tack to the point of claiming that blacks were racially inferior. Like many eighteenth-century Europeans, Du Pratz did not justify slavery on racial grounds; slavery was merely part of the natural order of the universe. Indeed, when paternally discussing the housing for his "people" after he had settled on his concession at Natchez, Du Pratz lumped French engagés, Indian slaves, and black slaves together as indistinguishable members of his own "family" of laborers.[49] Du Pratz concluded his *Histoire de la Louisiane* by noting that "one may, by attention and humanity, easily manage negroes; and, as an inducement, one has the satisfaction to draw great advantage from their labors."[50] This remark is probably an accurate summation of enlightened French colonists' view of their black slaves: unsentimental, pragmatic, entrepreneurial, and not viciously racist.

A general census of the Illinois Country was conducted in 1726.[51] The total resident population of the area—whites, blacks, and Indians—was shown as 501, although it is evident that the census taker did not manage to record every human soul. Blacks (all slaves apparently)—men, women, and children—numbered 118, thus constituting some 24 percent of the entire population. The next known census of French Illinois was taken in 1732.[52] This was a detailed tabulation, conducted community by community. The total human population of the area—from Cahokia in the north to Kaskaskia in the south—was 471, although once again some residents managed to elude the census taker. The black slaves, adults and children, numbered 164, constituting more than one-third of the population in the Illinois Country. The Society of Jesus in Kaskaskia and Philippe Renaut at his lead mine in Missouri were the largest slaveholders, each commanding twenty-two blacks. Renaut's black slaves were the first African inhabitants of what is today the state of Missouri. They were not, however, permanent residents on the west side of the Mississippi River, for the lead-mining operations there were only seasonal in nature, and Renaut's enterprise soon collapsed.[53] The 1737 census of the Illinois Country listed a total of 314 blacks, indicating that the black population of the region had almost doubled in five years. This marked increase was due largely to continuing imports of Africans from Lower Louisiana rather than an exploding birth rate within the existing population of Illinois, for the ratio of children to adults was approximately the same in 1732 and 1737. Nonetheless, life for French slaves was probably less harsh in the Illinois Country than on the Caribbean Islands; blacks were not reproducing rapidly in Illinois during the 1730s, but at least they were not dying in droves, as they did on the notorious sugar plantations in the West Indies.[54]

In 1747 Governor General Vaudreuil issued an order forbidding all shipments of blacks and mulattoes from "New Orleans and other places on the lower river to Illinois."[55] Vaudreuil argued that slaves shipped north up the Mississippi could not readily be replaced in the lower colony (war with England was disrupting commerce on the high seas) and that the slaves working in the New Orleans region were being used more efficiently than was possible in Illinois; presumably Vaudreuil meant that the larger the agricultural enterprise, the more efficient slave labor was, and plantations on the lower Mississippi therefore got first priority in the allocation of black slaves. It is not known how effective Vaudreuil's order was, but the almost continuous warfare between England and France for the duration of the French regime in Louisiana meant that there was a general shortage of slaves in the colony and that few were shipped north to the Illinois Country.[56] Increases in the black slave population of Illinois after 1747 were therefore generated largely by reproduction within the existing population. It seems apparent that the birth rate of black slaves in the Illinois often exceeded the death rate,[57] which means that many of these blacks had a level of material subsistence and health that surpassed many free peasants living in metropolitan France during the eighteenth century.

Edmund Flagg, an early nineteenth-century newspaper man who traveled widely, wrote that he had never seen a group of "sleeker, fleshier, happier-looking set of mortals" than the blacks who inhabited the former French villages in Illinois.[58] This remark may have been prompted because Flagg had seen black slaves in the Anglo-American Southeast whose material conditions of life were less good than those of the slaves in the middle Mississippi Valley. At the turn of the nineteenth century, it was accepted knowledge that slaves in Upper Louisiana were better treated than elsewhere in North America. The comte de Volney described St. Louis at this time as consisting of "half a dozen wealthy families, five hundred poor, idle, and sickly whites, and a few blacks, the property of the rich, who treat them well."[59] There were more than a few black slaves in St. Louis at the turn of the nineteenth century (the 1800 census lists 305 black and mulatto slaves out of total population of 1,039),[60] but Volney may well have been correct about their treatment. The fact that there was never a hint of slave rebellion in the Illinois Country, and that slaves there often carried firearms, suggests that French slaves in Upper Louisiana were living about as well as any slaves in the world during the eighteenth century.[61]

In 1752 Major Macarty drafted the most comprehensive and detailed census ever done of French Illinois. Although containing many inaccuracies, this document is an extremely valuable source (see table 1). Whites and blacks were listed as residents in all six communities—Kaskaskia, Fort de Chartres (including the village of Chartres), St. Philippe, Prairie du Rocher, Cahokia, and Ste. Genevieve. Ste. Genevieve, only recently founded on the west bank of the Mississippi, had but two blacks in its fledgling population. The 446 black slaves in the Illinois Country in 1752 made up 32 percent of the total population; thus, the ratio of blacks in the population of the region remained more or less constant between 1732 and 1752.[62] Perhaps underlying economic structures—to-

Table 1. Distribution of Population, Illinois Country, 1752

	Adults		Children					
	Male	Female	Male	Female	Male	Female	Volontaires	Totals
Kaskaskia								
White	66	58	100	51			77	
Black slave	102	67	45	32				
Indian slave					31	44		
Chartres								
White	33	41	43	46			35	
Black slave	35	25	16	13				
Indian slave					13	23		
St. Philippe								
White	15	14	15	20			6	
Black slave	20	10	7	8				
Indian slave					1	6		
Prairie du Rocher								
White	10	11	12	6			14	
Black slave	18	8	8	6				
Indian slave					4	4		
Cahokia								
White	19	14	19	23			15	
Black slave	11	6	4	3				
Indian slave					11	12		
Ste. Genevieve								
White	8	4	3	4			3	
Black slave	2							
Totals								
White	151	142	192	150			150	785
Black slave	188	116	80	62				446
Indian slave					60	89		149
								1380

Source: HMLO, 426.

Note: In this tabulation, soldiers and missionaries are included as part of the adult male population, and soldiers' wives are included in the adult female population. The nameless volontaires, adult males who did not own property, are listed as a separate category. The census lists Indian slaves only by gender without regard to age.

tal wealth, amount and distribution of agricultural land, and so on—of the Illinois Country contrived to establish that approximate ratio.[63]

This census of the six Illinois communities reveals that of the 167 heads of household (including soldiers, missionaries, and widows), 69, or 41 percent, owned one black slave or more. This was a higher percentage of slave owners relative to the total population than the American South had on the eve of the Civil War, where fewer than 30 percent of the families owned at least one slave. Slaveholding was therefore a rather democratized institution in the Illinois Country. Brackenridge's description of habitants and black slaves trudging together out to the grain fields at Ste. Genevieve reinforces the impression of a rather leveled slave-owning society, with many habitants owning a few slaves,[64] as does Finiels's remark that any habitant who owned two or three slaves considered himself a giant.[65] Nonetheless, it must be observed that on the 1752 census eight owners (4 percent) owned 216 (49 percent) of the black slaves. Two of the largest holders of black slaves in the Illinois Country were the Jesuits in Kaskaskia (thirty-four) and the Seminary of Foreign Missions in Cahokia (nineteen). Antoine Bienvenu owned an astonishing number of blacks, fifty-five at his residence in Kaskaskia and ten more at his plantation near Prairie du Rocher. Bienvenu was the only slaveholder in French Illinois who operated large, slave-worked agricultural enterprises similar to the cotton, tobacco, and indigo plantations of the Anglo-American South.

French settlers in the Illinois Country used their black slaves principally as agricultural laborers. On the earliest detailed Illinois census, that of 1732, appears a habitant—La Rose—and his wife at Kaskaskia. They owned a substantial amount of agricultural land, four linear arpents, and two black female slaves.[66] Very likely La Rose of this census was the André Deguire *dit* La Rose who in 1737 rented for one year from widow Lefèvre a black male slave for the sum of 1,500 livres worth of flour.[67] Surely La Rose intended to use this rented male slave for agricultural labor on his extensive holdings, and perhaps, if he still owned two female slaves and no males, he was hoping to use the rented male for breeding purposes. In any event, extant records indicate that as early as the 1730s, habitants who owned substantial amounts of agricultural land also tended to be slave owners.

French colonial censuses reveal that Kaskaskia, which had the largest agricultural production of any of the Illinois villages, had the largest number of black slaves, both in absolute terms and in proportion to the total population. Moreover, there was a strong direct correlation between the amount of real estate owned and the number of slaves owned. In 1732, for example, the Jesuit fathers at Kaskaskia owned nine linear arpents of agricultural land valued at 150 livres, and they held twenty-five black slaves; Jean-Baptiste Lasource and his wife owned four arpents of land valued at 100 livres, and they held eight black slaves; Thuillier *dit* Desvignets and his wife owned five arpents of land valued at 100 livres, and they held ten black slaves. There were some important exceptions, however. Jean-Baptiste Bauvais and his wife owned four arpents of land valued at 100 livres, but they held no black slaves whatsoever. Bauvais and his wife did own two Indian slaves, however, and in this case it would be fair to assume that the Indian slaves were used as agricultural laborers.

In 1752, as in 1732, Kaskaskia had the highest proportion of black slaves; indeed, Africans composed over 40 percent of the community's total population in 1752. From 1732 to 1752 the Jesuit agricultural holdings had decreased somewhat, from nine to six arpents (valued at 130 livres), but the number of black slaves they owned had grown significantly, from twenty-five to thirty-four. The combination of less land, more value per arpent of plowland, and larger numbers of black slaves suggests more intensive agriculture at the Jesuit establishment in Kaskaskia. Antoine Bienvenu was the only habitant in the Illinois Country in 1752 who ran a larger agricultural operation than the Jesuits. He owned thirty arpents of land—valued at 500 livres—at Kaskaskia, where he held fifty-five black slaves, and he also had a plantation at Prairie du Rocher that consisted of eight arpents of land valued at 100 livres and was worked by ten black slaves. Bienvenu's total holdings of slaves, sixty-five, was by far the largest number of African American slaves ever owned by a single individual in the Illinois Country during the entire colonial era.

Raphaël Bauvais presents an unusual case from the 1752 census. He was a member of the large and well-known Bauvais clan, whose members came early and in numbers to the Illinois Country from Montreal. Raphaël owned no agricultural land but was the master of five African American slaves. Moreover, he owned a substantial amount of livestock—sixty hogs, ten cows, five horses, two oxen, and two bulls. Land as recorded on French censuses in the Illinois Country was *arable* land, and it is possible that Raphaël Bauvais produced livestock without raising any cereal grains. He could have used the Kaskaskia commons for pasture, and in addition he may have operated what we today would call a feed-lot business. That is, he may have had a sizable enclosure of nonarable land in which he kept and fed his livestock, preparing them either for sale or for slaughter. In 1739 Raphaël had been in a position to offer for sale seventy-seven yoke of oxen at one time, an extraordinary number.[68] This suggests that livestock production, not crop cultivation, was his principal occupation. If that was the case, Raphaël Bauvais's five black slaves would have functioned as animal husbanders, certainly an agricultural occupation even though not directly connected to tilling the soil.

The only extant censuses of Illinois Country communities from the British period of sovereignty, 1763–83, were compiled for the commanding general of British North America, Thomas Gage, in 1767. Enumerations of two villages, Kaskaskia and Vincennes, are known (see table 2).[69]

For Lieutenant Thomas Hutchins, who was with the British garrison in the Illinois Country during the mid-1760s, the African presence in Kaskaskia was even more pronounced than these census figures indicate. He estimated that Kaskaskia contained "about 500 white inhabitants and between four and five hundred negroes."[70] In any case, the crude enumerations of 1767 reveal important differences between Kaskaskia and Vincennes, two Creole com-

Table 2. 1767 British Censuses, Kaskaskia and Vincennes

	Kaskaskia	Vincennes
Free inhabitants (both sexes, all ages)	600	232
Negroes		
Men	142	
Women	81	
Boys	80	
Negro slaves		10
Indian slaves		17
Strangers		168

Source: NR, 469–70.

munities in British Illinois: Kaskaskia was significantly larger and had a much higher percentage of black slaves (34 percent), which suggests that Kaskaskia's economy was more agriculturally based. Vincennes had a significant number of Indian slaves and "strangers" (i.e., voyageurs), which meant that this community's economy was still heavily dependent on the Indian fur trade. These impressions, based on categories of people listed in the censuses, are borne out by the tabulations of grain production in the respective villages— in 1767 Kaskaskia produced nearly five times as much maize as Vincennes and nearly three times as much wheat.

Moving to the other side of the Mississippi, and to a later time period of the colonial era, very similar patterns emerge. Of the two principal towns in Spanish Illinois, St. Louis and Ste. Genevieve, the latter was the more agricultural. Therefore, all the Spanish censuses of the twin towns indicate that Ste. Genevieve had largest number of black and mulatto slaves, both in absolute and proportional terms, and produced the most cereal grain. On the first Spanish census of the twin towns, compiled in 1772, nearly 38 percent of the total population of Spanish Illinois was made up of black and mulatto slaves (see table 3).[71] This decreased to 30 percent by 1791.[72]

In St. Louis and Ste. Genevieve the relatively democratized ownership of slaves, which also characterized the older communities on the east bank of the Mississippi, persisted. In 1787 and 1791 roughly one-half of the grain-producing habitants in the twin towns of Spanish Illinois owned at least one black or mulatto slave, and only Gabriel Cerré, with forty-three slaves (an unusually high number), owned more than fifteen. Cerré was also the largest grain producer at St. Louis. Other large grain producers in St. Louis— widow Marie-Thérèse Bourgeois Chouteau, Charles Gratiot, Joseph Brazeau, Antoine Morin—also had substantial numbers of slaves. Widow Chouteau, in a sense doubly widowed because both René Chouteau and Pierre de

Table 3. Free and Slave Populations, St. Louis and
Ste. Genevieve, 1791

	Male	Female
St. Louis		
White	505	332
Free colored	18	19
Slave colored	167	147
Ste. Genevieve		
White	361	219
Free colored	18	8
Slave colored	178	139
Totals		
White	866	551
Free colored	36	27
Slave colored	345	286

Source: SRM, 2:365–86.

Laclède Liguest were dead, is a good example of how a wealthy widow might assume high status in the Illinois Country, and she is not the only example. In any event, St. Louis was different from any other community in the region on either side of the Mississippi, for its principal raison d'être had never been agriculture. The village had been founded exclusively as a trading outpost in 1764, and when the Spaniards arrived in Upper Louisiana, they made it a political and administrative center. These circumstances meant that there were wealthy persons in St. Louis—including Auguste Chouteau and Louis Dubreuil—who owned numbers of black or mulatto slaves (fifteen and ten, respectively) and yet who were not personally engaged in agriculture. Exactly how these men used their slaves we do not know, but given that both Chouteau and Dubreuil were merchants, they probably used slaves as boatmen for commercial trips between St. Louis and New Orleans, which were notoriously backbreaking ventures.[73] St. Louis was an unusual case, however, and at Ste. Genevieve there was a very close correlation between agricultural production and slave ownership: the large grain producers—the brothers François and Jean-Baptiste Vallé, the brothers Jean-Baptiste and Vital Bauvais, Louis Bolduc, Jean-Baptiste Pratte, and François Moreau—were also the large slaveholders. Moreover, quite unlike at St. Louis, no one in Ste. Genevieve who owned significant numbers of slaves was not engaged in agriculture.

In the Illinois Country black slaves were a good index of economic status. Settlements with populations composed of poorer habitants had fewer slaves per capita. By 1791 Carondelet had emerged as an agricultural suburb of St. Louis. As its nickname, Vide Poche (Empty Pocket), suggests, this was a relatively poor community. Finiels described it in the late 1790s as being composed of French Canadians and Creoles who raised grain, "generally were poor," and lived in "paltry wooden cabins."[74] Early maps of Carondelet reveal that the land in the community was allocated for the three classic Illinois Country uses: nuclear village, compound of arable strips, and true commons for pasturage. The Spanish census of 1791 lists thirty heads of household for Carondelet, of which only five were not grain producers.[75] Nonetheless, despite the fact that Carondelet produced significant amounts of both maize and wheat, there were only three black slaves in the entire community, and two of these were women. Carondelet, a community of yeomen farmers practicing open-field agriculture, was the first village in the Illinois Country (at least since very early Kaskaskia) to have become a sizable producer of cereal grains without the assistance of substantial numbers of black slaves.

SLAVE VALUES

Values of black and mulatto slaves depended on age, health, sex, and the market circumstances of supply and demand at any given time. In the parlance of colonial Louisiana slave markets, a *pièce d'Inde* (from the Spanish *pieza de India*) was a unit of labor with an understood value.[76] In practice, healthy, young adult blacks of either sex qualified as pièces d'Inde in Upper Louisiana; that is to say, female slaves were just as valuable as male slaves. The 1732 census of the Illinois Country categorizes adult black slaves of both sexes as "pièce d'Inde."[77] Some female slaves no doubt functioned as domestic servants in the households of the wealthier residents of the Illinois Country— the Bauvaises and Ménards in Kaskaskia, the Jarrots and Moulins in Cahokia, the Vallés and Bolducs in Ste. Genevieve, and the Chouteaus and Cerrés in St. Louis. Many female slaves—unlike their free counterparts—must have worked in the agricultural fields, although there is no direct evidence to support this contention.[78] Indeed, African slave women of the Illinois Country are, in the extant documentation, a largely invisible group, except for the sacramental records of their burials, the baptisms of their children, and, occasionally, their marriages.

The inflation that afflicted Louisiana during the eighteenth century was reflected in slave prices in the Illinois Country. At Kaskaskia in 1724 pièces d'Inde were fetching 1,000 livres; by 1740 the price had risen to 1,500 livres; by 1747 it reached 2,000 livres; and by the end of the French regime in Illinois, pièces d'Inde were bringing 3,000 livres, and occasionally even more.[79] The inflated prices of 1763 probably stemmed from disruptions to the trans-Atlantic slave trade caused by the French and Indian War and the devaluation of French currency during this time period. In the Illinois Country on the other side of the Mississippi, at Ste. Genevieve and St. Louis, similar prices obtained. Indeed, the settlements on both sides of the river continued to constitute a closely integrated economic and commercial community despite the political changes wrought by the French and Indian War. In 1775, for example, Gabriel Cerré, who had not yet moved from Kaskaskia to St. Louis, sold to Louis Boisleduc (i.e., Bolduc) of Ste. Genevieve a black slave named Mailler, pièce d'Inde, for 2,500 livres.[80] The transaction was recorded by Lieutenant Governor Pedro Piernas in St. Louis, and no problems arose because the sale was being consummated across an international frontier—Kaskaskia being in British Illinois, and Ste. Genevieve in Spanish.

The 2,500 livres that Louis Bolduc paid for Mailler in 1775 was at the high end of the price range for pièce d'Inde during the 1770s. In Ste. Genevieve during the 1760s and 1770s, pièces d'Inde usually fetched 1,500–2,000 livres if they were "sound and free of all illnesses." In 1768 at Ste. Genevieve, Antoine Renaud gambled and purchased an ill, twenty-two-year-old black male slave named Michel for "400 pounds of good tobacco," which was worth approximately 160 livres. If Michel recovered from his illness, Renaud had struck a good bargain; if not, he would have to work his tobacco field with extra diligence the next year.[81] At Ste. Genevieve in 1783, several Vallé family slaves were valued at 2,000 livres each, and in 1788 a healthy thirty-five-year-old male sold there for 2,500 livres.[82] Slave prices (in French livres) rose a bit in the Illinois Country during the 1780s. This may have been due to increased demand or to economic dislocation wrought by the American Revolution. With the coming of the Spanish regime in Louisiana, the piastre and peso (both usually pegged at five French livres or one American dollar) were used as well as the livre in Ste. Genevieve and St. Louis.[83]

An interesting slave sale occurred in 1789 when Daniel McDuff, an early American resident of Kaskaskia, was forced to sell seven slaves to raise money to cover a debt that he had incurred with Jacques Clamorgan, a St. Louis merchant.[84] The group of black slaves consisted of two men, Will and Charles, and two women, Foëby and Cati, all of whom were "about twenty years of age." In addition these four adults had three children, two of whom were about two years old and one who was a three-month-old infant. All seven were natives of the "United States of America" and were sold to Louis Dubreuil, a merchant and large slaveholder from St. Louis, for 1,800 piastres (9,000 livres). This sale suggests that the practice of keeping slave families intact while children were prepubescent, which was mandated by the French Code Noir,[85] was generally adhered to in Upper Louisiana throughout the eighteenth century.

Gabriel Cerré fled Kaskaskia after the arrival of George Rogers Clark and his Virginians and established himself as a prominent trader in St. Louis. Cerré traded in slaves, in addition to numerous other commodities. In 1794 he sold to Nicolas Lecompte, "master armorer in St. Louis," a one-eyed female mulatto slave named "Geny" (i.e., Jenny), "native of America," and her two children, a five-year-old girl named Rosalie and a two-year-old boy named Étienne. Lecompte paid Cerré 400 piastres (2,000 livres) for this rather pathetic family.[86] None of these three slaves qualified as a pièce d'Inde, but if Lecompte was lucky, the two children would mature into that status and become valuable property. This was a gamble for Lecompte, and in the meantime Geny, who was sold with no guarantee of sound health, would serve as mother to the two children in whom he had invested.

Six years later a similar transaction occurred in St. Louis. A Negro women, Céleste, and her two mulatto children, an eight-year-old girl and a boy four or five years old, were sold to Joseph Brazeaux, who appears as a well-to-do "labrador" on the 1787 Spanish census of St. Louis, for 750 pesos (3,750 livres) in peltries.[87] The seller of these slaves was one Philip Pheins, who was illiterate and a recent arrival in Spanish Illinois. The slave family that Pheins sold to Brazeaux, like the one in the preceding paragraph, came from the "partida Americana" of the Illinois Country. Documentation on slave sales in the Illinois Country at the end of the eighteenth century strongly suggests that there was a flow of slaves across the Mississippi from east to west and that slaves were more valuable on the Spanish side of the river than on the American. This may have been because of persistent rumors, which were based on fragmentary knowledge of the Northwest Ordinance of 1787 and how it would be enforced, that the U.S. republican government was intending to liberate all slaves in American Illinois.[88] Slave prices reckoned in livres and piastres were remarkably stable in Spanish Illinois during the 1770s, 1780s, and 1790s, pièce d'Inde usually fetching between 400 and 500 piastres (2,000 to 2,500 livres). Right at the beginning of the nineteenth century, however, there was a perceptible increase in the value of slaves on both sides of the Mississippi River. By 1803, for example, prime male and female slaves sold in Ste. Genevieve for 3,000 livres.[89]

On the U.S. side of the Mississippi, the Northwest Ordinance had not succeeded in eradicating slavery in the regions that eventually became the states of Indiana and Illinois, for Article 6 of the ordinance was construed as not having been intended to apply to the French slaves, who had been in Illinois long before the region became U.S. territory.[90] Territorial governor General Arthur St. Clair wrote to President George Washington in 1790, saying, "I have thought proper to explain the Article [Article 6 of the Northwest Ordinance] respecting slaves as a prohibition to any introduction of them, but not to extend to the liberation of those the people were already possessed of."[91] President Washington did not take issue with St. Clair's reading of the Northwest Ordinance, and this interpretation was generally accepted in the Indiana and Illinois Territories. That is, "French slaves" were deemed beyond the reach of Article 6 of the Northwest Ordinance. Article 6 of the first Illinois Constitution was based on the same premise and was manifestly intended not to encroach upon preexisting property rights in slaves.[92]

Commerce in French slaves was therefore perfectly permissible in the Illinois Country under U.S. jurisdiction. At Cahokia in 1800 Auguste Clermont and his wife, Marianne Lepage, sold a twenty-seven-year-old black slave named Antoine to Jean Dehay (John Hay) for $660.00.[93] Two years later, also at Cahokia, a typical territorial commercial transaction occurred: Louis Peltier and his wife, Susanne Cécire, sold a fifty-year-old male slave named Ginga to Étienne Pinçonneau for $400.00, payable in deerskins reckoned at 2½ pounds per dollar.[94] Deerskins were a traditional form of currency in the Illinois Country, although they were often pegged at a higher rate than in this transaction.

In addition to the "old French slaves," new supplies of black bonded labor were introduced to early nineteenth-century Illinois through the legal practice of long-term indentures. Territorial laws of Indiana repeatedly sanctioned such indentures,[95] and when Illinois became a territory in its own right in 1809, the laws of the Indiana Territory were adopted wholesale in the new territory.[96] Numerous African Americans were brought into southern Illinois during the late eighteenth and early nineteenth centuries and put under long-term indentures.[97] In 1798, for example, Shadrach Bond Sr., who would eventually become first governor of the state of Illinois, purchased in Kentucky a slave named Harry, brought him north across the Ohio River, and placed him under a fourteen-year indenture.[98] Just as old French slaves could be bought and sold in Illinois, so indentured servants were considered marketable properties. Thus at Kaskaskia in Randolph County in 1812, Alexander Stuart sold a black female indentured servant named Lucy and her young son Moses to Shadrach Bond Jr. "for value received."[99] Less than two years earlier, Stuart and Lucy had agreed to an indenture that bound the thirty-three-year-old Lucy for a term of twenty-five years, which in that era was for all intents and purposes bondage for life.[100] Moreover, according to the laws of the Indiana and Illinois Territories, Moses, who seems to have been en ventre sa mère when Lucy agreed to her indenture in January 1810, was legally bound to servitude until the age of thirty years.[101] This provision in the territorial laws meant that Alexander Stuart did good business by indenturing the pregnant Lucy, keeping her until she bore her child, and then selling Lucy's indenture, which legally included the young Moses, to a third party. Significantly, long-term indentures were never used to engage *white* laborers in early Indiana or Illinois.

Black servitude, both slavery and indentured servitude, diminished in importance in Illinois during the early nineteenth century. No community in nineteenth-century Illinois had the high percentage of bondsmen that, for example, Kaskaskia had at the time of the 1752 census. Nonetheless, black servitude of one kind or another, outright slavery or extended indentureship, persisted well after Illinois became a state in 1818. The U.S. census of 1820 listed 917 slaves in Illinois, and many of these were from the counties along the Mississippi—Randolph, Monroe, and St. Clair—where the old French settlements were located.[102] A census of Randolph County in 1825 listed 3,489 free white persons, 91 free persons of color, and 240 colored slaves or indentured servants.[103] The fact that the local census taker lumped slaves and servants together in the same category reveals that colored persons who were held under long-term indentures were deemed tantamount to slaves.

HIRED AGRICULTURAL LABOR

Hired help of one kind or another made up a significant proportion of agricultural labor in the Illinois Country. With some exaggeration, Philip Pittman commented that "at the Illinois a man may be boarded and lodged the year round on condition of his working two months, one month in ploughing the land and sowing the corn, and one month in the harvest."[104] Despite its importance in colonial Illinois, hired labor is more difficult to study than is slave labor. Documentation on hired help is less abundant, and the absence of a consistent nomenclature makes it more difficult to analyze in a rigorous fashion.

The French word *volontaire*, like the English *volunteer*, was a word most often applied to soldiers who had volunteered to serve in the military. In the colonial Illinois Country, however, it never appears in a military context, and the most accurate and succinct definition of *volontaire* is "a free man who owned no land"; such a person was therefore not a habitant in the way in which that word was customarily used.[105] Major Macarty's 1752 census of the Illinois Country contains an enumeration of 150 men labeled "volontaires," and every one of the six communities included in the census contained some volontaires; in fact, more volontaires than habitants were listed. Comparing the Illinois Country with French Canada, in 1752 volontaires constituted only 1.9 percent of the total free population in Illinois, whereas Greer found that in 1765 hired labor made up 4.1 percent of the population in the three rural Quebec parishes that he studied.[106] On the other hand, 43.7 percent of all households in the Illinois Country in 1752 had at least one volontaire in residence, whereas Greer found that in 1765 only 13.5 percent of the households in his parishes had at least one servant. In rural Quebec, therefore, relatively few families engaged relatively large numbers of hired servants, whereas in Illinois servants were more evenly distributed, most families having a small number of hired hands.

A more obvious difference between Greer's Canadian parishes and those in the Illinois Country was the existence of numerous slaves, both African and Indian, in the latter. If one includes slaves along with the volontaires, most habitants of the Illinois Country had much more nonfamily assistance with agricultural labor than did their counterparts in the St. Lawrence Valley; in the Illinois Country a whopping 67.7 percent of the households had some sort of nonfamilial help—that is, at least one volontaire, black slave, or Indian slave. Owners of large numbers of African slaves, such as Antoine Bienvenu and the Jesuit fathers, ordinarily used few volontaires, relying instead on slave labor; the 1752 census lists only one volontaire chez Bienvenu and none at the sizable Jesuit establishment in Kaskaskia.

Macarty's 1752 census enumerated volontaires namelessly, always as residents of someone else's household. Volontaires seem always to have been free white (or sometimes perhaps mulatto or mixed blood) males who worked for wages, and likely many of the volontaires listed on the census were engagés. Engagés worked under the terms of *contrats d'engagement,* labor contracts, that usually (but not always) specified the tasks to be done and the duration of the contract period. Contracts were often used in French Atlantic seaports for sending laborers to New France (just as indentured servants were sent from Britain to the thirteen British colonies), and the usual contract period was three years. This led to the general term *trente-six-mois* for contract workers who came to Canada from France.[107] In French Canada such labor contracts were used from the earliest days of the colony to hire fishermen on the coast and canoemen for the fur trade,[108] and they became popular for a wide assortment of tasks throughout French North America. In the Illinois Country they were used to engage men for rowing bateaux, mining lead, driving cattle, domestic service, cutting wood, carpentry, agricultural labor, and sometimes simply generic day labor. The association between volontaires and engagés is apparent in the language used in a great many contracts, where a standard phrase—"s'est volontairement engagé," that is, "has voluntarily engaged himself"—often appears.[109]

The 1752 census is the only such document from colonial Illinois to use the term *volontaire* to define a category of person enumerated, and *engagé* was never used as a defining term on any census in colonial Illinois. A number of source documents, however, use *journalier* or its Spanish equivalent *jornalero* to designate the occupations of various individuals. *Journalier* derived from *journée*, which, depending on the context, could mean "day," "daytime," or "a day's worth of work." Twenty-one out of the 175 men (12 percent) listed on the Ste. Genevieve militia muster roll from 1779 were identified as "journaliers," day laborers.[110]

More interesting, however, is the 1787 Spanish census of St. Louis and Ste. Genevieve, for this document reveals specific occupations in which the journaliers of the Illinois Country may have been employed.[111] There were large numbers of "jornaleros" listed in both of the twin towns of Spanish Illinois, 102 in Ste. Genevieve and 286 in St. Louis. The apparent reason for these large numbers is that sons of the family who were still living in their parents' households were listed as "jornaleros." The day laborers enumerated who were not members of the nuclear family represented the hired help. In both communities about 80 percent of the grain-producing households included at least one jornalero, and in both towns about 80 percent of all the jornaleros listed lived in households that produced either wheat, maize, or both. Whatever the errors in the 1787 enumeration, this census provides strong evidence that much of the hired help in the Illinois Country was employed in agricultural labor.

The 1732 Illinois census did not have categories for enumerating volontaires, journaliers, or engagés, but the census taker did note that in addition to the persons listed on the census, there were "always about fifty voyageurs coming and going."[112] One might well suppose that many of these voyageurs—when they were not plying the rivers in bateaux, pirogues, and canoes—were employed as contract laborers in sundry other tasks within the various communities. In September 1738, for example, Claude Alarie, "voyageur," engaged himself to Daniel Legras of Kaskaskia for one year to work as a farm laborer, to build two plows, and to perform various other tasks.[113] Legras appears on the 1732 census of Kaskaskia as the owner of two linear arpents of agricultural land and an Indian slave couple, but Legras needed extra help and he engaged Alarie. Alarie's remuneration for the year's labor was to be one-third of Legras's agricultural profits for the year. On the other hand, it seems likely that at least some of the numerous volontaires listed on the 1752 census and many of the jornaleros on the 1787 censuses were voyageurs who took to the rivers once the harvest was in and the agricultural season had ended. Neither of these censuses, which are loaded with mentions of volontaires and jornaleros, each according to its language, makes any mention of voyageurs as residents of the Illinois Country; probably the census takers subsumed the voyageurs within other categories of hired labor.

Many volontaires listed on the 1752 Illinois census, journaliers of the 1779 Ste. Genevieve militia muster roll, and jornaleros of the 1787 Spanish census were probably engagés of one sort or another; that is, they were contract laborers whose terms of contract, either written or verbal, varied a great deal. Pedro (Pierre) Lacroix, for example, who is listed as a "jornalero" in the 1787 census of Ste. Genevieve, appears as Pierre Lacroix in a contract signed at Ste. Genevieve in 1791.[114] There is an interesting assortment of extant engagement contracts from the Illinois Country on both sides of the Mississippi, and many of these pertain specifically to various kinds of agricultural labor. Indeed, these contracts shed light not only on agricultural labor practices but on diverse aspects of agriculture and society in the region during colonial times.

In March 1725, in the office of du Vernay, the royal notary at Fort de Chartres, one Jean-Baptiste André bound himself to serve Pierre Melique, lieutenant in the French marines, for one year. Most French labor contracts in the Illinois Country were for terms of one or two years and only rarely three, which was the usual term for laborers departing France for the New World. As was usual in these contracts, André committed himself to do everything he was ordered to do, although domestic work and gardening were specified as his particular tasks. André's wages for one year of service were to be the first calf to issue from a cow that he tended for Melique, if the calf were a heifer; if not, Melique committed himself to exchanging a heifer of the same age for the bull calf. Lastly, André agreed that should he decide to sell the heifer, Melique would have first right of refusal to purchase it.[115] This contract reveals the high value of female cattle in the Upper Mississippi Valley at that early date (1725). Also remarkable for that period of time, Jean-Baptiste André was a free black man who, after appearing with his mark in this labor contract, disappears forever from the extant records of the Illinois Country. Lieutenant Melique himself was soon to be killed by Indians on an exploratory expedition up the Missouri River. The hopes of each of these men—one white and from France and the other black and from Africa—to become cultivators of the richest land in the empire of the Bourbon monarchy of France were therefore short-lived.

On November 13, 1739, Antoine Bienvenu, one of the wealthiest citizens in Kaskaskia, engaged Jean Missuë (he often signed his name "Missuy") for a term of three years. This contract is informative enough to be presented in detail:

> Before the royal notary of Illinois [Barrois], province of Louisiana, was present a resident of Kaskaskia, parish of the Immaculate Conception, Sieur Jean Missuë, a volontaire living in this town. He acknowledges by those present to have engaged himself and put himself in the service of Sieur

Antoine Bienvenu, an artisan living in this town. He accepts the said Sieur Jean Missuë as his servant, who in this position will do for his said master everything that is asked of him that is legal and honest during a term of three consecutive years. His engagement will commence the first of next March [i.e., March 1, 1740] and will finish March 2, 1744 [*sic*]. During these said three years he will sow the plowlands of his master with wheat as well as maize ["bled froment que de mailly"] or other seed grain; in his master's absence he will work his master's black slaves and other servants to do the sowing and harvesting and all other work that will be useful to him; and finally to do everything that can and must reasonably to expected of a good an loyal servant and overseer. . . . In addition the servant [i.e., Missuë] must assist at the Saline, leading and commanding his master's men, in order to produce 150 minots of salt . . . each year.[116]

Missuë's remuneration for his labor as servant and overseer consisted of the right to plant twenty minots of wheat each year on Bienvenu's land and to have his harvest milled into flour at Bienvenu's expense. Moreover, Missuë was to receive eighteen minots of salt for himself each year, which constituted a 12 percent cut of each 150 minots produced for Bienvenu at the Saline, the well-known salt springs that were located on the west side of the Mississippi near the mouth of Saline Creek. Lastly, Bienvenu was to provide for the laundering and mending of Missüe's clothes, for like most volontaires, Missüe was not married.

This engagement between Antoine Bienvenu and Jean Missuë is at the same time both usual and unusual. It was customary for such contracts to be drawn up in royal notary's office, as this one was, and it was standard boilerplate for them to include the catchall phrase that required engagés to do anything that was "legal and honest." On the other hand, the duration of the contract, three years, was longer than usual—not to mention the notary's slip of pen that turned it into a four-year agreement. It was also unusual in the Illinois Country to find a volontaire who, like Missuë, could sign his name. Missuë was apparently a cut above the usual volontaires who bound themselves to others for servitude, which explains why Antoine Bienvenu engaged him as an overseer. By 1752 Bienvenu was, with sixty-five slaves, the largest slave owner in the history of colonial Illinois, and this 1739 contract to engage an overseer suggests that already by that time he was using large numbers of slaves as agricultural laborers. Jean Missuë, like Jean-Baptiste André before him, disappears from view after having signed his contract of engagement in 1739. Brief appearances and then sudden disappearances were not unusual for the volontaires of the Illinois Country, for these landless men often led nomadic lives as boatmen, hunters, and trappers.

In the contract that Bienvenu signed with Missuë in 1739, the royal notary, Jean-Baptiste Bertlot *dit* Barrois (he always signed his name simply "Barrois"), identified Bienvenu as an "artisan," although *habitant* might have been a better designation for him, given the fact that he was a wealthy resident agriculturist. Perhaps Barrois, who had come to the Illinois Country from Canada, was reluctant to describe Bienvenu using *habitant*, which in Canada meant peasant. But an alternate explanation is provided in another contract that Bienvenu signed at Kaskaskia six years later, in 1745.[117] On this occasion the engagé, one Jacques Marthin, was once again a volontaire who, like Missuë before him, bound himself for three years to oversee slave agricultural workers "at the St. Philippe concession." This indicates that Bienvenu, who was identified as a resident of Kaskaskia, was involved in a large agricultural operation at Philippe Renaut's former concession at St. Philippe. Early GLO surveys[118] reveal that in 1736 Antoine Bienvenu and Joseph Buchet, who was storekeeper at Fort de Chartres, owned 16½ facing arpents of agricultural land at St. Philippe. This was a massive chunk of real estate that, according to the early American surveys, constituted over 1,300 acres and had once been the core of Renaut's St. Philippe concession. Although Bienvenu signed the engagement with Jacques Marthin in 1745, the terms of the contract make it clear that he was signing on behalf of "Bienvenu et Compagnie." Bienvenu and Buchet were therefore partners in a large slave-operated agricultural enterprise at St. Philippe, and the royal notary thought that *artisan* was a better designation for Bienvenu than *habitant;* even better might have been *bourgeois* or *marchand,* which terms were sometimes used in later contracts.[119]

The Bienvenu-Buchet partnership was a striking example of early Illinois agribusiness. Bienvenu lived in Kaskaskia, and Buchet at Fort de Chartres, and as partners they hired volontaires as long-term engagés to oversee the agricultural plantation at St. Philippe, which was worked largely with black slave labor. This partnership lasted for a decade and was amicably dissolved in September 1746 when Bienvenu sold out to Buchet. This sale was consummated for 20,000 livres, which was the value placed on Bienvenu's one-half share in the following real and personal property at their St. Philippe concession: "Arable land, meadows, woods, house, barn, stables, water and horse mill, and other buildings constructed on said concession, furniture, cattle, plows, carts, and all the utensils belonging to said concession, and all of the crops of this year [1746], five Negroes, pièces d'Inde, a Negro woman, four Negro boys, her children, and such as the whole now stands."[120] Some of the black slaves whom Jacques Marthin was hired in 1745 to oversee may be seen in this inventory. When the Bienvenu-Buchet partnership was dissolved in 1746, Marthin still had two years to serve in his three-year engagement, and presumably he stayed on at St. Philippe, working exclusively for Buchet rather than for Bienvenu and Company.

In any event, we see that Antoine Bienvenu preferred relatively long engagements; his contracts with both Missuë and Marthin were for three years. Marthin was to receive 650 livres per year, plus laundry and tobacco, his wash to be done by one of the "Negresses" working under his direction. The long-term contracts, however, together with the endemic diseases of the Mississippi Valley (most importantly malaria),[121] impelled Bienvenu to include an unusual clause in his contract with Marthin: each day that Marthin was ill and unable to perform his duties would be added to the term of his contract; i.e., should Marthin be incapacitated for thirty days with intermittent autumnal fevers, his contract would run for three years and thirty days with no increment in wages. So much for eighteenth-century sick leave. However, Bienvenu and Company magnanimously committed themselves to feed Marthin during any forthcoming period of illness.

The 1752 Illinois Country census, compiled seven years after Antoine Bienvenu's labor contract with Jacques Marthin, lists one volontaire and twenty-eight African slaves at the St. Philippe "concession de Monsieur Buchet."[122] Remarkably Buchet, who had been Bienvenu's partner at this concession, had increased the number of black slaves at St. Philippe almost threefold, from ten to twenty-eight, between the time that his partnership with Bienvenu was dissolved in 1746 and the time that the census was taken in 1752. We do not know, however, who the overseer at St. Philippe was in 1752, for Jacques Marthin's contract had expired in 1748, and he apparently did not renew it. The 1752 census lists Marthin, one of the rare volontaires who can be traced through time, as married and living at Cahokia. Indeed, Marthin's first child was born at Cahokia in December 1748,[123] which means that he had moved to Cahokia shortly after the expiration of his contract with Bienvenu and Company.

Barrois, the royal notary of Canadian origins, lived at Kaskaskia during the 1740s and 1750s. He drafted many of the contracts of engagement in the Illinois Country during that time period, and persons who lived elsewhere came to his office in Kaskaskia to have such contracts drawn up. One of these persons was Augustin Langlois, another man of Canadian background, who arrived in the Illinois Country during the 1730s and settled down at Prairie du Rocher when the community was emerging as a nuclear village. Langlois became *the* preeminent habitant in Prairie du Rocher, and the 1752 census indicates that he owned ten facing arpents of plowland, as well as more slaves than any other resident of this village.[124] He also had more volontaires (five) associated with his residence than anyone else, and probably they were working for Langlois under the terms of various contracts.

On September 21, 1745, one Louis Charente, "volontaire of the Illinois Country," engaged himself to Langlois "for the purpose of cultivating the fields."[125] His term of one year was to begin at "St. Michel's Day next" (Sept. 29, 1745), and he was to earn fifty écus (150 livres)—plus a pair of leggings ("mitasses"), a "braquet" (?), and a "chemise de service," which was some sort of standard-quality shirt used by the French in colonial Louisiana. On May 2, 1750, Thomas Deslauriers engaged himself to Langlois for one year "to work at cultivating the land and at all other tasks that his master assigns him, including threshing."[126] Deslauriers's wages were to consist of 300 livres in addition to six minots of seed wheat, which he could plant on Langlois's land and the fruits of which Langlois would help him to mill into flour. It appears that volontaires, who by definition did not own arable land, often wanted the right to plant grain on their master's land when they signed on as engagés.

Extant records do not permit us to determine whether either of Augustin Langlois's engagés were part of the group of five volontaires shown as associated with his household on the 1752 Illinois census. In any case, there is no evidence that either Louis Charente nor Thomas Deslauriers ever progressed from being single, landless men to become established Illinois habitants with wives, children, village residences, and outlying plowlands. As with so many eighteenth-century volontaires, they either drifted on or died before they had a chance to settle down, get inscribed in the local records, and become long-term subjects for future historians; their presence in the history of the Illinois Country will never be more than fleeting.

Few extant contracts of engagement from the 1750s and 1760s remain for the Illinois Country. It is impossible to say whether this is because fewer were drafted or because fewer notarial records have survived. With the coming of the French and Indian War and the ensuing end of the French regime in Louisiana, the entire French way of doing things eroded. In addition, the French legal practice of hiring contract labor doubtless declined to some degree. On the other hand, a substantial number of French-style contracts remain from the 1770s and 1780s, and these contracts were drafted by notaries in French even though French sovereignty had long since disappeared from the Illinois Country.

As the American Revolution was ending, Richard Winston was serving as county lieutenant, on behalf of the state of Virginia, of the Illinois Country on the east side of the Mississippi River.[127] That is to say, insofar as civil government existed at all in the region, Winston was the executive head of it. In December 1782 Pierre Langlois, who was a French Creole native of the Illinois Country, persuaded Winston to commission him notary at Kaskaskia. Langlois was soon busy drafting notarial documents in rather the same fashion as they had been done under the French regime, which had ended two decades earlier.[128] In September 1783 Langlois drew up a labor contract between Jacob Grots (or Groot) and Cristhome Kinter in which Kinter bound himself to work one year for Grots for wages of fifty-six piastres (280 livres) in "specie, animals, or merchandise."[129] Grots was an American farmer who had migrated to the Illinois Country as the American Revolution was ending, and presumably he engaged Kinter to do agricultural labor.[130] It is interesting to compare and contrast this labor contract with similar documents from the Illinois Country dating from the French regime. As with the earlier contracts, this one was drafted in French, uses the phrase *engagé volontairement,* and is short-term, being for only one year. On the other hand, it is rather different from the earlier contracts: most obviously, neither of the contracting parties was French or French Creole; they were Americans (perhaps Pennsylvania Germans), who most likely could not read the contract that they signed. Second, their contract is missing the standard boilerplate of earlier contracts that obliged the engagé to do everything "legal and honest" that the master ordered. That traditional limiting phrase, which had remained in use in the Illinois Country throughout the French and British regimes, disappeared in American Illinois.[131] Third, there is no mention in this 1783 contract of specific tasks for the engagé Cristhome Kinter. Traditional French contracts always specified the *principal* work that the engagé was to perform. Lastly, Kinter's wages were defined in terms of Spanish piastres, which had the same value as American dollars, instead of French livres.

Despite these qualifications, which are in fact rather minor, the contracts that the notary Pierre Langlois was drafting in Kaskaskia during the 1780s are fundamentally the same as those dating from the French regime; they are short-term agreements between persons who, though of different social status, came from basically the same social grouping—free white males. These types of contracts persisted on through the 1790s in places such as Ste. Genevieve on the Spanish side of the Mississippi.[132] During the 1790s, however, the traditional French contract of engagement totally disappeared in American Illinois, to be replaced by the sort of bonded-labor contract examined earlier in this chapter. This latter variety was long-term, exclusively between white masters and black servants, included no wages, and was specifically intended to circumvent the legal prohibition of slavery contained in Article 6 of the Northwest Ordinance.[133]

An early Anglo-American described the "wretched hovels" of the Illinois Country habitants as being "ready to tumble down on the heads of starving Indians, French and negroes, all mixed together."[134] This nasty blend of ethnocentrism and racism includes a snide allusion to the presence of many persons of mixed-blood heritage within the French Creole population of the Illinois Country. The fact of the matter was that many of these habitants had succeeded rather well as agriculturists, that they had cultivated their fields for a century alongside Native Americans and African Americans, some slave and some free, with modest success and in relative harmony. The crops they raised and how they raised them are examined in the following chapter.

The French Post of the Illinois is, of all the colony, that in which
with the greatest ease they grow wheat, rye and other like grain, for
the sowing of which you need only to turn the earth in the slightest
manner; that slight culture is sufficient to make the earth produce
as much as we can reasonably desire.
—Antoine Simon Le Page du Pratz, *History of Louisiana*

5 TILLING THE LAND IN COLONIAL ILLINOIS

In 1746 an official in King Louis XV's Ministry of Foreign Affairs
drafted a lengthy document entitled "Memoir concerning the Colony [Upper
Louisiana]." The anonymous author remarked that "they sow much wheat for
flour; they have much livestock; they have a salt spring that supplies the colony
and even parts of neighboring Canada [Detroit?]; and abundant lead mines
are being exploited."[1] If the author had mentioned peltries, his summary of the
Illinois Country's economy would have been complete. Wheat, it is noteworthy, was the first component of the economy enumerated.

The first English commentary about agriculture in the Illinois Country
dates from the period immediately following the French and Indian War,
when the east bank of the Mississippi had become British territory. Captain
Philip Pittman, who arrived in Illinois with British troops in 1765, was effusive in his praise of the region's richness: "The soil of this country in general is very rich and luxuriant; it produces all sorts of European grains, hops,
hemp, flax, cotton, and tobacco, and European fruits come to perfection. The
inhabitants make wine of the wild grapes, which is very inebriating, and is,
in colour and taste, very like the red wine of Provence."[2] Pittman's enthusi-

asm for horticulture, rather unusual and charming in a professional military officer, distorted the accuracy of his observations, for the Illinois wine made from local wild grapes was never so good as the red wines of Provence, which are themselves generally mediocre. But the Illinois Country's soil and climate were well suited for several varieties of agriculture, especially the production of cereal grains. Indeed, the Illinois Country was unique among French regions of colonization anywhere in the world, for it was the only one that was truly well suited for producing large quantities of cereal grains. The St. Lawrence Valley, with its thin soils and bitter climate, was satisfactory for dairy farming, but it was not a bountiful area for raising wheat and oats, much less maize. Lower Louisiana's boggy lands and blazing heat were fine for rice, indigo, and sugarcane, but the wheat bread baked in New Orleans was made with imported grain, much of it coming from the Illinois Country.

French explorers and missionaries who first entered the Illinois Country from Canada during the last quarter of the seventeenth century did not come in quest of arable lands for raising wheat or maize. Jolliet, La Salle, and Tonti; Marquette, Hennepin, and Gravier—these men journeyed west and south in pursuit of pelts and souls, not plowlands. Forts St. Louis I and II on the Illinois River (the first at Le Rocher, now Starved Rock, and the second at the lower end of Lake Peoria) were above all else trading outposts. Kaskaskia was located on an alluvial plain that ultimately proved to be superb for cereal-grain production, but there is no evidence that the rich soil of the bottomland attracted the first settlers to that site. The Kaskaskia Indians *may* have had their sights set on the agricultural potential of the alluvial peninsula that lay between the Mississippi and Kaskaskia Rivers, but the only certain facts about Kaskaskia's founding are that the Kaskaskia tribe was in flight from stronger tribes to the north and that the Frenchmen who accompanied them in 1703 were, first and foremost, missionaries and traders.

The transformation of the Illinois Country from a region of mission centers and fur-trading outposts into a major grain-producing region was the most important change to occur during the French regime in North America. This was of larger moment than the franchise over it given to the Royal Indies Company in 1717, the governing structure brought to it by Commandant Boisbriant in 1719-20, or its reversion to crown-colony status in 1731. Although the colonial villages in the Illinois Country continued to serve as mission centers and to function as entrepôts for trade in peltries (especially white-tailed deer skins), agriculture assumed a significant role in the lives of these communities during the first quarter of the eighteenth century.

Precisely when market agriculture emerged in the Illinois Country cannot determined, for the early decades of the eighteenth century are poorly documented. Illinois Indians certainly taught French Canadians to plant maize for subsistence, if the Canadians had not brought this knowledge with them from the St. Lawrence Valley. Henri Joutel, a survivor of La Salle's ill-fated last expedition, arrived at Fort St. Louis in the autumn of 1687 and re-marked that "Indian and even European corn thrives very well."[3] However, the leadership that urged the local residents (Indians, métis, and French Canadians) to take up agriculture seriously—to plant both wheat and maize, to employ draft animals for large-scale production, and to build gristmills— probably came from the local missionary priests: Seminarians at Cahokia and Jesuits at Kaskaskia, especially the latter. Missions of the Society of Jesus had become famous (and some, such as the one in Paraguay, infamous) around the world, and Jesuit fathers often excelled at secular endeavors as well as conversion of souls *ad majorem gloriam dei*. Jesuits often had some techni-cal training, and in New France they had already proven themselves to be persistent promoters of agriculture.[4] Moreover, the Jesuits in North America had never been attracted to the fur trade, for this commerce inevitably meant debauching the Indians in some fashion, either with alcohol or with priapic voyageurs. Enslave the Indians, yes, for as slaves they could be converted to Christianity and raised in the presence of good role models, but do not de-bauch them with brandy or sexual license. Therefore, the material basis of the Jesuit establishment in Kaskaskia was agricultural rather than commer-cial. The Jesuits introduced draft animals to the Illinois Country; they built several gristmills, including the first windmill in the region; and they were likely the first to use slaves for agricultural labor in Kaskaskia.

An engraved advertisement appeared in Paris in 1735 that touted the vir-tues of Illinois wheat and claimed that a "donné" of the Jesuits had first cul-tivated it there in 1718.[5] Substantial evidence exists, however, that market agriculture had commenced in Illinois before that date. As early as 1710, well before the founding of New Orleans in 1718, French officials at Mobile dis-cussed the importance of shipping grain and flour down the Mississippi from the Illinois Country.[6] André Pénicaut, a French soldier who traveled from the Gulf Coast to the Illinois Country in 1711, reported three gristmills (one wind-mill and two horse mills) at Kaskaskia,[7] and gristmills imply significant cereal-grain production. In the autumn of 1713 French officials at Mobile learned of a bumper wheat crop in the Illinois Country and were delighted that the habitants there were preparing to ship quantities of flour downriver to the Gulf Coast.[8] No later than 1715, then, the Illinois Country possessed all the necessary components for developing the agricultural system that would dominate the region for the remainder of the eighteenth century: seed maize and wheat, draft animals, plows and harrows, various technologies for milling grain, knowledge of elementary agricultural techniques, and enough habitants to till a significant portion of arable land.

By the early 1720s agriculture was firmly established in the Illinois Country. A memoir written in New Orleans in 1720 claimed that Illinois habitants had planted 525½ minots of wheat and 36½ minots of peas and beans that year, and that "when they have received the resources intended for them, they will easily be able to supply the foodstuffs needed in the lower colony."[9] A colonial official in 1722 characterized the Illinois post as having been established by voyageurs, but then, significantly, switching his perspective from fur trading to agriculture, claimed that wheat grew there as well as in France and that gristmills were being built to produce flour.[10] In the same year, the commissioners of the Royal Indies Company in Paris issued a regulation creating a provincial council to govern the Illinois Country, and this document referred to the "large number of French habitants" who lived in the region.[11] The commissioners' use of the word *habitants* rather than *voyageurs* reveals that already in 1722 these Frenchmen conceived of the Illinois Country as a region inhabited by tillers of the soil. In 1723 Diron d'Artaguiette, an official of the Royal Indies Company, claimed that Kaskaskia was "composed entirely of farmers,"[12] and in 1724 Boisbriant wrote to the company's directors that "everyone here [i.e., the Illinois Country] is devoted to agriculture."[13] These comments were exaggerated, but the fact they were made reveals the kind of economic transformation that was occurring in the Illinois Country.

By the mid-1720s local civil records from the Illinois Country provide specificity and concreteness not available in administrative documents. Barristers were forbidden in French Louisiana,[14] but local notaries did yeomen's service in handling legal paperwork—property transactions, marriage contracts, slave sales, estate inventories, and so forth. Among the variety of notarial documents from the Illinois Country, estate inventories are the most voluminous. By the mid-1720s, even for persons one would assume to have been traders, these inventories consisted largely of agricultural land, agricultural products, and agricultural tools. Take, for example, the estate of Michel Philippe and his wife, Marie Rouensa 8cate8a, daughter of a Kaskaskia Indian chief. The inventory was compiled in 1725 on the death of Marie, who left to her husband and six children a large estate that included two barns, many draft animals, much agricultural land, numerous agricultural instruments, and quantities of whole grain and flour.[15] Although Michel Philippe had journeyed from Canada to the Illinois Country as a voyageur and had married an Indian woman, the inventory of his estate demonstrates that he had settled down in Kaskaskia, taken up agriculture, and developed sedentary habits.

CLIMATE AND SOIL

The villages of the Illinois Country, from Kaskaskia in the south to St. Louis in the north, lay between thirty-eight and thirty-nine degrees north latitude, Kaskaskia falling just below the thirty-eighth parallel and St. Louis just below the thirty-ninth. The modern climate of this region is continental, and there is no reason to suspect that it was significantly different in the eighteenth century. Summers are hot and humid, and winters are cold with occasional snowfall. Nicolas de Finiels, who experienced the winter of 1797–98 as a resident of St. Louis, remarked that in the Illinois Country "the cold is just as bitter as that in Holland, and the heat just as burning as that which annually desiccates most of the fertile plains of the Antilles."[16] Finiels, who was experiencing for the first time in his life a thoroughly continental climate, was exaggerating little if any. In the eighteenth century, when there were no diesel-powered ice-breakers, the Mississippi was sometimes solidly frozen over at St. Louis; conversely, with no moderating ocean breezes, dog-day afternoons in St. Louis can be almost as stifling as those in New Orleans.

The growing season is generally a few less than 200 frost-free days, and the average last date of killing frost falls on April 15. Although the French colonists of the eighteenth century did not maintain records and compile such data, it is no mere coincidence that April 15 became the date most often set for village syndics to inspect the fencing surrounding the arable fields; trial and error had established a date that was just as valid as one ascertained by modern statistical evidence. This fact strongly suggests that the climate in the eighteenth century was indeed similar to that in the late twentieth century.

Mean annual precipitation ranges between 107 and 120 cm and is usually distributed rather evenly throughout the year, although not over the short term. Finiels bemoaned the Illinois Country's climate as "fickle and capricious," with torrential rains that could rot the seeds in the soil and droughts that could sap the earth of all its "nourishing nectars."[17] Finiels concluded that crops in the Illinois Country could not "compete in excellence with those produced by the temperate climate of the Old World."[18] The notion that fauna and flora had "degenerated" in the New World had been commonplace among European intellectuals since the publication of Buffon's *Histoire Naturelle,* and Finiels was here merely aping the famous French natural scientist.[19] Whatever Finiels's opinions, the incontrovertible fact remained that the climate of the Illinois Country was the best in French North America for the production of cereal grains.

An alluvial floodplain runs on the east side of the Mississippi River from the mouth of the Kaskaskia River upstream to just below present-day Alton, Illinois. This relatively flat floodplain, which can be as much as three miles wide, became known in the early nineteenth century as the American Bottom, but in colonial times it was thought of as the granary of French Louisiana. The west side of the Mississippi in the Illinois Country presented a more diverse landscape. At Ste. Genevieve there was a vast expanse of floodplain similar to the American Bottom on the east side of the Mississippi. Upriver from Ste. Genevieve, however, and north all the way to St. Louis along the west bank of the Mississippi, there was little bottomland except near the mouth of the Meramec River. At St. Louis and Carondelet, the arable fields were laid out on higher ground than at Ste. Genevieve or Kaskaskia. This higher ground was less fertile than the alluvial bottomlands, and it was harder for primitive plows to break, but it did possess the distinct advantage of being less vulnerable to spring flooding of the Mississippi. Terry Norris, an archaeologist with the U.S. Corps of Engineers in St. Louis, argues persuasively that the river was most unruly and destructive during the nineteenth century, after steamboats led to deforestation of the riverbanks.[20] Nevertheless, the Mississippi did frequently destroy crops sown on the floodplain during the eighteenth century, and the great flood of 1785 ("l'année des grandes eaux") prompted the relocation of Ste. Genevieve to higher ground.[21]

Arable agriculture in the colonial Illinois Country was practiced largely on the floodplain of the Mississippi River. In the eighteenth century this floodplain was not as pervasively and dramatically agricultural as it appears now. Swamps have been drained, scattered coppices of trees cut down, brush cleared away, and protective levees erected. Even the early GLO maps, and the field notes recorded by the land office surveyors who compiled the data on which the maps were based, do not fully convey to us the topography of the region as the French first experienced it; it was a wilder and less domesticated landscape than that which now meets our eyes. Furthermore, the floodplain was in perpetual flux. The main channel of the Mississippi was constantly shifting, oxbow lakes were left behind, and new sloughs and coulees were created. Nevertheless, the Illinois Country had the best soil in French North America, as it had the best climate, for the production of cereal grains.

French colonists and publicists did not take long to recognize this. Early on the Illinois Country was celebrated as "an earthly paradise": "they grow wheat, rye, and other like grain, for the sowing of which you need only to turn the earth in the slightest manner";[22] "the earth is very fertile, the climate salubrious, the women fecund."[23] To some extent these encomiums were part of a propaganda campaign sponsored by the royal government to help promote the colony. Later in the eighteenth century, Finiels excoriated all the rose-tinted visions of Louisiana that circulated in metropolitan France.[24] Nevertheless, for French peasants accustomed to pitifully small plots and even more pitiful seed-to-yield ratios, as well as to Canadian habitants accustomed to the usual thin soils and always bitter climate of the St. Lawrence Valley, the easy cultivation possible in the Illinois Country did make the region seem like a sort of terrestrial paradise.

AGRICULTURAL BASICS

Commandant Boisbriant's correspondence provides some of the earliest detailed comments about agriculture in the Illinois Country. In October 1720 he wrote from Kaskaskia to the directors of the Royal Indies Company that "clearing of the land is easy with Negroes [i.e., black slaves]. The prairie sod is taken up with a mattock ['pioche'], after which the land is easy to work. Several habitants plow it with one horse."[25] It is interesting to note that Boisbriant viewed slaves as integral to Illinois agriculture as early as 1720 and that he spoke of horses rather than oxen as the usual draft animals. Oxen soon came to dominate as draft animals in the Illinois Country, to the virtual exclusion of horses, for the heavy alluvial soils of the Mississippi and Kaskaskia bottomlands made the sturdier oxen the beasts of choice. Both oxen and horses were employed in the St. Lawrence Valley, sometimes, improbably, even in mixed teams.[26] Boisbriant, who was born and raised in Canada, may simply have slipped when he wrote of horses as draft animals in Illinois, or perhaps the transition to oxen was not complete in 1720. The shift in the other direction, from oxen to horses as draft animals, that occurred in some regions of France during the High Middle Ages, and also in eighteenth-century Canada, never occurred in colonial Illinois;[27] probably the alluvial soils of the region were too heavy for horses, which can plow faster than oxen but are less powerful.

If prairie grass had to be uprooted with mattocks before the Kaskaskia and Mississippi bottomlands could be cultivated, the work must have gone slowly at first. An observer at Kaskaskia in 1721, Monsieur Lallemant, commented that "it is a pity that only a quarter of a league of fields are being cultivated. . . . The little prairie at Kaskaskia alone has produced all of the wheat ['blé françois']."[28] It is difficult to know what Lallement meant by "a quarter of a league." However, if he was saying that the plowlands at Kaskaskia stretched along the Kaskaskia River for that distance and if we reckon a

French league at 2.76 miles,[29] that amount of land represented a not incon-
siderable extent of cultivation. Marc Bloch explained that until recent times
the French word *blé* had a generic meaning, like the English *corn*, which
defined any cereal grain.[30] Therefore Lallemant called wheat "blé françois"
to distinguish it from maize, which the French called either "maïs," from the
Spanish *maiz*, or "blé d'Inde," Indian corn.[31] An alternative designation for
wheat was *blé froment*, or often simply *froment*. Although the French in North
America likely had access to several different varieties of wheat, agricultural
nomenclature in the existing documents from the Illinois Country does not
permit us to identity these.

The plowing implement of the French habitants in the Illinois Country
was the *charrue*, the wheeled plow. Etymologically related to the French word
char, which is now popularly applied not only to military tanks but also to
virtually any wheeled vehicle, charrues had been used in various regions of
northern Europe since early medieval times.[32] By the High Middle Ages, the
charrue was the fundamental implement of tillage in northern France.[33] Early
Illinois governor and later enthusiastic amateur historian John Reynolds
remarked that the old traditional plows in Illinois were "of French descent, I
presume, as I saw the same species in Old France."[34] Later in the same volume Reynolds commented that the plows he saw in northern France in the
mid-nineteenth century were "exactly the same class of plows the French used
in Illinois fifty years since."[35]

French Canadians only reluctantly forsook the mattock and adopted the
charrue.[36] The St. Lawrence Valley frontier—with its hilly, rocky, stumpy, thin
soil—was not hospitable terrain for the charrue, which was the implement
par excellence of the northern European plain. Once the land had been thoroughly cleared, however, the charrue was widely adopted in Canada,[37] and
from Canada it soon made its way to the Illinois Country. André Pénicaut
was taken aback to see how widespread the charrue was in Illinois as early as
1711. He commented that of all the Indians he had seen during his travels,
including those of the entire lower Mississippi Valley, the Kaskaskias of Illinois were the only ones using the charrue.[38] Pénicaut further observed that
the Jesuits at Kaskaskia had trained the Indians to use this implement.
Pénicaut's observations are especially revealing because they suggest both
intensive and extensive agriculture in early French Illinois; intensive because
of the use of the charrue and extensive because Indians as well as French were
using this implement.

Co-aration—communal plowing with a communally owned team of
draft animals and plow—was apparently practiced in some regions of medieval Europe, as well as in early New England.[39] Marc Bloch, however, found

no evidence of communal plowing in the regions of medieval France that he studied,[40] and surely the independent-minded habitants of the St. Lawrence Valley never engaged in it. The French and French Creole residents of the Illinois Country would likely have worked within the French and French Canadian traditions, each habitant plowing by himself with his own plow and team. Estate inventories, which reveal that virtually every substantial habitant in the Illinois Country owned a team of oxen and charrue of his own, confirm this assumption.

A good team of draft oxen was a precious possession for any habitant. At Kaskaskia in 1725 good oxen were worth 1,200 livres a pair, and a solid charrue cost 250 livres, while a town lot containing two vertical-log houses was appraised at 5,500 livres.[41] On the other side of the Mississippi River and two generations later, Pierre Verrau died at Ste. Genevieve in 1786 and left an estate worth 1,435 livres, 10 sols. His team of oxen ("boeufs à tire") was evaluated at 250 livres, his old charrue with wheels missing at 60 livres, and his small vertical-log residence at 300 livres;[42] Verrau's house must have been in an advanced state of decay. Three years later Joseph St. Aubin's estate in Ste. Genevieve contained a pair of oxen valued at 300 livres, a plow (wheels included) worth 100 livres, and a new vertical-log house appraised at 4,000 livres.[43] Draft oxen were therefore worth about four times as much in the mid-1720s as they were sixty years later, and charrues were worth at least twice as much in the earlier period; residential properties, on the other hand, maintained fairly constant values across that time span. These relative values suggest that in the 1720s, when an agricultural economy was fast developing in the Illinois Country, implements and animals for tilling the soil had inflated values; sixty years later, with a fully matured agricultural system in place, these specialized items were worth relatively less.

The charrue was a heavy instrument that had a forestructure (*avant-train*) mounted on two wheels, two handles, and a fixed moldboard for laying aside the freshly cut slabs of soil. A difficult, nearly impossible implement in rugged country, it was well suited to the flat topography and alluvial soils of the Mississippi bottomlands. Indeed, it may have been better suited to the Illinois Country than to the undulating grain fields of northern France. There is no evidence that this implement evolved during the course of the eighteenth century, a century that saw much experimenting in Europe with the technology of plowing; charrues in the Illinois Country kept their medieval configurations. John Reynolds described French plows that he had seen at work in the fields near Kaskaskia in the early nineteenth century: "The plows were honored with only a small point of iron on the front in the ground, and that tied on to the wood with raw hide straps. The beams of the plows rested on axles, supported by small wheels, also without iron, and the whole concern hauled on by oxen—horses were not used in the plows by the French in pioneer times—and the oxen were yoked to the plows by the horns. Straps of untanned leather tied a straight yoke to the horns of the oxen, and a pole or tongue coupled the yoke to the wheel carriage, on which rested the beam of the plow."[44]

Other descriptions of French colonial plows come from disparate areas of French settlement outside the Illinois Country proper. At Green Bay an early American immigrant described the French and their agricultural practices: "Their manners and customs were of the most primitive character. They never used the yoke for their oxen; but instead, fastened sticks across the oxen's horns, to draw by. . . . Their plows were very uncouth, the plow-shares being about as large as a smoothing-iron; while the beam was about twelve feet long, with a pair of wheels near the fore end."[45] One detects a trace of ethnocentrism in this description, and some nineteenth-century Anglo-American observers went so far as to ascribe to racial deficiencies the peculiar (to American eyes) French technology in the Illinois communities. John Snyder called the inhabitants of these villages "mainly of primitive Canadian French stock, [who] seemed to be well contented with their condition and surroundings."[46] Snyder also called the prosperous Barbeau family of Prairie du Rocher a specimen of the "non-progressive exotic Creole race,"[47] which, like the other French families in Illinois, had not been much influenced by the example of "an incoming progressive, enterprising and industrious race" but instead were "stationary or gradually retrograding."[48] Snyder's ethnic comments must be seen as benign manifestations (they were not *all* benign) of increasing racial consciousness in the nineteenth century, for his father was of Alsatian stock and his mother was herself a member of the "non-progressive Creole race" who could not speak English when she married Snyder's father in 1820.[49]

Bela Hubbard, a resident of the Michigan Territory during the early nineteenth century, presented a rather different view of Franco-Americans and their technology. Although acknowledging that French agricultural technology was indeed inferior to that of the Anglo-Americans, Hubbard admired the French Canadians, who "accommodated themselves . . . gracefully to the mutations of their fate" and who "in their own way continued to prosper."[50] With regard to French Canadian agricultural implements, Hubbard expressed admiration: "The plow was of wood, except the share. Its long beam and handles extended ten or twelve feet, and it had a wooden mould-board. In front were two wheels, also of wood, of different sizes: a small one to run on the unplowed side, and a larger one in the furrow. . . . And a very good,

though shallow, plowing was performed by this rude but ingenious implement."[51] Hubbard described the furrows cut by French Canadian charrues
as "shallow," and Peter Kalm claimed that the grain fields of the St. Lawrence
Valley were characterized by "shallow furrows."[52] Henry Brackenridge, however, observing late colonial Ste. Genevieve, remarked that the local habitants
broke up the ground with "a kind of wheel plow, which enters deep into the
soil."[53] In any case, as Haudricourt has analyzed in detail,[54] French charrues
cut distinctly deeper furrows than the scratch plows (*araires*) that preceded
them in the history of agricultural technology.

The front wheels of different sizes described by Hubbard kept the beam
of the charrue level, for the smaller wheel ran on the unplowed ground while
the larger one ran in the adjacent furrow. Not all French colonial charrues
had wheels of differing diameters, however. An alternative, which was apparently employed often, was to adjust the plow's beam on the axle connecting
the wheels so as to keep it the correct distance from the ground even though
the axle itself was not.[55] This technical feature seems to have been what John
Reynolds was describing when he wrote that "holes in the beam of the plow
permitted the instrument to be so regulated on the axle that it would make
the proper depth of furrow."[56]

Reynolds called the French agricultural technology in Illinois "defective,"
and he may well have been alluding to the ox-horn yoke. As previously noted,
Ebenezer Childs described the French at Green Bay as using the same simple
device. The stick yoke at first strikes one as unworkable, cruel, or both; apparently, however, it was neither. It may be seen functioning satisfactorily in
late medieval France in Jean duc de Berry's "Les Très Riches Heures" illuminated manuscript for the month of March.[57] The horn yoke served the French
settlers in the Illinois Country well enough for at least one hundred years,
and according to some authorities, it was used in some regions of France until
recent times.[58]

The configuration of the plowlands that were worked with charrues has
been a topic of interest and controversy ever since Marc Bloch's *Les Caractères
originaux de l'histoire rurale française* appeared in 1931. Bloch argued that
charrues were, more than any other factor, responsible for the division of
plowlands in northern France into long, narrow strips.[59] For him, agricultural
technology—the difficulty of turning a heavy, wheeled plow at the end of each
furrow—produced the long furlong fields. Other historians of agriculture (e.g.,
the Orwins) explained the long, narrow, arable strips in traditional English
agriculture as a result of a complex interrelationship between the fixed moldboard plow and societal desire to ensure an equitable distribution of
plowlands.[60] Most recently Joan Thirsk has argued that the division of arable

lands into long strips was largely the result, over time, of partitioning rural real estate through inheritance.[61] In any case, it is perhaps reasonable to assume that heavy wheeled plows with fixed moldboards at least *encouraged* plowmen to minimize turns by tilling plots that were long and narrow.[62] Perhaps the cadastral longlots of the Illinois Country reinforced this tendency, although these longlots may in no way be considered as products of plowing patterns; longlots, which descended to the Illinois Country from Canada, certainly antedated French arable agriculture in the Mississippi Valley.

Agricultural technology and practices in the Illinois Country, which were essentially medieval, likely did have *some* effect on the configuration of the plowlands. Unfortunately, plowing patterns in the colonial Illinois Country remain unknown. It may perhaps be deduced from the ubiquitous charrues that the Illinois habitants plowed in relatively long, narrow strips. Furthermore, these plowmen probably used their fixed moldboard plows to practice "labour en refendant,"[63] which meant that they commenced plowing along one edge of their field, finished that furrow, crossed over to the other side of the field to return, and thereby plowed in ever smaller circles, concluding with a pronounced ditch down the middle. This pattern of plowing had two distinct advantages for the Illinois habitant: it lightened the burden of turning the charrue and the team of oxen after each furrow, and it facilitated drainage on the alluvial bottomlands where arable agriculture was practiced. But there is very little knowledge of how the long furrows cut by the charrues fit within the configuration of the larger, cadastral longlots that composed the arable compounds throughout the entire Illinois Country. With the exception of the early pattern at Cahokia, as described in chapters 2 and 3, there is no direct evidence that the long axes of the plow strips ran *consistently* parallel with the long axes of the larger longlots; furrows may conceivably have run on a bias or even perpendicular to the main axes of the cadastral longlots. The narrowest Illinois longlots tended to be two arpents in breadth (approximately 384 feet), and charrues could accommodate themselves easily to furrows of that length. Indeed, the topography of the land probably had more influence on the orientation of the furrows than did the direction of the longlots.

Two eighteenth-century maps convey some idea of plowlands in the Illinois Country, Broutin's of 1734 and Finiels's of 1798.[64] These maps were drafted by excellent cartographers; they stand on either end of a wide chronological span, more than sixty years; and they deal with the Illinois Country on both sides of the Mississippi—Broutin's depicting only the east side, and Finiels's being most accurate for the west side, which interested him most. Both these maps show clusters of plowlands consisting of elongated strips

Agriculture in eighteenth-century France from Denis Diderot's *Encyclopédie*. In the Illinois Country oxen rather than horses were used as draught animals for plowing.

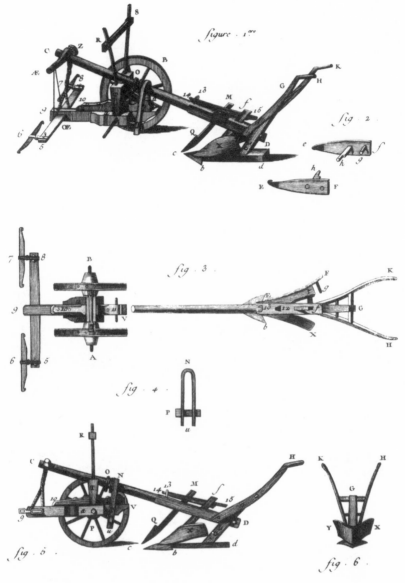

French plows (*charrues*) from Denis Diderot's *Encyclopédie*. The wheel plows in the Illinois Country were similar to these and were scorned by Anglo-Americans as primitive.

The month of March from Jean de Berry's fifteenth-century *Très Riches Heures* shows oxen hitched to a *charrue* with a stick yoke. This technique was ubiquitous in the Illinois Country. Original illuminated manuscript by the Limbourg brothers located in the Château de Chantilly.

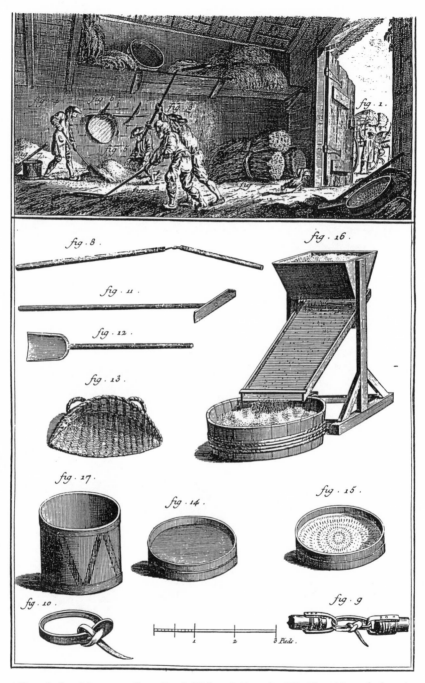

A French threshing scene from Denis Diderot's *Encyclopédie*. Threshing of wheat in the Illinois Country was also done in barns (*granges*).

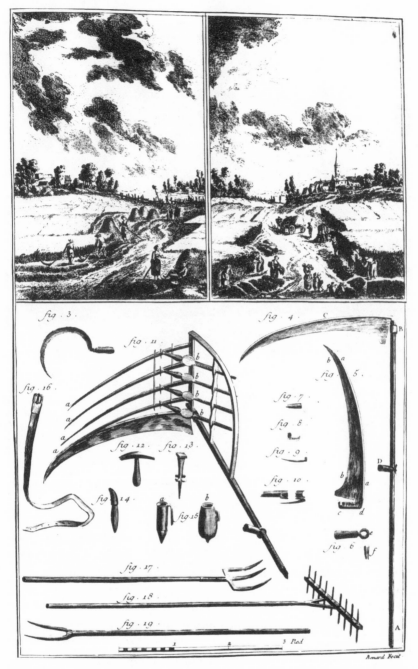

Eighteenth-century French harvest scenes from Denis Diderot's *Encyclopédie*. Women are shown helping with the harvest, but in the Illinois Country Creole women rarely worked in the grain fields.

Traditional agricultural implements as displayed at the Louis Bolduc House in Ste. Genevieve, Missouri.

whose orientations seem to bear little or no relationship to the longlot concessions. That is, there were longlots within longlots, but the two distinct varieties of longlots—one cadastral and one agricultural—existed quite independently of each other. The portrayal of plowlands on these maps is surely not uniformly accurate, but in any case they both suggest that the habitants of the Illinois Country did not consistently cut their long furrows to suit the dimensions of their cadastral longlots. As noted earlier, longlots in the region were seldom devoted exclusively to arable agriculture, even when they made up part of an open-field complex. A longlot at St. Philippe, which was three arpents wide and ran from the Mississippi back to the bluffline, was described in 1741 as consisting of "prez, bois, [et] terre labourable," that is, meadow, woods, and plowland.[65] It is difficult to imagine precisely how the plowlands fit into this tangled landscape, but the furrows of the arable may have gone in just about any direction.

The clusters of plowlands depicted on the Broutin and Finiels maps resemble the *quartiers* or *faisceaux* (furlongs in England) of the open fields from northern France, as illustrated in Bloch's seminal study. Nonetheless, even though both France and the Illinois Country displayed many similar components—charrues, longlots, open fields, community regulations, common pasture on the stubble, and nuclear villages—the resemblance does not run very deep. In France the individual strips that composed the quartiers were owned (though not en franc alleu) by different peasants; that was by definition how the quartiers were constituted. Second, crop rotation by quartiers, whether biennial or triennial, which was central to traditional open-field agriculture in France, was never practiced in the colonial Illinois Country.

CROPS IN THE ILLINOIS COUNTRY

All early visitors to the French Illinois Country commented about the locally produced wheat: in 1711 André Pénicaut remarked that "wheat grows there [Kaskaskia] as fine as any in France."[66] A decade later the inspector general of Louisiana, Bernard Diron d'Artaguiette, remarked that "French wheat grows very well there and of a fine quality."[67] A half-century later, in 1769, and from the other side of the Mississippi, the Spanish lieutenant governor in St. Louis, Pedro Piernas, remarked about the agriculture at Ste. Genevieve that "the chief crop is wheat, which yields abundantly."[68] The most important item of diet in the Illinois Country was wheat bread. Writing about traditional society in Europe, Fernand Braudel remarked that "the trinity of grain, flour, bread is to be found everywhere. . . . It was the major preoccupation of towns, states, merchants, and ordinary people for whom life meant eating one's daily bread."[69] In 1995 the French minister of agriculture, Philippe Vasseur, proclaimed, "Bread is part of our national identity; . . . if there isn't any left, we won't know who we are."[70] These remarks are wholly applicable to French Creole society in colonial Louisiana. Wheat certainly constituted the single largest component of their total caloric intake,[71] and it was a universally accepted fact that the best wheat in North America came from the Illinois Country; throughout the French regime, convoys of Illinois flour were eagerly awaited in New Orleans.

Each spring the habitants of the Illinois Country would decide which portions of their arable lands to devote to wheat and which to other crops such as maize. They would plow the designated wheat lands with charrues and then work them with harrows (*herses*) to break down the clumps of earth and smooth out the fields before sowing the grain. The seed wheat was broadcast, and then the fields would be harrowed again to cover the seeds. John Reynolds's treatise "The Agricultural Resources of Southern Illinois" contains the most accurate and humane description of French Creole wheat production:

> The wheat crop was generally sown in the early spring, and tolerably well plowed in with the ox team. It was cut with the sickles, or reap hooks, as no [grain] cradles existed in those times. They bound the sheaves with grass cut for the purpose, hauled the crop home in their horse or ox carts, and stowed it away in barns. The ancient custom was, at "harvest home," to tie together some nice straws of the wheat in the shape of a cross, and place it over the gate of the husbandman. This exhibition was in praise to providence for the harvest, and also to show that the crops were housed in the barns.[72]

Reynolds went on to note that "in the winter the wheat was threshed out in the barns with flails." An inventory from August 1725 confirms this observation, for the extensive wheat crop of one family from Kaskaskia, valued at 3,300 livres, was listed as "in sheaves in the barn ['en gerbe et en grange']."[73] Despite some planting of winter wheat, spring-sown wheat remained the principal crop in the Illinois Country until long after France surrendered sovereignty over the region. Potatoes were not planted at all until late in the eighteenth century, and cereal grains constituted the basic source of carbohydrates for the inhabitants for the entire colonial period. French Canadian habitants sowed mostly wheat and oats,[74] while those in the Illinois Country confined themselves overwhelmingly to wheat and maize; maize was much better suited to the Mississippi Valley than to the St. Lawrence Valley. In Illinois, as in Canada, wheat remained the favorite, the fundamental ingredient in the large, brown loaves of bread (*miches*) that were the staff of life for French colonists all the way from Quebec to Kaskaskia.

American Indians whom the French colonists encountered in the St. Lawrence Valley cultivated what the French called at first "blé de Turquie," then "blé d'Inde," and finally "maïs." The Jesuit missionary Paul le Jeune remarked in 1633 that the Montagnais Indians who lived northeast of Quebec were making "sagamite" from water and pulverized "bled d'Inde."[75] Perhaps Indians taught French Canadian habitants to plant maize, as according to hoary tradition they also taught the English Pilgrims at about the same time. But it is also conceivable that Frenchmen brought seed maize to the St. Lawrence Valley. Maize was carried back to Europe from America by Spaniards in the sixteenth century, and from Spain maize production spread slowly to other regions of Europe.[76] It was planted in Languedoc early in the seventeenth century, and in the 1670s John Locke reported seeing maize near

Saintes in western France.[77] In any case, unlike settlers in New England, the French in Canada were not much attracted to maize, always preferring wheat and oats as cereal grains.[78] Probably both taste and climate played roles in determining this preference; the French had no appetite for maize, and the Canadian climate was not well suited for its cultivation.

In early Louisiana, well before the founding of New Orleans, French colonists were chronically short of food and were obliged to consume maize raised by local Indians. The French, however, especially French women, did not like to eat what seemed to them a coarse and unpalatable grain. Governor Bienville reported from Mobile in 1704 that "the men who are in Louisiana are accustoming themselves to maize, but the women, who for the most part are natives of Paris, are very reluctant to consume it."[79] Bienville returned to the subject years later, remarking that a shipload of sickly African slaves who had just arrived in Louisiana required only a diet of maize to restore their health.[80] Maize was deemed suitable food only for African slaves and Indians. Le Page du Pratz spent several pages describing the cultivation and consumption of maize by Indians in Lower Louisiana, but he never once mentioned the French eating it.[81] In the Illinois Country there were few if any Parisian women, who were said to be the most discriminating and demanding of all French people, but sources suggest that ethnic French people of whatever sex or place of origin were slow in learning to appreciate maize as a foodstuff.

Documentation about maize is sparse during the early years of French settlement in the Illinois. Visitors to Kaskaskia during the first two decades of the eighteenth century always commented on the wheat grown there, not the maize. Since the earliest days of the settlement, however, some maize was surely cultivated, by the Indian wives of the French habitants if no one else.[82] In September 1752 Commandant Jean-Jacques Macarty reported that drought had much reduced the maize harvest in Illinois, which would be a great misfortune for "pork and for feeding animals."[83] The commandant did not bother to mention whether this shortage had any effect on human diets in the region. During the winter of 1797, the residents of New Madrid were isolated by ice floes on the Mississippi and as a consequence were "reduced" to eating corn bread for sustenance.[84] Looking back from the nineteenth century, John Reynolds observed that maize was consumed by Creole voyageurs engaged in the Indian trade and used by Illinois habitants to "fatten the hogs" but that the latter group "did not use it to any extent for bread."[85]

Despite all these disparaging comments about maize, by 1767 a crude British census of Kaskaskia showed the maize harvest to have been nearly twice as large as that of wheat,[86] and Spanish censuses from the end of the colonial era indicate that maize production was consistently higher than wheat production in Upper Louisiana by that time.[87] French Creole habitants in North America seem to have adjusted to maize rather slowly and reluctantly at first, but once they discovered that the alluvial bottomlands of the Illinois Country were incomparably well suited to its cultivation, they adapted and began producing relatively more maize and relatively less wheat. They fed it to their animals and to their slaves, they made whiskey from it, and they even debased themselves by eating corn bread.

Once again John Reynolds provides the best description of how the Illinois French cultivated maize: "I presume for more than one hundred years the French plowed in their corn about the 1st of June, and turned under the weeds and not many grew until the corn was up out of the reach of them. They planted the seed corn in the furrows as they broke the ground, and turned the furrow on the corn planted; plowed a few furrows more and planted another row of corn; and so on, until the field was all planted."[88] Unlike seed wheat, which was broadcast, individual grains of corn were planted in more or less evenly spaced rows. The folk art of Olaf Kranz reveals that Swedish female immigrants in mid-nineteenth-century Illinois were adept at sowing maize,[89] but once again there is no evidence from colonial Illinois that French or Creole women worked in the arable fields.[90]

Throughout the upper Mississippi Valley during the eighteenth century and into the nineteenth, French settlers sowed most of their arable fields in wheat and maize; these grains constituted the two staple crops on the alluvial bottomlands throughout the entire region. The rye, tobacco, hemp, pumpkins, beans, or turnips that were occasionally planted were seldom more than incidental crops. Even at remote Prairie du Chien on the upper Mississippi, the agricultural pattern was the same. U.S. Indian agent Nicolas Boilvin remarked in 1811 that the French Canadian habitants there raised "considerable quantity of surplus produce, particularly wheat and corn."[91]

There is better documentation pertaining to agriculture at colonial Ste. Genevieve than at St. Louis, or for that matter at any other village in the Illinois Country on either side of the Mississippi River. Ste. Genevieve was first, last, and foremost an agricultural community. The town was founded by agriculturists, and at the end of the colonial period grain production remained the largest component in the town's economy. Most adult males in eighteenth-century Ste. Genevieve were directly involved in agriculture, working the land themselves or overseeing their hired and slave labor. Visitors to colonial Ste. Genevieve were struck by the primacy of agriculture in the life of community. Perrin du Lac remarked that "The inhabitants of Ste. Genevieve are exclusively occupied with cultivation. . . . They possess a portion of the earth whose fertility transcends the imagination; in a few days they can sow and harvest their subsistence of the entire year."[92] Du Lac, a Frenchman accustomed to the tiny plots of exhausted land in France, was awestruck by the productive capacity of the Grand Champ, the enormous expanse of arable land at Ste. Genevieve that was enclosed by a single common fence.

Henry Brackenridge, the Anglo-American who as a schoolboy lived in Ste. Genevieve during the 1790s, remarked that the fence around the arable lands of the Grand Champ enclosed 7,000 acres and that "the principal employment of the inhabitants is agriculture." Brackenridge's description of Ste. Genevieve is the best eyewitness account of agricultural practices there:

> As the agriculture of St. Genevieve, is carried on more extensively, than in any of other villages, I shall take this opportunity of giving a description of it. One fence encloses the whole village field, and this is kept up at the common expense. The river side is left open, the steepness of the bank rendering any enclosure unnecessary. This field is divided into a number of small lots of an equal size; a certain number of arpents in front, and a certain number in depth. The more wealthy possess and cultivate several of these lots, while some of the poorer class do not own one entire. But nearly all the inhabitants have a share in them; they were ceded by the Spanish government, as an appendage to the possession of every residenter in the village. This mode has been practiced from the earliest settlements on both sides of Mississippi, and perhaps has it origins from necessary precaution against the Indians. Their agricultural labors commence in the month of April, when the inhabitants, with their slaves, are seen going and returning, each morning and evening, for eight or ten days, with their plows, carts, horses, &c. The ground is broken up with a kind of wheel plow, which enters deep into the soil. Corn, pumpkins, and spring wheat, compose the usual crop. It is now left entirely to nature, and no further attention is paid to it until harvest, when each villager, but without that mirth and jollity, which usually takes place on such occasions, in other countries, quietly hauls in his own crop.[93]

This description encompasses every essential element of French Creole agriculture in Upper Louisiana: the cadastral pattern, the open-field system of land usage, the agricultural calendar, the farm implements, the mixed (free and slave) labor supply, and the variety of crops. There is no such comprehensive description of eighteenth-century agriculture from east of the Mississippi, but Brackenridge's words would serve well to describe any one of the communities in the Illinois Country dealt with in this study.

In 1769 the Spanish lieutenant governor at St. Louis, Pedro Piernas, reported that Ste. Genevieve had "extensive fields and meadows suitable for all kinds of crops. The chief crop is wheat, which is yielded abundantly."[94] The lieutenant governor also mentioned that the habitants at St. Louis produced "much wheat." Piernas was probably correct in designating wheat as the principal crop in Spanish Illinois at that time. Although there are no harvest records from that year, it is likely that the habitants at Ste. Genevieve and St. Louis concentrated on wheat production, just as their kinsmen did in the villages on the east side of the Mississippi. Piernas's and de Leyba's comments came from an era when St. Louis and Ste. Genevieve were the only villages in Spanish Illinois. By the end of the eighteenth century, however, there were more than a dozen nuclei of settlement in Spanish Illinois, running from Cape Girardeau and New Madrid in the south to St. Louis and St. Charles in the north.

On the basis of his sojourn in Spanish Illinois during 1797–98, Finiels commented that the agriculture in all the settlements in Upper Louisiana was confined to the cultivation of wheat, maize, and tobacco.[95] Spanish censuses, and a scattering of other sources, permit us a number of generalizations about agriculture in Spanish Illinois during the late colonial period.[96] If Lieutenant Governor Piernas was correct in remarking that wheat was the chief crop in 1769, thirty years later it had been supplanted by maize—and not just marginally. Censuses for the last decade of the eighteenth century (to which I appeal without crediting these primitive statistical records with much accuracy) reveal that maize production was about double that of wheat. The 1800 census shows the aggregate maize harvest for Upper Louisiana was more than three times as large as the wheat.[97]

This relative increase in maize production over wheat production was likely promoted by a variety of factors. Over time the French Creoles in the Illinois Country had no doubt become impressed with the fact that maize did better than wheat on the soggy bottomlands along the rivers, where most arable agriculture was practiced during the eighteenth century. Father Louis Vivier had remarked back in 1752 that sown wheat returned only "five to eightfold," whereas maize "yield[ed] a thousandfold."[98] The changing demography in Upper Louisiana during the 1790s also likely augmented maize production. The newly founded settlements with large components of Anglo-Americans—New Madrid, Cape Girardeau, New Bourbon, Marais des Liards (now Bridgeton, Missouri), and the Meramec Valley—produced proportionally the most maize. The corn-and-hog culture of the American upland South was evidently beginning to influence Spanish Illinois before the end of the eighteenth century. More exclusively French Creole communities like St. Charles, St. Ferdinand, and Carondelet often continued to produce more wheat during the 1790s. To some degree, however, the French and French Creoles in the Mississippi Valley became accustomed to maize and were increasingly willing to consume it instead of wheat for their basic carbohydrate.

Maize in the Illinois Country was plentiful; it was also reputed to be an es-pecially excellent variety. In 1795 Governor Gayoso de Lemos of the Natchez District wrote to François Vallé in Ste. Genevieve, asking him to send "three minots of seed corn to Natchez so that we might have Illinois corn there."[99]

Much that has been said about maize production during the course of the eighteenth century may also be said of the third component in the maize-wheat-tobacco triad. Tobacco was cultivated early on at all of the Illinois Country communities, for the French—as well as their Indian allies and black slaves—were addicted to smoking tobacco in the clay pipes whose fragments are ubiquitous components at French colonial archaeological sites.[100] When British soldiers arrived in the Illinois Country in the mid-1760s, they were especially impressed by the quantity and quality of tobacco grown at Vin-cennes. In 1765 Colonel George Croghan remarked about the Vincennes re-gion that "the Country is level and clear and the Soil very rich producing Wheat and Tobacco. I think the latter preferable to that of Maryland or Vir-ginia."[101] The same year Captain Thomas Stirling remarked that Vincennes had the "most excellent soil and produces very good wheat and other grain, and the Tobacco that grows here is greatly esteem'd for its flavor by the French and sells much dearer than any other at N. Orleans."[102]

The first statistical compilation to list tobacco production in Upper Loui-siana was the 1787 Spanish census of St. Louis and Ste. Genevieve.[103] There-after until the end of the colonial regime, every Spanish census included data on tobacco. Settlements outside St. Louis that were heavily Anglo-American, such as Marais des Liards and those along the Meramec, produced substan-tial quantities of tobacco by 1800.[104] Americans, especially those upland southerners who migrated in numbers to colonial Spanish Illinois late in the eighteenth century, had voracious appetites for chewing tobacco as well as smoking it. It is difficult precisely to compare the tobacco crops with the grain crops, for grains were measured in minots, whereas tobacco was weighed in livres. Nonetheless, it is certain that tobacco never seriously competed with wheat or maize for primacy in arable agriculture in Upper Louisiana; it was always third in the basic triad of crops.

High hopes were evinced for commercial production of cotton, flax, hemp, maple sugar, and corn whiskey in Spanish Illinois during the late co-lonial period.[105] The 1800 census lists quantities of all these products.[106] In-deed, cotton production in Spanish Illinois for the last year of the eigh-teenth century, 39,143 pounds, was a favorable portent for Missouri agriculture, in which cotton now claims an important place. Nevertheless, none of these products ever outstripped tobacco—much less maize or wheat—in colonial times.

CREOLE GARDENS AND THEIR PRODUCTS

In the vast open, arable fields French Creoles in the Illinois Country raised cereal grains, some hemp and tobacco, and according to some sources, a few vegetables. Early in the eighteenth century, Diron d'Artaguiette reported that Sieur Melique raised not only wheat and maize but also "beans, peas, pumpkins and other vegetables" at his plantation outside Kaskaskia.[107] Late in the eighteenth century, Brackenridge reported from the west side of the Mississippi that in the Grand Champ at Ste. Genevieve, the local habitants raised pumpkins as well as wheat and maize.[108] In the mid-nineteenth century Reynolds commented that the old Creoles on the east of the Mississippi sometimes planted "strange looking Indian pumpkins" along with the corn. More rarely, according to Reynolds, "turnips were sown between the corn rows."[109] Peter Kalm reported from the St. Lawrence Valley in the mid-eighteenth century that French Canadians were very partial to pumpkins (*citrouilles*) and dedicated the "chief part" of their kitchen gardens to their production.[110] The descendants of these Canadians in the Illinois Country apparently shared this partiality to the extent that they moved production of pumpkins from kitchen gardens to arable fields.

Most vegetables for domestic consumption, however, were grown in the large kitchen gardens that were associated with every substantial residence in the various towns of the Illinois Country. As John Brinckerhoff Jackson has pointed out, the word *horticulture* derives from the Latin *hortus,* meaning "garden" or "enclosure."[111] Horticulture is the "science and art of growing fruits, vegetables, and flowers or ornamental plants,"[112] and most vegetable production in the Illinois Country was horticulture in the etymological sense of the word; that is, it was confined to the gardens that lay behind the dwelling houses in each village. The tradition of kitchen gardens was brought to the Mississippi Valley from French Canada, for according to Kalm, each farm between Quebec City and Montreal had a kitchen garden in which onions, pumpkins, carrots, beans, lettuce, cucumbers, and currants were raised for household consumption.[113] Reynolds, writing about old French customs on the east side of the Mississippi, acknowledged that "it must be awarded to the French, and particularly to the ladies, that they expended much labor and showed much taste in making nice gardens. They received not only much profit and comfort of living out of their gardens, but they also enjoyed the pleasure of rearing and seeing the beautiful plants and flowers growing in their gardens, which is so congenial to French taste."[114] Reynolds, himself an Irish American from Pennsylvania, frequently observed that French Creoles in Illinois sought comfort, pleasure, and aesthetic enjoyment to a greater extent than Americans, who were driven by ambition to pursue more strictly utilitarian goals.

Many observers noted that Creoles in the Illinois Country practiced an unusual and primitive style of agriculture in their open arable fields, but *all* observers commented on their skill as horticulturists. The results of this skill were abundant, luxurious, and aromatic gardens. When British troops arrived to garrison the Illinois Country following the French and Indian War, the expedition from Fort Pitt was led by Captain Thomas Stirling of the famous Black Watch Regiment (the forty-second regiment of foot). When Stirling first set eyes on "Kuskusquias" in 1765, he noted that "the vacant spots [are] made into Gardens and etc; which makes it look very well in the summer."[115] Later commentators—early Illinois governors and historians Thomas Ford, John Reynolds, and John F. Snyder; French military engineer Nicolas de Finiels; and American schoolboy Henry Brackenridge—were uniformly impressed by French gardening in the Illinois Country. Moreover, their observations came from diverse communities on both sides of the Mississippi. Ford remarked about the old French towns on the east side of the river that the "houses were generally placed in gardens, surrounded by fruit-trees of apples, pears, cherries, and peaches; and in the villages each enclosure for a house and garden occupied a whole block or square."[116] Reynolds, who was the closest American observer of Creole agriculture, claimed that "in horticulture, they excelled the Americans. The lettuce, peas, beans, beets, carrots, and similar vegetables were cultivated considerably in the French gardens. In this necessary branch of culture the pioneer Americans did not rival their French neighbors."[117] Snyder recalled from a boyhood trip the Kaskaskia of 1839 and observed that "the dwellings . . . were of the ancient French pattern, made of wood, one story and attic, . . . and all surrounded with porches, having around each ample, well-kept gardens with fruit trees, shrubbery, and profusion of flowers."[118] This description is remarkable in that it shows French patterns of life tenaciously persisting in southern Illinois, for the village landscape that Snyder observed at Kaskaskia in 1839 was that of a town that had been under American sovereignty for well over fifty years and that had already served as the capital of the Illinois Territory from 1809 to 1818 and of the state of Illinois in 1818.

From the other side of the Mississippi at Ste. Genevieve, Brackenridge rhapsodized about the garden of the Vital St. Gemme Bauvais residence, where he lived as a schoolboy: "It was, indeed, a garden—in which the greatest variety, and the finest vegetables were cultivated, intermingled with flowers and shrubs: on one side of it, there was a small orchard containing a variety of the choicest fruits."[119] Finiels observed that in colonial St. Louis "each resident must have a substantial garden in order to be able to lay in a supply of vegetables for the winter"[120] and that "they cultivate all varieties of vegetables and several European fruits—apples, pears, peaches, grapes, tart cherries, and currants."[121] Gardens constituted integral parts of the residential complexes in the colonial Illinois Country. They were deemed as important as any other part of the built environment surrounding the dwelling houses. When Jean-Baptiste Bauvais's residence was sold in April 1776 in Ste. Genevieve, it was described as having a "kitchen garden ['jardin potager'] already planted."[122] Any Creole family that purchased a residence in the spring of the year was sure to want its seasonal supply of vegetables already to have been sown; no garden, no home.

Early observers of Creole gardening in the Illinois Country never mentioned potatoes and tomatoes. John Reynolds even remarked that "potatoes were not raised to much advantage; not sufficient for the consumption of the people—I mean the French inhabitants of olden times."[123] Indeed, it seems apparent that potatoes were not cultivated in the Illinois Country during most of the colonial period. In 1770 the British merchant George Morgan ordered seed potatoes shipped to Kaskaskia from Pennsylvania; there were apparently none available in the immediate vicinity. In 1797 the French émigré Pierre Delassus de Luzières described experiments in raising "patates anglaises" (English potatoes) near Ste. Genevieve;[124] potatoes were evidently a new and experimental crop at that time. As for tomatoes, they remained virtually untouched by human lips during the eighteenth century, for they were usually deemed to be downright poisonous.

Flower cultivation falls under the general rubric of horticulture, and it composed an important component of gardening for the French Creoles in the Illinois Country. Brackenridge pointed out that "flowers and shrubs" were intermingled with the vegetables in the rear-lot garden of the Vital Bauvais residence in Ste. Genevieve. The tradition of flower growing persisted (indeed, still persists) in Ste. Genevieve after the colonial era. According to a newspaperman, in the early days of American commerce on the Mississippi, "flatboatmen drifting down the river by night could know when they were passing Ste. Genevieve by the perfume of the flowers wafted across the water."[125] Old French horticultural habits thus provided olfactory delight for American frontiersmen who otherwise would not have enjoyed such refined sensual experience.

CEREAL-GRAIN PRODUCTION

Cereal grains were the basis of the economy in the Illinois Country for much of the eighteenth century. For the early decades, our knowledge of wheat and maize production is based on only anecdotal evidence provided by occasional visitors; by midcentury extant sources contain some rough data, and by the end of the century there are, for the Spanish side of the Mississippi, numerous (although probably not very precise) statistical compilations. These sources provide a basis for determining overall rates of grain production; production ratios of wheat and maize; and the amount of grain and flour shipped to posts down the Mississippi, especially New Orleans. The last point addresses the issue of the extent to which the Illinois Country was engaged in a market economy that transcended the immediate locality.

The earliest commentators on agricultural productivity in the Illinois Country were content to remark about the fertility of the land, which was astonishing to men accustomed to the exhausted arable lands of metropolitan France and the rocky, lean soils of the St. Lawrence Valley. As early as 1711, André Pénicaut remarked that the Illinois region was "one of the finest in all Louisiana and one of the best for fertility of the soil."[126] In 1721 Lallemant noted that "the soil refuses nothing to the care of the plowman ['laboureur']."[127] Two years later Diron d'Artaguiette commented that the habitants in the Illinois Country raised a "fairly large quantity" of wheat, "which they sell for the subsistence of the troops."[128] Diron's comments reveal that as early as 1723 arable agriculture in the region had transcended mere subsistence farming and was supplying a regional market at Fort de Chartres. A much larger provincial market for Illinois agricultural products existed in Lower Louisiana, and soon convoys of bateaux and pirogues loaded with agricultural produce would be making their way down the Mississippi to New Orleans.

Outside observers often commented about the careless and slothful habits of Creole cultivators in the Illinois Country. John Jennings, a British merchant from Philadelphia, arrived at Kaskaskia in the spring of 1766 and observed that the soil there produced "very fine Crops of every thing that's sow'd on it, tho' the French are very bad Farmer's."[129] Two years later another English visitor at "Keskeskee" remarked that "here they plant Indian Corn in the Spring and never touches it 'til fall when they go fitch it home."[130] These English opinions did not merely represent Anglo prejudice against the French. Some thirty years after Jennings, a visitor from metropolitan France, François-Marie Perrin du Lac, remarked that the "habitants of Ste. Genevieve appear to be born without ambitions or desires" because subsistence agriculture was so easily practiced on the Grand Champ.[131] A half-century later Reynolds made much the same observation about Creole farmers on the east side of the Mississippi: "The early French immigrants were not good farmers. . . . The soil was exceedingly fertile and easily cultivated. A very small amount of labor raised much produce."[132] Henry Brackenridge claimed that once the land had been seeded at Ste. Genevieve, "it . . . [was] left entirely to nature, and no further attention [was] paid to it until harvest."[133] Both du Lac and Reynolds attributed the laziness of the Illinois Country cultivators to the ease with which they could extract subsistence from the rich soil of the Mississippi bottomlands; not being compelled to work hard, they chose not to work hard. Another metropolitan Frenchman, Nicolas de Finiels, also called these habitants slothful but thought that this sloth had been induced by another facet of the environment in the Illinois Country, "the uncertainty of the harvests, which generally makes the habitants hostile to unrequited labor."[134] It is noteworthy that all these commentators attributed the laziness of Creole farmers in Illinois to environmental causes, either rich soil or fickle weather; none of them accused the Creole cultivators of harboring inherently slothful natures.

Describing French agriculture from the Detroit region, Bela Hubbard commented that it was a "very imperfect culture," that the plowlands were "never manured," and that "high culture was little understood or regarded."[135] The high culture of which Hubbard spoke was the intensive agriculture pioneered by the Dutch and the English.[136] This meant systematic manuring of arable fields and regular rotation of crops that included nitrogen-fixing plants (e.g., legumes) such as clover and sweet peas. Indeed, as Hubbard correctly remarked, early French settlers in North America, whether in the St. Lawrence Valley or the Mississippi Valley, never practiced precisely this type of agriculture.[137] Henry Hamilton, the British officer who opposed George Rogers Clark at Vincennes during the American Revolution, with a supercilious English sneer, commented about Creole agricultural practices in the Wabash Valley near Vincennes: "They use no manure even for Tobacco, tho the quantity of filth about their houses would furnish great abundance."[138] Hubbard's observations about French agriculture in the Detroit region are perhaps more accurate than those of Hamilton about Vincennes, for at the latter site communal grazing on the stubble and fallow *did* provide a modicum of systematic manuring of the arable fields; indeed, that was one of the virtues of the old-fashioned common-field agriculture practiced throughout the Illinois Country.

John Jackson, although not remarking specifically on Creole agriculture in the Illinois Country, succinctly summarized the mind-set that underlay traditional open-field agriculture in general: "Farming was a strictly disciplined, highly conservative undertaking, and once a man was familiar with it he was not likely to be taken by surprise or be confronted by a problem which was new. . . . New crops, new tools, new methods were resisted, not simply out of conservatism but because they often threatened to disorganize the layout of the fields, alter the farming calendar, and in general raise havoc with a highly organized work system of interlocking, interdependent roles."[139]

Whether this absence of "high culture" in the Illinois Country led to serious soil depletion is debatable. The open arable fields of the Illinois Country did receive regular, if not exactly comprehensive, manuring through the practice of communal grazing on the stubblefields. Moreover, from time to time, the Mississippi overflowed its banks, sometimes destroying crops and even houses but also rejuvenating the soil, as the Nile did in Egypt. Cairo, Illinois, founded on the low-lying peninsula at the confluence of the Mississippi and Ohio Rivers, was named with a sound rationale, for the ancient and modern Cairos were both built on the alluvia of great rivers. Thomas Hutchins remarked in 1784 that "the slime which the annual floods of the river Mississippi leaves on the surface of the adjacent shores, may be compared with that of the Nile, which deposits a similar manure."[140] In the middle of the nineteenth century, Reynolds commented about the soil of the Mississippi bottomlands that "some of it has been cultivated for more than one hundred and fifty years, . . . and it yet yields excellent crops."[141]

In 1752 Major Jean-Jacques Macarty claimed that residents from the east side of the Mississippi were abandoning their lands there and moving to the new settlement at Ste. Genevieve on the west side of the river because "the fields on this side are worn out."[142] It is difficult to ascertain the accuracy of Macarty's claim. At the very least, however, it was probably hyperbole, an excuse for not sending more flour and grain downriver to New Orleans, as the governors general there always urgently desired. The same year, 1752, Father Vivier also wrote from Kaskaskia that "wheat, as a rule, yields only five to eightfold, but it must be observed that the lands are tilled in a very careless manner, and . . . have never been manured during the thirty years while they have been cultivated." But Vivier also acknowledged that "the soil is fertile" and that "this poor success in growing wheat is due still more to the heavy fogs and too sudden heats." The miracle of the Illinois Country for Vivier was "maize, . . . which grows marvelously; it yields more than a thousandfold."[143] A French promotional advertisement claimed that the first bushel of wheat sown at Kaskaskia in 1718 yielded a ninety-bushel harvest.[144] These were wild exaggerations engendered by enthusiasm and promotional energy, but seed-to-yield ratios in the Illinois Country were no doubt superior to those in Europe—and also to those in Canada, where the estimated overall ratio was only 1:5.8.[145]

Whatever the richness of the alluvial soils in the Illinois Country, harvests and the consequent flour production were exasperatingly inconsistent during the entire eighteenth century. Both wheat and maize harvests were adversely affected by floods, droughts, hailstorms, insects, diseases, rodents, and birds, but there was also human savagery with which to contend. In 1780 the remaining contingent of Virginians in Kaskaskia was commanded by Cap-

This promotional piece for Illinois wheat, printed in Paris, claims that in Illinois ninety bushels of spring wheat were harvested for every bushel they had planted. In France a usual seed-to-yield ratio for wheat was about one-to-five. Reproduced courtesy of the Bibliothèque Nationale de France.

tain John Rogers, and in November of that year six magistrates of Kaskaskia complained to Rogers that the Virginians had slaughtered their beasts of burden, which made it impossible for them to cultivate their lands.[146] The habitants of Cahokia sent a similar complaint to the U.S. Continental Congress four years later, complaining that they had not been properly paid for supplies they had furnished American troops and that, moreover, Indian incursions and flooding by the Mississippi had totally destroyed their grain crops.[147]

Toward the end of the colonial era in Upper Louisiana, Zénon Trudeau, Spanish lieutenant governor in St. Louis and a keen observer of life in Spanish Illinois, observed that the habitants of Ste. Genevieve and St. Louis claimed that they lost two out of three harvests to rampaging floodwaters from the Mississippi but that they nonetheless continued to sow their crops exclusively on the floodplain of the river, for "such is the power of custom."[148] Finiels, who lived in Upper Louisiana during Trudeau's tenure in office, observed much the same thing, remarking that a habitant in "this region of fickle and capricious climate can only rarely count on harvesting the fruits of his labors."[149] The tendency of farmers to exaggerate their plight is universal and eternal, but the evidence is incontrovertible that floods often played havoc with the crops and the lives of Ste. Genevieve's habitants. In 1778 de Leyba reported that constant rain during the harvest in Spanish Illinois had ruined one-half of the wheat crop,[150] and floods were more devastating than heavy rains. In 1785, 1794, and 1797 the rampaging Mississippi River destroyed virtually all the crops sown on the Grand Champ.[151] Anglo-Americans, who were beginning to immigrate in numbers to Spanish Illinois during the 1790s, were, according to Trudeau, "more experienced and prudent." These savvy and aggressive newcomers did not confine themselves to tilling the river bottoms but sowed grain on the uplands, "where they gain an abundant harvest of grain of a superior quality."[152] Trudeau's prose suggests that he was a bit frustrated with the conservative habits of his beloved Creole compatriots.

For the last decade of the colonial period, there is a good deal of evidence, both statistical and impressionistic, about the size of the grain harvest from Ste. Genevieve's Grand Champ. In June 1795 de Luzières wrote to Carondelet from New Bourbon and predicted a better harvest of wheat and maize than had been "seen in thirty years."[153] The prediction proved to be correct, for the recorded harvest of 1795 for Ste. Genevieve and New Bourbon totaled nearly 52,000 minots of wheat and maize.[154] The harvest of 1796 went even higher, jumping to nearly 60,000 minots of grain,[155] and that of 1800 rose to 64,000 minots.[156] These three years were remarkable in view of the fact that in 1787, which was also a satisfactory harvest year, approximately only 29,000 minots of wheat and maize were harvested by Ste. Genevieve's habitants.[157] The abundant harvests of 1795, 1796, and 1800 were probably due largely to favorable weather, although new acreage being sown on the uplands by recent immigrants perhaps also contributed to the healthy harvest figures.

Despite the newly broken plowlands on higher ground, however, Ste. Genevieve's Grand Champ remained the breadbasket of Spanish Illinois throughout the colonial period. This was apparent in 1797, when the Mississippi wiped out the grain crops on the alluvial bottomlands and the harvest from the upland fields could not prevent a genuine disaster from descending on the Ste. Genevieve and New Bourbon districts. The horror began on June 4, 1797, when the Mississippi stormed over its banks and swept across the Grand Champ. The habitants' pitiable efforts to stop the river's destructive progress were futile, and soon the young wheat and maize plants were entirely submerged. Delassus de Luzières reported from New Bourbon on June 12 that the surface of the "*plaine basse* was one vast sea" and that the wheat and maize crops were "totally" destroyed.[158] The same day François Vallé described the inhabitants of Ste. Genevieve scurrying to the outlying regions of the district in search of grain, for they knew that they were going to face famine during the coming winter.[159] Indeed, during the winter of 1797–98, numerous habitants of Ste. Genevieve and New Bourbon were reduced to slaughtering their livestock and taking grain given in charity by those few fortunate enough to have reserves. François Vallé described "the cruel distress caused by a lack of food,"[160] and Delassus de Luzières called the situation "truly disastrous."[161] The Spanish government at first sold foodstuffs at reduced prices and finally donated flour to the neediest families.[162] These government actions tided over the communities until the 1798 harvest, which was apparently a good one. Then in 1799 and 1800 there were bumper crops and the crisis of 1797–98 was soon forgotten. When the Grand Champ at Ste. Genevieve was generous, it could be extravagantly so, but if the Mississippi swept over it at the wrong time of year, Ste. Genevieve's economy was temporarily devastated and the townspeople were pushed to the brink of starvation.[163]

Table 4 is intended to place agricultural productivity from colonial Illinois into a rough comparative context. Data in this table are not precise or reliable, especial those from the eighteenth century; nevertheless, the figures are useful for providing a relative perspective on colonial agriculture in the Illinois Country.[164] Not surprisingly, by 1840 American agriculture in the Midwest was more efficient than French Creole agriculture had been in colonial times. This improvement doubtless had a variety of causes: more advanced technology, improved strains of livestock, better seed grain, and perhaps even systematic manuring of plowlands. The production figures from

Table 4. Cereal-Grain Production, Bushels per Capita

Ste. Genevieve County, Missouri, 1840	80
Ste. Genevieve and New Bourbon, 1796	57
Knox County, Indiana, 1840	79
Vincennes, 1767	49

Sources: For Ste. Genevieve and Knox Counties in 1840, Compendium of the Enumeration... from the Returns of the Sixth Census (Washington, D.C.: Thomas Allen, 1841); for Ste. Genevieve and New Bourbon, the 1767 Spanish census (SRM, 2:140–43); for Vincennes, the 1767 British census (NR, 469–70).

colonial times are certainly not contemptible, however, which suggests that during the eighteenth century the bottomland soils of the Mississippi and Wabash Rivers were not being seriously depleted by the open-field agriculture practiced on them.

ANIMAL HUSBANDRY

Bovine livestock—"bêtes à cornes," or horned beasts—were allegedly introduced to the Illinois Country from Canada by Jesuit missionaries at an early date.[165] Antoine de Lamothe Cadillac brought oxen from the St. Lawrence Valley to Detroit as early as 1704,[166] and cattle probably arrived in the Illinois Country not long after that. Reynolds recorded that "French cattle were emigrants from Canada, and were a small, hardy breed, with generally black horns. They stood the winter better, without grain, than the American cattle, gave less milk in the summer, and kicked more all the time."[167] André Pénicaut reported in 1711 that on the prairies near Kaskaskia, he saw "a great deal of livestock, such as bullocks, cows, etc.,"[168] and an estimate from 1721 placed one hundred cattle and fifty horses at Kaskaskia.[169] Swine, which soon became the most numerous domesticated animals in the Illinois Country, were probably brought in about the same time, and also from Canada. Of French horses in Illinois, Reynolds claimed that "they were generally small, but of pure Arabian stock, from Spain."[170] Unlike cattle and swine, horses in the Illinois Country probably arrived from the Spanish Southwest via Native American traders rather than from Canada. Pénicaut reported that the habitants at Kaskaskia bought horses from the "Cadodaquioux," that is, from the Caddo Indians, who inhabited the region where the states of Texas, Arkansas, and Oklahoma now come together.[171] Pénicaut's observation makes sense, for the Caddo tribe had long been in contact with Spaniards north of the Rio Grande River, and perhaps also with the French Arkansas Post. Thomas Hutchins observed in the mid-1760s that the French habitants at Vincennes had "a fine breed of horses (brought originally by the Indians from the Spanish settlements on the western side of the River Mississippi) and large flocks of Swine and Black Cattle."[172] The introductions of all three species of agricultural animals were momentous events in the history of the Illinois Country, for development of animal husbandry was fundamental to establishing an agricultural economy in the region.

Production of livestock—to use as draft animals, for dairy products, for domestic meat consumption, and for shipment of salted meat down the Mississippi—was a high priority with French Creoles in the Illinois Country. The first commandant at Fort de Chartres, Boisbriant, wrote from Kaskaskia in 1720 that "after the convoy arrives we will establish a farm ['métairie'] on the other side of the river [Mississippi] facing the settlement. We can raise more hogs there than we can use. That location, which is full of oak and walnut trees, is an ideal spot for raising these animals. Moreover, this entails no expenses and will place the settlement [i.e., the Illinois Country] in a position to supply hog bellies ['lard'] to the entire colony [Louisiana] within three years."[173] There is no evidence that Boisbriant's hog farm on the west bank of the Mississippi ever came into being, and agricultural exploitation of that side of the river would have to wait for another thirty years or so, until the founding of Ste. Geneviève circa 1750. Nonetheless, Boisbriant's letter reveals the ambitions that French colonial administrators had for developing extensive animal husbandry in the Illinois Country.

Writing from Kaskaskia in 1721, just one year after Boisbriant had sketched out his ideas about hog farming, Sieur Lallement reported only "about a hundred head of cattle and about fifty horses" at that community and went on to complain, "They would be able to have more cattle if they had more fields to cultivate."[174] This rather cryptic comment may suggest that the bottomlands were more heavily forested than usually thought and that fields had to be carved out of the woodlands; alternatively, it may mean that the extensive prairies surrounding Kaskaskia simply had not yet been broken by the plow. In any case, Lallement's estimate of cattle and horses was probably a bit low. Although census taking was a relatively new and crude device of European governments in the eighteenth century, the various censuses conducted between 1726 and 1752 provide us with the best data on the increase of livestock in the French Illinois Country. Table 5 gives aggregates for the entire region.[175] These figures, crude and imprecise though they are, reveal that the livestock population had increased tenfold between 1726 and 1752. During the same period, the nonslave human population did not quite triple, which suggests that the French Illinois Country was a more fecund environment for farm animals than for humans. Between 1732 and 1752 swine multiplied faster than any other animals. This may have been both because the

Table 5. Livestock in Illinois Country

	1726	1732	1752
Cattle	362		
Cows		431	714
Heifers			349
Bull calves			408
Horses	121	202	519
Mares			180
Oxen		407	777
Pigs		563	1682

Sources: Ser. G1, 464, ANC; HMLO, 426.

Illinois Country was fine country for raising pigs and because the local habitants purposefully set about increasing swine production, both for domestic consumption and for export of salted pork downriver; cured hams became a specialty of Illinois and were much prized in New Orleans.[176] Cattle flourished in the Illinois Country as well, however, and in 1768 an English observer remarked that the French habitants "have the great quantity of black cattle—the plains for miles are Covered with them."[177]

In the Illinois Country west of the Mississippi, reasonably good livestock statistics (given the time and place) are available for Spanish Upper Louisiana from 1796 and 1800. Swine, which were surely the most numerous domestic animals, were not enumerated in the censuses of those years. This was probably because swine ranged freely on the commons and in the woods and would have been virtually impossible for the census enumerator to tally. The censuses excluded the most outlying communities, such as New Madrid and Cape Girardeau, but included newer settlements, such as New Bourbon, Carondelet, and St. Charles. The 1796 census tallied 3,863 bovines and 618 horses; the 1800 census increased these figures to 8,918 bovines and 1,455 horses.[178] These figures from the end of the eighteenth century suggest, as do those from the early eighteenth century previously mentioned, that in the Illinois Country, whether from the east side of the Mississippi or the west, livestock multiplied faster than human beings. Father Louis Vivier remarked on the health of livestock in the Illinois Country, claiming that they "are not subject to any diseases; they live a long time, and, as a rule, die only of old age."[179]

Father Jean-Baptiste Mercier at Cahokia commented as early as 1735, "It is said that sheep would find fat pasturage here, to which I agree."[180] For reasons that are not entirely clear, however, sheep were never introduced to the Illinois Country during the French colonial regime. French mercantile policy probably discouraged cloth production in the colonies, and therefore there was no demand for raw wool to be spun and woven. Reynolds commented that the French Creoles of the Illinois Country were like "the lilies of the valley, they neither spun nor wove any of their clothing, but purchased it from the merchants."[181] The extensive listings of fabrics—limbourgs, beauforts, molletons, mazamets, and so forth—in estate inventories reveal that the habitants of the Illinois Country and their wives imported their cloth from Europe throughout the eighteenth century.[182] Perhaps this was simply a matter of habit and custom, or perhaps the laissez-passer, open-range system of raising livestock in the Illinois Country was not suitable for sheep, which require a good deal of care.[183] Finiels reported that sheep were finally introduced to the Spanish Illinois Country in 1797,[184] when he was a resident of St. Louis, but they did not multiply quickly enough ever to be enumerated on any census—French, British, or Spanish—during the colonial era on either side of the Mississippi.

Cattle, horses, and even swine were all left to graze pretty much at will, except in the arable fields from planting time to harvest. Owners branded their animals with their own distinctive marks and cropped their ears in different shapes so that livestock could be identified. All the Illinois Country communities except St. Genevieve had commons areas specifically designated for pasturing. Describing the practice at Kaskaskia in 1752, Vivier commented that "the working animals graze on a vast common around the village; others, in much larger numbers, which are intended for breeding, are shut up throughout the year on a peninsula over ten leagues in extent, formed by the Mississippi and the river of the Tamarouas [the Kaskaskia]."[185] The extensive St. Louis Commons, lying southwest of the town, was reckoned in 1859 to encompass about 4,000 acres,[186] and it was even larger in colonial times. In addition to using the pasturage provided by the commons, habitants at St. Louis made use of wastelands near the banks of the Mississippi and Missouri Rivers. Hogs often took to the woods and competed with the squirrels for the acorns that fell in the autumn. Mast not merely provided the hogs with subsistence; acorn-fattened pigs had been highly valued for their taste for centuries.[187] After the fall harvest was complete, the gates in the fences surrounding the arable compounds in Illinois Country communities were flung open and livestock were free to graze on the stubblefields. Even then, however, the animals were hard to control, for the fences surrounding the plowlands were generally not maintained between fall harvest and spring planting.

The nuisance of permitting livestock to have the run of the community promoted a certain change in the pattern of maintaining livestock during the early nineteenth century. Brackenridge described the way in which the "principal inhabitants" of Ste. Genevieve had begun to develop stock farms some distance outside town: "The greater part of the stock formerly seen about this place, has been removed to the country farms; in consequence of which, the passengers are enabled to go through the streets without danger of being jostled by horses, cows, hogs, and oxen, which formerly crowded them."[188] As the threat of Indian depredations declined in the Illinois Country, outlying stock farms became a viable option for livestock production.

Toward the end of the colonial era, Finiels remarked that a shortage of livestock had been "a persistent problem in the Illinois Country." He claimed that they were vulnerable to diseases and to the harsh climate of "burning heat" and "bitter cold." Moreover, Indian raids had done much to thwart the multiplication of animals, and the general shortage had adversely affected both subsistence and agriculture in the region. In brief, he found "this shortage of animals one reason for the continuing lethargy of the settlements in the Illinois Country."[189] It is difficult to assess the validity of Finiels's claims in this case. In other comments[190] he presented figures on the numbers of animals in Spanish Illinois that correspond roughly to extant census data and that suggest livestock production throughout the region was quite satisfactory—that, as in earlier times, domestic beasts were multiplying more rapidly than human beings. Finiels's impressions, as opposed to the relatively hard statistical data he presented, may have been distorted because he lived in the Illinois Country during a time when there had been a major crop failure (1797) and subsequent shortage of grain. Slaughtering in late autumn or early winter was traditional in French Canada in normal times[191] and probably in the Illinois Country as well; more slaughtering than usual was done in the autumn of 1797, both to provide food and to reduce demand on an inadequate fodder supply. In any case, the comparative figures in table 6 suggest that Finiels's point regarding shortages of livestock in the Illinois Country may have had some validity.[192] They also indicate that colonial Vincennes had a significantly larger number of animals per capita than did colonial Kaskaskia; the difference may simply reflect unreliable data, or it may reflect an agricultural economy at eighteenth-century Vincennes that was more pastoral than was Kaskaskia's. The previously adduced cereal-grain production figures suggest that the latter was likely the case.[193]

Boisbriant's prediction in 1720 that within three years the Illinois Country would be supplying the entire colony of Louisiana with hog bellies was a gross exaggeration. Nevertheless, salted beef and pork and cured hams continued as agricultural exports of the Illinois Country throughout the colonial era. Two hundred quintals of beef and 600–700 hams arrived in New Orleans from the Illinois Country in 1732.[194] A half-century later, in 1788, the

Table 6. Livestock per Capita

Kaskaskia, 1752	3.7
Randolph County, Illinois, 1840	7.0
Vincennes, 1767	5.8
Knox County, Indiana, 1840	5.9

Sources: For Ste. Genevieve and Knox Counties in 1840, *Compendium of the Enumeration . . . from the Returns of the Sixth Census* (Washington, D.C.: Thomas Allen, 1841); for Kaskaskia, the 1752 census (HMLO, 426); for Vincennes, the 1767 British census (*NR*, 469–70).

notorious John Dodge, a recent immigrant to Spanish Illinois from the American side of the Mississippi shipped a vast quantity of agricultural products to New Orleans; these included 10,000 pounds of bacon and hams,[195] Illinois products that were always highly prized in the colonial capital.

In addition to the salted and cured meats that went by bateau and pirogue from the Illinois Country villages to New Orleans, livestock on the hoof were sometimes dispatched to other French outposts in overland drives. In the spring of 1739, a large drive conveyed both horses and cattle from Fort de Chartres to Fort St. Francis in Arkansas, where a logistical outpost was being established for Governor Bienville's campaign against the Chickasaw Indians.[196] In 1746 there was a large cattle drive from the Kaskaskia to Detroit, where agriculture and animal husbandry were not practiced on the scale of the Illinois Country.[197] Records regarding the export of meat, either in barrels or on the hoof, from the Illinois Country are relatively scarce, however. Documentation regarding the downriver traffic in flour is much more plentiful, for it was (as grain is today) the largest item of commerce between the upper Mississippi Valley and the port of New Orleans. The flour trade down the valley is the topic of the following chapter.

CONCLUSION

The agriculture practiced in the Illinois Country by French Canadians, French immigrants, and their immediate descendants was sui generis. That is, the particular geography, soil, and other environmental conditions—including the threat of Indian attack—conspired to create an agricultural system that was unlike those that obtained either in France or French Canada. It was also radically different from the Anglo-American system that swept into the Mississippi Valley at the turn of the nineteenth century. Early in the eighteenth century, Illinois habitants planted substantially more wheat than maize, but as they became more accustomed to the latter crop and discovered how well suited the region was for it, they raised proportionately more maize. By 1800 the maize crop in Spanish Illinois was five times as large as the wheat crop.[198] In the St. Lawrence Valley, wheat and, to a lesser extent, barley and rye were consistently the principal crops, with only relatively small amounts of maize being raised.[199]

Although the communal, open-field system made agriculture in the Illinois Country more similar to that of France than to that of the St. Lawrence Valley, the absence of crop rotation and fallow in the Illinois Country distinguished this region from both France and French Canada. France's traditional rotation patterns are well known, chiefly through the seminal work of Marc Bloch, and French Canadians also rotated crops and left portions of the arable lie fallow each year, usually in a two-field system.[200] There is no evidence that the habitants of the Illinois Country ever rotated crops or left land to lie fallow for the purpose of preserving or rejuvenating its fertility. The rich alluvial soil, the relatively brief period of time that the region had been cultivated, the periodic flooding of the Mississippi, and the practice of vaine pâture all contrived to obviate the need for crop rotation and fallow in the Illinois Country. If the land was losing some of its fertility, as Major Macarty claimed, it was not losing enough of it to cause much consternation among the area's habitants.

Agriculture in the Illinois Country was also distinguished from that in northern France and the St. Lawrence Valley by the fact that little if any land in colonial Illinois was set aside for meadows to be mowed for winter fodder; there was little making of hay, which was a central feature of agriculture in French Canada. Henry Hamilton observed in 1779 about the French settlement at Vincennes that "very extensive meadows supply abundance of pasture Cattle in Summer, the hay is sweet and strong, and their Cattle could easyly be fodderd thro' the Winter, but the people are in general too lazy to make sufficient provision."[201] Hamilton considered the French lazy by definition, but his observation about the absence of haymaking at Vincennes was generally valid for the entire Illinois Country. There is fragmentary evidence that habitants at St. Ferdinand, just outside St. Louis, harvested some hay from the meadows in their commons.[202] In general, however, lands with the best soils were dedicated to arable fields, and the marginal lands (usually low lying and swampy) went to pasture, with little or none being allotted as meadowland for mowing. The relatively short and mild winters of the Illinois Country meant that livestock could forage for themselves without being provided with winter forage. Even though this may not have been the best animal husbandry, it was the easiest and most convenient way to handle cattle during the winter. Finiels described in some detail winter pasturing practices at St. Louis during the late 1790s: "Animals graze far from the vil-

lages—on the lowlands that border the Missouri, or the Grande Isle or the
Isle à Cabaret. . . . On these low, damp lands the cattle graze on horsetail
['presle'] that grows in the shady woods, and which is their *sole source of food
during the winter.*[203] In keeping with their reluctance to store supplies of
winter fodder for livestock, the habitants of the Illinois Country no doubt
did their slaughtering in the autumn, as had their medieval forebears,[204] when
the cattle were fattest and pasturage was getting thin.

Nuclear villages, open fields, and vaine pâture meant that Illinois Country habitants would have felt quite at home tilling the land near a traditional
agriculture village in medieval France, although they would have been bitterly disappointed with the desperately low seed-to-yield ratios from the
overworked fields in France.

Illinois . . . is located expressly to provide subsistence for New Orleans, where it can send grain and meat in all seasons, despite all the naval forces in the world.
—Comte Roland-Michel de La Galissonière, governor general of New France, 1747–49

6 Agricultural Commerce in the Mississippi Valley

The history of Upper Louisiana commerce has traditionally focused on the fur trade,[1] and with the exception of several pages in Nancy M. Miller Surrey's classic but outdated book,[2] no study has dealt with agricultural commerce emanating from the colonial Illinois Country. Indeed, a recent publication has discounted commerce between Upper and Lower Louisiana in colonial times, claiming that it was unpredictable before the last quarter of the eighteenth century and arguing that the Illinois Country was economically more attached to the Great Lakes region than to Lower Louisiana.[3] Source documents, both local and administrative, present a rather different picture. Agricultural commerce was eminently predictable well before the last quarter of the eighteenth century, and virtually as soon as New Orleans was founded in 1718, habitants of the Illinois Country understood that the new metropole of French Louisiana would be the focal point for their commerce in agricultural products. Although this is not principally an economic study, some analysis of the flour trade down the Mississippi during the eighteenth century is warranted.

At the beginning of his study of early commerce on the lower Mississippi River, Norman Walker made a remarkable observation: "Although the early French settlements were made altogether on the Mississippi or its chief tributaries, . . . the Mississippi was of no importance whatever as a commercial factor. The great valley which today clothes and feeds so large a proportion of the world, was actually not self-supporting."[4] Walker's principal point was that the earliest French settlements in Louisiana were not self-sustaining because they were not based on agriculture. This argument is valid only if Louisiana is viewed historically from the perspective of the Gulf Coast, which was Walker's native land. When he claimed that the Mississippi River was of no commercial importance, however, he revealed his ignorance of the colonial Illinois Country and its economic relationship with Lower Louisiana. In any case, during colonial times the lower part of the colony was most certainly not self-sufficient in foodstuffs.

Records from early Louisiana, well before New Orleans was founded, are replete with references to subsistence problems; there was never an adequate supply of flour for the basic life-sustaining element of French diets—wheat bread. Marcel Giraud remarked: "Wheat, more than other cereal, was the one that the population wished to introduce into Louisiana. This is evidence that the colonists broke away from the habits of the French countryside only with difficulty."[5] Flour was shipped from France to the French colonial communities on the Gulf Coast but often in inadequate amounts. French colonial officials at Mobile Bay were repeatedly reduced to begging for foodstuffs at the Spanish entrepôt of Veracruz in Mexico, despite the fact that the Spanish and the French were competing for colonial empires in the Caribbean and Gulf of Mexico.[6] During the years 1708–10 the French in the Gulf Coast region tried to raise their own wheat, some with seed grain sent from Illinois. They chose to sow it in an area bordering Lake Pontchartrain, at Bayou St. Jean, near where New Orleans would be established a decade later.[7] This agricultural experiment, for which there were high hopes, proved to be a dismal failure; the Gulf Coast region possessed neither the good soil nor a favorable climate for raising cereal grains. Although the wheat plants progressed well during their early development, the extreme summer heat and humidity induced a reddish brown fungus ("rust") that destroyed the grain before harvest time.[8] When in his *History of Louisiana* Le Page du Pratz discussed agricultural crops in eighteenth-century Louisiana, he did not even bother to mention wheat.[9] Nicolas de La Salle, a native Frenchman with long experience in North America, succinctly stated his views about wheat and its place in Louisiana toward the end of his tenure as commissaire at Fort Louis at Mobile in 1710: "As I know by my experience that it is impossible to live without it [wheat], . . . it would be wise to settle those persons interested in cultivating it on good lands along the banks of the Mississippi; for example, at Natchez, Tunica, the mouth of the Wabash River [i.e., Ohio], and at the Tamaroa."[10] Tamaroa meant Cahokia, and by Cahokia La Salle doubtless was referring to the Illinois Country as a whole. Nicolas de La Salle had accompanied Robert Cavelier de La Salle (apparently no relation)[11] and Henri Tonti on their epic trip down the Mississippi in 1682, and therefore he had at least some passing knowledge of the land and climate in the Illinois Country. The region was not yet prepared to export flour when La Salle wrote in 1710, but his vision for its future was prophetic.

Antoine de La Mothe Cadillac, who had founded the French outpost at Detroit in 1701, was appointed governor of Louisiana in 1713. When he arrived in the colony, he learned of the earlier experiments with wheat near Lake Pontchartrain, and he wrote pessimistically back to France that "wheat does not grow at all on this continent."[12] Cadillac's commissaire-ordonnateur in Louisiana, Jean-Baptiste Duclos, who disagreed with the governor about virtually everything, was not as pessimistic as Cadillac, and he expressed hope that the abundant wheat harvest in the Illinois Country in 1713 would provide relief for food shortages at Fort Louis at Mobile. Duclos claimed to have heard that the Illinois French had a gristmill and were preparing to ship a quantity of flour down the Mississippi to the French settlements on the Gulf Coast.[13] Cadillac was surely not thinking about the Illinois Country when he wrote categorically that wheat could not be produced in North America. Perhaps he changed his mind after his journey up the Mississippi to the Illinois Country in 1715, although his principal interest in the region was to reconnoiter the mineral resources on the west side of the Mississippi.[14]

By the early 1730s it had become axiomatic that Lower Louisiana was ill suited for cereal-grain production and that the mission of the Illinois Country within the province was to produce wheat. When Bienville was reappointed governor general of Louisiana in 1732, his official instructions from Louis XV stated categorically: "We cannot hope at all that this crop [wheat] will ever succeed [in Lower Louisiana]. But we also have this advantage that it succeeds well at the Illinois."[15] The king was correct—indeed, more correct than he knew. Bienville agreed with the royal analysis and offered a layman's explanation why the environs of New Orleans were ill suited for wheat production. "The fogs that are caused by the forests and the lakes of these quarters make it rust as soon as it is in the head, but the Illinois will furnish it in abundance in proportion to the number of inhabitants that are established there."[16]

Indeed, in 1731 the then governor general of Louisiana, Étienne Périer, and the commissaire-ordonnateur, Edmé-Gatien Salmon, drafted a document entitled "Mémoire sur le païs des Islinois." These men, both of whom wished to promote the development of French Louisiana and discover ways to harness the Illinois Country for this task, spelled out the relationships between agricultural produce from Illinois, commerce in French North America, and the economic welfare of Louisiana: "This country [Illinois], which by its fertility can supply grain, meat, and other foodstuffs to the colony, can be sustained only by commerce. . . . Transportation between this post and Canada is very difficult, whereas it is very easy with New Orleans via the river St. Louis [i.e., the Mississippi]."[17] These two French officials were the first to describe a commercial artery that today is responsible for carrying much of the cereal grain produced in the United States.

French colonial administrators long debated whether the Illinois Country should fall within the jurisdiction of Canada or Louisiana,[18] and the royal ordinance of 1717 that officially incorporated the Illinois Country into Louisiana did not end the debate.[19] In 1748 Jérôme Phélypeaux, comte de Maurepas, Louis XV's minister of marine and colonies, several times wrote to Governor General Vaudreuil in New Orleans questioning whether it might not be more workable to attach Illinois to Canada rather than to Louisiana. This reversal of what had been effected back in 1717 was never implemented, and soon the French and Indian War erupted and wreaked havoc with all French plans for North America. In any event, after Minister Maurepas had raised the issue of restructuring the administration of the French colonies, he concluded his discussion by observing "that whatever opinion one has on that issue, the habitants [of the Illinois Country] will always continue to market their flour in Louisiana. Indeed, we should seek ways to encourage them to increase their cultivation and their exports."[20]

Flour shipments from the Illinois Country to Lower Louisiana began as early as 1713, five years before the founding of New Orleans.[21] By the 1730s records of these shipments appeared regularly in administrative correspondence, although records regarding flour shipments were never maintained in a systematic or comprehensive manner.[22] In 1730 there was a bountiful harvest in the upper Mississippi Valley, and in the spring of 1731 bateaux from the Illinois Country carried more than a 100,000 livres of flour to New Orleans.[23] For that level of production, every variety of gristmill—water, wind, and horse (mostly horse)—in every Illinois community must have been spewing out flour.[24] The Illinois flour was a godsend in New Orleans, and it prompted Governor General Étienne Périer to wax enthusiastic about the importance of the Illinois Country. Assistance for the metropole was sure to be forthcoming from that region "every year," and it was very important that Illinois be defended with "troops and with good stone forts." The welcome flour from Illinois had spawned some fanciful thinking in Périer, for the Illinois Country was not destined to produce an agricultural surplus every year, and the stone version of Fort de Chartres was not built for another quarter-century.

For the time being, however, Périer's delusions were reinforced; the Illinois harvest in 1731 was even better than the previous year. The spring convoy of 1732, consisting rather oddly of "twenty-five to thirty pirogues or canoes," with no mention of the larger bateaux,[25] carried 200,000 livres of flour, as well as an assortment of the other delicacies that the Illinois Country often supplied to the lower colony: salted bacon and beef, cured hams, bear oil (always items that were much in demand in French Louisiana), and tallow.[26] Indeed, the Mississippi Valley was the only region in the French global empire that could supply these animal-based products in abundance.[27] The bounty of the region was spread far and wide in the spring of 1732, for other French outposts in the Mississippi Valley that were less productive than Illinois—such as Arkansas Post, the Tonicas, Natchez, and Pointe Coupée—were also resupplied by the descending convoy. Indeed, Minister of State Maurepas felt that Natchez had gotten *more* than its share of produce from upriver, and he was irate with the "exorbitant" demands of that post's commandant.[28]

Numerous flour contracts struck by Illinois entrepreneurs in New Orleans during the course of 1736 suggest that the 1735 wheat harvest had been bountiful. In January 1736 François La Croix, one of the principal habitants at Philippe Renaut's concession at St. Philippe, contracted in New Orleans to supply 2,715 livres of flour to the king's storehouse at Natchez,[29] which was still struggling to recover from the Natchez Indian revolt of 1729. The 1732 census[30] shows two La Croix households in St. Philippe, La Croix *père* and La Croix *fils*, both of whom owned agricultural land and barns. Although neither of them owned a gristmill, two other residents of St. Philippe did operate mills; Philippe Renaut himself and François Mercier. Renaut's concession at St. Philippe, which had been founded to serve as a logistical base for Renaut's lead-mining operations west of the Mississippi, had become, at least for the time being, a producer of flour for export from the region. The mines were being worked only sporadically, and the community at St. Philippe was producing an agricultural surplus. The same month Jean-Baptiste Crély signed an agreement to supply Gatien Brédit *dit* Touranjot, the royal gardener, with 1,000 livres of flour and two hams.[31] Crély was an up-and-coming Illinois habitant at this time. He and his wife appear on the 1732 census as a simple two-person family,[32] whereas by 1752 their household consisted of thirteen persons: husband and wife, two sons, one day laborer, six black slaves, and two Indian slaves.[33] Jean-Baptiste's family had done well in the twenty years between these two censuses, using hired and slave labor to work his six arpents of arable land and shipping agricultural produce downriver to New Orleans.

Five months after agreeing to supply flour to Natchez, La Croix contracted to supply Illinois agricultural products to both Arkansas Post and Natchez— 6,000 livres of flour to the former and 2,715 livres of flour and 215 livres of bacon to the latter.[34] The La Croix family of St. Philippe had evidently organized a small agribusiness consisting of both production and export capabilities. One member of the family oversaw agricultural production at St. Philippe, and the other worked up and down the Mississippi, striking contracts with government officials in New Orleans and delivering Illinois products at French colonial outposts that were not agriculturally self-sustaining. Natchez was a consistent consumer of foodstuffs from the Illinois Country. On June 1, 1736, two habitants of the Illinois Country, Joseph Huet *dit* Dulude and Thomas Chauvin, promised to deliver large amounts of flour there.[35] Dulude spent the summer of 1736 in New Orleans conducting business, for on August 14 he was partner in yet another contract in which he, Jean-Baptiste Guillon, and Louis Langlois agreed to furnish the royal storehouse with 70,000 livres of Illinois flour. Guillon of Kaskaskia had the lion's share of this commitment, agreeing to supply 50,000 livres.[36]

The spring convoy from Illinois arrived in New Orleans the evening of June 21, 1737, and Commissaire-ordonnateur Edmé-Gatien Salmon rushed to get a letter off to Paris via a royal ship that had already left New Orleans but was still waiting for the tide to cross the bar at the mouth of the Mississippi. His news for the royal minister was not good, however, meaning that the harvest in the Illinois Country in 1736 had been mediocre. The convoy carried only 40,000 livres of flour, less than one-fourth of that expected, and of this total 6,000 had been dropped off at Arkansas Post and 27,000 at Natchez.[37] Commanders of the convoys from Illinois were encouraged to supply flour to outlying posts on their way down the river, for it was much more efficient to deliver flour on the way downriver than, in case of emergency, to send foodstuffs upriver from New Orleans.[38] Furthermore, it was best to get the flour consumed before it spoiled, given that the flour shipped downriver from the Illinois Country was often not properly packed.[39] Flour was a necessity of life for all the French outposts in the Mississippi Valley; maize and rice might serve as stopgap substitutes, but they were clearly deemed inferior grains.[40]

After an auspicious beginning, Illinois crops in 1736 were attacked by a parasite, a "ground bug ['punaise de terre']" that totally devastated the maize fields and damaged the wheat plants as well.[41] This meant that Illinoisans had little flour to send downriver in the spring of 1737. After several years of scarcity, however, the harvest of 1737 was bounteous. The first convoy to descend the Mississippi in 1738 arrived in New Orleans toward the end of April and consisted of several "bateaux du Roy," as well as some "pirogues des particuliers." These vessels carried 100,000 livres of flour, which confirmed Governor Bienville's hopes that there had been an "abundant harvest in that region," that is, the Illinois Country.[42]

Linking local records to Louisiana administrative correspondence reveals some of the personal characteristics of the "particuliers" (private individuals) from Illinois who shipped flour to New Orleans in the spring of 1738. Charles Neau (sometimes Nault or Naud) was a well-to-do habitant of the village of Chartres, which lay outside the fort. In addition to owning his residence in the village, Neau had agricultural property that consisted of six running arpents of arable land, a team of oxen, nine pigs, four horses, and one of five gristmills listed at Chartres in the census of 1732.[43] In short, Charles Neau, with some 250 acres of arable land, a plowteam of oxen, horses, and a mill (probably a horse mill), was well equipped to participate in the Louisiana flour trade. Neau contracted with two other residents of Chartres, Louis Levasseur *dit* Despagne and Charles Eslie, to serve as hired labor on the commercial excursion to New Orleans and back.[44] Wages for each were 200 livres (the currency of New Orleans), in addition to which Levasseur and Eslie were entitled to transport commodities for themselves on the return trip. Levasseur would take back seventy pots (one pot equaled approximately two U.S. quarts) of brandy, and Eslie would carry fifty pots of brandy plus other European merchandise that he would purchase with his wages in New Orleans. There is no evidence of any mishap on this commercial river trip—no foundering of riverboats on Mississippi snags, no knife fights on the docks or in the brothels of New Orleans, no ambush by Chickasaws near Chickasaw Bluffs. Charles Neau and his two engagés all survived the four-month round-trip to New Orleans and lived to enjoy their fresh supply of French brandy during the Illinois winter of 1738–39.

Bienville's dispatch of April 26, 1738, which had announced the arrival of that spring's first convoy from Illinois, mentioned that two larger convoys were expected later that spring and summer. At least one of these did arrive in New Orleans, at the end of May, carrying 50,000–60,000 livres of flour.[45] Charles Legras, a merchant who lived in Kaskaskia with his wife, four children, and an Indian slave couple, had at least one bateau in this convoy.[46] On April 29, 1738, he engaged François La Boissière to accompany him back and forth to New Orleans.[47] Boissière's wages were a bit higher than his counterparts' from Chartres—257 livres compared to 200 livres—and he also had the right to bring back in Legras's boat merchandise purchased in New Orleans.

One wonders whether Legras's male Indian slave might not also have participated as a boatman on this commercial trip. The second convoy of 1738 was not so large as had been expected and moreover was apparently not followed by a third one, as had been predicted in April. Nonetheless, as Bienville and Commissaire-ordonnateur Salmon later wrote, "the 1737 harvest was abundant in the Illinois."[48] Salmon complained that 1738's harvest had been poor, however, for "wheat that had looked fine produced much straw and little grain."[49] Nevertheless, New Orleans did receive 300,000 livres of Illinois flour from the 1738 harvest, and there were high hopes for that of 1739.

In 1739 Bienville mounted a major military expedition against the Chickasaws, perennial enemies of the French, and more than 500 marines were dispatched from France to support this campaign.[50] Nearly 800,000 livres (7,646 quintaux) of flour were also sent from France, for Illinois was not producing enough to supply the demand at that time.[51] Salmon remarked that the flour received from Illinois could hardly satisfy the annual consumption by the troops in the colony, supposing that those recently sent from France would remain into 1740, which was a foregone conclusion. Indeed, even without the additional troops for the Chickasaw expedition, the royal garrison in New Orleans usually received 3,600 quintaux of flour annually from France.[52] A bitter winter in 1739–40 aggravated Bienville's problems, and ice floes on the Mississippi meant that no flour convoy left Illinois until the end of February.[53] The pressure was soon off, however, because for three years running—1739, 1740, and 1741—there were abundant harvests in Illinois, and flour came down the Mississippi by bateau and pirogue in quantities.

Harvests in the Illinois Country varied a great deal from year to year, not merely because of flood damage from the Mississippi, but also because of droughts, hailstorms, parasites, and so forth. Good harvests were gathered in 1736 and 1737 but were followed by a lean one in 1738; the next three years were good ones, but 1742, when persistent rains drenched the harvest, was a bad one. Pierre Messager, a trader and merchant from Kaskaskia, was in New Orleans in August 1742 and rented a black slave named Sans Quartier to return with him to Illinois and help to bring a convoy of flour downriver. A year later Messager had still not returned to New Orleans with Sans Quartier and the promised flour, and his creditor pursued the issue before the Superior Council.[54] Precisely when Pierre Messager did return to New Orleans, if ever, is unknown, but it seems apparent that the metropole received little or no flour from Illinois during 1743.

According to Le Page du Pratz, Illinois convoys carried a whopping 800,000 livres of flour downriver to Lower Louisiana in 1748.[55] This seems like an extraordinary amount, but there is some corroborating evidence for du Pratz's extravagant figures. Governor Vaudreuil reported from New Orleans on March 20, 1748, that the convoy from Illinois was expected imminently and that the 1747 harvest upriver had been bountiful.[56] Talk of a harvest of mythical proportions in the Illinois Country persisted for years in Louisiana, for in the mid-1760s Thomas Hutchins reported that "about the year 1746 there was a great scarcity of provisions at New Orleans, and the French settlements at the Illinois . . . sent thither upwards of eight-hundred thousand livres of flour."[57] These sources suggest that the 1747 harvest in the Illinois Country was one of the great harvests of the century. Once again, every gristmill in the region must have been churning out flour during the winter of 1747–48 to have produced that magnitude of surplus for export to the famished metropole of Louisiana.

Such largess from Illinois was rare, however. Records from the late 1740s are replete with data concerning shipments of flour *from France* to Louisiana; that is, the Illinois Country was often unable to supply the needs of the colonial capital at New Orleans. The usual French ports of lading for flour shipments to Louisiana were La Rochelle and Rochefort, and flour arrived both on government vessels such as the *Chameau* and *Union* and on privately owned vessels such as the *Triomphant, Duc d'Aiguillon,* and *Néréide*. In the spring of 1746 a fleet of bateaux (apparently not an official government convoy) from Illinois delivered almost 100,000 livres of flour to New Orleans, but the merchant ship *Triomphant* out of Rochefort arrived at about the same time with almost 270,000 livres.[58] Governor Vaudreuil remarked that these shipments were welcome because the province had been in a state of "indigence."[59] The same year, 1746, the *Néréide* and *Duc d'Aiguillon* were loaded in La Rochelle with over 252,000 livres of flour bound for Louisiana,[60] even though the Illinois commandant, Charles de Bertet, claimed that the harvest looked good for that year.[61] Agonizingly slow communications meant that flour destined for Louisiana was loaded in Rochefort while officials were in total ignorance of what the harvest in Illinois held in promise for that year.

After the royal flute ship *Chameau* arrived in New Orleans in the spring of 1747, a naval clerk, Louis le Bretton, went to the royal warehouse to investigate the unloaded cargo. He discovered one barrel ("un quart")[62] of flour "pierced by rats," which had eaten the entire contents, 203 livres of flour; a swarm of very fat rats must have scurried onto the docks at New Orleans when the *Chameau* tied up there in March 1747. This was not a calamity, however, for 499 barrels (totaling about 101,297 livres of flour) survived the ocean voyage from France without providing fodder for vermin.[63] In March 1749 the royal frigate *Union* arrived in Louisiana loaded with nearly 150,000 livres of flour, but only two months later Commissaire-ordonnateur Auberville complained of being very short of flour in New Orleans. This was particularly disturbing because the Illinois harvest was poor in 1748, following the abundant one of 1747. Auberville pleaded for a prompt flour shipment from France to supply not only the French troops but also the Indians at New Orleans and Mobile who had become dependent on French food supplies.[64]

The Illinois harvest of 1749 was a good one, although there is no evidence that flour from that harvest arrived in New Orleans until late in the summer of 1750; perhaps spring floods held up a downriver convoy. In any case, Governor Vaudreuil wrote to Versailles on September 24, 1750, that he was sending a convoy up the Mississippi to the Illinois Country that would consist of a small detachment of royal marines along with a group of "voyageurs et habitants" from Illinois who had arrived earlier in New Orleans with "a rather considerable quantity of flour."[65] The harvest of 1750 was a poor one, however, and in the spring of 1751 a convoy was dispatched upriver from New Orleans to supply flour to Natchez and Arkansas Post;[66] presumably there was at least enough flour in Illinois to sustain the residents there. In September 1752 Commissaire-ordonnateur Michel reported that "Illinois has furnished much flour; that is, more than the usual amount, and downriver outposts, including Natchitoches, have even been supplied with some of it."[67] The Illinois flour of Michel's report would have been from the harvest of 1751, which evidently was better than average, and the commissaire hoped that increased flour shipments from Illinois would make Louisiana less dependent on flour sent from France.

This was not to be, however, for while Michel was reporting the good harvest of 1751, Illinois commandant Jean-Jacques Macarty wrote that the wheat harvest in Illinois for 1752 would have been "very good if the rust ['la rouille'] had not got in part of the wheat,"[68] which he said meant that Detroit could expect few provisions from him that year. Virtually nothing is known about the flour trade from the Illinois Country to Detroit, but Macarty's comments suggest that it may have been substantial at certain times, despite the fact that Detroit itself was to some extent an agricultural community.[69] Although Detroit fell manifestly within Canadian jurisdiction, it was sometimes easier to supply it with flour from Upper Louisiana than from Montreal. The same was true for other outposts in Upper Canada, for the Miami Post on the St. Joseph River southeast of Lake Michigan and Ouiatanon on the upper Wabash River both received provisions from the Illinois Country, including pork, flour, lead, and tobacco.[70] Moreover, Macarty was expected to provide foodstuffs for military expeditions sent from the St. Lawrence Valley into the *pays d'en haut,* or Upper Canada. In 1753 he dispatched "provisions all kinds" up the Wabash River, although this convoy was frustrated in its attempts to rendezvous with the expedition from Canada.[71] Macarty suggested in 1752 that the harvest for that year was going to be poor, but the Illinois Country was clearly producing agricultural surpluses during the early 1750s. Indeed, the Jesuit father Louis Vivier reported in 1752 that Illinois produced three times as much food as it could consume, which doubtless was an exaggeration.[72]

On the eve of the French and Indian War, the governor general of New France, Roland-Michel, comte de La Galissonière, sent to Paris a well-known dispatch concerning the French strategic position in North America. Dispatch number 10, dated September 1748, argued that the Illinois Country was of virtually no economic value to France, that the region would continue to soak up crown resources, and that the settlers there could never become prosperous components of the French empire.[73] It was patently true that the royal government was not deriving any *direct* profits from the Illinois Country during the 1740s, and maintenance of the garrison at Fort de Chartres was a perennial expense. However, without the substantial flour shipments from Illinois during the 1730s and 1740s, the downriver outposts, including New Orleans, would have had difficulty surviving. Indeed, the hard-headed La Galisonnière concluded his strategic analysis of French North America by recommending that the crown retain the Illinois Country simply to protect the investment that it had already made there. Moreover, three years later La Galissonière drafted a memorandum in which he baldly stated that the Illinois Country "is located expressly to provide subsistence for New Orleans, where it can send grain and meat in all seasons, despite all the naval forces in the world."[74]

The French and Indian War (1754–63) brought turmoil and change, as the French were defeated on crucial battlefields and then prepared to dispossess themselves of their North American empire, with Spain acquiring sovereignty over the west side of the Mississippi and Great Britain obtaining the east side. Disruptions generated by these circumstances mean that data pertaining to agriculture and commerce from this era are sporadic at best. The last French census of the Illinois Country was that of 1752, and for the remainder of the French regime in the Illinois Country, there is little documentation concerning the size of cereal-grain harvests and the amounts of flour shipped downriver to New Orleans. Chickasaw and Cherokee Indians, provoked by their British allies, were threatening French outposts up and down the Mississippi River and interrupting the convoy system.[75] The French in Illinois were preoccupied with their own defense and were engaged in building the new stone version of Fort de Chartres. Furthermore, by late 1755 Fort Duquesne at the Forks of the Ohio had been cut off from Canada and required flour from Illinois to sustain its garrison.[76] The pattern of regular, if not always consistent, flour shipments from the Illinois Country to New Orleans that had characterized the 1730s and 1740s became sporadic during the 1750s and never recovered during the remainder of the French regime.

Administrative correspondence emanating from New Orleans during that decade reveals that Lower Louisiana was often in urgent need of flour and that Illinois was not able to supply it. Moreover, for each of the years 1751, 1755, and 1756, the naval ministry at Versailles earmarked over 9,000 quintaux of French flour for Louisiana, although it is not clear just how much of this ever arrived in New Orleans.[77] With Great Britain largely controlling the North Atlantic sea-lanes, however, these French supplies soon dried up.[78] In the spring of 1759, a Jewish merchant, David Dias Arias, sailed up the Mississippi to New Orleans flying a flag of truce on his British ship *Texel.* He wished to sell his cargo of flour in French Louisiana. Governor Kerlérec and Commissaire-ordonnateur Vincent-Pierre de Rochemore disagreed violently about the way to handle this delicate situation; after all, France and Great Britain were at war, and furthermore Jews were not welcome in the colony.[79] On the other hand, as Kerlérec cogently explained, Louisiana was in *dire* need of foodstuffs, and Arias was willing to sell his cargo of flour at a reasonable price. Kerlérec finally won out and wrote to the French minister that he was arranging to buy Arias's flour via a third party, a French merchant in New Orleans.[80]

As the French and Indian War was ending, the French command in New Orleans was at its wit's end trying to obtain foodstuffs from every quarter. In 1762 the commissaire-ordonnateur in New Orleans, Denis-Nicolas Foucault, dispatched a ship to the Spanish-Mexican port of Vera Cruz to seek flour, which he claimed the colony to lack.[81] By August 1761 France and Spain were wedded by the famous Pacte de Famille,[82] and the Spaniards did supply flour to alleviate food shortages in the metropole of Louisiana.[83] This was really just business as usual, for the French in Louisiana had been dispatching similar missions to Vera Cruz since the earliest years of their presence on the Gulf Coast. The last French governor of Louisiana, Charles-Philippe Aubry (who remained in New Orleans until the first Spanish officials arrived in early 1766), wrote to Versailles in August 1765, complaining, "For three years, the citizens and few troops here have subsisted only on English flour, and should we be deprived of this we would be forced to subsist on bread made of rice and maize."[84] Forced to live on a diet of rice and maize—a horrific thought for the poor French of New Orleans, whose refined palates did not seem to be willing to sacrifice much for the sake of *la patrie en danger.* English flour was preferable to no wheat flour at all.

English flour meant flour from Great Britain's American colonies. In June

1767 Foucault, the last French commissaire-ordonnateur of Louisiana,[85] ordered from the New York merchants Livingston, Randel, and Simpson 1,200 barrels of flour, 25 barrels of pork, and 25 barrels of salt beef for October delivery in New Orleans.[86] In his study of New Orleans's economy during the eighteenth century, John G. Clark observed that trade in flour and other foodstuffs was the basis for the first commercial connections between the Anglo-American colonies on the eastern seaboard and Louisiana;[87] as we saw in the case of David Arias and his ship *Texel,* these connections had begun before the end of the French and Indian War. In 1767 foodstuffs from the British colonies help to feed the French garrison that was still stationed in New Orleans, despite the fact that Louisiana had for some years been de jure a Spanish colony. Indeed, Clark claims that during the *entire* period of the Spanish regime, Englishmen and Americans supplied New Orleans with the major portion of its foodstuffs.[88]

A variety of circumstances caused New Orleans to become largely dependent on flour supplies from outside Louisiana, including faraway British New York. The 1767 British census for Kaskaskia, for example, indicates a poor wheat harvest that year,[89] while at the same time British garrisons throughout the Old Northwest were demanding the foodstuffs produced in the Illinois Country.[90] Nonetheless, the turbulence and dislocation that descended on the region during the 1760s were probably the most important factor in the diminution of flour shipments. There was little effective government on either side of the Mississippi; the French and French Creoles despised the newly arrived British troops; the Jesuit Order, which had been a stabilizing and civilizing influence in the Illinois Country for more than a half-century, was suppressed in 1763; and flocks of local habitants were either selling or abandoning their lands on the east side of the Mississippi to take up residence on the west side, where they found the prospect of Spanish rule more hospitable than British rule.[91] Major Robert Farmar, British commandant at Fort Cavendish (formerly Fort de Chartres), complained about the lack of flour in the Illinois Country and ascribed this lack both to congenital Creole indolence (a favorite British topic) and to demoralization induced by the bleak circumstances of 1766.[92]

During the last decade of the French regime in Louisiana, the Illinois Country was unable to sustain itself *and* provide an adequate supply of flour for New Orleans. This had been true to greater or lesser degree ever since the founding of Louisiana's metropole, although during the 1730s and 1740s the downriver flour trade had been regular and voluminous enough to raise expectations that Illinois might one day become Louisiana's breadbasket. This ultimately did occur, but French sovereignty over Louisiana had long since disappeared by the time that the Mississippi River had become the world's largest artery for the grain trade.

THE LATE COLONIAL ERA

After 1770 the flour trade on the east side of the Mississippi was dominated by Anglo-American merchants and not by the French Creole habitant-merchants who had traditionally controlled it. In the spring of 1775 Thomas Bentley and the trading partners Richard Winston and Patrick Kennedy, three Anglo-Americans who eventually deserted Britain and sided with the United States, were all shipping agricultural products from Illinois down the Mississippi;[93] apparently 1774 had been a good harvest year in the Illinois Country. These entrepreneurs were not themselves agriculturists, nor were they boatmen. Rather, they were the financial intermediaries of the 1770s, men who had the resources to purchase flour from local habitants and then buy slaves and hire voyageurs to crew the bateaux that carried the flour downriver. Two members of the large Charleville clan of Kaskaskia, François and Louis, commanded the small convoy that descended the Mississippi to New Orleans in May 1775.[94] Unfortunately, there is no information concerning the amount of Illinois flour that this convoy carried.

Shortly after the American Revolution, John Edgar, a former British officer turned American, arrived at Kaskaskia and set up shop as a merchant. He and his wife, Rachel, brought with them a considerable fortune with which to take up business, and he eventually bought Pagé's water mill near Kaskaskia (circa 1795) and produced his own flour for export.[95] At the outset, however, Edgar did as Bentley, Winston, and Kennedy had done before him: he had the financial wherewithal to purchase flour from local habitants and then hire local voyageurs to transport the Illinois produce to New Orleans. By the spring of 1786, Edgar had accumulated enough agricultural produce to send a substantial convoy downriver, and in Kaskaskia he hired numerous Creole boatmen[96] and also rented at least one slave to man his fleet of bateaux.[97] Edgar's agricultural export business prospered in Kaskaskia, and he built what was reputed to be the finest residence in the region.

In the late 1780s the Anglo-American entrepreneur and ruffian John Dodge sold out and left Kaskaskia, moving west across the Mississippi to Ste. Genevieve in Spanish Illinois. He took payment for his substantial east-bank properties in agricultural produce because there was a shortage of hard currency in the region. In September 1788 Dodge requested permission of Spanish authorities to ship down the Mississippi to New Orleans 110 casks of tobacco, 50,000 pounds of flour, 10,000 pounds of bacon and hams, and 5,000 pounds of butter and cheeses.[98] The lieutenant governor in St. Louis, Manuel Pérez, granted Dodge's request because Dodge was a powerful person who was "very useful and necessary to the region and who devoted himself with much application and intelligence to all kinds of agriculture."[99] An entire small convoy was required to transport Dodge's Illinois produce.

Virtually all habitants in the Illinois Country produced cereal grains on their arable lands, but only a small minority were actively engaged in commerce in agricultural products. The merchants who conducted the export-import trade of the Illinois Country constituted a kind of power elite in the region. They exported the raw materials of Upper Louisiana—peltries, lead, and agricultural products—and in New Orleans they exchanged these for long lists of things that were in demand in the villages of the Illinois Country: fancy beverages, such as coffee, tea, wine, and brandy; household goods that ran the gamut from pewter utensils to faience and silver tableware; fabrics of all kinds, such as woolens, linens, cottons, and silks; firearms and bar iron; and luxury products such as refined sugar, fine soap, Havana cigars, and even parasols and anchovies.[100] This import-export trade between the Illinois Country and New Orleans started with the founding of Louisiana's metropole in 1718 and lasted throughout the eighteenth century.

Some of the men who made up this power elite of small-time merchant capitalists have already appeared in this study. A partial listing from the east side of the Mississippi includes François La Croix, Charles Neau, and Jean-Baptiste Charleville in the 1730s; Charles Legras and Antoine Bienvenu in the 1740s; Thomas Bentley, Richard Winston, and Patrick Kennedy in the 1770s; John Edgar and John Dodge in the 1780s; and Jean Dumoulin, Nicolas Jarrot, Pierre Ménard, and William Morrison in the 1790s and beyond. From Ste. Genevieve on the west side of the river, beginning in the 1750s, there were several generations of Vallés; also coming from this town were Louis Bolduc, Jean-Baptiste Pratte, Jean-Baptiste Datchurut, Simon Hubardeau, Daniel Fagot, and Henri Carpentier, to name only some of them. From St. Louis, beginning with its founding in 1764, there were the town's founder, Pierre Laclède Liguest, and the brothers Chouteau. Then, after the Spaniards chose St. Louis as their capital of Upper Louisiana, merchants multiplied there rapidly: Antoine Bérard, Gabriel Cerré, Sylvestre Labbadie, Bernard Pratte, Charles Sanguinet, Jacques Clamorgan, Régis Loisel, Charles Gratiot, and Manuel Lisa.

SPANISH ILLINOIS

The earliest records of flour shipments from Spanish Illinois to New Orleans date from the early 1770s. Although the Spaniards had acquired Louisiana in

1762, they did not assume command of it until 1769. By the early 1770s Spanish administrative correspondence was flowing between San Luis and Santa Genoveva and Nueva Orleans, the Spanish names for the French-founded towns. Ste. Genevieve's economy was always more agricultural than that of St. Louis, and sufficient documents exist to provide a fairly clear picture of the colonial trade between it and New Orleans.[101] That is, these documents permit an examination of the commercial network—participating merchants, products being exchanged, calendar of the convoys, and even something about the factors and bankers in New Orleans who facilitated this trade at the lower end.

The Illinois Country experienced a bumper grain harvest in 1769, and in June and July 1770 numerous bateaux assembled at Ste. Genevieve in preparation for the trip down the Mississippi.[102] Bateaux from Spanish Illinois destined for New Orleans often assembled at Ste. Genevieve rather than at St. Louis. The former was not only further downriver but was the natural entrepôt for agricultural products and lead. St. Louis, to be sure, supplied peltries for the New Orleans trade, but they were the less bulky items of the downriver trade. Every bateau that was licensed in Ste. Genevieve during the summer of 1770 carried at least some flour. According to a tabulation compiled by Spanish officials in New Orleans, 60,050 pounds of flour were shipped from Ste. Genevieve to the metropole during the single month of July 1770.[103]

Daniel Fagot, merchant of Ste. Genevieve, owned one of the bateaux that departed during the summer of 1770.[104] Fagot's was the *San Daniel,* for Illinois merchants often named their river vessels after their own patron saints.[105] Fagot did not himself descend to New Orleans but put his skipper ("patron") Armagnac (no doubt an alias based on the man's native French province) in charge. Fagot's cargo consisted of 104 packets of peltries, four sheets of lead, and 13,600 pounds of flour. The *San Daniel* had a diverse crew consisting of fourteen men: six engagés—four whites, one free black, and one free mulatto—and eight black slaves. This was a large crew for the trip downriver, and one suspects that the month-long journey to New Orleans was in fact a bit of a junket, coasting with the current through the steamy summer days and herbaceous summer nights of the lower Mississippi Valley. Hell for the boatmen would begin, however, once Fagot's bateau was loaded with imported commodities and started back upriver against the current in late August or early September.

In late July 1770 a bateau belonging to Patrick Kennedy, who at that time worked for the Philadelphia trading house of Baynton, Wharton, and Morgan, also was licensed at Ste. Genevieve.[106] At this time (1770) Spanish authorities were permitting British traders to navigate freely on the Mississippi and to use New Orleans as port of deposit. Kennedy's bateau would carry not only Kennedy himself but also nine passengers (five white men, three black male slaves, and one female Indian slave), forty-three bundles of peltries, and 27,800 pounds of flour. The slaves were likely intended for the New Orleans market, for they do not seem to have been part of the crew. The crew consisted of one Carbonneau as skipper plus ten engagés (nine white men and one free black).

The harvest of 1770 was also bountiful, and the summer of 1771 saw a succession of flour-laden bateaux departing Ste. Genevieve. François Vallé, captain of the militia in Ste. Genevieve, was one of the first to request a license for departure that summer.[107] Vallé himself did not make the trip but rather turned his bateau over to his skipper, Pierre Picard. François Drouart embarked as a paying passenger, and the crew consisted of ten voyageurs or engagés who had hired on for the trip to New Orleans. Vallé was a large agricultural producer, and his bateau carried more flour than any of the others that descended the river during the summer of 1770: 44,240 pounds. Picard was also to drop off 1,000 pounds of biscuits, as well as a quantity of bacon, at Arkansas Post, which continued to function more as a trading outpost than an agricultural settlement and therefore, like New Orleans, depended on shipments of foodstuffs from the Illinois settlements.[108] Vallé's cargo was rounded out with twelve packets of peltries and 1,800 pounds of lead.

Two weeks after Vallé's boat departed, the Spanish commandant in Ste. Genevieve, Lieutenant Louis Dubreuil de Villars,[109] informed officials in New Orleans that a loaded "berge" was about to depart for the markets of the metropole;[110] berges were a smaller variety of bateau. Antoine Bérard, merchant of St. Louis, was the owner of this vessel, although his berge was apparently being loaded in Ste. Genevieve. The cargo consisted of 14,300 pounds of flour and three packets of peltries. Vien was the skipper and commanded a crew of only four engagés. A crew that small would scarcely have been able to pull a loaded berge upstream against the current of the Mississippi, which meant that additional crew members had to be added in New Orleans if Bérard intended to bring a load of imported commodities back to the Illinois Country.

In February 1772 Daniel Fagot loaded his *chaland* (yet another version of the bateau) at the docks near the Old Town of Ste. Genevieve.[111] The ice had just disappeared from the upper Mississippi, and Fagot was planning a swift ride downstream to New Orleans on a river that was fully charged but not flooding. He in fact made excellent time, for he checked in with Spanish officials at Pointe Coupée on March 14 and a day later at Manchac. In all likelihood Fagot's chaland made the entire trip from Ste. Genevieve to New Orleans in less than three weeks. At the docks there his cargo was unloaded: fifty sheets of lead, each weighing seventy pounds; thirty-one barrels of flour; and a variety of skins, including nine bundles of beaver pelts, four packets of untanned buckskins, eleven packets of tanned buckskins, fifteen doeskins, and eighty-five buffalo robes.[112] The flour was doubtless turned into bread and consumed in New Orleans, but the animal pelts and skins may well have been loaded on sailing vessels and sent to Europe.[113] Rather curiously, the bateaux descending the Mississippi from Ste. Genevieve during 1770, 1771, and 1772 seem not to have traveled in convoys but departed individually as soon as they were licensed.

The calendar of flour shipments from the Illinois Country to New Orleans remained the same as it had been before mid-eighteenth century, when the French settlements on the east side of the Mississippi provided all the region's flour for export. That is, flour that was shipped in any given year represented wheat that had been harvested during the previous calendar year. The 125,000 pounds of flour shipped downriver from Ste. Genevieve and St. Louis in 1772 came from the 1771 harvest;[114] the 246,700 pounds in 1773, from the 1772 harvest;[115] and the 112,600 pounds in 1774, from the 1773 harvest.[116] Unfortunately, there is no way to determine the total of flour shipments from the entire Illinois Country (both sides of the Mississippi) to New Orleans and other downriver outposts at any time between the 1760s and 1803. The lack of stable and effective government in first British and then American Illinois during that entire period precluded systematic tabulations; what few government officials were in residence did not maintain systematic records. Moreover, New Orleans and the Illinois Country east of the Mississippi were subject to different governments, which meant that there was no integrated administrative correspondence or coordinated record keeping.

During the Spanish regime in Louisiana, the Illinois Country continued to supply flour not only to New Orleans but also to outlying posts. In July 1783, for example, a merchant from Arkansas Post, Francisco Ménard, loaded his bateau at Ste. Genevieve with fifty barrels of flour, weighing somewhat more than 11,000 pounds, and sundry other items. His crew consisted of eight rowers (presumably white engagés) and a number of black slaves. Heading down the Mississippi after loading, Ménard's boat hit a hidden snag fifteen leagues downstream from Ste. Genevieve that ripped a plank from its bottom. Although the river was placid, the rush of water through the fractured hull shifted the boat's cargo, and a four-pound cannon mounted on one side of the vessel compounded the imbalance. As a result, the bateau quickly capsized, its entire cargo was lost, four slaves and one engagé drowned, and

Ménard himself barely escaped with his life. With this loss of the flour intended for the garrison at Arkansas Post, the small contingent of Spanish
soldiers there was probably placed on reduced rations.[117]

During the 1790s Spanish Illinois continued to export flour down the
Mississippi, but the tabulated data for the last decade of the eighteenth century suggest a declining commerce. In 1796 Ste. Genevieve and St. Louis
shipped to New Orleans, from the 1795 harvest, 56,000 pounds of flour;[118] in
1800, from the 1799 harvest, they sent only 12,400 pounds.[119] Given that both
the 1795 and 1799 harvests in the Illinois Country were decent, the quantities of flour shipped downriver in 1796 and 1800 were remarkably small,
significantly smaller than those of the 1770s or the 1740s, for example. Finiels,
who lived in St. Louis in 1797–98, claimed that Upper Louisiana was engaged
merely in subsistence agriculture and that there was no surplus of grain to
export.[120] Although Finiels was not an entirely reliable observer on economic
issues, his basic point was accurate enough: the era when the Illinois Country served as the principal granary for New Orleans and other parts of Lower
Louisiana, which had lasted for more than seventy-five years, had apparently
ended by the mid-1790s. What had happened?

In November 1795 the Spanish lieutenant governor in St. Louis, Zénon
Trudeau, wrote to Governor General Carondelet in New Orleans:

> The harvest of our settlement ["poblacion"] is such that it could produce
> at least 1,000 barrels [approximately 200,000 pounds] of flour. But no one
> invests in it due to the fact that there are not sufficient mills that can make it
> of good quality, and due to the exorbitant price of barrels, of boats, and of
> rowers, which make its cost so much that the Capitol [New Orleans] would
> not pay it. This comes about because of our small population, which occu-
> pies itself with the fur trade.[121]

Trudeau's last sentence suggests that he was referring specifically to the
settlement at St. Louis, for Ste. Genevieve remained heavily agricultural in
its economic orientation and was only tangentially involved in the fur trade.
In any case, Trudeau basically was observing that the old Creole communities in the Illinois Country were no longer producing flour for New Orleans
at competitive prices. As the lieutenant governor himself acknowledged,
however, this was not because wheat production had fallen off in Spanish
Illinois; rather, it was because the infrastructure was inadequate for milling
the grain and shipping the flour downriver. Such an infrastructure would
have required numerous gristmills, a plentiful supply of riverboats, *and* the
entrepreneurial will and capacity to invest in and manage milling and shipping operations. Trudeau was obliquely alluding to a veritable commercial

revolution that had occurred in the heartland of North America in the decade following the American Revolution. This revolution was the opening of the fecund Ohio Valley to settlement, to agriculture, and to the commercial network of the greater Mississippi Valley, with its thriving entrepôt at New Orleans. The revolution was fueled by the energy of American frontiersmen, who, according to Finiels, "grasped the advantages that they might derive from the natural indolence of the native habitants, and their industry has already opened avenues of business that indolence precluded."[122]

After France reacquired Louisiana by the Treaty of San Ildefonso in 1800, President Thomas Jefferson wrote to the American minister in Paris, Robert R. Livingston, about the importance to the United States of New Orleans and western river commerce: "There is on the globe one single spot, the possessor of which is our natural and habitual enemy. It is New Orleans, through which the produce of three-eighths of our territory must pass to market, and from its [the Ohio Valley's] fertility it will ere long yield more than half of our whole produce, and contain more than half of our inhabitants."[123] Jefferson, who possessed the broadest strategic vision of early American geopolitical thinkers, was especially succinct and penetrating in this observation. Thirty years before Jefferson expressed these thoughts, however, the British army officer, cartographer, and geographer Thomas Hutchins had foreseen all the possibilities of the Ohio-Mississippi commercial link and discussed it with an understated elegance:

> It may not, perhaps, be amiss, to observe, that large quantities of Flour are made in the distant (western) Counties of Pennsylvania, and sent by an expensive Land Carriage to the City of Philadelphia, and from thence shipped to South Carolina, and to East and West Florida. . . . The River Ohio seems kindly designed by nature, as the Channel through which the two Floridas may be supplied with Flour, not only for their own Consumption, but also for the carrying on an extensive Commerce with Jamaica and the Spanish Settlements in the Bay of Mexico. Millstones in abundance are to be obtained in the Hills near the Ohio, and the country is every where well watered with large, and constant Springs and Streams, for Grist, and other Mills.[124]

Hutchins made these observations before Anglo-American settlement had begun in earnest in the Ohio Valley. After the American Revolution, when floods of settlers crossed the Allegheny Mountains and descended into the Ohio Valley via the Allegheny, Monongahela, and Great Kanawha Rivers, Hutchins's remarks were a fortiori true. George Washington's plan to link the headwaters of the Potomac and Ohio Rivers by a canal were chimerical compared to Hutchins's farsighted commercial vision. "Continued extension was ingrained in the nature of the Anglo-American frontier, and the finger of destiny seemed to point down the Mississippi Valley."[125] Thus in 1927 wrote the great historian of the Spanish-American frontier Arthur Preston Whitaker, with a vestige of the nineteenth-century American concept of Manifest Destiny.

During the late 1780s and early 1790s, the flow of American agricultural products down the Ohio-Mississippi waterways to New Orleans was limited and halting. At that time settlers had not yet put to the plow all the rich lands of the Ohio Valley, and furthermore, there was chronic bickering between the United States and Spain over the use of the Mississippi River and the right of deposit on the docks in New Orleans. At this early time in the American history of the Ohio Valley, it was not even entirely clear what major products the region was going to develop for export. Tobacco, for example, loomed large among early exports from the region,[126] and Cincinnati (founded in 1788) had not yet become hog butcher to the world, a role that it would play for decades before Chicago began to compete for the honor in mid-nineteenth century. Illinois continued to participate in this agricultural and commercial network. The Spanish official Gayoso de Lemos reported in 1795, "It is true that much wheat could be obtained from Kaskaskia, . . . and if they are paid regularly for their wheat, they will dedicate themselves to cultivating it."[127] At about this time, John Edgar's gristmill near Kaskaskia opened for commercial operation,[128] and soon it developed a reputation for producing "great quantities of flour for the New Orleans market which would compare well with the Atlantic flour."[129]

The Spanish governor in New Orleans, Francisco Hector Carondelet, was personally not averse to letting Americans navigate on the Mississippi and use the docking facilities in New Orleans. He reduced from 15 to 6 percent the duty on imports from the American West, and in a single year (1792) Kentuckians brought 14,000 barrels of flour down the rivers in their flatboats to New Orleans.[130] Once Pinckney's Treaty of 1795 gave Americans complete freedom of navigation on the Mississippi and duty-free right of deposit in New Orleans, shipments of agricultural produce from the upper Mississippi Valley and the Ohio Valley leaped upward. According to Norman Walker, who in the 1880s was commissioned to study the subject for the U.S. Congress, New Orleans *exported* $500,000 worth of agricultural products (mostly flour and tobacco) in the twelve months following Pinckney's Treaty.[131] These exports from New Orleans did not include the agricultural products that were consumed by the growing city itself. If Walker's figure is even remotely accurate, and probably it is little better than that, we see that an astonishing agricultural and commercial revolution had occurred in the greater Mississippi Valley in a short period of time. In the late 1760s New Orleans had been obliged to import foodstuffs from as far away as New York City. A quarter-century later New Orleans was itself a major exporter of agricultural products. No wonder that James Madison wrote, characterizing the American westerners, that "the Mississippi River to them is everything—it is the Hudson, the Delaware, the Potomac, and all the navigable waters of the Atlantic States formed into one stream."[132]

In studying the internal commerce of the United States, Walker assembled some interesting comparative data concerning shipments of agricultural products into New Orleans via the Mississippi River during the years 1801 and 1802. His conclusions were that the value of produce from the Ohio Valley outstripped the value of that from Upper Louisiana by nearly twenty to one during that period.[133] For Walker, Upper Louisiana in 1801–2 was of course *Spanish* Upper Louisiana, and the products from the Ohio Valley encompassed not only those from Kentucky, Tennessee, and western Pennsylvania but also those from the entire Northwest Territory, including the Illinois Country on the east side of the Mississippi. John Reynolds tellingly remarked: "In the first year or two of the present century [the nineteenth], several flat boats, laded with flour, sailed from Kaskaskia to New Orleans, while that city was in the hands of the Spanish government. The flour was made of Illinois wheat, . . . and was manufactured in the mill of General [John] Edgar a few miles northeast of Kaskaskia."[134] In 1807 the perceptive traveler from New York State Christian Schultz Jr. described the American Bottom[135] as a "prairie of such extent as to weary the eye in tracing its boundaries. On this tract there are some very considerable settlements, which raise large droves of cattle, and annually send off great quantities of corn, pork, and other produce, to New Orleans."[136]

Thomas S. Berry studied the early nineteenth-century New Orleans market to establish broad trends for the prices of diverse agricultural products in the pre–Civil War era. Berry lamented the absence of hard data for studying the late eighteenth and early nineteenth centuries: "It is unfortunate that no figures are available with which to measure the effects of the Treaty of Greenville, the Land Acts of 1796 and 1800, and the Louisiana Purchase upon western production."[137] He went on to comment that 1801 and 1802 were boom years for western agricultural production, thus confirming Walker's earlier assessment of those years (although Berry's conclusions may have been based on Walker's figures), and then remarked that incomplete figures indicate that New Orleans received 133,403 barrels of flour during that period, "much of which undoubtedly came from the upper Ohio Valley."[138] In 1808 Schultz visited a fleet of flatboats near New Madrid, Missouri Territory, that was almost as large as that of "Agamemnon before Troy." Schultz remarked on the diverse cargoes of these riverboats and their far-flung places of provenience: "The first two were loaded with tobacco from Green River; four with flower [*sic*] and whiskey from Cincinnati; . . . two with cotton and tobacco from Cumberland [i.e., Tennessee]; and two with lime in bulk from Virginia [now West Virginia]."[139] The research of Walker and Berry, together with impressionistic accounts such as Schultz's, demonstrates that even before the arrival of the first steamboat on the waters of the upper Mississippi in 1817, the old Illinois Country had been supplanted by the Ohio Valley as the principal supplier of agricultural produce to New Orleans. A commercial connection that had been of primary importance for three-quarters of a century became secondary as Anglo-American farms and river ports proliferated along the length of the Ohio Valley.[140]

Finiels attributed the commercial success of the Americans in the Mississippi Valley to their energy and entrepreneurial acumen, but surely the surge in agricultural productivity of the Ohio Valley at the turn of the nineteenth century depended more on demographic changes than on national character. Kentucky became a state in 1792, Tennessee did so in 1796, and Ohio acquired statehood in 1803, which means that by the time of the Louisiana Purchase, the population of the Ohio Valley far outstripped that of the old Illinois Country. It was that demographic revolution that transformed New Orleans almost overnight into a major entrepôt for agricultural products, obtaining them from upriver and exporting them on the sailing vessels that arrived from the Gulf.

FLOUR PRICES

Because French colonists in Louisiana deemed flour to be essential for human existence, the availability and price of flour were literally vital concerns to government officials in Louisiana, as they were also to royal officials in France.[141] Wholesale prices of flour in colonial Louisiana were almost always expressed in terms of flour's value per quintal or per quart. The French quintal, or one hundred livres, was equal to approximately 108 English pounds. The quart was a barrel designed so that two persons could handle it when it was full of flour. For most of the eighteenth century a quart was supposed to contain 180 French pounds (approximately 195 English pounds) of flour, but the amount varied considerably. Often quarts of flour weighed more than 200 pounds.[142] It is easiest, and perhaps accurate enough, to think of a quart as containing roughly two quintaux.

In the early days of French Louisiana, before the founding of New Orleans, flour was scarce and rather expensive, selling at Mobile for eighty livres per barrel. The Royal Indies Company fixed the price in 1719 at fifteen livres per hundredweight, or approximately thirty livres per barrel.[143] The company wished to stimulate development in the colony by holding prices down. It apparently succeeded to some degree; nevertheless, by 1731, when the company returned the colony to royal control, flour was selling at twenty-five livres per quintal, or about fifty livres per barrel.[144]

During the 1730s flour in Louisiana varied from as low as eleven livres per quintal in 1732 to as high as forty livres per quintal in 1737,[145] averaging somewhere in the neighborhood of twenty-five livres. In 1739 the royal intendant at Rochefort bought the flour that was sent to Louisiana for Bienville's Chickasaw campaign at seventeen livres and ten sols per quintal, to which would have to be added approximately five livres per quintal for shipping it to New Orleans.[146] During the 1740s the price of flour in the New Orleans market shot up because of the disruption in commerce provoked by King George's War. In 1740 flour in Louisiana's metropole was already bringing seventy livres per barrel (approximately thirty-five per quintal),[147] and by 1744 it had skyrocketed to 365 livres the barrel.[148] After this war prices settled back down, so that by 1752 flour had once again reached the more or less normal value of twenty livres per quintal.[149] Then, with the arrival of new and larger warfare in the form of the French and Indian War, prices again took off, climbing from forty livres per barrel in 1752, to 280 livres in 1757,[150] to an astronomic 600 livres for a short while in 1762.[151] Shortages of foodstuffs that such prices represent make it no wonder that the provincial authorities in New Orleans came to terms with David Dias Arias and bought his shipment of flour in 1759, even though Arias's ship was English.

Prices fell precipitously after the war ended in 1763, and by 1764 flour was back at forty-five livres per barrel.[152] When in 1766 the Philadelphia trading company of Baynton, Wharton, and Morgan was preparing to supply foodstuffs to the British garrison in Illinois, the partners were optimistic that the "vast Crops in the Neighborhood of Fort Chartres" meant that flour could be bought in that region for less than one dollar (five livres) per hundredweight.[153] Revealing the usual Anglo ignorance of the Illinois Country, they were badly mistaken. Two years later, when George Morgan was himself in Kaskaskia, he wrote back to his business partners in Philadelphia that "as to Flour[,] it is impossible to buy it without Negroes, Bills of Exchange or hard Dollars even at the monstrous price of 37/6 PCt [i.e., thirty-seven shillings and six pence per hundredweight]."[154] Apparently the Creole inhabitants of the Illinois Country did not want much truck with their British visitors, and Morgan finished his discussion by recommending that flour be sent to Illinois from Fort Pitt, at the head of the Ohio River. Indeed, the high hopes that

Baynton, Wharton, and Morgan had entertained for making large profits in western trade never materialized, and the company lost a bundle of money in the Illinois markets. When Morgan was about to depart Philadelphia for the Mississippi Valley in 1770, John Baynton summed up their company's view of the region at that time: "Mr. Morgan setts off to Day or to Morrow for that shocking Country the Illinois—My Familys Distress on this grevious Occasion beggars Description."[155]

In 1769 Father Pierre Gibault, a missionary priest who had arrived in the Illinois Country from Canada a year earlier, claimed that flour prices in the region were fixed at twenty-five livres per hundredweight, which was a more normal figure.[156] At Ste. Genevieve, on the west side of the Mississippi in Spanish Illinois, flour sold for fifteen livres per quintal in 1777, twenty livres in 1779, and thirty livres in 1782.[157] Although showing some inflation over this five-year period, flour prices at Ste. Genevieve during the late 1770s and early 1780s were about normal for Louisiana at any time during the eighteenth century when international warfare had not driven them through the roof. The relatively high price of flour in 1782, when merchants from Ste. Genevieve were supplying St. Louis with foodstuffs, was probably due to inflation generated by the American Revolution.

In the mid-1790s the habitants in Ste. Genevieve and St. Louis in effect pleaded for government price supports for flour; they asked Governor Carondelet to order all Spanish outposts on the lower Mississippi to accept good quality flour from Spanish Illinois at 22½ livres per quintal, or forty-five livres per barrel.[158] How Carondelet handled this plea is not known, but it may well have been prompted by increasing competition presented by American wheat and flour producers in the Ohio River valley, who, as I have already mentioned, were already shipping substantial amounts of flour to New Orleans by the early 1790s. Forty-five livres per barrel translated into about nine American dollars per barrel, because the U.S. dollar was pegged at a value equivalent to the Spanish piastre, which itself was worth five livres.

There is no evidence that the Spanish colonial government ever established price supports for flour. Spanish authorities in New Orleans could ill afford to do so when the local price of flour in the Ohio Valley was sometimes as low as five dollars per barrel and never higher than twelve.[159] Indeed, even before Pinckney's Treaty gave Americans unfettered access to New Orleans via the Ohio and Mississippi Rivers, Governor Carondelet had been favorably disposed to let Americans navigate on the Mississippi River and use the port of New Orleans.[160] An obvious reason for Carondelet's commercial liberalism was that Lower Louisiana stood to benefit by buying cheap flour from the Ohio River, even though that may not have squared with mercan-

tilist economic policies promulgated by the Spanish royal government in
Madrid. The Creole habitants of the Illinois Country were being undercut
in their traditional market, New Orleans, which for three-quarters of a century had been willing to purchase every livre of flour that could be sent
downriver—and more. The price of flour remained low in the Mississippi
Valley until finally driven up by inflationary pressures generated by the War
of 1812.[161]

Such a system [open-field agriculture] depended upon tremendous
social cohesion in a society whose deepest impulses were directed
toward the community.
—Marc Bloch

CONCLUSION: CHANGING TIMES, CHANGING MENTALITÉS

THE DEMISE OF THE OPEN-FIELD SYSTEM

The pattern of land usage, settlement, and agriculture that developed in the Illinois Country during the eighteenth century was unique in
North America. From the original settlements on the east side of the Mississippi—Cahokia, Kaskaskia, and Chartres—this system spread to the newer
communities on the west side of the river, such as Ste. Genevieve, St. Louis,
Carondelet, and Florissant. By the end of the eighteenth century it had become
ubiquitous on both the Spanish and American sides of the Mississippi from
St. Louis in the north to Kaskaskia in the south. Furthermore, the same system was fully developed at Vincennes on the Wabash and existed in attenuated
form further up the Mississippi Valley at Prairie du Chien, near the mouth of
the Wisconsin River. The inhabitants of these communities shared not only
their way of settling and exploiting the land but also their language and their
ethnicity; they were all francophone, and they were virtually all of French,
French Canadian, French Indian, or French Creole extraction. The origins of
communal management of agricultural land in the Illinois Country may be

seen in scattered early source documents from the region. These records demonstrate that the laws promulgated by the commandant at Fort de Chartres,
and in at least one instance by the governor general in New Orleans, originated
in response to problems, pressures, and demands at the local level: control of
livestock, maximum efficiency in exploitation of the arable land, equitable
access to pasturage and firewood, and so forth. As the system evolved and
matured, it assumed a morphology remarkably like that which generally obtained in northern France from the high Middle Ages until the French Revolution. This was a tripartite configuration consisting of compact villages, clusters of open arable strips, and outlying areas of common pasture lands.

The remarkable similarity between this traditional European pattern and
that which developed in the French Illinois Country was not mere coincidence. Although this pattern had not developed in the regions that stood as
intermediary colonies between metropolitan France and the Illinois Country—Canada and Lower Louisiana—it is apparent that familiarity with ancient French practices provided the cognitive basis of the system. That is, even
though French medieval practices had not, for a variety of reasons, taken root
in the St. Lawrence Valley or in the lower Mississippi Valley, the French people
who arrived in the Illinois Country via these regions carried with them to
the middle Mississippi area group memories of what they or their ancestors
had known in France. The Illinois agricultural regulations began as ad hoc
decrees by the commandants at Fort de Chartres during the 1720s and 1730s
and attained their fullest elaboration and complexity at Ste. Geneviève and
St. Louis during the 1770s and 1780s. This could mean that historians of traditional rural life in France may benefit by examining agricultural regulations
that were drafted in Spanish Illinois. The agencies of agricultural regulation,
however, whether in Old Regime France or the Illinois Country, were strik-
ingly similar. General assemblies of habitants—their composition, their election of syndics, and their remarkable degree of local autonomy—demonstrate that the in the Illinois Country were replicating, mutatis mutandis, a
traditional French system of village governance.

Open-field agriculture, which had disappeared before the turn of the
eighteenth century in New England, developed and continued to thrive in
the Illinois Country throughout that century and into the nineteenth. It did
so for a variety of reasons. Firstly, open-field systems are best suited to agriculture in which both cereal grains and livestock are produced but in which
grain production predominates. Agriculture in the Illinois Country met these
qualifications better than any other region in French North America. Sec-
ondly, open-field systems are generally seen as forms of local subsistence
agriculture that are ill-suited to regional market economies,[1] but the habi-

tants of colonial Illinois were resourceful enough to adapt their open-field agriculture to serve the major provincial market of New Orleans. Lastly, until Anglo-Americans began to arrive in the region in massive numbers in the 1790s, open-field agriculture was deeply embedded in the mental structures of the vast majority of the inhabitants. No influx of fresh blood with fresh ideas occurred, as it had done to undermine the open-field system in some New England communities.[2]

Under the influence of Anglo-American law and practices and the pressure of increased population, the open-field system of agriculture broke down during the first half of the nineteenth century. As this traditional system disintegrated, two issues were principally involved: disposition of the commons, which in some instances consisted of very large tracts of land, and enclosure of individual arable strips, which shattered the old open-field compounds. These events did not necessarily occur simultaneously in particular villages, nor did they occur at the same time in all the communities addressed in this study. In any case, the following examples show how the old system of land usage was dismantled in several of the former French Creole villages of the Illinois Country.

With the Peace of Paris (1783), the Illinois Country east of the Mississippi River became U.S. territory. To American politicians after the American Revolution, the new republic's far western lands bordering the Mississippi were largely terra incognita. The contradiction within the Northwest Ordinance regarding slavery and private property—Article 2 guaranteed all persons living within the Northwest Territory the absolute right to all their possessions, real and personal, and Article 6 declared all "slavery or involuntary servitude" illegal—is the most blatant example of this ignorance.[3] Given such egregious errors, it is no wonder that the U.S. government did not then see fit to legislate concerning intricate matters of land usage. Indeed, the issue of open-field agriculture in the Illinois Country was quite beyond the ken of the Continental Congress in 1787, as government under the Articles of Confederation was drawing to a close and the Constitution was being drafted. In March 1791 the First U.S. Congress began to grapple with the political geography of the old French settlements in the Illinois Country. Section 5 of Statue 3 of 1791 enacted

> that a tract of land, containing about five thousand four hundred acres, which for many years has been fenced and used by the inhabitants of Vincennes as a common, also a tract of land including the villages of Cohos [i.e., Cahokia] and Prairie du Pont, and heretofore used by the inhabitants of the said villages as a common, be, and the same are hereby appropriated to the use of

the inhabitants of Vincennes and of the said villages respectively, to be used
by them as a common, until otherwise disposed of by law.[4]

The notion of a town commons—a parcel of public domain to be used
by members of the community for pasturage, recreation, and socializing—
was not alien to the American legislators of the First U.S. Congress; the famous Boston Common comes speedily to mind as an example of the widespread practice in New England. Nonetheless, in 1791 the national congress
could not have envisaged the need to legislate on issues concerning a comprehensive system of communal agriculture that included large compounds
of open fields. By 1799, however, the government of the Northwest Territory
recognized the existence of "common fields" in the Illinois Country, and a
territorial law of that year, "An act to regulate the enclosing and cultivating
of communal fields,"[5] spelled out the manner in which these fields were to
be regulated. This act contains very little that was incompatible with fencing regulations as they had evolved and functioned under the French and
Spanish colonial regimes on both sides of the Mississippi—with one absolutely fundamental exception. The first section of the 1799 act, which addressed for the first time in U.S. statute law the issue of open-field communes,
contained an essential caveat: "Any person who is a proprietor in any common field may, at any time hereafter, separate his, her, or their land from such
common field, by fencing the same, subject only to making and keeping in
repair fences in like manner as persons having enclosures adjoining the common field, as by this law directed."

This section of the territorial statute was in fact an American enclosure
act and carried within it the seed of ultimate destruction for the compounds
of open fields created by French and French Canadian settlers in the Illinois
Country. The enclaves of open-field communities, with their binding communal regulations, were anomalies within the philosophical matrix of American individual rights. The social and legal ethos of early nineteenth-century
American society viewed communally controlled property as eccentric. A
generation later, a small minority of Americans dabbled in communal settlements, but circa 1800 that romantic or religious communitarianism had not
yet taken root on American soil. Surely no individual could be *compelled* to
submit his or her land to the will of the local community. This issue had never
been raised explicitly or implicitly, as a practical or legal issue, under the
French or Spanish colonial regimes; no one dreamed of questioning the
power of the community to force individuals to turn their land into communal property for one-half of the year, from the end of the harvest season

to the beginning of the sowing season. Mandating practices substantially similar to those Philip J. Greven described as occurring in early colonial Massachusetts, the colonial Illinois system required that villagers view their agricultural lands not as individual parcels to be allotted and sold merely for short-time profit but as a resource to be managed and utilized in accordance with regulations established and enforced by communal assemblies.[6] This practice was fundamentally un-American, however, and the very first U.S. statute to deal with the subject of open-field agriculture, the territorial act of 1799, unequivocally addressed this fact. The following brief case studies show how communal agriculture collapsed in the former Illinois Country under the pressure of the American way of doing things.

VINCENNES

Vincennes was the first of the old French villages to dismantle its open fields. On Sunday, August 16, 1807, the Creole habitants of Vincennes met at the residence of Madame Pagé. This meeting constituted a general assembly of habitants, although its purpose was not to discuss communal fencing. Rather, the habitants met to "draw a petition and remonstrance, to the [territorial] legislature in the name of the proprietors of land in the lower prairie [i.e., the largest of the three compounds of arable fields at Vincennes], setting forth, that the existing laws respecting common fields, are inapplicable to the circumstances of the said inhabitants, and praying the repeal of those laws, and the passage of a law to authorize them to enclose and embank their said lands."[7] Precisely what circumstances impelled these habitants to want to enclose their individual strips, thereby destroying one of the open fields in their community, is not known. The habitants were a bit confused about the laws involved, apparently not being aware of the Northwest Territory Act of 1799, but in any case their petition to the Indiana territorial legislature received speedy action.

Until 1800 the original Northwest Territory was still intact as one vast, undifferentiated parcel of national real estate. In that year, however, the U.S. Congress, in creating the Ohio and Indiana Territories, began the process by which various states were eventually carved out of the Northwest Territory. William Henry Harrison was appointed governor of Indiana Territory, and Vincennes became its seat of government. Harrison's restored executive mansion, federal-styled Grouseland, still stands near the campus of Vincennes University. Within less than a month after receiving the petition from the French Creole habitants of Vincennes, the Indiana Territory legislature enacted a law that repeated verbatim the 1799 act from the Northwest Territory dealing with open-field agriculture.[8] These laws frankly acknowledged the persistence of this ancient European agricultural system in the American Midwest. More important, however, they contained the critical enclosure provision, which gave every individual the right to break with the communal system. Therefore, as of September 1807 it was manifestly apparent throughout the Illinois Country that any of the open-field compounds in any of the various communities where they existed was vulnerable to the whims of any individual proprietor. This was the American way. And at Vincennes, at least for the "lower prairie" compound, a majority of the proprietors wished to enclose their elongated parcels of plowland.

The commons was an issue discrete from that of the common fields, and after Vincennes became American territory, the Creole habitants in the village resolved to maintain their traditional communal pasturing rights. In May 1789 twenty of these habitants petitioned the U.S. commandant of Vincennes, Major John F. Hamtramck, to halt encroachments made into the commons by persons who were seizing plots of land illegally. Hamtramck was sensitive to local feelings about communal practices, and he accommodated the petitioners with alacrity: within twenty-four hours he issued an executive order forbidding further incursions into the commons.[9] Hamtramck's action was the background to the U.S. statute of 1791 that officially created a Vincennes commons of 5,400 acres.[10]

After the old French habitants at Vincennes began to enclose their plowlands, they nonetheless wanted to preserve their communal pasturing rights. In 1807 a proposal emerged to convey the entire Vincennes commons to Vincennes University, which had been created by the Indiana Territory legislature the year before. This proposal was likely a descendant of the provision in the U.S. Land Ordinance of 1785 that set aside one section in each township for the support of public schools. In any case, the board of trustees of Vincennes University first agreed to petition the U.S. Congress to grant the commons to the university and then quickly reversed itself.[11] This was a hotly contested issue in Vincennes, and opinion pieces appeared in the local newspaper, the *Western Sun,* in favor of the "poor illiterate French people of Vincennes" who "enjoyed and derived so much advantage" from the commons.[12] This campaign on behalf of an older way of life at Vincennes succeeded, and the commons survived, if only for another decade.

On October 12, 1818, in quaint English, fifty-nine inhabitants of Vincennes signed (most of them left their marks) a petition protesting the sale of the commons. The petitioners claimed that their rights to the commons dated back to mid-eighteenth century, to the time when Louis St. Ange de Bellerive had been French commandant at Vincennes, and that these rights had been confirmed by the "amariquen Gouvernment." Of the fifty-nine signatories, only two, George Walker and Anas Blum, did not have French names.[13] The petition was to no avail. The town trustees of Vincennes hired one William Green as surveyor and engineer to subdivide the commons, and the "poor illiterate" French habitants were dispossessed of their traditional communal pastureland.[14]

In 1951 the *Vincennes Sun-Commercial* told the last chapter in the story of the Vincennes Commons. By 1870 proceeds from the common land sales totaled $24,224.69, of which $15,500 had been spent for draining the pond. But there was no record that the remaining $8,724.69 had ever gone to Vincennes University, as specified by the federal statute of 1818. This issue was resolved in 1951 when the city council agreed to convey to Vincennes University "considerable property in the old water works area which was not now being used."[15] This amicable resolution to an ancient claim constituted the last legal action in the United States to derive from French colonial agricultural practices.

CAHOKIA

When the habitants met at Cahokia in January 1808 to draft the last communal fencing regulations for that village, a curious thing occurred at the last minute—the wealthiest member of the community, Nicolas Jarrot, formally withdrew himself from the community of cultivators.[16] Here was a man who had arrived rather recently in Cahokia in flight from the revolution in France. He was neither born nor raised in the Illinois Country and was probably not accustomed to the communal practices employed there. Moreover, he had a markedly entrepreneurial bent of mind. John Reynolds described his "incessant application to business. . . . He was like the honeybee."[17] Jarrot was not someone who wished to be fettered by the old-fashioned French Creole community of habitants at Cahokia. He was through and through a free-enterprise businessman of a modern stripe, and his individualistic agricultural practices were just as American as his federal style mansion that still ornaments the town of Cahokia. When Jarrot quit the community of habitants at Cahokia, he exempted himself from the village's communal fencing regulations. Therefore, in accordance with the laws of the Northwest and Indiana Territories, he was free to enclose the arable strips that he owned within the open-field compound. This sounded the death knell of open-field agriculture at Cahokia, for when a major landowner broke with the system, the system was doomed to unravel very quickly. Soon the entire compound of open fields at Cahokia was literally slashed to ribbons by private fencing.

KASKASKIA

Once the Anglo-American invasion of the Illinois Country commenced in earnest, life in Kaskaskia was quickly revolutionized by new customs and economic structures. The village that had been founded in 1703 as a Franco-Indian missionary outpost became in the early nineteenth century the commercial and political capital of territorial Illinois, where the new American frontier power elite congregated and resided. The Creole system of open-field agriculture at Kaskaskia was alien to these newcomers and crumbled rather quickly under American influence. That is, the vast unenclosed compound of arable fields that had existed at Kaskaskia since the 1720s was, soon after the turn of the nineteenth century, fenced in, broken up, and converted into individual parcels whose exploitation was governed by no community regulations. While communal agriculture still reigned across the Mississippi River at Ste. Genevieve, the common field at Kaskaskia was torn asunder. In 1824 the *Kaskaskia Republican Advocate,* one of the earliest newspapers in Kaskaskia, listed a 120-acre parcel of agricultural land for sale in the "old Common Field" that was "under good fence."[18] Any kind of fencing made open-field agriculture difficult; good fencing rendered it impossible. The expression *common field* was still understood at Kaskaskia in 1824, but the use of the field for communal agriculture had disappeared.

The commons for pasturage survived longer at Kaskaskia than did the open-field plowlands. As described earlier (chap. 2), the traditional commons at Kaskaskia was located in the low-lying areas on the peninsula between the Kaskaskia and Mississippi Rivers. In 1743 Louisiana governor Vaudreuil officially designated this land as commons, and it remained intact as such until mid-nineteenth century. Article 11 of the 1848 Illinois constitution decreed that any commons that had been granted to the inhabitants "by any government having power to make such a grant [i.e., including the defunct French monarchy]" would remain as commons until a majority of the citizens in any particular community decided to subdivide and sell the land.[19]

In January 1851 the General Assembly of Illinois passed a private "Act to provide leasing the lands granted as a Common to the inhabitants of the town of Kaskaskia, . . . for school and other purposes."[20] The act defined "school" as education in reading, writing, arithmetic, grammar, and geography for the children of Kaskaskia; rather curiously (and perhaps unconstitutionally), the "other purposes" turned out to be "for the support and advancement" of religion. In any case, five men—Dennis Kavanaugh, Savinien St. Vrain, Joseph Baronowski, George W. Staley, and Edmond Ménard—were named to serve as trustees of the Kaskaskia commons. These men still had some sympathy for the idea of a village commons, and on a motion by Edmond Ménard, son of former lieutenant governor Pierre Ménard, the trustees unanimously resolved that it was "unnecessary, inexpedient, and improper to lease any portion of the Commons lying south of, or below, the southern boundary line of the common field."[21] In keeping with Ménard's motion, less than half the Kaskaskia commons was surveyed into five-, ten-, twenty-, and forty-acre parcels for long-term leasing. Over time the entire commons was leased to private individuals, and early in the twentieth century the plots were finally sold to individual proprietors.[22] When all the former Kaskaskia commons had been subdivided and converted into private property, the public trustees of communal property became supernumerary. By 1911 the "Record Book of Minutes for the Kaskaskia Commons" had outlasted its time, and it now gathers dust in the Illinois State Archives, a last documentary reminder of an ancient pattern of land usage, communal practices, and *mentalités* in the Illinois Country.[23]

ST. LOUIS

The basically medieval settlement pattern—compact village, unfenced arable fields, and commons—that characterized all the major communities of the Illinois Country during the eighteenth century was not so firmly implanted at St. Louis as in the region's other major settlements—Cahokia, Kaskaskia, Ste. Geneviève, and Vincennes. St. Louis was founded relatively late, agriculture was never the principal occupation of its inhabitants, and the French peasant *mentalité* on which the medieval pattern depended was less pronounced in a community whose raison d'être was commerce and government. A structure that had never been deeply embedded was already beginning to disintegrate by the end of the colonial period. In a long jeremiad of 1798, Lieutenant Governor Trudeau complained that St. Louis had but a few ignorant cultivators, that the system of enclosing the arable fields with common fencing was no longer efficient, that the common fences were in disrepair, and that the crops were being destroyed by errant livestock. Trudeau's solution to all these difficulties was that the traditional system of communal agriculture "be done away with in order to further the prosperity of the inland plantations. And their animals abandoned to themselves, as in Natchez, they [the local habitants] will begin each one to enclose their farms."[24] Trudeau was thus envisaging a more thoroughly individualistic and American system of agriculture, in which each cultivator would fence his own arable fields and independent farmsteads ("inland plantations") would proliferate. The lieutenant governor was waxing prophetic, for this indeed was the wave of the future for agriculture in the American Midwest.

By the 1830s the open arable fields that had once surrounded St. Louis were long gone. When Henry Shaw, the future public benefactor, was purchasing land in the former Prairie des Noyers at that time, all this land, much of which had been cultivated in colonial times, had reverted to prairie grass and wild flowers and was being used for pasture. Ironically, the central portion of the former Prairie des Noyers, which was once treeless, now comprises Tower Grove Park, one of the most diverse urban forests in the United States.[25]

The St. Louis commons was doomed to distinction along with the open fields. Sales of land in the commons began in the mid-1830s, but the nationwide economic slump of 1837 put a virtual end to them. Many purchasers reconsidered and concluded that they had paid inflated prices for their parcels and refused to pay taxes on them. The city of St. Louis's legal counsel, A. W. Manning, published notice that under section 10 of a Missouri General Assembly act of 1835, tax delinquent land from the commons could be repossessed.[26] By 1854 the city had indeed repossessed much of its former commons, and during the mid-1850s the best of this land was auctioned off for a total of $670,000. On Sunday, September 25, 1859, the *Missouri Republican* ran a commercial advertisement for the final sale of real estate from the once extensive St. Louis commons.[27] A news article in the same edition proclaimed that the "city of St. Louis . . . is about to dispossess herself of the last vestige of her Common," which would be sold off in "parcels of not less than one, nor more than forty acres." The city electorate decided what portion— one-half, one-fourth, or one-tenth—of the proceeds should be earmarked for public education. The voters, already possessed of a keen and dogged American suspicion of book learning, selected the lowest percentage. A vigorous national economy boosted land sales in 1859, and the last of the commons sold for an aggregate sum of $80,601.[28]

Although the last of the commons—and thereby the last of an ancient system of land usage, agriculture, and settlement—was being rapidly swallowed up, some areas that were once part of the St. Louis commons remained as public domain. Many of the public parks in the southwestern portion of St. Louis are vestiges of the old St. Louis Commons, among them: Lafayette, Compton Hill, Fox, Benton, Gravois, Marquette, and Wood. The best example in the St. Louis area of colonial common lands persisting as community property on into the modern era, however, is sizable Carondelet Park, all of which was part of the Carondelet commons in the late eighteenth century.

STE. GENEVIEVE

Ste. Genevieve, of all communities in French North America where open-field agriculture was practiced, had the most deeply embedded and enduring system. It was at Ste. Genevieve where the economic base was most thoroughly agricultural; where the most complex and elaborated open-field regulations were promulgated; where outside visitors were most awestruck by the vast, unbroken sweep of the grain fields; and where open-field laws, in the form of private laws of the State of Missouri, persisted on throughout the nineteenth century.

Open-field agriculture was so woven into the fabric of community life at Ste. Genevieve that the system continued throughout the entire territorial period with no debate; no one questioned the legality or appropriateness of an open-field system that obliged property owners within the Grand Champ at Ste. Genevieve to adhere to time-worn and hallowed community regulations that prevented individuals from enclosing their lands. The portion of the Louisiana Purchase that lay north of the thirty-third parallel was, until the Missouri Territory was created in 1812, called the District of Louisiana and was governed at first by officials of the Indiana Territory. However, the laws of neither the Northwest Territory nor the Indiana Territory were imposed on the District of Louisiana.[29] This anomalous arrangement was concocted to protect slavery in the District of Louisiana, for the territories east of the Mississippi had at least nominally abolished slavery and "involuntary servitude." It had other ramifications as well. With regard to open fields, the Northwest and Indiana Territory laws that conveyed to any landholder the right to enclose his or her own land were not applied west of the Mississippi. Indeed, no laws pertaining to agricultural fencing were passed during the entire period, from 1804 to 1821, during which time Ste. Genevieve fell within the District of Louisiana and then the Territory of Missouri.

Soon after Missouri became a state in 1821, however, the legal status of open-field agricultural on Ste. Genevieve's Grand Champ was dealt with by state statute. Legislators of the new state of Missouri no doubt realized that the open-field regulations at Ste. Genevieve were at odds with American notions about individual property rights, as well as with territorial laws on the east side of the Mississippi. The novel solution adopted by the state of Missouri was to create, by enacting a private law, a corporation at Ste. Genevieve composed of all proprietors of real estate within the Grand

Champ.[30] The corporation that perpetuated the open-field system at Ste. Genevieve throughout the nineteenth century was disbanded in 1907, and individual property owners now have the right to fence their own plowlands. Nonetheless, they choose not to do so, either out of deference to tradition or, more likely, because it is most practical to pursue arable agriculture there without fencing. The Grand Champ, of which there is still a magnificent view from the bluffs where New Bourbon once stood, is now dissected by roadways, levees, and a railroad line but not by fences. Although the communal discipline of open-field agriculture is now long gone, the vast unfenced Grand Champ at Ste. Genevieve, an agricultural artifact of a bygone way of village life, remains to be seen and admired.[31]

CULTURE CLASH

A tenacious truism of North American history is that when the French and the English arrived on the "new" continent in the seventeenth century, they were motivated by different purposes and settled in different ways—the French came for pelts and prosyletizing and settled sparsely over vast regions; the English came for agriculture and commerce and settled thickly along a relatively narrow strip of the eastern seaboard. This abstracted view of settlement in colonial North America has been pervasive in standard historical texts: "Unlike their English neighbors, whom the Appalachian barrier had so long confined to the coastal settlement, the French were encouraged by the great corridor of the St. Lawrence and the Great Lakes to disperse far into the interior in search of furs. . . . The lure of furs and fish inhibited true settlement and there were few new French immigrants ready to shoulder the backbreaking work of tilling the unrewarding soil."[32] The most recent reiteration of this traditional view states that "French colonists [in the Mississippi Valley] relied to an extraordinary extent and for an unusually long period of time on Indian communities for food supplies."[33] This generalization, that French colonists in North America shunned and eschewed even subsistence agriculture, has obscured a different manner of distinguishing French and English settlements in North America, one based on considering both ethnic groups as permanent settlers and agriculturists.

The Illinois Country of the late eighteenth century provides a remarkable historical laboratory in which to examine the clash of two different ethnic groups, two different systems of agriculture, and two different *mentalités*. French and French Creoles, with their distinctive mind-sets and approaches to exploiting the land, dominated the Illinois Country until after the American Revolution; the short-lived British presence (1765–72) and George Rogers

Clark's incursion in 1778 had only tangential impact on the traditional French Creole manner of life in the Illinois Country. As Reginald Horsman has put it, "by the summer of 1780 the British had no real foothold in the Illinois Country, . . . [and] George Rogers Clark's victories in 1778 were never built on."[34] By the late 1780s, however, a flood of Anglo-Americans began to arrive in the region via the Ohio Valley, and during the last decade of the eighteenth century the ethnic balance in the Illinois Country began to shift precipitously in favor of Anglo-Americans.[35] In the process of this demographic shift, fundamental differences between the two cultures—their settlement patterns, their agriculture, and their mind-sets—were cast into bold relief.

The open-field agriculture practiced by French Creoles in Illinois disappeared after U.S. laws on the east side of the Mississippi River explicitly gave agriculturists the right to fence their own strips of arable land.[36] Before American law did this, the habitants of the various French villages would not have dreamed of contesting the traditional regime of open fields by demanding the right to fence their plowlands. American laws that conveyed this right did not compel anyone to erect fences around his land. If there had been the community will (i.e., *unanimous* agreement from the individuals within the agricultural community) to do so, the open fields could have survived in perpetuity. Over time the will disappeared, however, and so did the open fields on both sides of the Mississippi River.

In his detailed study of colonial Andover, Massachusetts, Philip Greven dealt with this same issue for seventeenth-century New England: "Although it is impossible now to know why Andover altered its initial commitment to the open-field system of farming, several factors are likely to have influenced the change."[37] Greven then suggested that the rapid abandonment of the open-field system during the 1650s and 1660s may have been due to changing leadership in Andover; leaders who had been committed to the system either died or left the area, and newcomers arrived from regions of England where this system had not been generally practiced. Greven readily acknowledged, however, that this was mere speculation and that there is no one simple and sufficient answer as to why a particular community such as Andover abandoned its open-field system. The only certainty is that by the 1650s and 1660s "those who favored the open-field system were becoming a minority" in Andover.[38]

The traditional open-field system of agriculture in the Illinois Country disappeared as the region was swamped by Anglo-American settlers from the east. Clarence W. Alvord remarked that by 1790 "the roaring of the advancing tide of the Americans was already heard west of the Alleghenies, and with inexorable force the *waves of individualism* were to inundate the wilderness."[39]

These successive waves rolled on to the banks of the Mississippi, where they eroded the communal agriculture that had been practiced in the Illinois Country for most of the eighteenth century. Open-field cultivation demanded cooperative effort and a certain sense that agricultural land to some extent belonged to the community and was not utterly governed by the laws of freehold proprietorship. These notions conflicted with an American ethos of individual autonomy, liberty, and self-reliance; in short, they were incompatible with the American way of doing things.

A striking example of this incompatibility occurred even before Great Britain officially ceded the Illinois Country to the United States in the 1783 Treaty of Paris. A curious character from Connecticut, Richard McCarty, had immigrated to the British Illinois Country about 1775. This move itself was idiosyncratic, for there was nothing remotely approaching a migration from New England to the Illinois Country during the 1770s. In any event, McCarty settled down somewhere outside Cahokia on land that he neither purchased nor was granted; he simply squatted on it, preempted it, American frontier style. After McCarty served in the expedition against British Vincennes in 1778, George Rogers Clark awarded him a captaincy and appointed him American commandant at Cahokia.[40] In September 1779, apparently just before harvest time, fourteen of McCarty's free-grazing hogs, including "Several Sowes Just ready to Pig," were discovered inside the compound of arable fields at Cahokia and shot by the local habitants. McCarty, hearing that this had been authorized by Colonel John Todd, whom Governor Patrick Henry of Virginia had appointed county lieutenant in the Illinois Country, wrote to Todd in fractured grammar and a foul mood:

> The People of this Village [Cahokia] have Sowen Grain out in the open fields & meadows without Any fence or inclosure to preserve it as I am at Such a Distance from this Village it cannot be Supposed that I have Connections with them in the Town Laws Concerning their Commons, as I am Quite on the other Side of them. . . .
> I dont see yet through the Designe of a few Dispicable Inhabitants who say they are authorized by you, to parade themselves in the fields Destroying my property.[41]

McCarty's letter (if it can be taken at face value) suggests that the French Creole habitants at Cahokia still fenced in their animals, confining them to common pasturelands, rather than fully enclosing the arable lands with a fence to protect them against foraging animals. McCarty made it a point to explain that he was not a member of the traditional community at Cahokia; he lived at some distance from the compact village. This, McCarty readily acknowledged, meant that he did not understand or appreciate traditional land usage at Cahokia—village, common pasture, and open-field arable—but he *did* know that there were village regulations ("Town Laws") concerning the system, of which he patently did not approve.

Understanding that he was unlikely to get any satisfaction from Todd, with whom he was already at odds, McCarty also wrote to Colonel John Montgomery, American military commandant in the Illinois Country: "I think it would be a happy thing could we get Colo Todd out of the Country. . . . I have wrote him a pretty Sharp Letter on his Signing a Death Warrant against My poor hogs for Runing in the Oppen fields."[42] To add insult to injury, the carcasses of four of McCarty's hogs were taken to Cahokia village and sold (probably in front of the parish church), with the proceeds likely going to meet some parish need. Even in French Canada, where open-field agriculture was not practiced, ordinances dating back to the seventeenth century permitted the killing of vagabond hogs found in arable fields.[43] McCarty's anguish over his "poor hogs" and his disapproval of the communal agricultural and village practices of the habitants at Cahokia were short-lived. In the spring of 1781, he departed the Illinois Country and headed east for Virginia (which claimed Illinois until 1784), where he intended to deliver a petition to the governor of Virginia, Thomas Jefferson. Jefferson had already been warned that McCarty was a troublemaker and had "long since rendered himself disagreeable by endeavoring to enforce Military Law upon the Civil Department at Kohos [Cahokia]."[44] As it turned out, Governor Jefferson was spared the pain of having to cope face to face with McCarty, who was killed by Indians (probably Shawnees) somewhere in the Ohio Valley before reaching Virginia.[45]

In any event, Anglo-Americans had difficulty grasping the idea that the arable strips within the French colonial common fields in the Illinois Country were not precisely the same as freehold parcels of real estate. When in 1809 U.S. land commissioners described land usage in the Illinois villages, they understood the threefold nature of the communities, and they described the "Commons, Common Field, and Town Lots" as discrete entities for each community. Failing to see how the practice of l'abandon limited the full scope of freehold ownership in the arable strips within the common fields, however, the land commissioners described these strips as comparable to the residential plots in the villages, that is, as manifestly freehold parcels to be bought and sold and utilized by the individuals who had title to them.[46] The commissioners totally missed the concept, which was still fundamental to land usage in the French communities, that "ownership" of land in the common-field compounds was in fact largely the right of tillage, the right to sow and harvest crops, after which the community's rights to use the arable for common pasture took precedence over the property rights of individuals. Some outside observers who had not been born and raised in the Illinois Country noticed that the peculiar settlement pattern of nuclear villages with outlying arable fields was distinctly un-American. Captain Amos Stoddard, who took command of Upper Louisiana for the U.S. government in the spring of 1804, remarked that "the inhabitants of all the *compact* villages are . . . Creoles and Canadians [i.e., Franco-Americans]. But the *extensive* settlements about the country have been made by English Americans."[47]

Stoddard was himself "English American," but continental Europeans also noticed the same fundamental differences in settlement patterns. Jean Badollet was a French Swiss who had moved to America just after the American Revolution and wound up settling down at Vincennes on the lower Wabash. A boyhood friend of Badollet's from Geneva was Albert Gallatin, who also immigrated to America and eventually became Thomas Jefferson's secretary of the treasury. Despite their widely divergent paths in America, these two men remained friends and correspondents until Badollet's death at Vincennes in 1837. In 1806 Badollet wrote to his friend and compatriot, who was then serving in Jefferson's cabinet, and criticized his new place of residence:

> The population of this town is composed of ancient french inhabitants and of Americans. The first is an ignorant, harmless & indolent race exhibiting to the eyes of an observer an uncouth combination of french and indian manners. Their attachment to their old habits is such that the idea of living in the woods, that is to say on a farm, excites in them as much abhorrence as if they were dropped here from the middle of Paris. . . . They live cooped up in this village (the only place in America to which that name applies with the meaning it has in Europe).[48]

A native of Geneva and a man bred of French language and culture, Badollet had over a period of twenty years become acculturated in American ways to the point where he scorned European-style agricultural villages. The new way, the American way, the progressive way, was to live in rugged independence on one's own farmstead. As Oscar Handlin noted in discussing Anglo-American society: "The communal qualities of peasant agriculture never took root in America. Attempts to restore the village . . . failed miserably."[49] On any clear day a view of the Midwest from the air reveals the isolated farmsteads scattered over the rigorously rectangular grid of townships, ranges, and sections created by the Land Ordinance of 1785; and a clear night, in which the individual yard lights of the isolated farmsteads stand out, reveals even more dramatically the dispersed settlement pattern governed by the vast waffle-iron grid of the Land Ordinance. Bela Hubbard, an acute observer of French Canadian manners and *mentalités* from early nineteenth-century Michigan, claimed that "a Frenchman so situated would die of ennui. He must have facilities for regular and frequent intercourse with his neighbors."[50]

Alexis de Tocqueville, the most famous foreign observer of American life, was, like Jean Badollet, a friend of Albert Gallatin's. During his far-flung travels across much of eastern North America, Tocqueville had occasion to visit the recently founded town of Pontiac in the Michigan Territory. The view of this American town reminded him "of what M. Gallatin had said to me a month before in New York: that there is no village in America, at least in the sense which we give to that word. Here the houses of the cultivators are scattered in the middle of the fields. People only assemble in a place to establish a sort of market for the use of the surrounding population. In these so-called villages one only finds lawyers, printers, or traders."[51] This passage reveals that Gallatin in his conversations with Tocqueville had forgotten what Badollet had written to him years before concerning the settlement at Vincennes, for Badollet had described Vincennes as very much an Old World agricultural village situated in the middle of the North American continent. Tocqueville himself never traveled far enough west to visit Vincennes, or any other Illinois Country village. In any event, of these three Frenchmen—Badollet, Gallatin, and Tocqueville—only the first experienced life in a European-style village set in the American Midwest, and even he was not aware that what he observed about Vincennes was replicated in Vincennes's sibling settlements situated further westward in the Illinois Country.

John Reynolds, who spent much of his life in the region of Illinois first colonized by the French, wrote: "The French, by living together many ages, begin to think they could not exist out of a French village. Their social intercourse are so interwoven in their [the villages'] composition that to separate one from another are looked upon with a kind of horror."[52] From the west side of the Mississippi, Paul Wilhelm, duke of Württemberg, commented about Ste. Geneviève, which he saw in 1824, that "real, honest people of true Creole stock live there, people who dislike to leave their villages, . . . and would rather bear the consequences of the adverse location of Ste. Geneviève than abandon the place, which is sacred to their patron saint."[53] As late as 1839, Louis Joseph Papineau remarked about French Creoles that they "have no ambitions beyond their present possessions, & never want to go beyond the sound of their own church bells."[54] The agricultural villages in the Illinois Country were evidently viewed by early nineteenth-century observers as strange apparitions on the American landscape. Furthermore, the open-field agriculture that was characteristic of these communities was deemed down-right un-American by many Americans. Jonathan Jennings wrote from Vincennes in 1807 that "you may behold at one and the same time a hundred plows going, under one inclosure, which belongs to the French, who cultivate in Common. Their Customs are often very ridiculous and grating to the feelings of an American."[55] These American biases against an old-fashioned way of settling on and tilling the land were soon appropriated by immigrants from Europe, such as the Swiss Jean Badollet.

The comte de Volney traveled widely in North America during the 1790s and later published his observations in *A View of the Soil and Climate of the United States of America.* In this volume Volney compared the different *mentalités* of Anglo and French settlers in America. The Anglo-American "is nowise averse to sell his farm, . . . and move, even in old age, still farther into the forest, cheerfully recommencing all the labors of a new settlement." On the other hand, "to visit and talk are so necessary to a Frenchman, that along the frontier of Canada and Louisiana there is no where a settler of that nation is to be found, but within sight or reach of some other."[56]

MENTALITÉS

The first chapter of this study contained a brief discussion of possible relationships between settlement patterns, modes of agricultural exploitation, and the *mentalités* of French Canadian habitants. That is, in the St. Lawrence Valley the markedly independent-minded roturiers lived in a dispersed settlement pattern and exploited their own rotures individually. Of course, the tangled and complex relationships between mental structures and modes of existence virtually preclude the possibility of determining cause and effect with any certainty; that is, were Canadian habitants rugged individualists because they farmed independently, or did they farm independently because they yearned to do so? Virtually every historian of open-field agriculture has commented on the distinctive *mentalité* demanded by a cooperative and communal system of cultivating the earth. The Belgian historian Léopold Genicot, an authority on the medieval community in western Europe, recently noted: "Collective matters required collective decisions. . . . Such a system of [open-field] cultivation and the regulation of the activity of all the members of the village . . . strengthened the common spirit and attitudes."[57] Richard C. Hoffman has suggested that open-field agriculture was "more than just a way of raising crops[;] common fields were part of a way of life that combined social, legal, and purely agricultural institutions in a cultural unity."[58]

Long before Hoffman wrote this, one of the masters of European rural history, Marc Bloch, had already explained one component of the cultural unity that lay behind the open-field system: "Such a system depended upon tremendous social cohesion in a society whose deepest impulses were directed toward the community."[59] Bloch was especially interested in the ways that the physical bases of life shaped social *mentalités,* and he returned to this theme by remarking that "the existence of land that is collectively exploited . . . creates powerful bonds among members of the group."[60] More recently Robert Mandrou in describing the "solidarités fondamentales" of life in early modern France, defined the rural parish as a "group of peasants who worked the land together and led lives of the strictest solidarity."[61] This thesis may be buttressed with a distant cross-cultural comparison by adducing Richard Critchfield's comment about Third World agricultural villages in the late twentieth century: "Agriculture imposes its own rules of conduct upon people who live close to the soil and whose way of life . . . changed hardly at all, one generation to the next."[62]

Colonial Illinoisans recognized that a relationship existed between communal agricultural and a cast of mind oriented toward mutual cooperation and community well-being, and they articulated this in remarkably precise and penetrating language; that is, eighteenth-century people spoke best for themselves. When in April 1785 Antoine Girardin, "commandant and habitant" of Cahokia (then part of the United States but still largely francophone), urged villagers to adopt fencing laws to regulate the open-field agriculture practiced in the region, he remarked: "If there are objections to these just and equitable proposals, and a society of habitants cannot be maintained that is advantageous to everyone, then all bonds of the community shall be destroyed. Each habitant shall be free to enclose his own grain, and everyone shall be exempt from communal fencing, for it would be unjust for the industrious habitants to work to preserve the grain, while the others remain inert."[63] Girardin saw the issues with perfect clarity: if the habitants at Cahokia chose not to endorse open-field regulations then the very fabric of the community would be torn asunder; each individual had to agree to forsake some freedom if communal activities were to succeed. Girardin was persuasive on this occasion, and the villagers approved the proposed fencing laws.

What aspects of daily life demonstrate colonial Illinoisans to have been people whose strongest motives were directed toward community? If the subsistence basis—namely, communal agriculture—created cultural unity in this colonial society, a communal ethos should be apparent in facets of the society other than the cooperative efforts required to maintain an open-field agricultural system. A considerable body of evidence suggests that this ethos was indeed reflected in the aversion to physical violence that characterized the habitants of the Illinois Country.

John Reynolds wrote a good deal about the French Creole society that he had seen firsthand as a youth in Illinois, and he returned time and again to note that French Creole citizens had been remarkably law-abiding people. Their manner of life, he wrote, "has almost entirely secured them from any infractions of the penal laws of the country." Moreover, "there never was a Creole Frenchman hung in Illinois since the earliest settlement of the country. . . . No Creole was ever sentenced to the penitentiary of this State." Finally, he wrote, "I believe the records of the courts in Illinois do not exhibit an indictment against a Creole Frenchman for any crime higher than keeping his grocery open on a prohibited day of the week."[64] Reynolds went even further by observing that French Creoles not only avoided violating statute laws but also were free of crimes *malum in se,* offenses against natural law. It was not so much that Creoles were compulsively law-abiding out of respect for the state; rather, they simply shunned violence: "In common broils and personal combats the French rarely engaged. They detested a quarrelsome, fighting man."[65]

On the western side of the Mississippi, Frederick Bates, territorial secretary in Upper Louisiana after the purchase, was brazenly confident about his knowledge of French Creoles in the territory. "I speak with certainty arising from intimate knowledge of their general character. They are blameless and inoffensive for the most part, but they know nothing of the duties of a soldier, and could never be *dragged* into action either with Spaniards or Indians."[66] Bates was notably contemptuous of Creoles for lacking martial spirit, although he never bothered to ask himself why the French Creole character was, in his eyes, so pusillanimous relative to that of the Anglo-American. Other things that Bates wrote about the Creoles of Upper Louisiana[67] suggest that he believed their deficiencies of character to be indelibly engraved into their souls rather than perhaps stemming from certain economic and social conditions.

Rufus Easton, another Anglo-American who later became a Missouri Territory representative, arrived in St. Louis shortly after the Louisiana Purchase and wrote to President Thomas Jefferson about the new American citizens who resided west of the Mississippi. Jefferson must have been gratified to learn that the French Creoles of Upper Louisiana were "a civil quiet people" who could be "easily governed."[68] Easton, although he was not aligned politically with the Creole faction in St. Louis, did not seem to think that an absence of aggressiveness necessarily constituted a character deficiency in the Creole citizens.

Remaining civil records from the Illinois Country reveal remarkably little physical violence between habitants during colonial times. Many of these documents have been lost, and moreover, altercations no doubt occurred that for one reason or another were never recorded. French Canadian habitants generally preferred to settle their disputes outside the framework of the official legal system,[69] and likely those in the Illinois Country did as well. In any case, the best-documented case of violent crime from the east side of the Mississippi during colonial times occurred at Kaskaskia in 1738. One December evening at about seven o'clock, after numerous "coups de vin" in the residence of one Henri Catin, a brawl ensued between Catin and two of his drinking companions, Jean-Baptiste Richard and Daniel Richard, who, despite their common surname, do not seem to have been related. The result of this drunken fracas was that Henri Catin eventually died of wounds to his arms, back, and buttocks inflicted with an ash scoop (*pelle à feu*) and an ax. Other members of the community had been present in Catin's house, but with the wine flowing and the sun long down, these persons were not entirely clear about what had transpired. Depositions and an extensive inquest by authorities from Fort de Chartres could not determine precisely what had happened that cold December night; the interior of Catin's house was obviously a murky and chaotic place that evening. Unable to conclude definitively whether Catin's death resulted from an accident, a murder, or an act of self-defense, or even whether Jean-Baptiste Richard or Daniel Richard, or both of them, had inflicted the fatal blows, the royal officials Flaucourt and Buchet settled the issue with a compromise that from the perspective of Anglo-American jurisprudence seems odd. Neither of the Richards was found guilty of murder, yet their behavior had contributed to a man's death. Therefore, they were each fined a modest 100 sous (five livres), and the aggregate of 200 sous went to help sustain "the poor of the parish of the Immaculate Conception" in Kaskaskia.[70]

It is important to observe that, at the time of the brawl that led to Catin's death, none of the three principals was a well-established member of the agricultural community in Kaskaskia. (William Eccles has observed that in French Canada, Montreal, a fur-trading outpost and military base, was much more violent than Quebec, which had a less transient population.)[71] Jean-Baptiste Richard *dit* le Parisien, who did not appear on the 1732 census, had probably only recently arrived from Paris. Although the 1752 census lists him as the owner of one arpent of agricultural land, he was principally a merchant rather than a habitant in the regional sense of the word; he was identified as a merchant born in Paris on his widow's marriage record in 1758.[72] The other two were distinctly marginal types. Daniel Richard appears on no Illinois

census and never became a significant landowner in the Kaskaskia area. Henri
Catin's life in the Illinois Country was brief. He seems to have arrived in the
region only in 1737, and a year later he died in great agony in his own bed of
wounds inflicted by his drinking companions.

Of the various agricultural communities on both sides of the Mississippi
in the Illinois Country, Ste. Genevieve has, up to this time, been the most
closely examined. In perusing the large, though not complete, documentary
record of criminality in colonial Ste. Genevieve, an interesting fact emerges:
there is no written record of a single instance in which a habitant is accused
of committing a crime of physical violence against a fellow habitant. Domestic violence, such as spousal abuse, is a rather different matter, and that surely
did occur in Ste. Genevieve,[73] as well as in the other French Creole villages
of the Illinois Country. The most violent confrontation on record between
habitants from Ste. Genevieve occurred in 1789, when Jean-Baptiste Becquet
publicly accused Simon Hubardeau of being a "damned, fucking faggot
['sacré, foutu Berdache']." Both men were notoriously brash and slightly
eccentric members of the community in Ste. Genevieve. Becquet had engaged
in a flamboyant elopement to acquire his first wife, and Hubardeau had a
reputation for public displays of exquisitely bad taste.[74] Remarkably these two
men never came to physical blows following Becquet's provocative epithets.

Extant documentation reveals unmistakably that violent crimes increased
dramatically as the ethnic composition of Upper Louisiana began to change
during the 1790s; murders and rapes appear in local records for the first
time.[75] Moreover, dueling, which was unknown among the traditional Creole habitants, became a common occurrence in Upper Louisiana after the
purchase. In 1807 Joseph McFerron shot and killed William Ogle at Cape
Girardeau; in 1810 Dr. Bernard Farrar shot and killed James Graham on
"Bloody Island," which was located in the Mississippi River and was the favorite venue of Anglo duelists at St. Louis; a year later Thomas Crittenden
shot and killed Dr. Walter Fenwick on Moreau's Island, near Ste. Genevieve.[76]
Dueling likewise became a problem on the east side of the Mississippi shortly
after the turn of the nineteenth century, bred partly by squabbles between
rival political factions in the Indiana and Illinois Territories. American-style
representative government and adversarial justice, in conjunction with
American frontier mores, contained seeds for generating public disorder of
a murderous variety. When Rice Jones and Shadrach Bond Jr., members of
opposing political factions, dueled in 1808, the affair ended without bloodshed on the field of honor outside Kaskaskia. But one of Bond's seconds, Dr.
James Dunlap, was not satisfied with this result, and he pursued the issue until
he finally shot and killed Jones in cold blood on a street in midtown

Kaskaskia;[77] this was curious behavior for a man who had presumably taken the Hippocratic oath. Dunlap fled the area and was never brought to justice, and in 1810 the Illinois Territory legislature adopted an antidueling statute that mandated death by hanging for anyone found guilty of killing an opponent in a duel.[78]

Europeans and Creoles in the Mississippi Valley viewed Anglo-Americans as ruffians who were hot-headed, lawless, and addicted to strong drink; "Whiskey Boys," one French observer called them.[79] When the Englishman William Blane visited Illinois in 1822, he was taken aback by the violent ways of what he called the "Backwoodsmen." "Drinking, fighting, etc., and, when fighting, 'gouging' and biting. . . . The object of each combatant is to take his adversary by surprise; and then, . . . either to 'gouge' him, that is, to poke his eye out, or else to get his nose or ear into his mouth and bite it off. . . . This abominable practice of gouging is the greatest defect in the character of the Backwoodsmen."[80] Another British observer of the western American frontier, James Flint, agreed with Blane: "Fights are characterized by the most savage ferocity. Gouging, or putting out the antagonist's eyes, by thrusting the thumbs into the sockets, is a part of the *modus operandi*."[81] Mark Twain's *Huckleberry Finn* is replete with tales of murder and mayhem in Mississippi River communities during the mid-nineteenth century. The savage and bloody Grangerford-Shepherdson feud described in the novel was based on the real-life Darnell-Watson bloodlettings that Twain himself came near to witnessing as a cub riverboat pilot on the Mississippi. Twain's biographer, Albert Bigelow Paine, claimed that Samuel Clemens had witnessed no fewer than four murders while he was growing up in the small river town of Hannibal, Missouri.[82] The indisputable fact is that this kind of red-blooded American behavior, which was endemic on the Anglo-American frontier, did not occur on the French Creole frontier in the Illinois Country. No young person in colonial Kaskaskia or Ste. Genevieve ever witnessed cold-blooded murders on their village streets, as young Clemens did in Hannibal.

Francis S. Philbrick vigorously disputed the many claims about the high level of violence on the Anglo-American frontier,[83] but more recently Elliott J. Gorn has colorfully documented and carefully analyzed the savagery of "rough-and-tumble" frontier brawling.[84] Significantly, Gorn's study deals largely, though not exclusively, with southern frontier culture, and many of the early Anglo-American settlers in the Illinois Country arrived from the upland South. Neither of these scholars attempted to draw a cross-cultural comparison by examining the Anglo-American frontier in relation to the Franco-American frontier that had preceded the former in the Mississippi Valley. It is interesting to note Gorn's observation, however, that in analyzing the society that "nourished rough-and-tumble fighting, . . . the best place to begin is with the material base of life and the nature of daily work."[85] Gorn goes on to remark that "where work was least rationalized and specialized, domesticity weakest, legal institutions primitive, and the market economy feeble, rough-and-tumble fighting found fertile soil."[86] In virtually every regard this constitutes an inverse definition of the highly regulated agricultural society of habitants in the French Creole villages of the Illinois Country.

John Reynolds had a simpler but not simple-minded explanation for Americans' violent tendencies: "This idea of liberty gave them a personal independence, and confidence in themselves that marked their actions throughout life. This notion of excessive independence frequently brought them into conflicts and personal combats with each other. Bloody noses and black-eyes were the results."[87] Reynolds's Americans were less savage than William Blane's, for they merely blackened eyes instead of gouging them out, but the two authors were in fundamental agreement about the singular strain of violence in the character of American frontiersmen. Reynolds thought that this component in the American psyche was rooted in the very hallmark of American civilization—liberty, a liberty that Reynolds believed led to "excessive independence." Reynolds did not make a final analytical leap and suggest that the Anglo-American spirit of independence may have been associated with the manner in which Americans settled the land and practiced agriculture—on isolated farmsteads and with individually fenced fields. More recently, however, a cultural geographer, William N. Parker, has remarked that "Midwestern individualism, as it showed itself in farming and in business achievement, was rooted in the family organization brought into the region and reinforced by the conditions of rural settlement on isolated farmsteads."[88] John Mack Faragher, discussing the early settlement at Boonesborough, commented about the "settler's unwillingness to adopt collective measures. . . . Many of the settlers had come west precisely to escape hierarchy and control, and in their radical notions of independent action they resembled no group more than the Indians."[89]

Reynolds's conclusions that excessive liberty and independence created a violent strain in the American character are of course simplistic and overly abstract. Complex and specific causes generated the violence of the American frontier, and U.S. frontier historians have expended considerable effort explaining these causes. It is beyond the scope of this study to delve deeply into them,[90] for the other side of the coin is more germane here: why were the French Creole habitants of the Illinois Country so reluctant to engage in physical violence? If the roots of the violent Anglo-American frontier were complex, so doubtless were the factors that created the relatively pacific

French Creole society in the middle Mississippi Valley. These may have included a sense of community cohesiveness going back to peasant life in metropolitan France, the hierarchical nature of Creole political and religious institutions, the absence of an adversarial system of justice, and the powers of moral suasion exercised by local parish priests within compact villages. But perhaps Marc Bloch's previously adduced observation about communal agricultural life also provides part of the answer: open-field agriculture required tremendous social cohesion. It would be too strong to characterize the French Creole society of the middle Mississippi Valley in terms that have been used to describe other rural communities that had "a pervasive ethic of mutual aid . . . so deeply engrained that it assumed a quasi-religious role."[91] Much bickering and litigation went on in the villages of the Illinois Country, but physical violence represents a heightened level of rivalry and animosity between individuals. Since their very subsistence depended on cooperating with their neighbors—maintaining communal fencing and obeying the open-field regulations—habitants were little inclined to murder or maim each other, or even challenge one another to a duel. This is not to argue that the Illinois villages were idyllic communities in which all habitants were governed by an ethos of mutual respect and affection; it is merely a possible explanation for the relative lack of interpersonal violence and bloodshed in these colonial communities.[92]

When during the spring of 1787 Thomas Jefferson traveled through the Champagne country of northeastern France, he remarked that there were "no farm houses, all the people being gathered in villages. Are they thus collected by that dogma of their religion [Roman Catholicism] which makes them believe that, to keep the Creator in good humor with his own works, they must mumble a mass every day? Certain it is that they are less happy and less virtuous in villages than they would be insulated with their families on the grounds they cultivate."[93] Jefferson had difficulty restraining his anticlericism when he served in France as American minister, and his comments here reflect the opinions of a staunch deist. Although it is always dangerous to disagree with someone as intelligent and perceptive as Jefferson, my argument in this study—which is that village and parish life in colonial Illinois did in some sense make the inhabitants of the Creole villages there more rather than less virtuous, if part of virtue consists in respecting the lives and limbs of one's neighbors—is diametrically opposite to his.

Appendix: Gristmills and River Vessels

GRISTMILLS

Steven Kaplan remarked in his *Provisioning Paris:* "It was not enough for the provisioning trade to assure a regular and ample supply of grain—bread was made from flour, not wheat."[1] Over the decades of the eighteenth century a good deal of trial-and-error experimentation went on with regard to gristmill technology in the Illinois Country. All available sources of power—wind, water, horse, and human—were employed for milling.[2] Nevertheless, extant records clearly demonstrate that efficient milling of cereal grains into flour was a persistent problem everywhere in the Illinois Country throughout the colonial period. That is, milling technology never kept pace with increasing grain production.

In 1711 the royal marine André Pénicaut observed that there were three gristmills at Kaskaskia, a "windmill belonging to the Jesuit Fathers, which is used quite often by the residents, and two others, horse mills, owned by the Illinois [Indians] themselves."[3] Eleven years later Bernard Diron d'Artaguiette, royal inspector general of Louisiana, echoed Pénicaut's comments, remarking that Kaskaskia had several horse mills and a "windmill made of wood, belonging to the Reverend Jesuit Fathers."[4] The Jesuits were evidently leaders in developing mills in the Illinois Country,[5] although they probably never functioned as manorial seigneurs, compelling the habitants to use their mill in exchange for a fixed amount of flour. Seigneurs in French Canada sometimes imposed this ancient right of *banalité* on their censitaires,[6] but it is unlikely that this vestige of manorialism ever appeared in the Illinois Country. The number of mills quickly multiplied, and the 1732 census listed fourteen mills at Kaskaskia, five at Chartres, and two at Philippe Renaut's settlement at St. Philippe.[7]

Most of the mills listed in this 1732 census were horse mills, which remained the most common type of mill in the Illinois Country throughout the eighteenth and into the nineteenth century.[8] This device dates back to Babylonian times, before wind and water power had been effectively harnessed. Lynn White Jr. has explained that water mills existed in the ancient world as early as the first century before Christ.[9] The technology of water mills was difficult to master, however, and numerous documents pertaining to the building and repair of horse mills reveal this ancient device's popularity in the Illinois Country throughout the eighteenth century.[10] In 1728 Sieur Hébert, a habitant of the early village at Chartres, contracted with Mathurin Charruaud to have a horse mill built that was to be completed "before the next harvest." Hébert himself was to supply the dressed lumber and was to compensate Charruaud for his labor with 100 minots of wheat, one cow, and one heifer and to provide cartage to transport 800 posts for him.[11] In 1753 Commandant Macarty complained that horse mills were the *only* gristmills in the Illinois Country, but that a floating ("sur bateau") mill was being developed.[12] There is no evidence that such a contraption every came to fruition to solve milling problems in the Illinois Country.

After the mid-eighteenth century, the horse mill continued as a fundamental attribute of Creole technology in the communities on both sides of the Mississippi. In 1777 the *lieutenant particulier* in Ste. Genevieve, François Vallé I, bought at auction from Madame Rocheblave a horse mill "all ready to grind flour."[13] In 1779 the townspeople in Ste. Genevieve were afraid they would not be able to mill into flour the grain from their harvest because Osage Indians had stolen twenty horses.[14] At the very end of the colonial era, Nicolas de Finiels reported that the recently founded community of Carondelet, just outside St. Louis, was still grinding its grain with a horse mill.[15] It is apparent that most of the flour produced in St. Louis during the colonial era was milled with horse mills,[16] and a map drawn of St. Louis at the time of the Louisiana Purchase located no fewer than five horse mills within the town limits.[17] Indeed, Philander Draper recalled that when he came to Missouri Territory as a small boy in 1815, his family first ground grain with a handmill, and that they were all "immensely relieved" when a horse mill was finally established fifteen miles from their home.[18]

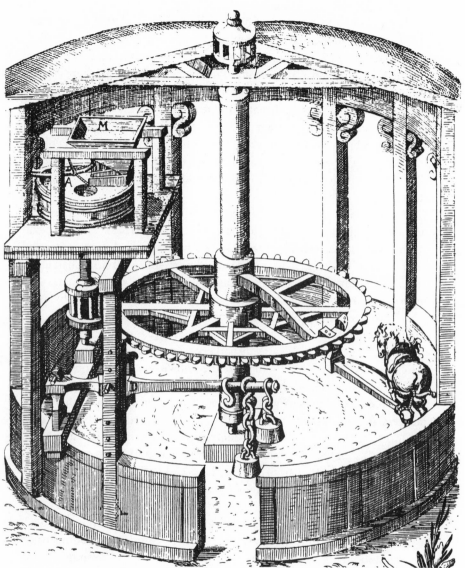

A horse-powered gristmill from Renaissance Europe. Horse mills were the most common type of gristmill in the Illinois Country throughout the eighteenth century. Printed in Agostino Ramelli's *Le Diverse et Artificïose Machine*, 1620.

Despite the continued use of horse mills, habitants in the Illinois Country began early in the eighteenth century to experiment with more sophisticated machinery for milling. These attempts, especially as they proliferated during the 1730s and 1740s, are good evidence of expanding cereal-grain production in the Illinois Country—more grain required more and better mills. Windmills had been invented in Europe during the twelfth century,[19] and the technology of such mills was well known to eighteenth-century inhabitants of the Illinois Country. The Jesuit windmill that Pénicaut had seen in 1711 evidently functioned for a number of years, for Diron d'Artaguiette noticed the Jesuits' wooden windmill when he visited Kaskaskia in 1723.[20]

A better windmill was constructed at the Grande Prairie (the agricultural area located on the Mississippi floodplain between Kaskaskia and Prairie du Rocher) in 1731–32. Jean-Baptiste Lalande, a substantial habitant, contracted with Charles Gossiaux, "master mason in Illinois," and Mathurin Charruaud, "master carpenter in Illinois," in August 1730 to build a windmill that was to be ready to produce flour by the end of September 1731. This was obviously a major construction project, and Lalande hired experienced men for the job: Philippe Renaut, the mining engineer from France, drafted the plans, and Mathurin Charruaud, who already had experience building horse mills, did the carpentry. They were also to make the millwheels and fashion the metal fittings, although Lalande himself was to provide the canvas for the "wings." Four black slaves supplied by Lalande were to assist on the project, three male laborers and one female "servante," the latter presumably to serve as cook, laundress, and so forth. The remuneration for Gossiaux and Charruaud would consist of the three male slaves, whom they could keep on the termination of the project, a pair of oxen, and two casks of brandy.[21] The building of this windmill was one of the largest and most complex construction projects to occur in the Illinois Country during the entire colonial era.

The map that Thomas Hutchins drafted of the Illinois Country, which was first published in 1771 but was based on Hutchins's observations when he was stationed as an ensign at Fort de Chartres (Fort Cavendish to the British) during the mid-1760s, shows an "Old Wind Mill" at Grande Prairie.[22] This was perhaps the mill that Gossiaux and Charruaud had erected for Lalande in 1730–31, but it probably was not in service when Hutchins saw it thirty-five years later. Philip Pittman, another British officer who was stationed in the Illinois Country at the same time as Hutchins, made it a point to comment on mills, and he found no functioning windmill in the region.[23] A windmill was mentioned near Fort de Chartres in 1757,[24] but this also was apparently out of service by the time British observers arrived in the mid-1760s, for none of them mentions it.

Toward the end of the Spanish colonial era in Louisiana, Nicolas de Finiels observed from the west side of the Mississippi that there was a functioning windmill on the Missouri River at St. Charles, which was "the only one that has succeeded in the Illinois Country, and it had several false starts before it began to function. There was an attempt to build one of wood in St. Louis on the slope of the plateau where the fort is located, but in this case ingenuity tried to liberate itself by blazing a trail beyond its capacities."[25] This unsuccessful windmill was undoubtedly that built by Joseph Motard, which Henry Gratiot fondly remembered in 1825, claiming that he had "a perfect knowledge of the situation of Motard's windmill, for when a Boy he has frequently played Ball against this same mill."[26] Toward the end of the colonial era, Antoine Roy built a windmill with a round stone base near the Mississippi at the north end of town, but, like Motard's, its fame was as a local landmark rather than as a steady producer of flour.[27]

In early Illinois water mills for grinding grain, and sometimes cutting lumber, apparently were more successful than windmills. Father Jean-Baptiste Mercier, the Seminarian father superior at Cahokia, discussed water mills at some length when he described his mission in 1735.[28] Indeed, Mercier's discussion is the longest and most detailed description of mills from eighteenth-century Illinois. He explained that he was carefully selecting a site for his mill because sudden freshets had rendered virtually useless the water mill built three years earlier (1732) by the Jesuits at Kaskaskia (the Jesuits' windmill was apparently unserviceable by this time). Therefore, Mercier and his assistants were placing their water mill at a stream on the bluffline and engineering a network of races that would feed water to the millwheel and yet prevent its destruction by heavy rains or melting snows. Mercier's description of these races suggests that the wheel, which he claimed was nineteen English feet in diameter, was of the overshot design, a more powerful variety than the undershot type.[29] The millstones were a little more than five feet in diameter, the builders "not having found any larger ones," Mercier explained. This mill, which Mercier called "le moulin de la côte de St. Michel" on his 1735 plan of the settlement at Cahokia, may have been the one that Pittman witnessed functioning there in the 1760s and described as "a very good mill for corn and planks."[30]

In the 1790s Jean Emmanuel Dumoulin, who immigrated to the Illinois Country from Switzerland via Canada, operated a water mill on the Mississippi bluffline southeast of Cahokia; this wealthy landowner had an ideal name for an owner of a gristmill. Although Mercier's mill had no doubt fallen into disuse before Dumoulin arrived in the Illinois Country, the latter's mill was perhaps located at the same site as Mercier's much earlier mill.[31] The 1730s witnessed much experimentation with water mills in the Illinois Country. In May 1737 a partially constructed water mill located "near the [Kaskaskia] Indian village" was sold to Urbain Gervais and his wife, Catherine Baudreau Gervais,[32] but two months later this couple sold it to Pierre Aubuchon.[33] Pierre and his descendants operated this mill for a considerable period of time, for the first American surveyors in the area called the creek that flowed out of the bluffs into the Kaskaskia River "Obishan's Creek";[34] one still encounters this phonetic spelling of *Aubuchon* in the region. The market in gristmills was active in 1737, perhaps because of the abundant harvest that year, and in September one-third interest in a water mill and its "dependencies" in the hills of Prairie Chassin (near Prairie du Rocher) was auctioned off after mass at the door of the parish church of Ste. Anne in the village of Chartres.[35]

In 1751 Governor General Vaudreuil ordered Jean-Jacques Macarty to improve the quality of Illinois flour by encouraging the region's residents to build more water mills, since "there are very proper sites for them near Kaskaskia."[36] Macarty had at least some success, for Prisque Pagé (also Paget or Pagget) did develop a productive water-driven gristmill near the village of Kaskaskia during the 1750s. In his description of Kaskaskia from the mid-1760s, Philip Pittman observed: "Mons. [Prisque] Paget was the first who introduced mills in this country, and he constructed a very fine one on the river Cascasquias, which was both for grinding corn and sawing boards. . . . The mill proved fatal to him, being killed as he was working in it, with two negroes, by a party of Cherokees, in the year 1764."[37] Pittman was incorrect to credit Prisque Pagé with having been the first to introduce water mills in the Illinois Country. Moreover, Pagé's mill was not located directly on the Kaskaskia River; rather, it lay on a small tributary that entered the river just upstream from the village of Kaskaskia.[38] Pittman's skillfully drafted plan of Kaskaskia village includes a roadway leading north out of the village that he labeled "Roadway to Madme Paget's Mill."[39] John Reynolds told a slightly modified version of Pagé's death, claiming that he and several of his black slaves were killed at his mill by Indians during the French and Indian War and that "the head of Paget was cut off and thrown into the hopper of his mill."[40] Nineteenth-century writers liked to attribute a grisly sense of humor to American Indians, and this story may well be apocryphal. In any case, Pagé's mill survived his death as the best-known gristmill in the Kaskaskia area.

American GLO surveyors called the stream on which Pagé's mill had been located "Edgar's Mill Run,"[41] for in the territorial period John Edgar bought, rebuilt, and enlarged Pagé's mill. Edgar was a former British army officer who adopted the American cause during the Revolution and wound up on the far western frontier of the United States in 1784.[42] Reynolds, commenting about early nineteenth-century Illinois, remarked that "Edgar's mill, . . . was, for the time, a fine flouring mill, with French buhrs, and made excellent flour."[43] Masonry vestiges of Edgar's mill are still visible along the bank of this stream, not far from the Pierre Ménard House State Historic Site in Randolph County. Despite perpetual experimentation with water mills at Cahokia and Kaskaskia, most of the eight gristmills shown on the 1767 British census of Kaskaskia were surely traditional horse mills.[44]

The British census of 1767 listed three mills at Vincennes, without specifying whether they were driven by water, wind, or horses.[45] Twelve years later, when Major Henry Hamilton descended from Detroit to Vincennes to attempt to cope with George Rogers Clark's invasion of British Illinois, Hamilton noted that the horse mills at Vincennes were "expensive and tedious." He opined that "floating Corn mills might easyly be employed as the current of the river Ouabache is strong most part of the Year," and he noted that there was one water mill located on a small stream east of Vincennes that was operated by "one Cartier (almost the only industrious man among them)."[46] This was likely the mill, known locally in the early nineteenth century as Snapp's Mill, that was situated on Mill Creek just outside Vincennes.[47]

Water mills were also built in the Illinois Country on the west side of the Mississippi after the mid-eighteenth century. Pittman noted in the 1760s that at Ste. Genevieve there was "a very fine water-mill, for corn and planks, belonging to Mons. Valet [François Vallé]."[48] Other persons also attempted to construct and operate water mills on the various streams that flowed out of the hills and across the Grand Champ toward the Mississippi at Ste. Genevieve.[49] Nevertheless, the horse mill remained the principal device for milling flour in colonial Ste. Genevieve. After Osage braves slipped into town and stole twenty horses in 1779, the townspeople feared that they had lost the motive power to mill their wheat.[50] In 1794 Lieutenant Governor Zénon Trudeau wrote from St. Louis that remains of a water mill (apparently that of François Vallé mentioned by Pittman thirty years earlier) could be seen near Ste. Genevieve but that conflicts over proprietorship were impeding its rebuilding.[51] Whether this water mill was ever rebuilt remains unknown, and in the meantime the habitants in Ste. Genevieve were compelled to use their horse mills or send their grain to St. Louis to be milled.

Shortly after the founding of St. Louis in 1764, Joseph Taillon (or Tayon) built a water mill just outside town. The town's founder, Pierre Laclède, purchased this mill from Taillon and, according to Billon,[52] spent large sums of money rebuilding the dam and improving the machinery. After Laclède died in 1778, his protégé and stepson, Auguste Chouteau, acquired the pond and the mill from Laclède's estate. Chouteau was by then St. Louis's premier citizen, and the eight-by-forty arpent (approximately 270 acres) parcel of land on which the pond and mill were located was called "Chouteau's Mill Tract."[53] Indeed, in late colonial and territorial times, Chouteau's Pond was a well-known landmark at St. Louis, and it looms large and clear on plans drawn in the 1790s.[54] Finiels provided a description of this mill that is brief but nonetheless the best there is from the colonial Illinois Country: "It is one of the area's busiest and most important for milling wheat and maize. Both grains are milled at the same time by using millstones and pestles that run off the same drive shaft. It is driven by a horizontal wheel that is fitted with scoops requiring a good deal of water. The flour produced is often burned by the excessive speed of its action."[55] In 1794, several years before Finiels saw this mill, Lieutenant Governor Trudeau wrote, "Monsieur Chouteau has just sent grindstones to his mill which is today in condition to grind a hundred-thousand livres of flour a year,"[56] and eighteen months later Trudeau proudly reported, "The water mill is in perfect working order and produces flour that is as good as the finest in Philadelphia and that tastes even better."[57]

For modern minds, which are accustomed to vertical waterwheels, Chouteau's mill, with its horizontally placed wheel, was an exotic contraption. A horizontal wheel with a vertical drive shaft was a primitive configuration that descended from the first water mills in Europe.[58] This setup obviated the need for gears to transfer the flow of power from water wheel to millstones through a right-angle turn in the drive shaft. The buhrstones for this mill may well have been limestone rather than the harder and preferable granite. Limestone was certainly the original material for millstones in the Illinois Country, because no source of granite was close at hand,[59] and it is difficult to determine when imported granite supplanted the local limestone. A cursory comparison of eighteenth-century French mills, as described by Kaplan,[60] with those from colonial Illinois makes it apparent that the art of producing and maintaining high-quality millstones was much more developed in metropolitan France than in French Illinois. The best French stones, for example, were composed of several finely cut components bound together with a circular iron strap. This advanced millstone technology was never used in the colonial Illinois Country.[61] Chouteau's mill was probably the largest and most productive in the middle Mississippi Valley at the turn of the nineteenth century. Indeed, perhaps its primitiveness kept it functioning while more complicated mills, being more ticklish and difficult to maintain, broke down more often; even the simple technology of Chouteau's mill did not keep it steadily in service. In 1795 Gayoso reported: "Chouteau has a mill in St. Louis that grinds all the flour of that district and of San Carlos and much wheat that comes from Ste. Genevieve; in spite of this it is stopped half the time."[62]

Whatever the success of Chouteau's mill at St. Louis, the problem of milling the grain that the rich arable lands of the Illinois Country produced was never satisfactorily resolved in colonial times. In the mid-1790s a French engineer-entrepreneur, Barthélémy Tardiveau,[63] contracted with the Spanish colonial government to build water mills at both New Madrid and Ste. Genevieve.[64] In what was probably a reference to this enterprise, Pierre Delassus de Luzières wrote from New Bourbon (neighboring village to Ste. Genevieve) in 1797 that water mills to produce both flour and lumber were being built at Ste. Genevieve, New Bourbon, and New Madrid. De Luzières expected that these mills would produce "fine market flour, which up to this time the horse mills have not been able to accomplish."[65] Tardiveau never fulfilled the terms of his contract,[66] however, and the fine gristmills that de Luzières naively envisioned never materialized. At the end of the colonial era, four well-known entrepreneurs from St. Louis—Manuel Lisa, Charles Sanguinet, François Benoist, and Grégoire Sarpy—proposed building a new gristmill at St. Louis.[67] What little evidence we have about this initiative suggests that when Lewis and Clark first arrived in the area in December 1803 to prepare for their expedition up the Missouri River, the proposed mill was not yet functioning because of persistent bickering among the four entrepreneurs.[68]

In his *Pioneer History* John Reynolds noted how popular the horse mill remained well into the nineteenth century. Water mills were difficult to build and maintain, and according to Reynolds, a certain Thomas Kirkpatrick built one "many times on Cahokia Creek." In Reynolds's view these early mills were "like faith without works, not worth much." Indeed, this observer of pioneer life in Illinois thought that the "want of mills retarded the improvement of the country in early times more than all other considerations. Schools and preaching could be dispensed with better than corn-meal."[69] The primitive technology of the Illinois Country meant that the problem of milling grain into flour or meal was never fully solved during the colonial era.

RIVER VESSELS

Commerce between the Illinois Country and New Orleans was conducted in a wide variety of river vessels. *Voiture* was the generic term for a river vessel of any size or shape in eighteenth-century Louisiana. Nancy M. Miller Surrey described the range of voitures used by the French in the Mississippi

Valley—bark canoes, pirogues (dugouts), cajeux (makeshift log rafts), flatboats, shallops, bateaux, and so forth.[70] Marquette and Jolliet in 1673 and La Salle and Tonti in 1682 used birchbark canoes produced in Canada on their historic voyages down the Mississippi, and bark canoes were undoubtedly important in the fur trade. But birchbark canoes were seldom if ever used for commerce between the Illinois Country and New Orleans.[71] Besides the crafts' relative fragility, the paper or canoe birch tree (*Betula papyrifera*) does not thrive south of the Great Lakes.[72]

The vessels of choice for the Illinois trade during the eighteenth century were bateaux and pirogues. The royal government, the Royal Indies Company, and private individuals all used both, and virtually every convoy that passed between the Illinois Country and New Orleans was composed of both varieties. The following discussion of eighteenth-century Mississippi River craft is confined to pirogues and bateaux and is based principally on examples taken from the Illinois Country.

Young George Morgan—representing the Philadelphia trading house of Baynton, Wharton, and Morgan—traveled down the Mississippi River from the Illinois Country to New Orleans in the autumn of 1766. Soon after leaving Kaskaskia, he saw for the first time Louisiana-style pirogues: "Their Perriogues generally contain or carry 3 to 5,000 Wt but I have heard of much larger."[73] Morgan's estimate of the carrying capacity of Creole pirogues was reasonably accurate, including his observation that they were occasionally larger than 5,000 livres burden. Norman Walker described the Louisiana pirogue in his nineteenth-century study of commerce on the lower Mississippi River: "The commercial pirogue of early Louisiana was generally . . . from 2 to 5 tons, and propelled by negro slaves, a mast and sail being occasionally used when the wind was favorable. In one of these as many as 20 bales of cotton or 30 barrels of molasses could be floated down to New Orleans."[74] Walker's observations hold true for the French Creole pirogues of the eighteenth century, although they would not have been carrying cotton and molasses in colonial times.

Nancy Surrey described Louisiana pirogues as generally made of cottonwood or cypress, propelled either by oars or by sails when the wind was favorable, and guided either with a steering oar or a "more pretentious rudder."[75] A nineteenth-century Frenchman described Louisiana pirogues succinctly: "Those [vessels] made of a single trunk are called pirogues. They can be 40 to 50 feet long, 6 feet wide, and 4 to 4½ feet deep. These pirogues are sometimes made of cottonwood or poplar trees, which in this region grow to enormous size. But most often they are made of cypress, which is just as light but stronger."[76]

In December 1725 Jean-Baptiste Turpin of Fort de Chartres traded St. Pierre Laverdure a pirogue of 4,500 livres burden, plus 400 pounds of flour, for a residential lot and a parcel of plowland.[77] Less than a year later, another resident of Chartres, Jean-Baptiste Lecomte, contracted to build a pirogue for Pierre Desroches *dit* Laverdure (obviously the same man as in the previous contract) and Jacques Bernard in exchange for 600 livres in trade goods and 100 livres worth of flour. This pirogue was to be hewn out of cottonwood, forty pieds long and three wide, and to have a carrying capacity of 7,000–8,000 livres.[78] Cottonwoods were the largest trees in Upper Louisiana, although cypresses had more rot-resistant wood and were preferable for water vessels. Cypresses grew as far north as the lower Ohio Valley but did not attain sufficient size in the Illinois Country to be used for commercial pirogues. The pirogue that Lecomte agreed to build at Chartres in 1726 perhaps qualified as "large-average" for the Mississippi Valley. When Commissaire-ordonnateur Edmé-Gatien Salmon ordered five cypress pirogues built at New Orleans in 1736, they ranged from thirty-six to thirty-eight pieds in length and three to four pieds in width. These dimensions suggest that cypress trees did not grow quite as large as cottonwoods, even in Lower Louisiana.[79] Lecomte's contract obligated him to include a rudder, three oars, and one paddle with the pirogue—but not the fittings for the rudder. These would have been fashioned of metal, and metal of any variety was relatively rare and dear in the Illinois Country. To have included the fittings for the rudder in this contract would have changed the nature of the agreement, even though Lecomte as a master smith had the ability to make the fixtures.[80] Lecomte had until the end of September 1726, roughly seven weeks, to complete the pirogue. If Lecomte finished the vessel on schedule, Laverdure and Bernard may well have used it to ship Illinois produce—flour, salted meat, lead, and deer skins—to New Orleans in the fall convoy of 1726.

Twenty years later Jean-Baptiste Aubuchon, featured rather grandiosely as "constructeur des voitures au pays des Illinois," contracted at Kaskaskia to make two pirogues of the same size, 17,000 livres burden, one for André Roy and one for Jacques Godefroy.[81] The latter two were identified as "voyageurs-négociants" who usually resided in Detroit but who were, for the time being, in Kaskaskia. These vessels were very large for pirogues, for the 17,000 livres burden was not to include the weight of the oarsmen or their food. The specifications for these two vessels are detailed, and they reveal something about the configurations of larger pirogues. Each was to include basically two parts, the hull and the upper decking (*rehausse de bordage*). It is therefore apparent that some pirogues, like some bateaux, were at least partially decked over to afford a modicum of protection for the cargoes. Aubuchon was obliged to include oars, seats, and rudders; the purchasers, Roy and Godefroy, agreed to furnish the nails, metal fixtures for the rudders, oakum, and tar. As merchants they had better access to these imported materials than did the local carpenter, Aubuchon. Aubuchon had from the date of the contract, November 22, 1746, until the end of January 1747 to have the two pirogues "well caulked and ready to sail." Roy and Godefroy were to pay a total of 1,200 livres, 600 per vessel; 600 livres could purchase a decent residence in Kaskaskia as that time. This sum was to be cobbled together from 200 livres in paper redeemable in New Orleans ("bons de la caisse"), 400 livres in merchandise, and 600 livres worth of flour. In colonial Louisiana, where specie was always in short supply, this kind of mix was typical for payment of obligations throughout the eighteenth century.

While *voiture* was a generic term for rivercraft, *pirogue* was used exclusively for dugout vessels of all sizes. *Bateau* could be applied to any boat, large or small, equipped with sails or oars and used on rivers or the sea, but it was used generally for larger vessels only—virtually never for a canoe or pirogue. The bateaux that carried the commerce between New Orleans and the Illinois Country were the largest river vessels in North America.[82] In the nineteenth century Walker noted that bateaux were "generally in use in the upper country, and meant for longer voyages than the pirogues. They were of rough plank, long in proportion to their breadth, and something in the shape of a coffin."[83] Although *bateaux* is much used to describe water transportation in colonial Louisiana, the image of the crafts' appearance has been diffuse and often confused.[84] Walker's coffin metaphor leaves a sharp and indelible impression of an elongated, boxy, flat-bottomed vessel.

Pirogues were used by the French on the lower Mississippi River from the earliest days of Louisiana, and according to Walker, they continued in commercial use on the lower river until as late as 1830. Bateaux required sawed—albeit roughly—planks and probably came into use somewhat later than pirogues. Surrey remarked that Iberville *proposed* the building of flatboats as early as 1700, but the first contract for any such vessel was struck in 1708, and "the number of such boats did not increase rapidly."[85] When flour shipments from Illinois increased in frequency and size during the early 1730s, more bateaux were built. In 1733 a sixteen-ton model was built in New Orleans for the Illinois trade, but it was damaged by flotsam drifting down the rain-swollen Mississippi and did not get started upriver until 1734.[86]

By the late 1730s, with the Illinois–New Orleans trade booming, many contracts for bateaux were drafted by royal notaries in Louisiana. In the summer of 1737, Commissaire-ordonnateur Salmon ordered no fewer than fifty bateaux, all of which were to be forty pieds long and nine wide, at a cost of

1,550 livres per hull and 3,440 livres when the caulking, rigging, and metal-work were completed.[87] In December 1737 two woodworkers at Fort de Chartres, Michel Vien and Michel Le Jeune, collaborated on a contract with Louis Giscard de Benoist to construct the hull of a bateau that would carry 30,000 livres. The contract specified that Vien and Le Jeune were to construct only the hull of this vessel and were not required even to caulk it. Benoist was to supply the nails for the project, provide two laborers to assist Vien and Le Jeune, and compensate them with 500 livres worth of flour and brandy on the completion of the work.[88]

Although the records do not reveal it, one suspects that Benoist of the aristocratic name who ordered the bateau at Fort de Chartres in December 1737 was the commander of the royal convoy in 1737–38 and that the bateau he was ordering at Fort de Chartres would constitute part of the government contingent of boats in the spring convoy that descended the Mississippi.[89] Illinois had an abundant wheat harvest in 1737, and the convoy that arrived in New Orleans in late April 1738 carried 100,000 livres of flour. The hull of black walnut that Vien and Le Jeune contracted to build in December 1737 was to be delivered ready for caulking on the shore of the Mississippi by April 1, 1738. If they finished their work on time, this walnut craft was likely one of the vessels that glided into the docks at New Orleans in late April loaded with Illinois flour. The downriver run was often swift and easy, and Governor Bienville was delighted with the success of this convoy when it arrived in his provincial capital.[90]

The contractors who built Benoist's walnut bateau, Michel Vien and Michel Le Jeune, were apparently making other vessels during the spring of 1738, for at Fort de Chartres in May 1738 they agreed that the latter would sell in New Orleans the oak-and-walnut bateau that they had built as partners.[91] We know that several convoys descended from the Illinois Country to New Orleans during the spring and summer of 1738, and it seems that Michel Le Jeune exchanged temporarily his shipwright's bonnet for a voyageur's ban-danna and headed downriver with one of the later convoys. In New Orleans he sold the bateau that he and Vien had built earlier in the spring, no doubt along with the flour they had received as part of their contract. In exchange for these items, Le Jeune would acquire imports from France required in the Illinois Country—coffee, sugar, wine, guns, gunpowder, shoes, cloth, cloth-ing, and so forth.

The price of labor was reputed to be high in the Illinois Country. None-theless, contracts for bateaux made at New Orleans and Fort de Chartres in 1737 suggest that riverboats might be had more cheaply in Upper Louisiana than in Lower; perhaps lumber suitable for constructing them was simply more plentiful in the upper colony. In any event, the same "constructeur des voitures" who built a pirogue at Kaskaskia in 1746, Jean-Baptiste Aubuchon, contracted to build five bateaux for the French royal government at Kaskaskia in October 1756.[92] This means either that boats for the Mississippi Valley trade could be built more cheaply in Illinois or that they were specifically needed in that place at that time to dispatch Illinois foodstuffs to Fort Duquesne, at the Forks of the Ohio. By this point in the French and Indian War, the British had cut off Fort Duquesne from its sources of supply in Canada and the French commandant there was urgently requesting foodstuffs from the Illinois Country.[93]

When at the end of the war the British acquired control over the Illinois Country east of the Mississippi, they immediately had to procure river transportation to their newly acquired settlements in the heart of the continent. Early in 1763 the British commander-in-chief in North America, Sir Jeffrey Amherst, ordered three shipwrights to travel from Philadelphia to Fort Pitt to build twenty "Batteaux" for use on the Ohio River.[94] Amherst's orders were duly carried out, for in the summer of 1764 his replacement as commander-in-chief, General Thomas Gage, complained that the British had at Fort Pitt only twenty-three "Batteaus" and that building more of them would cost a "monstrous price."[95] British officers consistently used French nomenclature when discussing river vessels, but it is impossible precisely to describe the "Batteaux" built at Fort Pitt in 1763.

British merchants also had to cope with the problem of inland-waterway transportation. Baynton, Wharton, and Morgan of Philadelphia was the largest of the British trading companies that engaged in western commerce following the French and Indian War. By 1766 merchants from this company were following the practice initiated by the British army, dispatching sawyers and shipwrights from Philadelphia to Fort Pitt to construct "Battoes" for the Ohio River trade.[96] The shipwrights were paid eleven pounds Pennsylvania currency per month; the sawyers, eight pounds. Moreover, the skilled craftsmen received "Meat, Drink and Washing," but the common laborers received only "Sufficient Meat." The shipwrights seem to have been Englishmen—Rambo and Beverley—whereas the pit sawyers were more usually Irish and Scotsmen—Cornelly, Fitzpatrick, Lynch, Evans, and Andrews. As interesting as these 1766 labor contracts are, they do not provide any detailed descriptions or specifications for the "Battoes" that were being built at Fort Pitt. The persistent use of the French name, however, suggests that these vessels very much resembled the French bateaux of the Mississippi Valley.

General Gage considered the cost of constructing riverboats "monstrous." Baynton, Wharton, and Morgan reckoned the price of building forty-five

"Batteaus" at Fort Pitt to be fifty-five pounds Pennsylvania currency per vessel.[97] Translating this amount into roughly 750 French livres suggests that the cost of building bateaux at Fort Pitt compared favorably with costs anywhere else within the extended Mississippi watershed. The boats built at Fort Pitt were made of green timber, however, and were expected to last only one year in service.[98] Moreover, Baynton, Wharton, and Morgan needed many of them to carry on their western commerce; they were hoping to prepare a convoy of sixty-five boats to descend the Ohio River in the autumn of 1766 with supplies for the British garrison in the Illinois Country.[99] The unexpectedly high price of river vessels was one reason for the financial difficulties that this famous trading company experienced in conducting commerce between Pennsylvania and the Mississippi Valley.

British merchants traded down the Mississippi with New Orleans as well as up the Ohio with Fort Pitt. In February 1775 the trading partners Patrick Kennedy and Richard Winston[100] commissioned Louis Chauvin-Charleville of Kaskaskia to have a bateau constructed for a commercial journey to New Orleans. This vessel was to accommodate sixteen to eighteen oarsmen and to carry 30,000 to 35,000 livres of freight.[101] The fact that this contract was signed February 16 and the vessel was to be completed on March 10 reinforces the impression that bateaux were rather primitive, flat-bottomed vessels, for it is hardly conceivable that a sophisticated vessel with full keel, ribs, and planking could have been built in less than four weeks.

The bateau developed by the Louisiana French early in the eighteenth century as their river vessel of preference continued as the standard craft for the commercial route between Illinois and New Orleans long after the French regime had ended in Louisiana. In 1782 a master carpenter in Kaskaskia (at that time still de jure British but controlled by Virginia), André Sabourin, contracted to built a bateau for Joseph Delière dit Bonvouloir for 1,500 livres.[102] The American Revolution had inflated the price of bateaux along with that of flour and everything else. Sabourin agreed to furnish all the wood, caulking, and tar for the boat; Bonvouloir would supply all the metal parts: 810 nails, the fixtures for the rudder, and the iron ring for the anchor. Metal components were still rare and dear in the Illinois Country, and they were doled out with great care and precision.

Eighteenth-century Louisiana was not a place where people were addicted to precision, uniformity, and standardization. Remarkably, however, the bateau that Sabourin built at Kaskaskia in 1782 had *precisely* the same dimensions as the fifty vessels that Commissaire-ordonnateur Salmon ordered built in New Orleans a half-century earlier—forty pieds long and nine wide. This suggests that a standard bateau for use in the Illinois Country–New Orleans trade developed rather early in the eighteenth century and that it performed well enough to remain standard for the entire century. Indeed, Norman Walker claimed that the first boats built by Americans in the entire Mississippi watershed were thirty bateaux constructed near Pittsburgh in 1787 for the U.S. government—once again, the dimensions were precisely the same, forty feet by nine feet.[103] The bateaux ordered at New Orleans in 1737 were each to be of twelve tons burden.[104] Michel Vien and Michel Le Jeune agreed to build a single bateau designed to carry 30,000 livres (fifteen tons) at Chartres during the winter of 1738. The standard eighteenth-century bateau was therefore about forty pieds long, nine pieds wide, and carried somewhere between twelve and fifteen tons. These coffin-shaped vessels continued in use until as late as 1825, according to Walker,[105] before being entirely supplanted by the larger American-style flatboats, sometimes called Kentucky boats, that as early as the 1790s began to descend the Ohio River to the Mississippi and thence to New Orleans.

Like good gristmills, serviceable riverboats were chronically scarce in colonial Louisiana. In 1797 Lieutenant Governor Trudeau remarked that when Chouteau's water mill in St. Louis got fitted with a saw, in addition to its millstones, it would be able to produce planks for building "chalands," flat-bottomed riverboats.[106] These vessels would then, Trudeau hoped, facilitate the transport of flour from Spanish Illinois to New Orleans, which, he said, "will some day be provisioned entirely by us." This would eventually happen, although not in Trudeau's lifetime. It is not known whether Chouteau's mill ever got fitted out for sawing planks, but this had not yet been accomplished when Finiels saw it in 1797. In a section entitled "Observations" attached to the New Bourbon census of 1797,[107] Delassus de Luzières complained about the shortage of commercial rivercraft in Upper Louisiana and suggested that the Spanish colonial government lure boat builders from the United States by offering to pay their moving expenses and guaranteeing them work. There is no evidence that Spanish officials in New Orleans ever acted on de Luzières's suggestion, and the colonial period in Upper Louisiana ended with the region still being plagued by a shortage of river vessels.

During the eighteenth century, the time required to travel the Mississippi River between the Illinois Country and New Orleans depended on the water level in the river, the weather, the state of Indian relations, blind luck and, most important, the direction of the current. A good rule of thumb was that the trip upriver required about four times as long as that downriver. Usually the descent to New Orleans from Kaskaskia or Ste. Genevieve could be made in three to four weeks, whereas it often took three to four months of cursing and pulling to bring a bateau upriver. Trips upriver were often nightmarish.

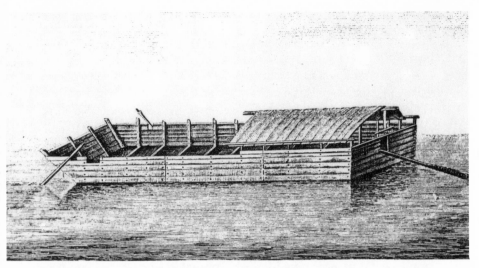

American-style flatboat of the type used on the Ohio and Mississippi Rivers. Creole bateaux were smaller but similar in style and appearance. Illustration by Charles Warin from Georges-Victor Collot's *Journey in North America*, 1924.

In April 1781 a Spanish convoy was bushwhacked by Chickasaw Indians ("Chis") near the mouth of the Arkansas River, and the ensuing month that was required to reach the safety of Ste. Genevieve was a living hell for the Spanish troops. Josef de la Peña, one of the officers, described this escapade and noted that from the commander on down, every man in the convoy remained armed day and night, "enduring fatigue, discomfort, continual rain, and frequent alarms."[108] De la Peña doubtless wished many times during this nightmare that he was back in his native sunny Spain.

Two decades later Perrin du Lac traveled on the Mississippi and described the daily lives of boatmen:

> No trips are more arduous than those on the Mississippi. The men who row up it are exposed to the weather, sleep on the ground, and eat nothing but maize and bacon. On long voyages . . . they suffer indescribably. They wear nothing except what is required for decency, and their skins, burned by the sun, are continuously peeling. . . . It is not unusual for them to succumb to fatigue and die oar in hand. The incredible number of mosquitoes that infest the riverbanks increases their torment and prevents them from obtaining the rest at night that is required to restore their strength.[109]

Parisians like Perrin du Lac were amazed by the swarms of mosquitoes that throve in the Mississippi Valley, for these insects were virtually unknown in northern France. Mosquito netting was sometimes used by boatmen in the eighteenth century,[110] but it was never adequate to prevent festering bites and malaria.[111]

A bateau built at Kaskaskia in 1775 called for places for sixteen to eighteen men.[112] Sixteen rowers may have been adequate for the trip downriver, but Governor General Vaudreuil insisted in 1751 that twenty-four soldiers per bateau, in addition to the "patron" (i.e., the skipper), were required to pull a royal convoy upriver from New Orleans to the Illinois Country.[113] The crews that endured the hardships of propelling and guiding bateaux on the Mississippi in colonial times were composed of engagés, slaves, and royal troops (French, Spanish, or British).[114] Given that ascending the river was far and away more onerous than descending, slaves were sometimes leased in Lower Louisiana specifically for making the trip upriver to the Illinois Country. In 1736, for example, Pierre Boucher de Monbrun of Kaskaskia leased two slaves (Jacques and Petit Jean) from Messieur Tixerant in New Orleans for a fee of 3,000 livres of flour, Monbrun mortgaging all his real and personal property as security.[115] Three years later Monsieurs Bienvenu and Mathurin leased a slave (Jacob) in Pointe Coupée from Madame François Baron, but ascending the Mississippi their bateaux was attacked by Indians (probably Chickasaws) who killed Mathurin and abducted Jacob, which left a financial mess resulting in a lawsuit.[116]

Although slaves commonly rowed bateaux and poled pirogues, engagés likely constituted the largest category of boatmen in the colonial Mississippi Valley. The Kaskaskia Manuscripts contain numerous contracts of engagement for boatmen,[117] and the militia muster roll for Ste. Genevieve in 1779 lists "voyageur" as the largest occupational category in town.[118] When a bateau belonging to Henri Carpentier was preparing to ascend the Mississippi from New Orleans to Ste. Genevieve in 1768, the crew consisted of the skipper, eighteen engagés, and two black slaves.[119] British use of French terms for riverboats and their crews included the curious "Batteau Men." The "Batteau Men" whom the British employed were often French Canadian or French Creole engagés, as were the voyageurs employed in the fur trade. When shipping supplies and trade goods down the Ohio River in bateaux, the British normally used a crew of five men, but when they utilized these vessels to transport personnel, they could hold "at least 25 Men each."[120] These names and numbers suggest that on the Ohio River the British used French-style bateaux that were somewhat smaller than the largest of the vessels that usually plied the Mississippi between New Orleans and the Illinois Country.

Notes

INTRODUCTION

1. Pierre Pluchon, *Histoire de la colonisation française, des origines à la Restauration* (Paris: Athème Fayard, 1991). This volume does contain, however, a truly bizarre map that shows *two* Kaskaskias (one located on the site of St. Louis) but no other villages in the region.

2. Gregory H. Nobles, *American Frontiers: Cultural Encounters and the Continental Conquest* (New York: Hill and Wang, 1997), 90–91.

3. Clarence Walworth Alvord, *Illinois Country, 1673–1818*, The Centennial History of Illinois, vol. 1 (Springfield: Illinois Centennial Commission, 1920).

4. Ibid., 190.

5. Concerning the fur trade in the middle Mississippi Valley, consult the splendid bibliography in William E. Foley, *The Genesis of Missouri: From Wilderness Outpost to Statehood* (Columbia: University of Missouri Press, 1989).

6. Throughout this study I will use the French *mentalité* rather than the English *mentality* because, as Robert Darnton explains (*The Kiss of Lamourette: Reflections in Cultural History* [New York: Norton, 1990], 257), "*mentalité* conveys a broader idea than its English counterpart."

7. John G. Clark, *New Orleans, 1718–1812: An Economic History* (Baton Rouge: Louisiana State University Press, 1970); Nancy M. Miller Surrey, *The Commerce of Louisiana during the French Regime, 1699–1763* (New York: Columbia University Press, 1916).

8. Marc Bloch, *Les Caractères originaux de l'histoire rurale française*, 2 vols. (Paris: A. Colin, 1964), esp. 1:46; Léopold Genicot, *Rural Communities in the Medieval West* (Baltimore: Johns Hopkins University Press, 1990), 45; Richard C. Hoffman, "Medieval Origins of the Common Fields," in *European Peasants and Their Markets: Essays in Agrarian Eco-*

nomic History, ed. William N. Parker and Eric L. Jones (Princeton, N.J.: Princeton University Press), 24; Robert Mandrou, *Introduction à la France moderne: Essai de psychologie historique (1500–1640)* (Paris: A. Michel, 1961), 125.

9. For examples, see Jacqueline Peterson and Jennifer S. H. Brown, eds., *The New Peoples: Being and Becoming Métis in North America* (Lincoln: University of Nebraska Press, 1985); Judith A. Franke, *French Peoria and the Illinois Country, 1673–1846,* Illinois State Museum Popular Science Series, vol. 12 (Springfield: Illinois State Museum Society, 1995); Tanis C. Thorne, *The Many Hands of My Relations* (Columbia: University of Missouri Press, 1996); Richard White, *The Middle Ground: Indians, Empires, and Republics in the Great Lakes Region, 1650–1815* (New York: Cambridge University Press, 1991).

CHAPTER 1: FRENCH LONGLOTS IN NORTH AMERICA

1. Peter Kalm, *The America of 1750: Peter Kalm's Travels in North America,* ed. Adolph B. Benson (New York: Dover, 1964), 415.

2. It will be convenient throughout this study to spell *longlot* as a single unhyphenated word.

3. See Michael Roark, "Imprint of the French in North America: Long-Lots in the Mid-Mississippi Valley," in *French and Germans in the Mississippi Valley: Landscape and Cultural Traditions,* ed. Michael Roark (Cape Girardeau: Center for Regional History and Cultural Heritage, Southeast Missouri State University, 1988), 111–36. Although this article is weak on historical background, it is a useful introduction to longlots in the Illinois Country.

4. Terry G. Jordan, "Antecedents of the Long-Lot in Texas," *Annals of the Association of American Geographers* 64 (Mar. 1974): 70–86.

5. Jordan, "Antecedents," 71.

6. The great seminal study in this regard is August Meitzen, *Siedlung und Agrarwesen der Westgermanen und Ostgermanen, der Kelten, Römer, Finnen und Slawen,* 3 vols. (Berlin: W. Hertz, 1895). Much German scholarship has been done on medieval settlement patterns and field types since then. See, for examples, W. Abel, *Geschichte des deutschen Landwirtschaft* (Stuttgart: Ulmer, 1978); Werner Rösener, ed., *Strukturen der Grundherrschaft im frühen Mittelalter* (Göttingen: Vandenhoeck und Ruprecht, 1989).

7. Quoted in Georges Duby, *Rural Economy and Country Life in the Medieval West,* trans. Cynthia Postan (Columbia: University of South Carolina Press, 1968), 391–93. The width-to-length ratio of these twelfth-century German longlots, 1:24, was greater than that of most French longlots in North America.

8. See the map of settlement patterns at Green Bay on p. 18.

9. See examples from France and Germany in Marc Bloch, *Les Caractères originaux de l'histoire rurale française,* 2 vols. (Paris: A. Colin, 1964), 1: planche 1; Hans-Jürgen Nitz, "Siedlungsstrukturen der königlichen und adeligen Grundherrschaft der Karolingerzeit— der Beitrag der historisch-genetischen Siedlungsgeographie," in *Struckturen der Grundherrschaft im frühen Mittelalter,* ed. Werner Rösener (Göttingen: Vandenhoeck und Ruprecht, 1989), 479.

10. Bloch, *Caractères originaux*, 1:39. All translations from French and Spanish are mine unless otherwise noted.

11. Calvin Goodrich, *The First Michigan Frontier* (Ann Arbor: University of Michigan Press, 1940), 16.

12. This pattern of land usage for farms in the St. Lawrence valley is depicted graphically in R. Cole Harris, ed., *Historical Atlas of Canada* (Toronto: University of Toronto Press, 1987), 1: pl. 53.

13. Jordan, "Antecedents," 80–82.

14. On Sudbury, see Sumner Chilton Powell, *Puritan Village: The Formation of a New England Town* (Middletown, Conn.: Wesleyan University Press, 1963); on Rowley, see David Grayson Allen, *In English Ways: The Movement of Societies and the Transferal of English Local Law and Custom to Massachusetts Bay in the Seventeenth Century* (Chapel Hill: University of North Carolina Press, 1981).

15. Map printed in Allen, *In English Ways*, 35.

16. See Richard C. Harris, *Seigneurial System in Early Canada, A Geographical Study* (Madison: University of Wisconsin Press, 1966), 119.

17. Max Derruau, "À l'origine du 'rang' canadien," *Cahiers de Géographie de Québec* 1 (1956): 40–47.

18. Marcel Trudel, *Les Débuts du régime seigneurial au Canada* (Montreal: Fides, 1974), 173 n. 89.

19. Harris, *Seigneurial System*, 120–21.

20. Concerning Giffard's grant to Langlois, see Trudel, *Régime seigneurial*, 151, 173–74; Derruau, "À l'origine du 'rang' canadien," 44, 46; Harris, *Seigneurial System*, 119.

21. Trudel, *Régime seigneurial*, 151 n. 24.

22. Harris, *Seigneurial System*, 119.

23. Allan Greer, *Peasant, Lord, and Merchant* (Toronto: University of Toronto Press, 1985), 26.

24. Trudel, *Régime seigneurial*, 169–74; see also Pierre Deffontaines, *Le Rang, type de peuplement rural du Canada français*, Cahiers de Geographie no. 5 (Quebec: Les Presses de l'université Laval, 1953); Derruau, "À l'origine du 'rang' canadien"; Louise Dechêne, *Habitants et marchands de Montréal au XVIIᵉ siècle* (Paris: Plon, 1974), 259–60. In his glossary of French-Canadian nomenclature, Harris (*Seigneurial System*, 229–30) defined the roture as "a concession of land which could not be subconceded, and which was held by a *censitaire* from a seigneur," the côte as "a short line of settlement along a river or a road," and the rang as "a row of rectangular *rotures* with the short side fronting on the same river or road."

25. Marcel Trudel, *An Atlas of New France* (Quebec: Les Presses de l'université Laval, 1968), 172.

26. The plans of these three villages, two square and one a half-square, are shown in Harris, ed., *Historical Atlas of Canada*, 1: pl. 52; and Trudel, *Atlas of New France*, 166.

27. Deffontaines, *Le Rang*, 24.

28. Harris, *Seigneurial System*, 180. Harris defined a village as a "compact settlement of not more than five hundred people in which there were several commercial and ser-

vice functions" and identified only six villages in all of Canada at the end of the French regime; five of these were concentrated near Montreal (176).

29. Louis-Edm. Hamelin, "Le Rang à Saint-Didace de Maskinongé," *Notes de Géographie* 3 (May 1953): 5.

30. Ibid., 4.

31. Dechêne, *Habitants et marchands,* 263.

32. Ibid., 7.

33. On the development of Detroit as an agricultural community during the French regime, see Lina Gouger, "Montréal et le peuplement de Détroit, 1701–1765," paper presented at the annual meeting of the French Colonial Historical Society, Montreal, May 1992; Ernest J. Lajeunesse, ed., *The Windsor Border Region: Canada's Southernmost Frontier* (Toronto: The Champlain Society for the Government of Ontario, 1960).

34. Hamilton quoted in Goodrich, *The First Michigan Frontier,* 93.

35. *American State Papers, Public Lands* (hereafter *ASP, PL*), 9 vols. (Washington, D.C.: U.S. Government Printing Office, 1832), 1:282.

36. See letter from the governor general of Canada, Frederick Haldimand, to the lieutenant governor at Detroit, Jehu Hay, Aug. 31, 1784, printed in Lajeunesse, ed., *The Windsor Border Region,* 74.

37. *ASP, PL,* 1:264.

38. Ibid.

39. Dennis Au ("Maps and Archeology," 4–5) has pointed out that the French habitants at River Raisin in the Detroit region seldom if ever precisely measured off eighty arpents but rather simply proceeded on the premise that their longlots extended a considerable distance from front to back.

40. *Atlas of North America: Space Age Portrait of a Continent* (Washington, D.C.: National Geographic Society, 1985), 83 (inset).

41. Bela Hubbard, *Memorials of a Half-Century in Michigan and the Lake Region* (New York: G. P. Putnam's Sons, 1888), 116.

42. Au, "Maps and Archaeology."

43. British census of 1782 printed in *Report of the Pioneer and Historical Society of the State of Michigan,* 21 vols. (Lansing: Thorp and Godfrey, State Printers and Binders, 1888), 10:601–13.

44. See Richard Alan Sambrook, "Historical Lineaments in the Straits of Mackinac" (M.A. thesis, Michigan State University, 1980).

45. Cartographic Division, Michigan State Archives, Lansing, Michigan.

46. See Elizabeth M. Scott, *French Subsistance at Fort Michilimackinac, 1715–1781,* Archaeological Completion Report Series, no. 9 (Mackinac Island, Mich.: Mackinac Island State Park Commission, 1985), 13.

47. Sambrook, "Historical Lineaments," 59.

48. This map is reproduced in Wayne C. Temple, ed., *Indian Villages of the Illinois Country, Atlas,* Scientific Papers of the Illinois State Museum, vol. 2 (Springfield: Illinois State Museum, 1975), pl. 72.

49. Jonathan Carver, *The Journals of Carver and Related Documents, 1766–1770,* ed. John Parker (St. Paul: Minnesota Historical Society Press, 1976), 73–78.

50. Kerry A. Trask, "Community of LaBaye," *Michigan Historical Review* 15 (Spring 1989), 4.

51. Henry R. Schoolcraft, *Narrative Journal of Travels,* ed. Mentor L. Williams (East Lansing: Michigan State College Press, 1953), 242.

52. Jacqueline Peterson, "Many Roads to Red River," in *The New Peoples: Being and Becoming Métis in North America,* ed. Jacqueline Peterson and Jennifer S. H. Brown (Lincoln: University of Nebraska Press, 1985), 55, 57.

53. Trask, "LaBaye," 6.

54. Ibid.

55. *ASP, PL,* 5:97.

56. Ebenezer Childs, "Recollections of Wisconsin since 1820," in *Collections of the State Historical Society of Wisconsin,* 10 vols., ed. Lyman Copeland Draper (Madison: State Historical Society of Wisconsin, 1906), 4:166.

57. *ASP, PL,* 5:97.

58. Ibid.

59. Peterson, "Many Roads to Red River," 57.

60. Trudel, *Régime seigneurial,* 115–19.

61. Peterson, "Many Roads to Red River," 57.

62. Albert G. Ellis, "Fifty-Four Years' Recollections of Men and Events in Wisconsin," in *Wisconsin Historical Recollections,* 10 vols., ed. Reuben G. Thwaites (Madison: State Historical Society of Wisconsin, 1906), 7:215, 218.

63. Peterson, "Many Roads to Red River," 57.

64. Jay Higginbotham, *Old Mobile: Fort St. Louis de la Louisiane, 1702–1711* (Mobile, Ala.: Museum of the City of Mobile, 1977), 346.

65. This edict was printed in translation in the *Louisiana Historical Quarterly* 14 (July 1931): 347.

66. Pierre Deffontaines, "The *Rang*-Pattern of Rural Settlement," in *French-Canadian Society,* ed. Marcel Rioux and Yves Martin (Ottawa: McClelland and Stewart, 1964), 6.

67. Edward T. Price (*Dividing the Land: Early American Beginnings of Our Private Property Mosaic* [Chicago: University of Chicago Press, 1995], 303) argues that there was no "preordained" plan for riverain longlots in French Louisiana. *Preordained* may be too strong a word, but there certainly was a government plan for this cadastral practice that antedated the founding of New Orleans.

68. Superior Council of Louisiana to Directors of the Royal Indies Company, Sept. 30, 1725, ser. C13A, 9:241–42, Archives Nationales Coloniales (hereafter ANC), Paris. Microfilm from Library of Congress, Washington, D.C.

69. John Whitling Hall, "Louisiana Survey Systems: Their Antecedents, Distribution, and Characteristics" (Ph.D. diss., Louisiana State University, 1970), 25, 32.

70. In North America the French never measured agricultural land in toises, perhaps because the larger unit was more convenient for larger parcels of land or perhaps merely because of custom and habit.

71. William B. Knipmeyer, "Settlement Succession in Eastern French Louisiana" (Ph.D. diss., Louisiana State University, 1956), 32.

72. Hall, "Louisiana Survey Systems," 168.

73. Glenn R. Conrad, *The Attakapas Domesday Book: Land Grants, Claims and Confirmations in the Attakapas District, 1764–1826* (Lafayette: Center for Louisiana Studies, University of Southwestern Louisiana, 1991), 3.

74. Price, *Dividing the Land,* 302.

75. Although Prairie du Chien, located on the east bank of the Mississippi just above the mouth of the Wisconsin River, fell within Upper Canada, this study will consider it as part of the Illinois Country, for it participated in the same pattern of land usage that characterized the other Illinois communities.

76. Morris S. Arnold, *Unequal Laws unto a Savage Race: European Legal Traditions in Arkansas, 1686–1836* (Fayetteville: University of Arkansas Press, 1985), appendix 2. Concerning the colonial history of Arkansas Post, see also Morris S. Arnold's scrupulously researched and elegantly written *Colonial Arkansas, 1686–1804: A Social and Cultural History* (Fayetteville: University of Arkansas Press, 1991).

77. Arnold, *Unequal Laws,* 87.

78. Jordan, "Antecedents of the Long-Lot," 80.

79. Jordan's misapprehension concerning the use of longlots in the Illinois Country is understandable given the ignorance that prevails regarding the colonial history of the Mississippi River valley. D. W. Meinig, for example, in his magisterial *Shaping of America,* vol. 1, *Atlantic America, 1492–1800* (New Haven, Conn.: Yale University Press, 1986), 242–43, makes precisely the same mistake when he clumps the French longlots of Canada, Louisiana, and the Illinois Country together as identical phenomena.

80. Clarence Walworth Alvord, *The Illinois Country, 1673–1818,* The Centennial History of Illinois, vol. 1 (Springfield: Illinois Centennial Commission, 1920), 206–7.

81. See, for example, two recent studies, both of which perpetuate this confusion: Philippe Oszuscik, "French Creoles on the Gulf Coast," in *To Build in a New Land: Ethnic Landscapes in North America,* ed. Allen G. Noble (Baltimore: Johns Hopkins University Press, 1992), 142–43; Price, *Dividing the Land,* 8 (map), 286 (comments).

82. Jordan, "Antecedents of the Long-Lot," 72–74.

83. Roark ("French Imprint," 113–17) addresses this issue briefly and rather awkwardly. For example, he confuses European and French Canadian influences on the development of longlots in the Illinois Country.

CHAPTER 2: SETTLEMENTS IN THE ILLINOIS COUNTRY

1. Volney to Jefferson, Aug. 24, 1796, in Gilbert Chinard, ed., *Volney et l'Amérique d'après des documents et sa correspondance avec Jefferson,* Johns Hopkins Studies in Romance Literatures and Languages (Baltimore: Johns Hopkins University Press, 1923), 49.

2. Francis Parkman, *The Conspiracy of Pontiac* (Boston: Little, Brown, 1902), 245.

3. Sara Jones Tucker, ed., *Indian Villages of the Illinois Country, Atlas,* Scientific Papers of the Illinois State Museum (Springfield: Illinois State Museum, 1942), 1: pl. 1.

4. Ibid., pl. 7.

5. Ibid., pls. 9, 10.

6. "Règlement pour l'establissement d'un conseil provincial aux Illinois," ser. B, 43:103–4, ANC.

7. On Vaudreuil, see *Dictionary of Canadian Biography*, 1981 ed., s.v. "Rigaud, Pierre-François, marquis de Vaudreuil," by William J. Eccles; Guy Frégault, *Le Grand Marquis: Pierre de Rigaud de Vaudreuil et la Louisiane* (Montreal: Fides, 1952).

8. See Vaudreuil's memorial, Nov. 9, 1745, ser. C13A, 29:85–87, ANC.

9. St. Louis Recorded Archives (hereafter STLRA), no. 512, Missouri Historical Society Archives (cited hereafter MHS), St. Louis, Missouri.

10. See Arrêt du Conseil d'Etat, Sept. 27, 1717, Manuscrits français, nouvelles acquisitions 9310, Bibliothèque Nationale (hereafter BN), Paris; "Règlement sur le Régie des affaires de la colonie de la Louisiane," Sept. 5, 1721, ser. B, 43:28, ANC.

11. Jack P. Greene, *Imperatives, Behaviors, and Identities: Essays in Early American Cultural History* (Charlottesville: University of Virginia Press, 1992), 2.

12. See Carl J. Ekberg, "Marie Rouensa 8cate8a and the Foundations of French Illinois," *Illinois Historical Journal* 84 (Autumn 1991): 146–60, for a case study on one such early Illinois family. (The 8 in Marie Rouensa's name was apparently pronounced like the French *oui*.) The relationships between Frenchmen and Indian women have been recently explored at great length by Richard White (*The Middle Ground* [Cambridge: Cambridge University Press, 1991]), whose study focuses on the *pays d'en haut*, Upper Canada. The French never clearly defined the boundary between Upper Canada and Upper Louisiana, and White's study includes much of the Illinois Country.

13. Clarence Walworth Alvord, *The Illinois Country, 1673–1818*, The Centennial History of Illinois, vol. 1 (Springfield: Illinois Centennial Commission, 1920), chaps. 6–10, is still the best summary of this period of Illinois history, although his coverage of early settlement patterns and agricultural exploitation is minimal.

14. Marcel Giraud, *Histoire de la Louisiane française*, 5 vols. (Paris: Presses Universitaires de France, 1966), 3:372.

15. Order of the Royal Indies Company, Aug. 26, 1718, ser. B, 42:230–32, ANC. On the creation of the provincial government in the Illinois Country after the founding of New Orleans, see also Marcel Giraud, *A History of French Louisiana*, vol. 5, trans. Brian Pearce (Baton Rouge: Louisiana State University Press, 1991), 440–41. Volume 5 of this ambitious work is the first to deal with the Illinois Country in anything but cursory fashion (vols. 1, 2, and 5 have been translated into English). Giraud's massive work is indispensable to the student of French Louisiana, but it presents two serious problems for dealing with the Illinois Country. First, Giraud does not acknowledge the existence of *any* preceding scholarship, including the essential studies of Alvord (*The Illinois Country*) and Natalia M. Belting (*Kaskaskia under the French Regime* [Urbana: University of Illinois Press, 1948], 33 n. 30). Second, his knowledge of the Kaskaskia manuscripts is thin, and when he does cite them, he uses an antiquated and now useless method rather than the efficient system developed by Margaret Kimball-Brown and Lawrie C. Dean (concerning their organization and collation of the Kaskaskia Manuscripts, see note 32 of this chapter).

16. Alvord, *Illinois Country*, chaps. 9, 10.

17. See the comments by Governor General Bienville (ser. C13A, 21:60–62, ANC) from 1736 regarding the site selected for Fort de Chartres.

18. See Edward B. Jelks, Carl J. Ekberg, and Terrance J. Martin, *Excavations at the Laurens*

Site, Studies in Illinois Archaeology, no. 5 (Springfield: Illinois Historic Preservation Agency, 1989), 3–15.

19. Boisbriant was born in Montreal in 1675, the son of Sidrac-Michel Dugué de Boisbriant. For Boisbriant's family background, see René Jetté, ed., *Dictionnaire généalogique des familles du Québec* (Montreal: Presses de l'université de Montréal, 1983), 379; *Dictionary of Canadian Biography,* s.v. "Dugué, Pierre, sieur de Boisbriand," by W. Stanford Reid; William Bennet Munro, ed., *Documents Relating to the Seigniorial Tenure in Canada, 1598–1854* (Toronto: Champlain Society, 1908), 102 n. 2. The description of Boisbriant's status in the Illinois Country is contained in a letter written by one Monsieur Lallemant from Kaskaskia. This important letter is in the Archives du Service Hydrographique de la Marine (ser. 2 JJ 56, item no. 29), which is housed within the Archives Nationales in Paris; the Illinois Historical Survey in Urbana has a photostat of it.

20. Source documents from the early 1720s are scarce and scattered. The best introduction to this era is Alvord, *The Illinois Country,* chap. 8.

21. Sidney Breese, *The Early History of Illinois from Its Discovery by the French in 1673, until Its Cession to Great Britain in 1763* (Chicago: E. B. Myers, 1884), 286. The location of the manuscript of this important source document is unknown.

22. Ibid., 292.

23. Giraud (*Histoire de la Louisiane,* vol. 3) is overwhelmingly the best source on the Royal Indies Company's activities in Louisiana during the early eighteenth century.

24. For an introduction to early real estate conveyances in the Illinois Country, see Alvord, *Illinois Country,* 203–5.

25. See this concession in ser. B, 43:56, ANC.

26. See *ASP, PL,* 2:183.

27. Munro, *Seigniorial Tenure,* 102, 112.

28. Alvord, *Illinois Country,* 203–4, suggests that in the Illinois Country, unlike in French Canada, lands granted "en franc alleu" could indeed convey seigneurial tenure.

29. Jetté, *Dictionnaire,* 379. Alvord (*Illinois Country,* 204) and Breese (*Early History,* 179) both misidentified this man as Jean St. Thérèse Langlois.

30. Concerning Broutin's career as an engineer in French Louisiana, see Samuel Wilson Jr., "Ignace François Broutin," in *Frenchmen and French Ways in the Mississippi Valley,* ed. John Francis McDermott (Urbana: University of Illinois Press, 1969), 231–94. Broutin's map is located in ser. C11A 126:47, ANC, and has been reproduced in Tucker, *Indian Villages, Atlas,* 1: pl. 22.

31. Munro, *Seigniorial Tenure,* 112 n. 2.

32. Kaskaskia Manuscripts 34:2:19:1 (i.e., the first document from February 19, 1734), collated by Margaret Kimball-Brown and Lawrie C. Dean, French Collection, Randolph County Courthouse, Chester, Illinois. Cited hereafter as KM. Concerning the value of this collection, see Margaret Kimball-Brown, "Documents and Archaeology in French Illinois," in *French Colonial Archaeology,* ed. John A. Walthall (Urbana: University of Illinois Press, 1991), 78–84.

33. Richard C. Harris, *Seigneurial System in Early Canada, A Geographical Study* (Madison: University of Wisconsin Press, 1966), 106; Munro, *Seigniorial Tenure,* 91–94.

34. Theodore C. Pease and Raymond C. Werner, eds., *The French Foundations, 1680–1693*, Collections of the Illinois State Historical Library, vol. 23 (Springfield: Illinois State Historical Library, 1934), 28–31.

35. Morris S. Arnold, a historian as well as an erudite jurist, remarks on the seigneurial nature of concessions granted in early Illinois by La Salle in *Unequal Laws unto a Savage Race: European Legal Traditions in Arkansas, 1686–1836* (Fayetteville: University of Arkansas Press, 1985), 15.

36. "Records of the Superior Council," trans. Heloise H. Cruzat, *Louisiana Historical Quarterly* 5 (July 1922): 408.

37. John Reynolds, *The Pioneer History of Illinois* (Chicago: Fergus, 1887), 50. John F. McDermott noted about John Reynolds's books on early Illinois history: "They are frequently erroneous in matters of fact, as reminiscences are likely to be. Yet they are of real value, for they preserve the impressions of a sympathetic outsider who over a long period had many intimate contacts with the French of the Illinois Country" (McDermott, ed., *Old Cahokia: A Narrative and Documents Illustrating the First Century of Its History* [St. Louis: St. Louis Historical Documents Foundation, 1952], 45 n. 97).

38. Kaskaskia Record Book B:16, Illinois State Archives (hereafter ISA), Springfield, Ill.

39. Harris, *Seigneurial System*, 129.

40. Belting, *Kaskaskia*, 33 n. 30.

41. Chassin to Father Bobé Descloseaux, July 1, 1722, ser. C13A, 10:299, ANC.

42. Munro explained (*Seigniorial Tenure*, 251 n. 1) that allodial land tenure in New France could be either *en franc alleu noble* or *en franc alleu roturier*.

43. This seventeen-arpent parcel is shown on the plat done by the American surveyor William Rector in 1810 (*ASP, PL*, 2: plat map between 182 and 183). Rector seems to have seen the original conveyance, or a copy of it, and gives a date of June 25, 1722. This means that Chassin already had one-half of this tract when, one week later, he wrote about his expectations of receiving a twenty-arpent parcel.

44. Margaret K. Brown and Lawrie C. Dean, eds., *The Village of Chartres in Colonial Illinois, 1720–1765* (hereafter *VOC*) (New Orleans: Polyanthos, 1977), document K-8, 345–46.

45. KM 30:10:28:1. Agnes was the daughter of a Kaskaskia Indian woman, Marie Rouensa 8cate8a (see chap. 2, note 12) and Michel Philippe. See Carl J. Ekberg, "Marie Rouensa 8cate8a and the Foundations of French Illinois," *Illinois Historical Journal* 84 (Autumn 1991): 146–60.

46. Ser. G1, 464, ANC.

47. *VOC*, K-62, 390–91.

48. A translation of this document has been printed in McDermott, *Old Cahokia*, 63. The original manuscript seems to have disappeared, but later manuscript copies correspond very closely to one another. See Perrin Collection; Cahokia Record Book B:123–24, in ISA.

49. The endpaper plats in Harris, *Seigneurial System*, show this concession.

50. Harris, *Seigneurial System*, 63–69; Alvord, *Illinois Country*, 205; McDermott, *Old Cahokia*, 77.

51. Mercier's letter published in McDermott, *Old Cahokia*, 77.

52. Allan Greer, *Peasant, Lord, and Merchant* (Toronto: University of Toronto Press, 1985), chap. 5; Harris, *Seigneurial System*, chap. 5.

53. Concerning John Law and the Royal Indies Company during 1717–23, see Giraud, *Histoire de la Louisiane*, vols. 3 and 4.

54. Kaskaskia Record Book B:11, ISA.

55. See Munro, *Seigniorial Tenure*, xcvi, 8, 35, on the system of fiefs that was established in the St. Lawrence River valley.

56. Regarding Renaut's concession, see *ASP, PL,* 2:190; Kaskaskia Record Book B:11, ISA; ser. B, 247:301, ANC.

57. Document 952.14, ISA; see also *ASP, PL,* 2:189.

58. *ASP, PL,* 2:192–93.

59. *VOC,* K-146, 496–97. There are notarial lists of concessions granted by Renaut (KM 34:4:11:1–4) that do not refer to any known more complete written conveyances. Perhaps these lists are notations for concessions that were granted verbally by Renaut, which he certainly seems to have done.

60. Kaskaskia Record Book A:359, C:245–46, ISA.

61. See Clarence W. Alvord, ed., *Cahokia Records, 1778–1790,* Collections of the Illinois State Historical Library, vol. 2 (Springfield: Illinois Historical Library, 1907), xxii (hereafter *CR*), where he argued that land in colonial Illinois held en franc alleu was fundamentally the same as a fief.

62. According to Trudel, in Canada to hold a fief en franc alleu meant that the seigneurs had no obligations to any suzerain (Marcel Trudel, *Les Debuts du régime seigneurial au Canada* [Montreal: Fides, 1974], 39).

63. Munro, *Seigniorial Tenure*, 52 n. 2. More usually, due to subinfeudation, *foi et hommage* were rendered locally in Canada (see Trudel, *Régime seigneurial,* 3).

64. Concerning Bienville as governor, see *Dictionary of Louisiana Biography,* ed. Glenn R. Conrad (1988), s.v. "Bienville," by Caroly E. De Latte; Giraud, *Histoire de la Louisiane,* passim.

65. KM 25:1:30:1.

66. KM 24:5:2:3.

67. The 1726 Louisiana census lists three Héberts as heads of households in Illinois (ser. G1, 464, ANC).

68. "Records of the Superior Council," trans. Heloise H. Cruzat, *Louisiana Historical Quarterly* 5 (July 1922): 408.

69. Quincy [Ill.] *Bounty Land Register,* Mar. 18, 1836, p. 1. Microfilm in Illinois State Historical Library, Springfield.

70. Breese, *Early History,* 173.

71. Marc Bloch, *Les Caractères originaux de l'histoire rurale française,* 2 vols. (Paris: A. Colin, 1964), 1:56.

72. André G. Haudricourt and Mariel Jean-Brunches Delamarre, *L'Homme et la charrue à travers le monde* (Paris: Gallimard, 1955), 355.

73. Léopold Genicot, *Rural Communities in the Medieval West* (Baltimore: Johns Hopkins University Press, 1990), 33.

74. Reynolds, *Pioneer History,* 54–55.

75. The excellent new study of Franco-Fox relations (R. David Edmunds and Joseph L. Peyser, *The Fox Wars: The Mesquakie Challenge to New France* [Lincoln: University of Nebraska Press, 1993]) is focused on New France and deals with Upper Louisiana only tangentially.

76. Ser. C13A, 8:447, ANC.

77. See burial record published in Marthe Faribault-Beauregard, ed., *La Population des forts francais d'Amérique,* 2 vols. (Montreal: Éditions Bergeron, 1984), 2:197.

78. Concerning this major Fox defeat, see Edmunds and Peyser, *Fox Wars,* chap. 5.

79. Vaudreuil to Maurepas, Mar. 20, 1748, in Theodore C. Pease and Ernestine Jenison, eds., *Illinois on the Eve of the Seven Years' War,* Collections of the Illinois State Historical Library, vol. 29 (Springfield: Illinois State Historical Library, 1940), 55.

80. On Macarty, who served as commandant in Illinois from 1751 until 1760, see ibid., xiii–xiv n. 1.

81. Ibid., 427.

82. J. P. Dunn Jr., *Indiana: Redemption from Slavery* (New York: Houghton, Mifflin, 1905), 94.

83. Georges Duby, *Rural Economy and Country Life in the Medieval West,* trans. Cynthia Postan (Columbia: University of South Carolina Press, 1968), 55.

84. An original manuscript version of this plan is in the William L. Clements Library, Ann Arbor, Michigan. It is reproduced in Philip Pittman, *The Present State of the European Settlements on the Mississippi* (London, 1770; facsimile repr., ed. Robert Rea, Gainesville: University of Florida Press, 1973), facing p. 8. For an expert analysis of Pittman's plan, see F. Terry Norris, "Old Cahokia: An Eighteenth-Century Archaeological Site Model," *Le Journal* 2 (Fall 1984): 2–5.

85. Winstanley Briggs ("The Forgotten Colony: Le Pays des Illinois" [Ph.D. diss., University of Chicago, 1985], 74–75) has proposed a highly rationalized pattern of town-planning for the French colonial villages in the Illinois Country that is not warranted by the evidence.

86. Reynolds, *Pioneer History,* 70.

87. Porter Collection, folder 23, Indiana Historical Society, Indianapolis (hereafter IHS).

88. Henry Marie Brackenridge, *Views of Louisiana: Together with a Journal of a Voyage up the Missouri River in 1811* (Pittsburg: Cramer, Spear and Eichbaum, 1814), 119.

89. Nicolas de Finiels, *An Account of Upper Louisiana,* ed. and trans. Carl J. Ekberg and William E. Foley (Columbia: University of Missouri Press, 1989), 62. Concerning Finiels, see the introduction to this volume, 1–16.

90. Fernand Braudel, *The Structures of Everyday Life: The Limits of the Possible,* trans. Sian Reynolds (New York: Harper and Row, 1959), 486.

91. Bloch, *Caractères originaux,* 1:36.

92. John Brinckerhoff Jackson, *The Necessity for Ruins* (Amherst: University of Massachusetts Press, 1980), 20.

93. Ibid., 24.

94. Henry Marie Brackenridge, *Recollections of Persons and Places in the West* (Philadelphia: J. I. Kay, 1834), 24.

95. Quoted in Carl J. Ekberg, *Colonial Ste. Genevieve: An Adventure on the Mississippi Frontier* (Gerald, Mo.: Patrice, 1985), 285. Italics added.

96. Ibid., 286.

97. Duby, *Rural Economy*, 11.

98. Harris, *Seigneurial System*, 179–80.

99. Louise Dechêne, *Habitants et marchands de Montréal au XVIIe siècle* (Paris: Plon, 1974), 263–64.

100. Gilbert J. Garraghan, "New Light on Old Cahokia," *Illinois Catholic Historical Review* 9 (Oct. 1928): 99–146; idem, "Earliest Settlements of the Illinois Country," *Catholic Historical Review* 15 (1930): 351–62. The most comprehensive studies of early Cahokia are *CR*, xiii–clvi; Charles E. Peterson, "Notes on Old Cahokia," *Journal of the Illinois State Historical Society* 42 (Mar., June, and Sept. 1948): 7–29, 193–208, 314–43. Concerning the material culture of colonial Cahokia, see Bonnie L. Gums, *Archeology at French Colonial Cahokia*, Studies in Illinois Archeology, no. 3 (Springfield: Illinois Historic Preservation Agency, 1988); Bonnie L. Gums, William R. Iseminger, Molly E. McKenzie, and Dennis D. Nichols, "The French Colonial Villages of Cahokia and Prairie du Pont, Illinois," in *French Colonial Archaeology: The Illinois Country and the Western Great Lakes*, ed. John A. Walthall (Urbana: University of Illinois Press, 1991), 85–122; Norris, "Old Cahokia," 1–19.

101. In addition to consulting the two studies by Garraghan cited in the previous note, see "Arbitrage des évêques," copy in ser. C13A 4:123–24, ANC; Giraud, *Histoire de la Louisiane*, 1:52–55.

102. *CR*, 624–32; Clarence W. Alvord, ed., *Kaskaskia Records, 1778–1790* (hereafter *KR*), Collections of the Illinois State Historical Library, vol. 5 (Springfield: Illinois State Historical Library, 1909), 414–19. Concerning the flight of inhabitants from Kaskaskia to Spanish Illinois during the 1780s, see Ekberg, *Colonial Ste. Genevieve*, 431–33.

103. Charlevoix quoted in McDermott, *Old Cahokia*, 13.

104. Ser. C13A, 8:226, ANC.

105. Ser. G1, 464, ANC.

106. The original of this important map is located in the archives of the Seminary of Quebec. It is well reproduced in Tucker, ed., *Indian Villages, Atlas*, 1: pl. 23.

107. Harris, *Seigneurial System*, 43.

108. Letter printed in McDermott, *Old Cahokia*, 77.

109. McDermott, *Old Cahokia*, 79.

110. Reynolds, *Pioneer History*, 67.

111. Ibid., 129.

112. Girardin (1736–1802) either fled the St. Lawrence Valley toward the end of the French and Indian War or settled down to farm in the Illinois Country circa 1760. See *CR*, 632 n. 100.

113. Concerning the departure of the Seminarians and the sale of their property at Cahokia, see Clarence W. Alvord and Clarence E. Carter, eds., *The Critical Period, 1763–1765*, Collections of the Illinois State Historical Library, vol. 10 (Springfield: Illinois State Historical Library, 1915), 45–49 (hereafter *CP*); McDermott, *Old Cahokia*, 24, 80–83; Reynolds, *Pioneer History*, 129. It is not clear whether Girardin bought property directly

from the Seminarians at the time of their departure or acquired it from Jean-Baptiste Lagrange, who had purchased it from the Seminarians at a somewhat earlier date.

114. *CR*, xlvii.

115. Ibid., 89.

116. Ibid., 153, 564–67.

117. This extremely interesting case may be followed in ibid., 580–89. See also *ASP, PL,* 2:139.

118. *ASP, PL,* 2:194.

119. The most accurate depiction of this road during colonial times is contained on the map "Carte d'une partie du cours du Mississippi, depuis la rivière des Illinois jusqu'au dessous de la Nouvelle Madrid," done by Nicolas de Finiels at the end of the eighteenth century. This map is now located in the Archives du Service Historique de la Marine at the Château de Vincennes outside Paris and is reproduced, in small scale, in Wayne C. Temple, ed., *Indian Villages of the Illinois Country, Atlas,* Scientific Papers of the Illinois State Museum, vol. 2 (Springfield: Illinois State Museum, 1975), 2: pl. 79.

120. The GLO survey from 1809 indicates that the Jesuit plowlands consisted of over 183 acres of rich bottomland (ibid.), which was cultivated with black slave labor (see chap. 4).

121. See a listing of Jesuit seigneuries in Trudel, *Régime seigneurial,* 275–78.

122. Concerning the suppression of the Jesuit Order in Illinois, see *CP*, 62 n. 2; Clarence W. Alvord, ed., *Trade and Politics, 1767–1769,* Collections of the Illinois State Historical Library, vol. 16 (Springfield: Illinois State Historical Library, 1921), 136 n. 1 (hereafter *TP*).

123. For a sympathetic Jesuit account of their colony in Paraguay, see Pierre-François Xavier de Charlevoix, *The History of Paraguay,* 2 vols. (London: L. Davis, 1769).

124. Interestingly, there are no extant concessions to the Jesuit fathers.

125. J. Nick Perrin, *History of Illinois* (Springfield: Illinois State Register, 1906), 66.

126. Breese, *Early History,* 287–89.

127. Kaskaskia Record Book A:341, ISA.

128. Pease and Jenison, *Illinois on the Eve of the Seven Years' War,* 693.

129. Cahokia Record Book A:190–92, ISA.

130. When American GLO surveyors suveyed this land in 1809, this strip belonged to Antoine Bienvenue. *ASP, PL,* 2: following 182.

131. Concerning the large d'Artaguiette family and their activities in Louisiana, see Jay Higginbotham, *Old Mobile: Fort Louis de la Louisiane, 1702–1711* (Mobile: Museum of the City of Mobile, 1977), 319–21.

132. Original in the cartographic collection of the Archives du Service Historique de la Marine, Château de Vincennes, France.

133. Nicolas Ignace Beaubois, who was one of the Jesuit fathers in residence at Kaskaskia when Boisbriant made this decision, described it in a memoir that he addressed to the Royal Indies Company in 1729 (ser. C13A, 12:265, ANC). According to Beaubois, Boisbriant also arranged to relocate the Michegamea tribe, which had been living with the Kaskaskias, to an area just north of Fort de Chartres.

134. Original in ser. C11A, ANC. Reproduced in Tucker, *Indian Villages, Atlas,* 1: pl. 22.

135. Ser. G1, 464, ANC.

136. *VOC*, K-365, 827–28; K-416, 900–903; K-417, 903–4.

137. *ASP, PL*, 2: following 182.

138. Belting, *Kaskaskia*, 23.

139. For an early rope survey of agricultural land, see *VOC*, K-62, 391.

140. The plan of Kaskaskia printed in the *Randolph County Atlas of 1875* contains many of the basic features shown on Pittman's plan done more than a century earlier.

141. *ASP, PL*, 2: following 182.

142. Ibid.

143. Jelks, Ekberg, and Martin, *Excavations at the Laurens Site*, chap. 1.

144. Concerning the population of the Parish of Ste. Anne, see Paula Nelson, "Ste. Anne: The Populating of a Parish in the Illinois Country" (M.A. thesis, Illinois State University, 1993). This large thesis contains a scrupulous account of the ancestral backgrounds of the residents of this parish.

145. Giraud, *French Louisiana*, 5:457.

146. Genicot, *Rural Communities*, 93.

147. KM 24:5:2:3.

148. See ser. C13A, 4:931, ANC.

149. *VOC*, K-3, 339–40.

150. *ASP, PL*, 2: following 186.

151. KM 24:5:2:1.

152. KM 24:5:2:2.

153. KM 33:5:18:1.

154. See Ekberg, "Marie Rouensa 8cate8a," 154, 156.

155. Concerning the use of the Coutume de Paris in colonial Louisiana, see Hans W. Baade, "Marriage Contracts in French and Spanish Louisiana: A Study in 'Notarial Jurisprudence,'" *Tulane Law Review* 53 (Dec. 1978): 1–92; Ekberg, *Colonial Ste. Genevieve*, 186–95.

156. *VOC*, K-7, 344–45.

157. Ibid., K-380, 851–52.

158. Ibid., K-6, 341–44.

159. Ibid., K-10, 346–47.

160. Census of 1732 in ser. G1, 464, ANC. Gristmills, including wind-driven mills, are dealt with in the appendix.

161. Illinois State Highway 3 follows the approximate route of this ancient French road near Belle Fontaine.

162. Census of 1732 in ser. G1, 464, ANC.

163. Photocopy of original document in author's files. Concerning Joseph Michel *dit* Taillon's life in the Illinois Country, see Frederic L. Billon, ed., *Annals of St. Louis in Its Early Days under the French and Spanish Dominations, 1776–1804* (St. Louis: F. L. Billon, 1886), 414–15.

164. The Kaskaskia Manuscripts do in fact contain numerous documents from Chartres, in addition to those from Kaskaskia, and many of these have been published in *VOC*.

165. KM 1723–25:21.

166. Document 952.14, ISA.

167. Reproduced in Kaskaskia Record Book A:234, ISA; and *ASP, PL,* 2:183.

168. *ASP, PL,* 2:183.

169. "Croghan's Journal," in Clarence W. Alvord and Clarence E. Carter, eds., *The New Regime, 1765–1767,* Collections of the Illinois State Historical Library, vol. 11 (Springfield: Illinois State Historical Library, 1916), 32 (hereafter *NR*).

170. The best accounts of early Vincennes may be found in John D. Barnhart and Dorothy L. Riker, *Indiana to 1816: The Colonial Period* (Indianapolis: Indiana Historical Bureau and Indiana Historical Society, 1971), chaps. 1–3; and Frances Krauskopf, "The French in Indiana: A Political History" (Ph.D. diss., Indiana University, 1953), 1–100. See also Andrew R. L. Cayton, *Frontier Indiana* (Boomington: Indiana University Press, 1996), 45–69, for a recent and refreshing summary on early Vincennes.

171. Krauskopf, "The French in Indiana," 133–34, 148–49, 171.

172. See Macarty's instructions in Pease and Jenison, *Illinois on the Eve of the Seven Years' War,* 293–319.

173. "Aubry's Account of the Illinois Country," *CP,* 3.

174. *ASP, PL,* 3:384.

175. Ibid., 432.

176. According to U.S. Government documents (*ASP, PL,* 1:10), the Piankashaw Indians sold their land at Vincennes and had left the area by 1786.

177. On this issue, see Joseph P. Donnelly, *Pierre Gibault, Missionary, 1737–1802* (Chicago: Loyola University Press, 1971), esp. chap. 8.

178. Constantin-François Chasseboeuf, comte de Volney, *A View of the Soil and Climate of the United States of America,* trans. C. B. Brown (New York: Hafner, 1968 [1804]), 332.

179. Porter Collection, folder 23, IHS.

180. Knox County Records, IHS.

181. *ASP, PL,* 1:10.

182. R. Louis Gentilcore, "Vincennes and French Settlement in the Old Northwest," *Annals of the Association of American Geographers* 47, no. 3 (Sept. 1957): 293.

183. Leonard Lux (*The Vincennes Donation Lands* [Indianapolis: Indiana Historical Society, 1949], 431) noticed this aspect of French settlement at Vincennes but did not elaborate on it. Cayton (*Frontier Indiana,* 57) remarks that the French of Vincennes "did not live on isolated farms" but does not examine land usage in detail.

184. Lasselle Papers, Box 1, 14–10–89, Indiana State Library Archives (hereafter ISL), Indianapolis.

185. John D. Barnhart, ed., *Henry Hamilton and George Rogers Clark in the American Revolution* (Crawfordsville, Ind.: R. E. Banta, 1951), 160.

186. *ASP, PL,* 1:10.

187. Lasselle Papers, Box 1, 7–20–90, ISL.

188. *ASP, PL,* 1:10.

189. Clarence E. Carter, ed., *The Territorial Papers of the United States,* 27 vols. (Washington, D.C.: U.S. Government Printing Office, 1934), 2:341.

190. Porter Collection, folder 23, IHS.

191. Carter, *Territorial Papers*, 2:92.

192. Gayle Thornbrough, ed., *The Correspondence of John Badollet and Albert Gallatin, 1804–1836* (Indianapolis: Indiana Historical Society, 1963), 79.

193. See Pierre-Charles Delassus de Luzières, "Observations sur le caractère, qualités, et professions des habitans blancs du District de la Nouvelle Bourbon," appended to the New Bourbon census of 1797, in PC, legajo 2365, AGI.

194. These introductory paragraphs are based largely on the author's study *Colonial Ste. Genevieve*.

195. Finiels, *Account*, 46.

196. Guibourd Collection, MHS.

197. "The First Law Regulating Land Grants in French Colonial Louisiana," *Louisiana Historical Quarterly* 14 (July 1931): 346–47; Mémoires et documents, Amérique 8:261, Archives des Affaires Étrangères, Paris (hereafter AAE).

198. KM 53:11:28:1. Concerning the configuration of the Old Town of Ste. Genevieve, see F. Terry Norris's excellent analysis "Ste. Genevieve, a French Colonial Village in the Illinois Country," in *French Colonial Archaeology*, ed. John A. Walthall (Urbana: University of Illinois Press, 1991), 133–48.

199. Surveys and Plans, no. 75, Ste. Genevieve Archives (hereafter SGA); microfilm version in MHS.

200. KM 53:11:28:1, 58:7:26:1.

201. F. Terry Norris ("Ste. Genevieve," 140–41) and Winstanley Briggs ("The Forgotten Colony," 74–75) have suggested a more highly rationalized pattern of town planning in the colonial Illinois Country. This interesting discussion has not been concluded, but I believe that Norris and Briggs have exaggerated the degree of rational planning underlying village development in the Illinois Country.

202. Manuscript GLO plats of Ste. Genevieve may be found in the archives of the surveyor general's office in Rolla, Mo.; some photographic copies are available in the MHS map collection.

203. HMLO, 426.

204. Perrin Collection, Sept. 10, 1768, ISA.

205. Concessions, no. 57, SGA.

206. Pittman, *European Settlements*, 50.

207. Norris, "Ste. Genevieve," 133–48.

208. Brackenridge, *Views of Louisiana*, 127.

209. See Ekberg, *Colonial Ste. Genevieve*, chap. 13.

210. St. Pierre to Carondelet, Oct. 1, 1792, PC, legajo 206, AGI.

211. Letter of May 1, 1793, PC, legajo 214, AGI.

212. See Carl J. Ekberg, "A Map of Ste. Genevieve," *Mapline*, no. 45 (Mar. 1987): 1–3, for an analysis of this map.

213. Ernest E. Graf, former surveyor with the U.S. Corps of Engineers in St. Louis, discovered this scale.

214. Finiels, *Account*, 44–45.

215. Concerning the early history of St. Louis, see John Francis McDermott, "Myths and Realities concerning the Founding of St. Louis," in *The French in the Mississippi River Valley*, ed. John Francis McDermott (Urbana: University of Illinois Press, 1965), 1–16; William E. Foley, *The Genesis of Missouri: From Wilderness Outpost to Statehood* (Columbia: University of Missouri Press, 1989), chap. 3; William E. Foley and C. David Rice, *The First Chouteaus: River Barons of Early St. Louis* (Urbana: University of Illinois Press, 1983), chaps. 1, 2; James Neal Primm, *Lion of the Valley: St. Louis, Missouri* (Boulder, Colo.: Pruett, 1981), chap. 1. Patricia Cleary has recently analyzed the founding of St. Louis, emphasizing interactions between the Euro-American settlers and the neighboring Indian tribes ("Contested Terrain: Environmental Agendas and Settlement Choices in Colonial St. Louis," in *Common Fields: An Environmental History of St. Louis*, ed. Andrew Hurley [St. Louis: Missouri Historical Society Press, 1997], 58–72).

216. Billon, *Annals of Early St. Louis*, 92.

217. Charles E. Peterson correctly began his brief but illuminating study of colonial St. Louis with three sections devoted respectively to the village, the commons, and the common fields. See his *Colonial St. Louis: Building a Creole Capital* (Tucson: Patrice, 1993), 6–23. Concerning the configuration of early St. Louis, see also Primm, *Lion of the Valley*, 15–19.

218. GLO map from the archives of the Surveyor General's Office, Rolla, Mo.

219. *Missouri Republican*, Sept. 25, 1859, microfilm in MHS.

220. On deforestation near St. Louis, see Finiels, *Account*, 123–24.

221. Chouteau's deposition in "Hunt's Minutes," 2:165, MHS.

222. Peterson, *Colonial St. Louis*, 4–9, contains the best description of the physical plan of early St. Louis.

223. Billon, *Annals of Early St. Louis*, 19–20; Foley and Rice, *The First Chouteaus*, 5; Peterson, *Colonial St. Louis*, 5.

224. On the early planning of New Orleans, see Giraud, *Histoire de la Louisiane*, 4:398–412. This volume contains several useful plans of early New Orleans.

225. Concerning the planning of port cities in France, see Josef W. Konvitz, *Cities and the Sea: Port City Planning in Early Modern Europe* (Baltimore: Johns Hopkins Unversity Press, 1978), pt. 2.

226. Concerning the planning of New Orleans, see Samuel Wilson Jr., *Le Vieux Carré* (New Orleans: Historic New Orleans Collection, 1968).

227. The most detailed depiction of early St. Louis is the plan drawn in 1796, probably by Charles Warin, who was adjutant to the French general Victor Collot when they visited St. Louis. One version of this plan is in the Archives du Service Historique de la Marine at Vincennes and has been reproduced in Peterson, *Colonial St. Louis*, 91. Another version is an inset to Collot's map of the Illinois Country that is located in the cartographic section of the Bibliothèque Nationale in Paris.

228. See Vaudreuil to Maurepas, Mar. 20, 1748, in Pease and Jenison, *Illinois on the Eve of the Seven Years' War*, 55.

229. One consequence of this was that when George Rogers Clark and his Virginians arrived at Kaskaskia in July 1778, they simply walked into the village unopposed and virtually unnoticed. See Katherine W. Seineke, *The George Rogers Clark Adventure in Illinois*

(New Orleans: Polyanthos, 1981). In 1766 Captain Philip Pittman made a sketch of a defensive perimeter for Kaskaskia (map division, Clements Library), but the this proprosal was never implemented.

230. Concerning this attack, see John Francis McDermott, "The Myth of the 'Imbecile Governor': Captain Fernando de Leyba and the Defense of St. Louis in 1780," in *The Spanish in the Mississippi Valley*, ed. John Francis McDermott (Urbana: University of Illinois Press, 1974), 287–313; and Abraham P. Nasatir, "St. Louis during the British Attack of 1780," in *New Spain and the Anglo-American West: Historical Contributions Presented to Herbert Eugene Bolton*, 2 vols., ed. George P. Hammond (Los Angeles: privately printed, 1932), 1:239–61. Frederic L. Billon's map of St. Louis shows the early palisade and contains the remark that it was built after the "affair of May 26, 1780." See map at the end of "Hunt's Minutes," typescript in MHS.

231. See the introduction to Finiels, *Account;* James B. Musick, *St. Louis as a Fortified Town* (St. Louis: R. F. Miller, 1941).

232. This is certainly the thrust of the remarks made by the deponents of Theodore Hunt, recorder of deeds, in 1825. See especially the depositions of Jean-Baptiste Rivière and Jean-Baptiste Lorraine in "Hunt's Minutes," 2:102, 3:96, typescript in MHS.

233. *Atlas of North America: Space Age Portrait of a Continent* (Washington, D.C.: National Geographic Society, 1985), 98.

234. Henry R. Schoolcraft, *Narrative Journal of Travels,* ed. Mentor L. Williams (East Lansing: Michigan State College Press, 1953), 220; Stephen H. Long, "Voyage in a Six-Oared Skiff to the Falls of St. Anthony in 1817," in *Minnesota Historical Collections,* vol. 2, pt. 1 (St. Paul: Minnesota Historical Society, 1872), 640; James H. Lockwood, "Early Times and Events in Wisconsin," in *Wisconsin Historical Collections,* vol. 2, ed. Lyman Copeland Draper (Madison: Wisconsin Historical Society, 1903), 119.

235. Concerning the comments of Carver and Pond, see Mary Antoine de Julio, "The Vertefeuille House of Prairie du Chien: A Survivor from the Era of French Wisconsin," *Wisconsin Magazine of History* 80 (Autumn 1996): 38–39.

236. John Long, *Voyages and Travels in the Years 1768–1788* (Chicago: R. R. Donnelly and Sons, 1922), 185.

237. Carter, *Territorial Papers,* 16:154.

238. On all issues pertaining to Prairie du Chien in this chapter, I have relied heavily on assistance from Mary Antoine de Julio, a local history expert who resides in Prairie du Chien.

239. Peter Lawrence Scanlan, *Prairie du Chien: French, British, American* (Menasha, Wisc.: George Banta, 1937), 10.

240. This original of this Nicolas Bellin map is located in the National Map Collection, Public Archives of Canada, Ottawa.

241. Scanlan, *Prairie du Chien,* 13; Alice E. Smith, *From Exploration to Statehood,* 24–30, vol. 1 of William Fletcher Thompson, ed., *History of Wisconsin* (Madison: State Historical Society of Wisconsin, 1973).

242. Scanlan, *Prairie du Chien,* 27.

243. Ibid., 52.

244. *ASP, PL,* 3:385.

245. The map is reproduced in *ASP, PL,* 5:270–71.

246. *ASP, PL,* 5:308.

247. Long, *Voyages,* 185.

248. Louise Phelps Kellogg, ed., *The British Regime in Wisconsin and the Northwest* (Madison: State Historical Society of Wisconsin, 1935), 316–17; J. Leitch Wright Jr., *Britain and the American Frontier, 1783–1815* (Athens: University of Georgia Press, 1975), 174–75, 181. British regular military units did evacuate these outposts, but militia units loyal to Great Britain often remained.

249. Quoted in Ninian W. Edwards, *History of Illinois from 1788 to 1833 and the Life and Times of Ninian Edwards* (Springfield: Illinois State Journal, 1870), 99.

250. Cahokia Record Book B:590, ISA.

251. Dennis M. Au, "An Architectural Analysis: The Francois Vertefeuille House," unpublished ms., contains several pertinent paragraphs dealing with the complex settlement pattern at Prairie du Chien.

252. The original of this map is in the county clerk's office, Prairie du Chien, Wisconsin.

253. Cahokia Record Book B:576, ISA.

254. *ASP, PL,* 5:310–18.

255. For an anlysis of Rowley, see David G. Allen, *In English Ways: The Movement of Societies and the Transferal of English Local Law and Custom to Massachusetts Bay in the Seventeenth Century* (Chapel Hill: University of North Carolina Press, 1981), 33–40.

256. *ASP, PL,* 5:307.

257. Lucius Lyon, "Field Notes &c," 1828, collection of Villa Louis Historic Site, Prairie du Chien. I am indebted to Mary Antoine de Julio, curator of collections at the Villa Louis, for providing me with this document.

258. *ASP, PL,* 5:308.

259. The communal nature of agriculture at Prairie du Chien is made apparent in a Crawford County ordinance from 1828: "All Horses, mares, geldings, all Horned cattle and all other domestic animals shall be free commoners, and . . . all fences that are in common shall be put in good order by the twenty-fifth of April" (Election returns for 1828, Crawford County Courthouse, Prairie du Chien, Wisc.). I am indebted to Mary Antoine de Julio for providing me with this document.

260. "Hunt's Minutes," 3:3, typescript in MHS.

CHAPTER 3: OPEN-FIELD AGRICULTURE

1. Concerning open-field agriculture in seventeenth-century New England, see Sumner Chilton Powell, *Puritan Village: The Formation of a New England Town* (Middletown, Conn.: Wesleyan University Press, 1963); Philip J. Greven Jr., *Four Generations: Population, Land, and Family in Colonial Andover, Massachusetts* (Ithaca, N.Y.: Cornell University Press, 1970); David G. Allen, *In English Ways: The Movement of Societies and the Transferal of English Local Law and Custom to Massachusetts Bay in the Seventeenth Century* (Chapel Hill: University of North Carolina Press, 1981).

2. Some communal agriculture occurred on tidal marshlands in Acadia (see Andrew Hill Clark, *Acadia: The Geography of Early Nova Scotia to 1760* [Madison: University of Wisconsin Press, 1968], 161–62; Naomi E. S. Griffiths, *The Contexts of Acadian History, 1686–1784* [Ottawa: McGill-Queen's University Press, 1992], 56–57), but this was an eccentric case in an unusual environment and did not constitute open-field agriculture in the traditional European sense.

3. Pierre Goubert, *Beauvais et les Beauvaisis de 1600 à 1730: Contribution à l'histoire sociale de France du XVIIe siècle*, 2 vols. (Paris: S.E.V.P.E.N., 1960), 1:93 n. 43.

4. See Pierre Brunet, *Structure agraire et économie rurale des plateaux tertiaires entre la Seine et l'Oise* (Caen: Caron, 1960), 13–60; Robert Fossier, *La Terre et les hommes en Picardie jusqu'à la fin du XIIIe siècle* (Paris-Louvain: Béatrice-Nauwelaerts, Nauwelaerts, 1968), 432–35.

5. See, for example, the 700-page volume by Alan R. H. Baker and Robin A. Butlin, eds., *Studies of Field Systems in the British Isles* (Cambridge: Cambridge University Press, 1973).

6. Jean-Robert Pitte, *Histoire du paysage français* (Paris: Tallandier, 1983), 220, for example, contains an extensive index listing for *openfield*.

7. Joan Thirsk, "The Common Fields," *Past and Present* 29 (Dec. 1964): 3.

8. See Richard C. Hoffman, "Medieval Origins of the Common Fields," in *European Peasants and Their Markets*, ed. William N. Parker and Eric L. Jones (Princeton, N.J.: Princeton University Press, 1975), 24 n. 2.

9. Pierre de Saint-Jacob, *Documents relatifs à la communauté villageoise en Bourgogne du milieu du XVIIe siècle à Révolution* (Paris: Société des Belles Lettres, 1962), xi.

10. Ibid., vii.

11. Joan Thirsk, "Field Systems of the East Midlands," in *Studies of Field Systems in the British Isles*, ed. Alan R. H. Baker and Robin A. Butlin (Cambridge: Cambridge University Press, 1973), 232.

12. Hoffman, "Medieval Origins," 25.

13. Xavier de Planhol, *Géographie historique de la France* (Paris: Arthème Fayard, 1988), 161–67.

14. John Reynolds, *The Pioneer History of Illinois* (Chicago: Fergus, 1887), 49.

15. Logan Esarey, *A History of Indiana from Its Exploration to 1850* (Indianapolis: W. K. Stewart, 1915), 24.

16. KM 37:3:8:1.

17. KM 37:5:5:2.

18. Copy of Vaudreuil's and Salmon's decree dated New Orleans, Aug. 14, 1743, in Cahokia Record Book A:190, ISA.

19. *ASP, PL,* 2:194.

20. Reynolds, *Pioneer History,* 67–68.

21. Peter Kalm, *The America of 1750: Peter Kalm's Travels in North America*, ed. Adolph B. Benson (New York: Dover, 1964), 459.

22. Hildegard B. Johnson, *Order upon the Land* (New York: Oxford University Press, 1976), 228.

23. Louise Dechêne, *Habitants et marchands de Montréal au XVIIe siècle* (Paris: Plon,

1974), 311; Allan Greer, *Peasant, Lord, and Merchant* (Toronto: University of Toronto Press, 1985), 11–12.

24. Marc Bloch, *Les Caractères originaux de l'histoire rurale française*, 2 vols. (Paris: A. Colin, 1964), 1:42–49; Thirsk, "The Common Fields," 3; Hoffman, "Medieval Origins," 24–25; Pitte, *Histoire du paysage français*, 114, 119, 121; André Meynier, *Les Paysages agraires* (Paris: Armand Colin, 1958), 19. *L'abandon* meant that once the crops had been harvested, the arable fields were "abandoned" to the herds of livestock.

25. Bloch, *Caractères originaux*, 1:48–49.

26. Ibid., 42–43.

27. Ibid., 46.

28. Dechêne, *Habitants et marchands*, 312. Dechêne goes on to remark (313–14) that vaine pâture was an atavastic practice that was contracting rather than expanding and was evidently on its way to extinction.

29. Greer, *Peasant, Lord, and Merchant*, 25.

30. Bloch, *Caractères originaux*, 1:31.

31. Edmond Pognon, *Les Très Riches Heures du Duc de Berry*, trans. David Macrae (New York: Crown, 1979), 35.

32. Thomas Wien, "'Les Travaux pressants': calendrier agricole, assolement et productivité au Canada au XVIIᵉ siècle," *Revue d'Histoire de l'Amérique française* 43 (Spring 1990): 542.

33. Dechêne, *Habitants et marchands*, 301. This raises the intriguing question of who in France would have done this selecting of seed grains for Canada.

34. Ernest J. Lajeunesse, ed., *The Windsor Border Region: Canada's Southernmost Frontier* (Toronto: Champlain Society for the Government of Ontario, 1960), 261.

35. The original of Monsieur Lallemant's letter is in the Archives du Service Hydrographique de la Marine (series 2 JJ 56, item no. 29), which is housed within the Archives of the Service Historique de la Marine in the Château de Vincennes, just outside Paris. The Illinois Historical Survey in Urbana has a photostat. Lallemant's first name and position are unknown, but he resided in Kaskaskia long enough to witness a baptism (Mathe Faribault-Beauregard, ed., *La Population des forts français d'Amérique*, 2 vols. [Montreal: Éditions Bergeron, 1984], 2:147). Given Lallemant's calendar of sowing and harvesting, it is clear that the habitants at Kaskaskia were planting spring wheat at that time.

36. KM 1723–25:22.

37. Boisbriant's letter, 1724, ser. C13A, 8:447–50, ANC. Curiously, Marcel Giraud (*A History of French Louisiana*, vol. 5, trans. Brian Pearce [Baton Rouge: Louisiana State University Press, 1991], 459) commented on Boisbriant and wheat sowing in the Illinois Country without ever mentioning the related issue of open-field cultivation that was practiced in the region.

38. John Reynolds, *My Own Times, embracing also the history of my life* (Chicago: Fergus, 1879), 23; idem, *Pioneer History*, 69; idem, "The Agricultural Resources of Southern Illinois," in *Transactions of the Illinois State Historical Society for the Year 1917* (Springfield: Illinois State Historical Society, 1917), 147.

39. Reynolds, "Agricultural Resources," 147.

40. Henry Marie Brackenridge, *Views of Louisiana: Together with a Journal of a Voyage up the Missouri River in 1811* (Pittsburg: Cramer, Spear and Eichbaum, 1814), 127.

41. Trudeau to Carondelet, May 27, 1794, in Abraham P. Nasatir, ed., *Before Lewis and Clark,* 2 vols. (St. Louis: St. Louis Historical Documents Foundation, 1952), 1:215.

42. KM 37:3:8:1.

43. At Fort de Chartres in 1728, a fourteen-month old heifer was evaluated at 300 livres. See *VOC,* K-417, 904.

44. KM 37:3:22:2.

45. KM 37:5:5:2.

46. Copy of the regulation in Cahokia Record Book A:190, ISA.

47. Vaudreuil and Salmon did not go so far as to proclaim that the individual habitants in Illinois should actually enclose their strips of arable land, as was being done in some regions of France at the time, but clearly this provincial decree of 1743 was a step in the direction of enclosure. Concerning the beginnings of agricultural individualism in metropolitan France, see Bloch, *Caractères originaux,* 1:223–35.

48. Reynolds, *Pioneer History,* 68.

49. Georges Duby, *Rural Economy and Country Life in the Medieval West,* trans. Cynthia Postan (Columbia: University of South Carolina Press, 1968), 55.

50. Bloch, *Caractères originaux,* 1:182.

51. Hoffman, "Medieval Origins," 59.

52. Joan Thirsk, "Village Bylaws," in *Studies of Field Systems in the British Isles,* ed. Alan R. H. Baker and Robin A. Butlin (Cambridge: Cambridge University Press, 1973), 246.

53. Robert R. Palmer, *The Age of the Democratic Revolution, 1760–1780* (Princeton, N.J.: Princeton University Press, 1959).

54. Henri Babeau, *Les Assemblées générales des communautés d'habitants en France du XIIIᵉ siècle à la Révolution* (Paris: Arthur Rousseau, 1893).

55. It is rather curious that neither Marc Bloch, who discussed rural assemblies (*Caractères originaux,* 1:175–180), nor Georges Duby, who also discussed them (*Histoire de la France rurale,* vol. 2, *L'Age classique des paysans, 1340–1789* [Paris: Seuil, 1975], 284–94), made use of Babeau's seminal work.

56. Babeau, *Assemblées,* 14–16; Bloch, *Caractères originaux,* 1:175–76.

57. Babeau, *Assemblées,* 63.

58. Ibid., 81.

59. Babeau (81–85), Duby (*France rurale,* 2:284–88), and Bloch (*Caractères originaux,* 1:182–83) all acknowledged this, although the last argued that local seigneurs exercised substantial influence over the assemblies.

60. William J. Eccles (*The Canadian Frontier* [New York: Holt, Rinehart and Winston, 1969], 198 n. 28) adduces an interesting ordinance in which the intendant of New France ratified the election of two syndics by an assembly of habitants at Boucherville, just outside Montreal. In this instance the syndics were charged with overseeing the use of the common pasture in the seigneury of Boucherville.

61. "Requête des habitants de la Pointe Coupée," Jan. 9, 1779, French Archives no. 967,

Pointe Coupée Parishhouse Records. I am indebted to historian William D. Reeves of New Orleans for having brought this document to my attention.

62. Clarence Walworth Alvord commented briefly about the importance of village assemblies in the Illinois Country and noted that they elected church wardens and were heavily involved in regulating open-field agriculture (*The Illinois Country, 1673–1818,* The Centennial History of Illinois, vol. 1 [Springfield: Illinois Centennial Commission, 1920], 221).

63. Nicolas-Edm. Rétif de la Bretonne, *La Vie de mon père,* ed. Gilbert Roger (Paris: Éditions Garnier Frères, 1970), 123.

64. Perrin Collection for 1785, ISA.

65. Documents no. 27, SGA.

66. Babeau, *Assemblées,* 31–37.

67. Bloch, *Caractères originaux,* 1:178–79. It is possible that Bloch adopted this position because his perspective on the village assemblies was more medieval.

68. Rétif de la Bretonne, *La Vie de mon père,* 123.

69. William J. Eccles, *Canadian Frontier, 1534–1760* (Albuquerque: University of New Mexico Press, 1983), 81.

70. See Documents, no. 27, SGA.

71. "Règlemens entre les habitants des Cahos concernant les clôtures des terres," Perrin Collection, no. 32, ISA.

72. Precisely how Girardin became American commandant at Cahokia is a bit of a mystery. The 1780s were in general a period of anarchy in the Illinois Country, which was de jure under American sovereignty but where little government existed. See Alvord, *Illinois Country,* 358–78.

73. This law is printed in Theodore C. Pease, ed., *The Laws of the Northwest Territory, 1788–1800,* Collections of the Illinois State Historical LIbrary, vol. 17 (Springfield: The Illinois State Historical Society, 1925), 498.

74. Rétif de la Bretonne, *La Vie de mon père,* 123. Babeau (*Assemblées,* 2, 3, 23) used this passage, and so did Bloch (*Caractères originaux,* 1:185)—apparently without being aware that Babeau had used it earlier in the same context. Concerning the use of the parish church as a forum for secular activities in the Illinois Country, see Carl J. Ekberg, *Colonial Ste. Geneviève: An Adventure on the Mississippi Frontier* (Gerald, Mo.: Patrice, 1985), 318.

75. Duby (*France rurale,* 2:285) defined villages assemblies as "réunions des chefs de famille."

76. Jacob Piatt Dunn, ed., "Documents Relating to the French Settlements on the Wabash," in *Indiana Historical Society Publications,* vol. 2, no. 11 (Indianapolis: Bowen-Merrill, 1894), 407.

77. Andrew R. L. Cayton, *Frontier Indiana* (Bloomington: Indiana University Press, 1996), 48.

78. Bloch, *Caractères originaux,* 1:178–79.

79. See, for example, "Règlements des habitants de Ste. Geneviève," May 9, 1784, Official Document no. 5, SGA, which calls for the election of village syndics by "pluralité des voix."

80. Babeau, *Assemblées,* 51–53.

81. Duby (*France rurale,* 2:285) agreed that widows sometimes participated in the assemblies.

82. See "Règlemens entre les habitants des Cahos concernant les clôtures des terres," June 7, 1785, Perrin Collection no. 32, ISA.

83. Official Document no. 29, Feb. 17, 1788, SGA.

84. Babeau, *Assemblées,* 295.

85. Bloch, *Caractères originaux,* 1:37.

86. Reynolds, "Agricultural Resources," 146,

87. Christian Schultz, *Travels on an Inland Voyage . . . performed in the years 1807 and 1808* (New York: Isaac Riley, 1810), 2:55.

88. Brackenridge, *Views of Louisiana,* 125.

89. GLO plan of Ste. Genevieve and environs, archives of the Surveyor General's Office, Rolla, Mo.

90. Amos Stoddard, *Sketches, Historical and Descriptive of Louisiana* (Philadelphia: Mathew Curey, 1812), 216. Italics mine.

91. Surveys, no. 75, SGA.

92. Schultz, *Travels on an Inland Voyage,* 2:55.

93. Official Document no. 26, SGA.

94. See Gaines Post, "A Romano-Canonical Maxim, *Quod Omnes Tangit* in Bracton and the Early Parliaments," in Gaines Post, *Studies in Medieval Legal Thought: Public Law and the State, 1100–1322* (Princeton, N.J.: Princeton University Press, 1964), 163–238.

95. Léopold Genicot, *Rural Communities in the Medieval West* (Baltimore: Johns Hopkins University Press, 1990), 59.

96. Official Document no. 27, SGA.

97. Stephen E. Ambrose, *Undaunted Courage: Meriwether Lewis, Thomas Jefferson, and the Opening of the American West* (New York: Simon and Schuster, 1996), 161.

98. For Girardin's multifarious activities at Cahokia during the 1780s, see *CR,* passim.

99. Original ms. in Perrin Collection, ISA; a translation of this document, which contains some misleading errors, may be found in John F. McDermott, ed., *Old Cahokia: A Narrative and Documents Illustrating the First Century of Its History* (St. Louis: St. Louis Historical Documents Foundation, 1952), 116–20.

100. Thirsk, "Field Systems," 248–49; Allen, *In English Ways,* 33. See also Duby, *Rural Economy,* 141; Powell, *Puritan Village,* 94; C. S. Orwin and C. S. Orwin, *The Open Fields,* 2d ed. (Oxford: Oxford University Press, 1967), 132–33, 155.

101. Bloch, *Caractères originaux,* 1:186;

102. See Official Document no. 28, SGA.

103. See note 99.

104. Susan Reynolds, *Kingdoms and Communities in Western Europe, 900–1300* (New York: Oxford University Press, 1984), 144.

105. Duby, *France rurale,* 2:286.

106. Perrin Collection, ISA,

107. Quoted in Duby, *Rural Economy,* 407.

108. Cahokia Record Book B:421–23, ISA.

109. Pease, *Laws of the Northwest Territory,* 498–501. The following quotations are from this work.

110. In eighteenth-century Acadia, dikes were built and maintained as communal projects, but no open-field agriculture as it has been discussed in this chapter existed. See Griffiths, *Contexts of Acadian History,* 56–57; Clark, *Acadia,* 161–62.

CHAPTER 4: HABITANTS, SLAVES, AND ENGAGÉS

1. Allan Greer, *Peasant, Lord, and Merchant* (Toronto: University of Toronto Press, 1985), 20–48.

2. Peter Kalm, *Travels in North America,* trans. John Reinhold Forster (Warrington, Great Britain: William Eyres, 1770; repr., ed. Adolph B. Benson, New York: Dover, 1966), 458.

3. Edmond Pognon, *Les Très Riches Heures du Duc de Berry,* trans. David Macrae (New York: Crown, 1979), 27.

4. "Notes of a Tour into the Southern Parts of France, &c.," in *The Papers of Thomas Jefferson,* 26 vols., ed. Julian P. Boyd (Princeton, N.J.: Princeton University Press, 1955–95), 11:415. Jefferson served as U.S. minister plenipotentiary to France from 1784 to 1789, but his extended excursion through southern France in 1787 was not an official trip.

5. Nicolas de Finiels, *An Account of Upper Louisiana,* ed. and trans. Carl J. Ekberg and William E. Foley (Columbia: University of Missouri Press, 1989), 117.

6. Pierre de Saint-Jacob, *Documents relatifs à la communauté villageoise en Bourgogne du milieu du XVIIe siècle à la Révolution* (Paris: Société des Belles Lettres, 1962), viii n. 4.

7. KM 25:8:16:1. On rare occasions in the Illinois Country *habitant* was used also to mean "inhabitant." For example, in 1750 the Jesuit father Louis Vivier (*JR,* 69:144) remarked that "les habitans sont de trois espèces: des Français, des Nègres, et des Sauvages." Vivier was born and raised in France and was therefore more inclined to French usage. I am indebted to Judge Morris S. Arnold, who kindly provided me with this reference.

8. *VOC,* K55, 385; K176, 540; K192, 567; K200, 579.

9. Henry Marie Brackenridge, *Views of Louisiana: Together with a Journal of a Voyage up the Missouri River in 1811* (Pittsburgh: Cramer, Spear and Eichbaum, 1814), 127.

10. Censuses of 1726 and 1732 in ser. G1, 426, ANC; census of 1752 in HMLO, 426.

11. Militia roster for 1779, PC, legajo 213, AGI.

12. John F. McDermott, "The Myth of 'The Imbecile Governor' Captain Fernando de Leyba and the Defense of St. Louis in 1780," in John F. McDermott, ed., *The Spanish in the Mississippi Valley, 1762–1804* (Urbana: University of Illinois Press, 1974), 373–80.

13. *CR,* 624–32; *KR,* 414–20.

14. See Carl J. Ekberg, *Colonial Ste. Genevieve: An Adventure on the Mississippi Frontier* (Gerald, Mo.: Patrice, 1985), 188–89, on the Customary Law of Paris and inheritance practices in the Illinois Country.

15. The only known version of the 1787 census is in the archives of the Missouri Historical Society, and this is a copy of a copy done in 1906.

16. Marc Bloch, *Les Caractères originaux de l'histoire rurale française,* 2 vols. (Paris: A. Colin, 1964), 1:197–98. Concerning the status of laboureurs in French society, see also

Georges Duby, *Histoire du France rurale*, vol. 2, *L'Age classique des paysans, 1340–1789* [Paris: Seuil, 1975], 303–5.

17. De Luzières, "Etat and dénombrement de Nouvelle Bourbon," PC, legajo 2365, AGI.

18. Bloch, *Caractères originaux*, 1:198.

19. Greer, *Peasant, Lord, and Merchant*, 12–13.

20. Ibid., ix.

21. François Perrin du Lac, *Voyage dans les deux Louisianes et chez les nations sauvages dur Missouri* (Paris: Capelle and Renand, 1805), 172.

22. Census of 1787, MHS.

23. Quoted in Eugene Genovese, *Roll, Jordan, Roll: The World the Slaves Made* (New York: Random House, 1972), xv.

24. Boisbriant to the Royal Indies Company, Oct. 3, 1720, ser. A1, vol. 2592, folders 97–98, Service Historique de l'Armée, Vincennes (hereafter SHA). Boisbriant continued to complain about the shortage of slaves in Louisiana after he had left the Illinois Country (see Marcel Giraud, *A History of French Louisiana*, vol. 5, trans. Brian Pearce [Baton Rouge: Louisiana State University Press, 1991], 472).

25. "Édit concernant les Nègres à la Louisiane," *Publications of the Louisiana Historical Society* 4 (1908): 76.

26. Brackenridge, *Views of Louisiana*, 127. My italics.

27. Finiels, *Account*, 109.

28. Abraham P. Nasatir, "St. Louis during the British Attack of 1780," in *New Spain and the Anglo-American West*, ed. George P. Hammond (Lancaster, Penn.: Lancaster, 1932), 239–61.

29. The Illinois census of 1752 (HMLO, 426) lists 446 black slaves and only 149 Indian slaves.

30. James D. Hardy Jr., "The Transportation of Convicts to Colonial Louisiana," *Louisiana History* 7 (Summer 1966): 207–22.

31. There were a few African slaves in New France during the colonial period, but there is no evidence that any of these were taken to the Illinois Country. See Marcel Trudel, *L'Esclavage au Canada français: histoire et conditions de l'esclavage* (Quebec: Presses de l'Université Laval, 1960).

32. Daniel H. Usner Jr. "African Captivity to American Slavery: The Introduction of Black Laborers to Colonial Louisiana," *Louisiana History* 20 (Winter 1979): 25–28. John Mason Peck, an abolitionist, was the first person to present a history of slavery in Illinois. He did so in a series of newspaper articles written in 1847, and his first several articles dealt with slavery in the Illinois Country during the French regime (see Roger D. Bridges, ed., "John Mason Peck on Illinois Slavery," *Journal of the Illinois State Historical Society* 75 [Autumn 1982]: 179–217).

33. "État de la Louisiane au mois de Juin, 1720," ser. A1, 2592:93, SHA.

34. Bienville to the Royal Indies Company, Apr. 25, 1721, ser. A1, 2592:106–8, SHA.

35. Memoir of Bienville, 1725 or 1726, in Dunbar Rowland and Albert G. Sanders, eds., *Mississippi Provincial Archives*, 3 vols. (Jackson: Mississippi Department of Archives and History, 1927), 3:520.

36. Concerning slavery in the French colonial Caribbean, see the two standard studies: Gabriel Debien, *Les Esclaves aux Antilles françaises (XVIIe–XVIIIe siècles)* (Fort-de-France, Martinique: Société d'Histoire de la Martinique, 1974); Gaston Martin, *Histoire d'esclavage dans les colonies françaises* (Paris: Presses Universitaires de France, 1948).

37. "Édit concernant les Nègres," 75–90. For a recent succinct analysis of the Black Code in Louisiana, see Mathé Allain, "Slave Policies in French Louisiana," *Louisiana History* 21 (Spring 1980): 127–37.

38. Although the Code Noir was not officially promulgated until 1685, two years after Jean-Baptiste Colbert's death in 1683, this code resulted from legal reforms that he instituted on behalf of Louis XIV. See Allain's commentary on these issues in "Slave Policies," 127–30.

39. "Édit concernant les Nègres," 81.

40. Quoted in David P. Geggus, *Slavery, War, and Revolution: The British Occupation of Saint Domingue, 1793–1798* (Oxford: Oxford University Press), 24.

41. Carl A. Brasseaux, "The Administration of Slave Regulations in French Louisiana, 1724–1766," *Louisiana History* 21 (Spring 1980): 139–58.

42. Transcripts of baptismal records from many of the Illinois Country parishes are available in the archives of the Missouri Historical Society in St. Louis. Why French colonists in Upper Louisiana were more willing to baptize slaves than were those in Lower Louisiana is an interesting unanswered question, but Brasseaux ("Slave Regulations," 148) claims that the article of the Black Code that required baptism for slaves (article 2) was not enforced in the lower colony.

43. "Règlement," ser. C13A, 35:40–51, ANC. Concerning this decree and its enforcement in Lower Louisiana, see James T. McGowan, "Creation of a Slave Society: Louisiana Plantations in the Eighteenth Century" (Ph.D. diss., University of Rochester, 1976), 145–55; Brasseaux, "Slave Regulations," 156–58.

44. "Règlement," 50.

45. Ibid., 46.

46. Ibid., 49. Brasseaux ("Slave Regulations," 156–57) sees the Louisiana slave regulation of 1751 as a significant tighting up of control of slaves in the colony.

47. Louisiana State University Press published a facsimile version of the 1774 English edition of Du Pratz's work: Antoine Simon Le Page du Pratz, *The History of Louisiana,* ed. Joseph G. Tregle Jr. (Baton Rouge: Louisiana State University Press, 1975).

48. Du Pratz, *History of Louisiana,* 382.

49. Ibid., 27.

50. Ibid., 387.

51. Ser. G1, 464, ANC.

52. Ibid.

53. The old chestnut about Renaut having 500 slaves seems to have begun with John Mason Peck's serialized account of Illinois slavery that first appeared in 1847 (see Bridges, "John Mason Peck," 190). Peck's story was perpetuated in N. Dwight Harris, *The History of Negro Servitude in Illinois* (Chicago: A.C. McClurg, 1904), 2.

54. Census of 1737 in ser. C13A, 4:197, ANC. Living conditions for slaves on the French

Caribbean islands are described in Geggus, *Slavery, War, and Revolution*, 23–30. For a more comprehensive analysis, see Debien, *Les Esclaves aux Antilles*, 171–248.

55. Vaudreuil's order, May 1, 1737, in ser. F3, 243:13, ANC.

56. In a remarkable passage Marcel Giraud (*French Louisiana*, 5:472–73) criticizes the Royal Indies Company for not furnishing to the Illinois Country enough black slaves to ensure an adequate food supply for the lower colony.

57. The high birth rate among African slaves in French Louisiana has been remarked on by Gwendolyn Hall in *Africans in Colonial Louisiana: The Development of Afro-Creole Culture in the Eighteenth Century* (Baton Rouge: Louisiana State University Press, 1992), 175.

58. Edmund Flagg, "The Far West, 1836–1837," in *Early Western Travels, 1748–1846*, 32 vols., ed. Reuben G. Thwaites (Cleveland: A. H. Clark, 1906), 27:56.

59. Constantin-François Chasseboeuf, comte de Volney, *A View of the Soil and Climate of the United States of America*, trans. C. B. Brown (New York: Hafner, 1968 [1804]), 343.

60. *SRM*, 1: facing 414.

61. Ekberg, *Colonial Ste. Genevieve*, 185, 210, 237, 348–49.

62. For the purpose of colonial comparisons, it is interesting to note that this same ratio of blacks to whites obtained in Maryland at the time of the American Revolution. See John J. McCusker and Russell R. Menard, *The Economy of British America, 1607–1789* (Chapel Hill: University of North Carolina Press, 1985), 136.

63. The original of the 1752 census of the Illinois Country is in the Vaudreuil Papers (HMLO, 426). The census taker (presumably Commandant Macarty) erred in tabulating the slaves at Chartres; there were thirty-five rather than thirty-four adult males. This means that the grand total of slaves in 1752 should be 446 instead of 445.

64. Brackenridge, *Views of Louisiana*, 127.

65. Finiels, *Account*, 109.

66. Ser. G1, 464, ANC.

67. KM 37:10:23:1.

68. Natalia M. Belting, *Kaskaskia under the French Regime* (Urbana: University of Illinois Press, 1948), 65.

69. *NR*, 469–70.

70. Thomas Hutchins, *Topographical Description of Virginia, Maryland, Pennsylvania and North Carolina*, ed. Frederick C. Hicks (Cleveland: Arthur H. Clark, 1904), 108.

71. Censuses of 1772, *SRM*, 1:53–60.

72. Censuses of 1791, *SRM*, 2:365–77.

73. Black slaves were frequently used as oarsmen on commercial trips between New Orleans and the Illinois Country (see Hall, *Africans in Colonial Louisiana*, 174–75). I address this practice in the appendix.

74. Finiels, *Account*, 55.

75. Census of 1791, *SRM*, 2:378–86.

76. See Philip Curtin, *The Atlantic Slave Trade: A Census* (Madison: University of Wisconsin Press, 1969), 22.

77. Ser. G1, 464, ANC.

78. In many agricultural economies based on slave labor, larger proportions of female slaves than male slaves served as field hands. See Robert William Fogel, *Without Consent or Contract: The Rise and Fall of American Slavery* (New York: Norton, 1989), 45–46. I am indebted to Bruce Walker for calling this to my attention.

79. For examples of these prices, see bills of sale in KM 24:9:13:1, 40:2:20:1, 47:1:10:1, and 63:6:19:1. The highest prices ever paid for slaves under the French regime in the Illinois Country seems to have been at Fort de Chartres in September 1763, when the commandant, Neyon de Villiers, sold to Jean-Baptiste Lagrange and Étienne Layssard eleven slaves, nine African Americans and two Native Americans, for 40,000 livres. See the contract of sale in Miscellaneous French Records (81055–81058), Notarial Archives, Civil Courts Building, New Orleans.

80. St. Louis Recorded Archives, no. 166, MHS.

81. Slave Sales, no. 138, SGA.

82. Inventory of François Vallé estate, François Vallé Collection, Box 1, MHS; Slave Sales, no. 18, SGA.

83. During the Spanish Regime, slave prices were higher in Lower than in Upper Louisiana. At Natchitoches in the Red River valley, for example, the best slaves were valued at 800 piastres each in 1787. See the inventory of the Rachal estate in French Archives, Bundle 1787, Natchitoches Parishhouse Records, no. 2039, Natchitoches, Louisiana.

84. St. Louis Recorded Archives, no. 512, MHS.

85. "Édit concernant les Nègres," Article 43.

86. St. Louis Recorded Archives, no. 624, MHS.

87. St. Louis Recorded Archives, no. 810, MHS.

88. *CR*, cxli; Amos Stoddard, *Sketches, Historical and Descriptive of Louisiana* (Philadelphia: Mathew Curey, 1812), 225. The famous Article 6 of the ordinance forbade slavery and unvoluntary servitude in the Northwest Territory (Theodore Calvin Pease, ed., *The Laws of the Northwest Territory, 1788–1800* [Springfield: Illinois State Historical Library, 1925], 130), but this article was construed as not applying to French slaves or their descendents; see Bridges, "John Mason Peck," 94–95.

89. Simon Hubardeau estate, Estates no. 125, SGA.

90. The text of Article 6 is found in Pease, *Laws of the Northwest Territory*, 1:130. For recent commentary on this issue, see Paul Finkelman, "Evading the Ordinance: The Persistence of Bondage in Indiana and Illinois," *Journal of the Early Republic* 9 (Spring 1989): 21–57.

91. St. Clair to Washington, 1790, in Clarence E. Carter, ed., *The Territorial Papers of the United States*, 27 vols. (Washington, D.C.: U.S. Government Printing Office, 1934), 2:248. See also Harris, *Negro Servitude*, 6; Bridges, "John Mason Peck," 194–95.

92. See Harris, *Negro Servitude*, 22; Solon Justus Buck, *Illinois in 1818* (Chicago: A. C. McClurg, 1918), 281–82; Peter S. Onuf, "From Constitution to Higher Law: The Reinterpretation of the Northwest Ordinance," *Ohio History* 94 (Winter–Spring 1985): 5–34.

93. Bill of sale, Nov. 13, 1800, in Cahokia Record Book B:107, ISA.

94. Bill of sale, June 25, 1802, in Cahokia Record Book B:195, ISA.

95. See Francis S. Philbrick, ed., *The Laws of the Indiana Territory, 1801–1809*, Collec-

tions of the Illinois State Historical Library, vol. 21 (Springfield: Illinois State Historical Library, 1930): 42–45, 136–39, 523–26.

96. Harris, *Negro Servitude*, 12; Buck, *Illinois in 1818*, 215.

97. See Harris, *Negro Servitude*, 6–16; David E. Richards, comp., "Servant and Slave Records," 51–55, ISA. Many indentures may be seen in the Perrin Collection of the Illinois State Archives and in Cahokia Record Book B.

98. Contract of indenture, Dec. 24, 1798, Cahokia Record Book B:504, ISA.

99. Bill of sale, April 29, 1812, Cahokia Record Book B:617, ISA. Shadrach Bond Jr. was a nephew of Shadrach Bond Sr.

100. Ibid.

101. See paragraph 13 from territorial law of 1807 in Philbrick, *Laws of the Indiana Territory*, 526.

102. *Compendium of the Fourth Census of the United States*, Washington, D.C., 1821. Microfilm copy.

103. County Clerk's Office, Randolph County Courthouse, Chester, Ill.

104. Philip Pittman, *The Present State of the European Settlements on the Mississippi* (London, 1770; facsimile repr., ed. Robert Rea, Gainesville: University of Florida Press, 1973), 55.

105. John F. McDermott was the first scholar to apply this definition of *volontaire* for the Illinois Country (*Old Cahokia: A Narrative and Documents Illustrating the First Century of Its History* [St. Louis: St. Louis Historical Documents Foundation, 1952], 19 n. 41, 263 n. 29).

106. Greer, *Peasant, Lord, and Merchant*, 23.

107. See Gabriel Debien, "Les Engagés pour le Canada partis de Nantes (1725–1732)," *Revue d'histoire de l'Amérique française* 33 (Mar. 1980): 583–86; Peter N. Moogk, "Reluctant Exiles: Emigrants from France in Canada before 1760," *William and Mary Quarterly*, 3d ser., 46 (July 1989): 470–75; idem, "Manon Lescaut's Countrymen: Emigration from France to North America before 1763," in *Proceedings of the Sixteenth Meeting of the French Colonial Historical Society, Mackinac Island, May 1990*, ed. Patricia K. Galloway (New York: University Press of America, 1992), 31–32.

108. C. de La Morandière, *Histoire de la Pêche de la Morue dans l'Amérique septentrionales (des origines à 1789)*, 2 vols. (Paris: G. P. Maisonneuve et Larose, 1962), 2:665–75; Gratien Allaire, "Les Engagements pour la traite de la fourrure—évaluation de la documentation," *Revue d'histoire de l'Amérique française* 34 (June 1980): 3–26.

109. See, for example, Agreements and Contracts, no. 45, SGA.

110. Ste. Genevieve militia muster roll for 1779, PC, 213, AGI.

111. Manuscript copy in MHS.

112. Ser. G1, 464, ANC.

113. KM 38:9:13:1. Original ms. in Chicago Historical Society.

114. Agreements and Contracts, no. 44, SGA.

115. *VOC*, K-371, 842. Curiously, André is shown on the notorial lists as a "nègre," meaning that he was a free black man.

116. KM 39:11:13:1. Barrois mistakenly wrote "1744" when he should have written 1743 for the final year of the contract, for the duration of the contract, three years, was reiterated.

117. KM 45:4:19:1.

118. *ASP, PL*, 2: facing 192.

119. See for example, Contract no. 42, 1795, SGA. In France a person like Bienvenu might have been called a "marchand-laboureur." See Duby, *France rurale*, 2:304.

120. *VOC*, K-182, 548.

121. Concerning endemic malaria in the Illinois Country, see Ekberg, *Colonial Ste. Genevieve*, 250–58.

122. Census of 1752 in HMLO, 426.

123. Marthe Faribault-Beauregard, ed., *La Population des forts français d'Amérique*, 2 vols. (Montreal: Éditions Bergeron, 1984), 1:206.

124. Census in HMLO, 426; comment on Bienvenu's "habitation" by the census taker, Commandant Jean-Jacques Macarty.

125. KM 45:9:21:1.

126. KM 50:2:5:1.

127. See Clarence Walworth Alvord, *The Illinois Country, 1673–1818*, The Centennial History of Illinois, vol. 1 (Springfield: Illinois Centennial Commission, 1920), 346–47; comment on Virginia's short-term possession of the Illinois Country.

128. *KR*, 308 n. 1.

129. KM 83:9:24:1.

130. *CR*, 191; *KR*, 421.

131. The phrase continued in Spanish Illinois at least as late as 1770. See Contracts, nos. 43, 45, SGA.

132. See Contracts, nos. 42 and 44, SGA.

133. See for example, Cahokia Record Book B:278, ISA.

134. Richard Lee Mason quoted in William P. Strickland, *The Pioneers of the West; or, Life in the Woods* (New York: Carlton and Phillips, 1856), 56.

CHAPTER 5: TILLING THE LAND IN COLONIAL ILLINOIS

1. "Mémoire sur la colonie de la Louisiane en 1746," Mémoires et Documents, Amérique, 2:208, Archives des Affaires Étrangères (hereafter AAE), Paris.

2. Philip Pittman, *The Present State of the European Settlements on the Mississippi* (London, 1770; facsimile repr., ed. Robert Rea, Gainesville: University of Florida Press, 1973), 51.

3. Henri Joutel, *Journal of the Last Voyage Perform'd by de la Sale* (London: A. Bell, 1714; repr., Ann Arbor: University Microfilms, 1966), 172 (page references are to reprint edition).

4. *JR*, 4:268 n. 38.

5. Manuscrits français, nouvelles acquisitions 2552:161, BN. See also Mary Borgias Palm, "The First Illinois Wheat," *Mid-America* 13 (July 1930): 72–73.

6. De la Salle to minister, June 20, 1710, ser. C13A, 2:521, ANC.

7. André Pénicaut's "Relation," in *Découvertes et Établissements des français dan le sud de l'Amérique Septentrionale (1614–1754)*, 6 vols., ed. Pierre Margry (Paris: Maisonneuve frères et Charles Leclerc, 1887; repr., New York: AMS, 1974), 5:490. Concerning gristmills, see the appendix.

8. Du Clos to minister, Oct. 25, 1713, ser. C13A, 3:205–6, ANC.

9. "Mémoire sur la colonie de la Louisiane," Dépôt des Fortifications des Colonies, 9:13–14, Centre National des Archives d'Outre-Mer, Aix-en-Provence.

10. Drouot de Vale de Terre to minister, 1722, ser. C13A, 6:362–63, ANC.

11. Ser. B 43:104, ANC.

12. Diron d'Artaguiette, "Journal," in *Travels in the American Colonies*, ed. Newton D. Mereness (New York: Macmillan, 1916), 67.

13. Ser. C13A, 8:447, ANC.

14. Clarence Walworth Alvord, *The Illinois Country, 1673–1818*, The Centennial History of Illinois, vol. 1 (Springfield: Illinois Centennial Commission, 1920), 195.

15. KM 25:8:16:1.

16. Nicolas de Finiels, *An Account of Upper Louisiana*, ed. and trans. Carl J. Ekberg and William E. Foley (Columbia: University of Missouri Press, 1989), 125.

17. Ibid., 133.

18. Ibid., 134.

19. Buffon's ideas disturbed Thomas Jefferson, who refuted them at length in his *Notes on the State of Virginia*. See Thomas Jefferson, *Writings*, ed. Merrill D. Peterson (New York: Library of America, 1984), 169–82.

20. F. Terry Norris, "Where Did the Villages Go? Steamboats, Deforestation, and Archaeological Loss in the Mississippi Valley," in *Common Fields: An Environmental History of St. Louis*, ed. Andrew Hurley (St. Louis: Missouri Historical Society Press, 1997), 73–89.

21. Carl J. Ekberg, *Colonial Ste. Genevieve: An Adventure on the Mississippi Frontier* (Gerald, Mo.: Patrice, 1985), 418–24.

22. "Mémoire de Raymond Amyault, sieur d'Auseville," Jan. 20, 1732, ser. C13A, 14:237, ANC.

23. Mémoires et Documents, Amérique, 2:220, AAE.

24. Finiels, *Account*, 25–27.

25. Boisbriant's memorial, ser. A, 2592:97, SHA.

26. Louise Dechêne, *Habitants et marchands de Montréal au XVIIe siècle* (Paris: Plon, 1974), 307; Allan Greer, *Peasant, Lord, and Merchant* (Toronto: University of Toronto Press, 1985), 28.

27. Georges Duby, *Rural Economy and Country Life in the Medieval West*, trans. Cynthia Postan (Columbia: University of South Carolina Press, 1968), 200.

28. Concerning Monsieur Lallemant as a source for early Illinois agricultural history, see chap. 3, n. 35.

29. Regarding the length of a league in colonial Louisiana, see Finiels, *Account*, 29 n. 12.

30. Marc Bloch, *Les Caractères originaux de l'histoire rurale française*, 2 vols. (Paris: A. Colin, 1964), 1:22.

31. Dechêne, *Habitants et marchands*, 301. According to Dechêne, French Canadians

also sometimes called maize "blé de Turquie," which suggests that they were unaware that it was indigenous only to the New World.

32. A. G. Haudricourt and M. Jean-Brunhes Delamarre, *L'Homme et la charrue à travers le monde* (Paris: André-Georges, 1955), 351.

33. Bloch, *Caractères originaux*, 1:55–57; Duby, *Rural Economy*, 198–99.

34. John Reynolds, *My Own Times, embracing also the history of my life* (Chicago: Fergus, 1879), 23.

35. Ibid., 352.

36. Duby, *Rural Economy*, 202 n. 71; Dechêne, *Habitants et marchands*, 272–73.

37. Dechêne, *Habitants et marchands*, 307–8.

38. Pénicaut, "Relation," 5:489.

39. C. S. Orwin and C. S. Orwin, *The Open Fields*, 2d ed. (Oxford: Oxford University Press, 1967), 41; Warren O. Ault, *Open-Field Farming in Medieval England* (London: n.p., 1972), 20–21, 78.

40. Bloch, *Caractères originaux*, 1:47 n. 32. It is perhaps significant that the word *co-aration* does not exist in French, in which to discuss the issue one must use the phrase *labour en commun*.

41. KM 25:8:16:1.

42. Estates, no. 231, SGA.

43. Ibid., no. 211.

44. John Reynolds, "The Agricultural Resources of Southern Illinois," in *Transactions of the Illinois State Historical Society for the Year 1917* (Springfield: Illinois State Historical Society, 1917), 146.

45. Ebenezer Childs, "Recollections of Wisconsin since 1820," in *Collections of the State Historical Society of Wisconsin*, vol. 4, ed. Lyman Copeland Draper (Madison: State Historical Society of Wisconsin, 1906), 161.

46. John F. Snyder, *Selected Writings* (Springfield: Illinois State Historical Society, 1962), 92.

47. Ibid., 98.

48. Ibid., 100.

49. Ibid., 3–4.

50. Bela Hubbard, *Memorials of a Half-Century in Michigan and the Lake Region* (New York: G.P. Putnam's Sons, 1888), 115.

51. Ibid., 120.

52. Peter Kalm, *Travels in North America*, trans. John Reinhold Forster (Warrington, Great Britain: William Eyres, 1770; repr., ed. Adolph B. Benson, New York: Dover, 1966), 459.

53. Henry Marie Brackenridge, *Views of Louisiana: Together with a Journal of a Voyage up the Missouri River in 1811* (Pittsburg: Cramer, Spear and Eichbaum, 1814), 127.

54. Haudricourt and Delamarre, *La Charrue*, 330–35,

55. See illustration in ibid., 339.

56. Reynolds, *My Own Times*, 23.

57. Edmond Pognon, *Les Très Riches Heures du Duc de Berry*, trans. David Macrae (New York: Crown, 1979), 21.

58. Dechêne, *Habitants et marchands*, 307 n. 28.

59. Bloch, *Caractères originaux*, 1:55–57.

60. Orwin and Orwin, *Open Fields*, 39–51.

61. Thirsk, "The Common Fields," 12–14.

62. German authorities continue to associated long, narrow arable strips with primitive plows. See Hans-Jürgen Nitz, "Siedlungsstrukturen der königlichen und adeligen Grundherrschaft der Karolingerzeit—der Beitrag der historisch-genetischen Siedlungsgeographie," in *Struckturen der Grundherrschaft im Frühen Mittelalter*, ed. Werner Rösener (Göttingen: Vandenhoeck und Ruprecht, 1989), 470–71.

63. See Haudricourt and Delamarre, *La Charrue*, 335.

64. Concerning Broutin and Finiels and their respective maps of the Illinois Country, see chap. 2, notes 30 and 89.

65. Kaskaskia Record Book A:359, ISA.

66. Pénicaut, "Relation," 5:489.

67. D'Artaguiette, "Journal," 67.

68. Piernas to O'Reilly, *SRM* 1:70.

69. Fernand Braudel, *The Structures of Everyday Life: The Limits of the Possible*, trans. Sian Reynolds (New York: Harper and Row, 1959), 143.

70. Quoted in *Newsweek*, Dec. 25, 1995, p. 72.

71. Ekberg, *Colonial Ste. Genevieve*, 302–7.

72. Reynolds, "Agricultural Resources," 147.

73. KM 25:8:16:1.

74. Dechêne, *Habitants et marchands*, 301–2; Thomas Wien, "'Les Travaux pressants': calendrier agricole, assolement et productivité au Canada au XVIIe siècle," *Revue d'Histoire de l'Amérique française* 43 (Spring 1990): 540; Greer, *Peasant, Lord, and Merchant*, 38–39.

75. *JR*, 5:96.

76. Slicher van Bath (*The Agrarian History of Western Europe* [London: Edward Arnold, 1962], 265) remarks that "it is not certain that maize is of American origin," but most authorities agree that it originated in the New World, arriving in Europe only in the sixteenth century.

77. For a good introduction regarding the dissemination of maize from the New World to Europe, see N. J. G. Pounds, *An Historical Geography of Europe, 1500–1840* (Cambridge: Cambridge University Press, 1979), 184–85. Pounds quotes John Locke on the subject.

78. Dechêne, *Habitants et marchands*, 301; Wien, "Calendrier agricole," 540; Greer, *Peasant, Lord, and Merchant*, 38.

79. Jay Higginbotham, *Old Mobile: Fort Louis de la Louisiane, 1702–1711* (Mobile: Museum of the City of Mobile, 1977), 225.

80. Bienville to minister, Apr. 25, 1721, ser. A1, 2592:107, SHA.

81. Antoine Simon Le Page du Pratz, *The History of Louisiana*, ed. Joseph G. Tregle Jr. (Baton Rouge: Louisiana State University Press, 1975), 183–85.

82. Fifty minots of maize were tallied in the estate inventory of Marie Rouensa, Kaskaskia Indian wife of Michel Philippe, in 1725 (KM 25:8:16:1).

83. Macarty to Vaudreuil, Sept. 2, 1752, printed in Theodore C. Pease and Ernestine

Jenison, eds., *Illinois on the Eve of the Seven Years' War,* Collections of the Illinois State Historical Library, vol. 29 (Springfield: Illinois State Historical Library, 1940), 686.

84. Camille Delassus to Governor Carondelet, Mar. 6, 1797, PC, legajo 35, AGI.

85. Reynolds, "Agricultural Resources," 80, 147.

86. *NR,* 469.

87. Census of 1796 in *SRM,* 2:143; census of 1800 in ibid., 1: facing 414.

88. Reynolds, "Agricultural Resources," 146.

89. Olaf Kranz Museum, Illinois State Historic Site, Bishop Hill, Illinois. I am indebted to Edward Safiran of the Illinois Historic Preservation Agency for calling this to my attention.

90. Female black slaves, however, almost certainly worked as field hands during the sowing and harvesting seasons. See chap. 4.

91. Ninian W. Edwards, *History of Illinois from 1788 to 1833 and the Life and Times of Ninian Edwards* (Springfield: Illinois State Journal, 1870), 89.

92. François Perrin du Lac, *Voyage dans les deux Louisianes et chez les nations sauvages du Missouri* (Paris: Capelle and Renand, 1805), 172.

93. Brackenridge, *Views of Louisiana,* 127.

94. Piernas to O'Reilly, Oct. 31, 1769, *SRM* 1:70.

95. Finiels, *Account,* 70.

96. The most important of the Spanish censuses for dealing with agricultural production are those of St. Louis and Ste. Genevieve for 1772 (*SRM* 1:53–60), for 1787 (ms. copy in MHS Archives), and for 1791 (*SRM* 2:365–386).

97. *SRM,* 1: facing 414.

98. *JR,* 69:219.

99. Dec. 2, 1795, MHS Archives, François Vallé Collection, Box 2. A minot, dry measure, equaled approximately 1.1 bushels; see John Francis McDermott, *A Glossary of Mississippi Valley French, 1673–1850,* Washington University Studies, New Series, Language and Literature, no. 12 (St. Louis: Washington University, 1941), 104.

100. In 1797 Pierre-Charles Delassus de Luzières, a relative newcomer to the Illinois Country, complained bitterly about fires ignited in the fields, woods, and meadows by the "neglience of the numerous smokers of this country, whites, Indians, and slaves, . . . who always put down their pipes without taking care to extinguish them" ("Observations sur le caractère, qualités, et professions des habitans blancs du District de la Nouvelle Bourbon," attached to the 1797 New Bourbon census, PC, legajo 2365, AGI).

101. "Croghan's Journal," in *NR,* 32. Concerning the high quality of the tobacco produced at Vincennes, see also Thomas Hutchins, *Topographical Description of Virginia, Maryland, Pennsylvania and North Carolina,* ed. Frederick C. Hicks (Cleveland: Arthur H. Clark, 1904), 100.

102. See "Stirling's Journal," in *Broadswords and Bayonets,* ed. Robert G. Carron (N.p.: Society of Colonial Wars in the State of Illinois, 1984), 68.

103. Manuscript copy in MHS.

104. *SRM,* 1: facing 414.

105. De Luzières, "Observations."

106. *SRM*, 1: facing 414.

107. D'Artaguiette, "Journal," 68.

108. Brackenridge, *Views of Louisiana*, 127.

109. Reynolds, "Agricultural Resources," 146–47.

110. Kalm, *Travels*, 516–17.

111. John Brinkerhoff Jackson, *The Necessity for Ruins* (Amherst: University of Massachusetts Press, 1980), 21.

112. *Webster's New International Dictionary*, 2d ed. (1959), s.v. "horticulture."

113. Kalm, *Travels*, 510.

114. John Reynolds, *The Pioneer History of Illinois* (Chicago: Fergus, 1887), 111.

115. "Stirling's Journal," 90.

116. Thomas Ford, *A History of Illinois* (Ann Arbor: University Microfilms, 1968 [1854]), 36.

117. Reynolds, *My Own Times*, 22.

118. Snyder, *Selected Writings*, 92.

119. Brackenridge, *Recollections*, 24.

120. Finiels, *Account*, 62.

121. Ibid., 69.

122. Estates, no. 19, SGA.

123. Reynolds, "Agricultural Resources," 147.

124. De Luzières, "Observations." Antoine Parmentier's book about the virtues of potatoes had been published in France in the 1770s, but de Luzières gave no indication that he knew of this work.

125. *New York Times*, Aug. 22, 1935, p. 14.

126. Pénicaut, "Relation," 5:489.

127. Concerning Monsieur Lallemant and his informative 1721 letter from Kaskaskia, see chap. 3, note 41.

128. D'Artaguiette, "Journal," 67.

129. Jennings' "Journal," in *NR*, 177.

130. Butricke to Barnsley, Sept. 15, 1768, in Clarence W. Alvord and Clarence E. Carter, eds., *Trade and Politics, 1767–1769* (hereafter *TP*), Collections of the Illinois State Historical Library, vol. 16 (Springfield: Illinois State Historical Library, 1921), 411.

131. Perrin du Lac, *Voyage*, 172.

132. Reynolds, "Agricultural Resources," 146.

133. Brackenridge, *Views of Louisiana*, 127.

134. Finiels, *Account*, 134.

135. Hubbard, *Memorials*, 118.

136. See Slicher van Bath, *Agriculture*, 239–324.

137. Dechêne, *Habitants et marchands*, 305–6; Wien, "Calendrier agricole," 540.

138. Hamilton, "Journal," in John D. Barnhart, ed., *Henry Hamilton and George Rogers Clark in the American Revolution* (Crawfordsville, Ind.: R. E. Banta, 1951), 160.

139. Jackson, *Necessity of Ruins*, 26.

140. Thomas Hutchins, *An Historical Narrative and Topographical Description of Louisiana and West Flordia* (Philadelphia: Robert Aiken, 1784; repr., Gainesville: University of Florida Press, 1968), 27.

141. Reynolds, *Pioneer History*, 113.

142. Macarty to Vaudreuil, Sept. 2, 1752; Pease and Jenison, *Illinois on the Eve of the Seven Years' War*, 693.

143. *JR*, 69:219.

144. "Première Culture de Bled aux Illinois," Manuscrits français, nouvelles acquisitions 2552:161, BN.

145. Richard C. Harris, *Seigneurial System in Early Canada, A Geographical Study* (Madison: University of Wisconsin Press, 1966), 153. Dechêne (*Habitants et marchands*, 326–27) presents ratios of 1:4.5 to 1:6.5 for the region surrounding Montreal.

146. "Magistrates to Captain Rogers," Nov. 18, 1780, printed in *KR*, 207–8.

147. "Inhabitants of Cahokia to Congress," Nov. 10, 1784, printed in *CR*, 567–72.

148. Trudeau to Governor General Gayoso, Jan. 15, 1798, *SRM*, 2:248.

149. Finiels, *Account*, 133. Finiels no doubt socialized with Trudeau in St. Louis during the winter of 1797–98, and he may indeed have gotten this from the lieutenant governor.

150. De Leyba to Governor General Galvez, Nov. 16, 1778, *SMV*, pt. 2, 1:310.

151. See Ekberg, *Colonial Ste. Genevieve*, 138, on these floods and their consequences for crops in Spanish Illinois.

152. Trudeau to Governor General Gayoso, Jan. 15, 1798, *SRM*, 2:248.

153. De Luzières to Carondelet, June 9, 1795, PC, legajo 211, AGI.

154. Census data for 1795 in *SRM*, 1:326.

155. Census data for 1796 in *SRM*, 2:143.

156. Census data for 1800 in *SRM*, 1: facing 414.

157. Manuscript copy of 1787 census in MHS Archives. Ste. Genevieve seems to have had a relatively poor harvest in 1787, for according to the census figures, St. Louis produced more wheat and maize (33,000 minots) that year, which was very unusual. Or possibly the census figures are inaccurate, for this document at the Missouri Historical Society is a copy of a copy, and the original is not extant.

158. De Luzières to Governor General Carondelet, June 12, 1797, PC, legajo 212-A, AGI.

159. François Vallé to Trudeau, June 12, 1797, PC, legajo 214, AGI.

160. Vallé to Governor General Gayoso, Dec. 2, 1797, PC, legajo 214, AGI.

161. De Luzières to Gayoso, Jan. 7, 1798, PC, legajo 215-A, AGI.

162. Trudeau to Vallé, Nov. 30, 1797, François Vallé Collection, Box 2, MHS.

163. Ekberg, *Colonial Ste. Genevieve*, 140, 142.

164. The figures for Ste. Genevieve and Knox Counties for 1840 come from the *Compendium of the Enumeration of the Inhabitants and Statistics of the U.S. . . . from the Returns of the Sixth Census;* those for Ste. Genevieve and New Bourbon come from the 1796 Spanish census (*SRM*, 2:143); and those for Vincennes come from the 1767 British census (*NR*, 469–70). All cereal grains were included in these tabulations, and one minot was reckoned at 1.1 bushels.

165. Belting, *Kaskaskia*, 56.

166. Calvin Goodrich, *The First Michigan Frontier* (Ann Arbor: University of Michigan Press, 1940), 92.

167. Reynolds, "Agricultural Resources," 147.

168. Pénicaut, "Relation," 5:490; see also Belting, *Kaskaskia*, 13, 56.

169. Letter of Monsieur Lallemant from Kaskaskia. Concerning this letter, see chap. 3, note 35.

170. Reynolds, "Agricultural Resources," 147.

171. Pénicaut, "Relation," 5:489–90.

172. Hutchins, *Topographical Description*, 100.

173. Oct. 3, 1720, ser. A1, 2592:97, SHA.

174. Concerning Lallemant's letter, see chap. 3, note 41.

175. Census of 1726, ser. G1, 464, ANC; census of 1732, ibid.; census of 1752, HMLO, 426.

176. Reynolds, whose commentaries about agriculture in early Illinois are often accurate as well as interesting, was incorrect when he wrote that "the French never raised hogs in proportion to their other stock" ("Agricultural Resources," 148).

177. Butricke to Barnsley, Sept. 15, 1768, in *TP*, 411.

178. Census of 1796, *SRM*, 2:143; census of 1800, *SRM*, 1: following 414.

179. *JR*, 69:221.

180. Mercier letter in John F. McDermott, *Old Cahokia: A Narrative and Documents Illustrating the First Century of Its History* (St. Louis: St. Louis Historical Documents Foundation, 1952), 77.

181. Reynolds, *My Own Times*, 39.

182. See especially the Kaskaskia Manuscripts and the Ste. Genevieve Civil Records for detailed inventories.

183. It is interesting to note that the 1750 census of the Detroit region (reprinted in Ernest J. Lajeunesse, ed., *The Windsor Border Region: Canada's Southernmost Frontier* [Toronto: Champlain Society for the Government of Ontario, 1960], 54–56) lists no sheep, but that the 1782 census (*Report of the Pioneer and Historical Society of Michigan* [Lansing: Thorp and Godfrey, State Printers and Binders, 1888], 10:601–13) of that region lists 447, about half the number of cows enumerated.

184. Finiels, *Account*, 64.

185. *JR*, 69:221.

186. *Missouri Republican*, Sep 25, 1859, microfilm MHS.

187. See swine foraging on fallen acorns near an oak forest in the November illuminated manuscript of Jean duc de Berry's famous calendar (Edmond Pognon, *Les Très Riches Heures du Duc de Berry*, trans. David Macrae [New York: Crown, 1979], 39).

188. Brackenridge, *Views of Louisiana*, 128.

189. Finiels, *Account*, 132–33.

190. Ibid., 47, 49, 55, 69, 70, 75.

191. Greer, *Peasant, Lord, and Merchant*, 31.

192. The figures for Ste. Genevieve and Knox Counties for 1840 come from the *Compendium of the Enumeration of the Inhabitants and Statistics of the U.S. . . . from the Returns of the Sixth Census;* those for Kaskaskia come from the 1752 census (HMLO, 426); and those for Vincennes come from the 1767 British census (*NR*, 469–70).

193. John G. Clark has remarked that "from the beginning of settlement in Indiana less land and labor was devoted to wheat than to corn and hogs" (*The Grain Trade in the Old Northwest* [Urbana: University of Illinois Press, 1966], 23).

194. Nancy M. Miller Surrey, *The Commerce of Louisiana during the French Regime, 1699–1763* (New York: Columbia University Press, 1916), 289.

195. Dodge to Pérez, Sept. 23, 1788, PC, legajo 14, AGI.

196. See the Kaskaskia Manuscripts for May 1739; Margaret Kimball Brown, "Allons, Cowboys!" *Journal of the Illinois State Historical Society* 76 (Winter 1983): 273–82. Fort St. Francis, which turned out to be a short-lived installation, was located on the Arkansas River just downstream from the mouth of the St. Francis River (Morris S. Arnold, *Colonial Arkansas, 1686–1804* [Fayetteville: University of Arkansas Press, 1991], 202, 204).

197. KM 46:4:4:2.

198. Census of 1800, *SMR*, 1: following 414.

199. Dechêne, *Habitants et marchands*, 301; Wien, "Calendrier agricole," 537, 540.

200. Dechêne, *Habitants et marchands*, 303–5; Wien, "Calendrier agricole," 538–43.

201. Hamilton, "Journal," 160.

202. Frederic L. Billon, ed., *Annals of St. Louis in Its Early Days under the French and Spanish Dominations, 1776–1804* (St. Louis: F. L. Billon, 1886), 273.

203. Finiels, *Account*, 63. Italics mine.

204. Duby, *Rural Economy*, 149.

CHAPTER 6: AGRICULTURAL COMMERCE IN THE
MISSISSIPPI VALLEY

1. The bibliography on the fur trade is enormous. The best introductions to the fur trade in Upper Louisiana are found in William E. Foley and C. David Rice, *The First Chouteaus: River Barons of Early St. Louis* (Urbana: University of Illinois Press, 1983), and William E. Foley, *The Genesis of Missouri: From Wilderness Outpost to Statehood* (Columbia: University of Missouri Press, 1989).

2. Nancy M. Miller Surrey, *The Commerce of Louisiana during the French Regime, 1699–1763* (New York: Columbia University Press, 1916), 289–95.

3. Daniel H. Usner Jr. "The Frontier Exchange Economy of the Lower Mississippi Valley in the Eighteenth Century," *William and Mary Quarterly* 44 (Apr. 1987): 167. Usner modified his opinion somewhat in his subsequent fine book, remarking that "the Illinois Country eventually became one reliable source of wheat for the colonists downriver" (*Indians, Settlers, and Slaves in a Frontier Exchange Economy: The Lower Mississippi Valley before 1783* [Chapel Hill: University of North Carolina Press, 1992], 198).

4. Norman Walker, "The Commerce of the Mississippi River from Memphis to the Gulf of Mexico," pt. 3 (pp. 136–389) of "The Commerce of the Mississippi and Ohio Rivers," in *The Executive Documents of the House of Representatives for the First Session of the Fiftieth Congress* (Washington, D.C.: U.S. Government Printing Office, 1889), 178.

5. Marcel Giraud, *A History of French Louisiana*, vol. 1, trans. Joseph C. Lambert (Baton Rouge: Louisiana State University Press, 1974), 191.

6. See Jay Higginbotham, *Old Mobile: Fort Louis de la Louisiane, 1702–1711* (Mobile: Museum of the City of Mobile, 1977), 143–60, 225, 298–301, 387, 434–36.

7. Ibid., 346, 373.

8. La Salle to minister, June 20, 1710, Correspondance à l'arrivée en provenance de la Louisiane, ser. C13A, 2:520, ANC; Higginbotham, *Old Mobile*, 387.

9. Antoine Simon Le Page du Pratz, *The History of Louisiana*, ed. Joseph Tregle Jr. (Baton Rouge: Louisiana State University Press, 1975), 187–93.

10. La Salle to minister, June 20, 1710, ser. C13A, 2:521, ANC.

11. See Patricia Galloway, "Sources for the La Salle Expedition of 1682," in Patricia Galloway, ed., *La Salle and His Legacy: Frenchmen and Indians in the Lower Mississippi Valley* (Jackson: University of Mississippi Press, 1982), 18.

12. Lamothe Cadillac to Jérôme de Pontchartrain, Oct. 26, 1713, in Dunbar Rowland and Albert Godfrey Sanders, eds., *Mississippi Provincial Archives*, 3 vols. (Jackson: Mississippi Department of Archives and History, 1927), 2:166.

13. Duclos to minister, "Mémoire générale sur la Louisiane," Oct. 9, 1713, ser. C13A, 3:205–6, ANC.

14. See John E. Rothensteiner, "Earliest History of Mine La Motte," *Missouri Historical Review* 20 (Jan. 1926): 199–213.

15. King's instructions to Bienville, Sept. 2, 1732, in Rowland and Sanders, *Mississippi Provincial Archives*, 3:545.

16. Bienville and Salmon to minister, May 12, 1733, in Rowland and Sanders, *Mississippi Provincial Archives*, 3:600.

17. Étienne Périer and Edmé-Gatien Salmon, "Mémoire," ser. C13A, 13:28, ANC.

18. See Glenn R. Conrad's analysis of the French government's debate over the Illinois Country, "Administration of the Illinois Country: The French Debate," *Louisiana History* 36 (Winter 1995): 31–53.

19. Clarence Walworth Alvord, *Illinois Country, 1673–1818*, The Centennial History of Illinois, vol. 1 (Springfield: Illinois Centennial Commission, 1920), 151.

20. Maurepas to Vaudreuil, Nov. 4, 1748, ser. B, 87:15, ANC.

21. Duclos to minister, Oct. 9, 1713, ser. C13A, 3:205–6, ANC.

22. John G. Clark, in his useful study *New Orleans, 1718–1812: An Economic History* (Baton Rouge: Louisiana State University Press, 1970), claimed that "the Illinois was only of occasional value to New Orleans" (59), but he did not make a systematic study of the flour trade down the Mississippi River during colonial times. Surrey (*Commerce of Louisiana*, 289) states that "by 1732 there was a well-established trade between the Illinois country and Louisiana proper," but it seems likely that this trade was in fact well established a decade before that date.

23. Périer to Maurepas, Mar. 25, 1731, ser. C13A, 13:53, ANC. A French livre equaled approximately 1.08 English pounds. Flour shipped downriver from the Illinois Country was customarily packed in barrels.

24. For a detailed discussion of gristmills in the Illinois Country, see the appendix.

25. The largest pirogues, hewn out of cypress or cottonwood, could carry three or four tons, whereas bateaux generally carried fifteen or sixteen tons. For further discussion of river vessels, see the appendix.

26. Salmon to minister, May 15, 1732, ser. C13A, 15:133–34, ANC.

27. Animal products were exported from outposts such as the Arkansas Post, as well

as from the Illinois Country. See Morris S. Arnold, *Colonial Arkansas, 1686–1804* (Fayetteville: University of Arkansas Press, 1991), 59–64.

28. Minister to Salmon, Sept. 2, 1732, ser. B, 57:817–18, ANC.

29. Contract published in "Records of the Superior Council," trans. Heloise H. Cruzat, *Louisiana Historical Quarterly* 8 (Jan. 1925): 147.

30. Illinois "recensement" of 1732, ser. G1, 464, ANC.

31. Contract published in "Records of the Superior Council," *Louisiana Historical Quarterly* 8 (Jan. 1925): 147–48.

32. Illinois "recensement" of 1732, ser. G1, 464, ANC.

33. Illinois "recensement" of 1752 in HMLO 426.

34. Contract published in "Records of the Superior Council," *Louisiana Historical Quarterly* 8 (Apr. 1925): 290.

35. Contracts published in ibid., 8 (Apr. 1925): 293; ibid., 5 (July 1922): 381.

36. Contract published in ibid., 8 (July 1925): 487.

37. Salmon to minister, June 17, 1737, ser. C13A, 22:192–94, ANC.

38. Concerning agriculture at Arkansas Post and the demand for Illinois flour there, see Arnold, *Colonial Arkansas,* 59–64.

39. Minister to Salmon, Sept. 2, 1732, ser. B, 57:817, ANC.

40. Without providing any substantial supporting data, Gwendolyn Hall (*Africans in Colonial Louisiana: The Development of Afro-Creole Cultre in the Eighteenth Century* [Baton Rouge: Louisiana State University Press, 1992], 122–23) argues that colonial Louisiana *always* had plentiful supplies of rice. More data are obviously needed, but given the desperation with which authorities in New Orleans awaited flour shipments, from France as well as from the Illinois Country, Professor Hall's argument seems problematic.

41. Bienville to minister, Sept. 5, 1736, ser. C13A, 36:221, ANC.

42. Bienville to minister, Apr. 26, 1738, ser. C13A, 23:52, ANC.

43. Illinois "recensement" of 1732, ser. G1, 464, ANC.

44. KM 38:1:20:1; 38:3:21:1. Some of the original manuscripts of the civil records from French Illinois, including the two just cited, are located in the Chicago Historical Society. These manuscripts have, however, been catalogued and filmed as part of the large collection of Kaskaskia Manuscripts, which, after having been sorted, reorganized, and numbered by Margaret K. Brown and Lawrie D. Dean, are now housed in the Randolph County Courthouse in Chester, Ill.

45. Abstract of Bienville's dispatch of May 29, 1738, ser. C13A, 23:77–80, ANC.

46. Illinois "recensment" of 1732, ser. G1, 464, ANC.

47. Contract of engagement in KM 38:4:29:2. Original ms. in Chicago Historical Society.

48. Bienville and Salmon to minister, June 9, 1739, ser. C13A, 24:4, ANC.

49. Salmon to minister, June 3, 1739, ibid., 24:128.

50. For a general account of the Franco-Chickasaw relations during the eighteenth century, see Patricia D. Woods, *French-Indian Relations on the Southern Frontier, 1699–1762* (Ann Arbor: UMI Research, 1980). Concerning Governor Bienville's campaign against the Chickasaws during the late 1730s and early 1740s, see ibid., 111–46.

51. Jean Frédéric Phélypeaux, comte de Maurepas (minister of the marine) to intendant at Rochefort, Apr. 26, 1739, ser. 1E 129:273, Archives du Port de Rochefort, Service Historique de la Marine, Rochefort.

52. See Maurepas's "État des farines nécessaires pour les troupes des colonies 1738," Dec. 9, 1737, in ibid., 1E 127:411. Approximately the same amounts of French flour went to the garrisons on Martinique and St. Domingue.

53. Salmon to minister, June 3, 1739, ser. C13A, 24:128, ANC.

54. "Records of the Superior Council," *Louisiana Historical Quarterly* 11 (Oct. 1928): 647. Renting slaves in New Orleans to be used as boatmen for commercial trips to the Illinois Country was a common occurence in colonial Louisiana (see Hall, *Africans in Colonial Louisiana,* 174–75).

55. Le Page du Pratz, *History of Louisiana,* 162–63.

56. Vaudreuil to minister, Mar. 20, 1748, ser. C13A, 32:29, ANC.

57. Thomas Hutchins, *A Topographical Description of Virginia, Pennsylvania, Maryland, and North Carolina,* ed. Frederick C. Hicks (Cleveland: Arthur H. Clark, 1904), 90.

58. Commissaire-ordonnateur Le Normant to minister, Apr. 8, 1746, ser. C13A, 30:144, ANC.

59. Vaudreuil to minister, Apr. 12, ibid., 30:57.

60. "État des fonds à remettre au port de Rochefort pour payement du fret des farines," Nov. 10, 1746, ibid., 30:214–15, 219.

61. Vaudreuil to minister, Nov. 20, 1746, ibid., 30:71.

62. According to John Francis McDermott (*Glossary of Mississippi Valley French,* Washington University Studies, new series, Language and Literature, no. 12 [St. Louis: Washington University, 1941], 129), a quart was a barrel that usually contained 180 French pounds (approximately 195 English pounds). As with all eighteenth-century measurements, however, the contents of quarts varied a good deal according to time and circumstance.

63. "Procès-verbal du déchargement de la flûte du roi le *Chameau,*" Mar. 18, 1747, ser. C13A, 31:114–15, ANC.

64. Vaudreuil and Auberville to minister, May 4, 1749, ibid., 33:4; Auberville to minister, May 9, 1749, ibid., 33:115–16.

65. Vaudreuil to minister, Sept. 24, 1750, ibid., 34:277.

66. Major Macarty to minister, May 27, 1751, ibid., 35:362.

67. Michel to minister, Sept. 23, 1752, ibid., 36:270.

68. Macarty to Governor Vaudreuil, Sept. 2, 1752, in Theodore C. Pease and Ernestine Jenison, eds., *Illinois on the Eve of the Seven Years' War,* Collections of the Illinois State Historical Library, vol. 29 (Springfield: Illinois State Historical Library, 1940), 686.

69. Concerning French Canadian agriculture at Detroit, see Ernest J. Lajeunesse, ed., *The Windsor Border Region: Canada's Southernmost Frontier* (Toronto: Champlain Society for the Government of Ontario, 1960), lxvi–lxxv, 78–87.

70. See Macarty to Vaudreuil, Jan. 1752, in Pease and Jenison, *Illinois on the Eve of the Seven Years' War,* 465–66; Vaudreuil to St. Ange, Apr. 28, 1752, in ibid., 610.

71. Macarty to minister, Dec. 8, 1752, C13A, 36:313, ANC; Kerlérec to minister, June 23, 1754, ibid., 38:79.

72. Father Vivier, *JR*, 69:219.

73. This dispatch (Sept. 1, 1748, ser. C11A, 91:116–23, ANC) has been analyzed by William J. Eccles (*The Canadian Frontier, 1534–1760* [New York: Holt, Rinehart and Winston, 1969; rev. ed., Albuquerque: University of New Mexico Press, 1983], 155) and has been reanalyzed from the perspective of Louisiana by Glenn R. Conrad ("Administration of the Illinois Country: The French Debate," *Louisiana History* 36 [Winter 1995]: 31–53).

74. Mémoirs et Documents, Amérique, 24:136, Archives des Affaires Étrangères, Paris. A translation of this document is printed in Edmund B. O'Callaghan, ed., *Documents Relating to the Colonial History of the State of New York*, 15 vols. (Albany, N.Y.: Weed, Parsons, 1853–87), 10:220–26; see also Guy Frégault, *Le Grand Marquis: Pierre de Rigaud de Vaudreuil et la Louisiane* (Montreal: Fides, 1966), 328.

75. Administrative correspondence during the 1750s is rife with discussions of hostile Chickasaw activities. Jean-Baptiste Macarty, commandant in the Illinois Country, wrote in May 1753 that in the previous eighteen months, thirty men had been killed or seized by Chickasaws along the Mississippi (Macarty to minister, May 20, 1753, Pease and Jenison, *Illinois on the Eve of the Seven Years' War*, 817). In the fall of 1753, a convoy on its way from Ouiatenon on the Wabash to Kaskaskia in quest of foodstuffs was attacked by Chickasaws twelve leagues south of Kaskaskia, and seven men were killed (Duquesne to minister, Oct. 31, 1753, ibid., 844). In 1759 Chickasaws plundered the Jesuit plantation that was only a musket shot from Kaskaskia (Macarty to Kerlérec, Aug. 30, 1759, ser. C13A, 41:104–5, ANC).

76. See Dumas to Macarty, Nov. 10, 1755, ser. C13A, 39:171, ANC.

77. See the "États des approvisionnments à envoyer à la Louisiane," Archives de Rochefort, 1E 149:993; 1E 155:819, 995. This near tripling of the amounts of flour from France earmarked for New Orleans during the 1730s and 1740s was likely a consequence of lesser amounts coming down the Mississippi from Illinois and an increase of the size of the garrison in New Orleans in response to King George's War.

78. John G. Clark (*La Rochelle and the Atlantic Economy during the Eighteenth Century* [Baltimore: Johns Hopkins University Press, 1981], 150–57) has commented on the serious impact of warfare on such important French seaports as La Rochelle.

79. See Abraham P. Nasatir and Leo Shpall, "The Texel Affair," *American Jewish Historical Quarterly* 53 (Sept. 1963): 3–43, on this interesting episode in the commerical history of French New Orleans. Article 1 of the Louisiana Black Code forbade Jews from residing in Louisiana. See "Édit concernant les Nègres," *Publications of the Louisiana Historical Society* 4 (1908), 76.

80. Kerlérec to minister, May 7, 1759, ser. C13A, 41:57–58, ANC.

81. Foucault to minister, July 26, 1762, ibid., 43:146–47.

82. Gaston Zeller, *Les Temps modernes,* vol. 3 of Pierre Renouvin, *Histoire des relations internationales* (Paris: Hachette, 1955), 244, 270.

83. The Spaniards were not very successful in this endeavor, for much of the flour that arrived in New Orleans on Spanish ships had gone bad. There is some interesting documentation on this in the New Orleans Notarial Archives. See, for example, the letter of Lalande d'Apremont, assessor for the Provincial Superior Council, in "Miscellaneous French Records," 67-031, 67-032, Mar. 26, 1762.

84. Aubry to minister, Aug. 8, 1765, ser. C13A, 39:118, ANC.

85. Concerning Denis-Nicolas Foucault and his activities during the 1760s, see Marc de Villiers du Terrage, *The Last Years of French Louisiana*, trans. Hosea Phillips, ed. Carl A. Brasseaux and Glenn R. Conrad (Lafayette: Center for Louisiana Studies, 1982), 234–345.

86. See Livingston to minister, May 13, 1769, ser. C13A, 49:25, ANC.

87. John G. Clark, *New Orleans, 1718–1812: An Economic History* (Baton Rouge: Louisiana State University Press, 1970), 164.

88. Clark, *New Orleans*, 161–62.

89. The 1767 census shows the Illinois wheat harvest to have been only half that of maize. See *NR*, 469.

90. See George Croghan to Thomas Gage, Jan. 12, 1767, in *NR*, 479–81.

91. See Carl J. Ekberg, *Colonial Ste. Genevieve: An Adventure on the Mississippi Frontier* (Gerald, Mo.: Patrice, 1985), 40–43.

92. Farmar to Barrington, Mar. 19, 1766, in *NR*, 191.

93. John Fitzpatrick to Garret Rapalje, Manchac, Apr. 12, 1775, and Fitzpatrick to Winston and Kennedy, May 10, 1775, in Margaret Fisher Dalymple, ed., *The Merchant of Manchac: The Letterbooks of John Fitzpatrick, 1768–1790* (Baton Rouge: Louisiana State University Press, 1978), 186.

94. See François Charleville's contract of engagement, KM 75:5:12:1.

95. James H. Roberts, "The Life and Times of General John Edgar," *Transactions of the Illinois State Historical Society for the Year 1907* (Springfield: Phillips Bros., 1908), 70.

96. See contracts of engagement in KM for March 1786.

97. KM 86:4:8:1.

98. Dodge to Pérez, Sept. 23, 1788, PC, legajo 14, AGI.

99. Pérez to Miró, Oct. 12, 1788, PC, legajo 14, AGI.

100. There is no consistent documentation pertaining to commodities being shipped from New Orleans to the Illinois Country. A few bills of lading for bateaux heading upriver in July 1768 may be found in PC, legajo 188A, AGI. Finally, the François Vallé Collection in the archives of the MHS contains several manifests of merchandise that Vallé received from New Orleans during the 1790s.

101. Masses of this correspondence reside in the various *legajos* of the Papeles du Cuba section of the Archivo General de Indias in Seville. See James A. Robertson, *A List of Documents in Spanish Archives Relating to the History of the United States* (Washington, D.C.: U.S. Government Printing Office, 1910).

102. Many of the licenses for these bateaux are to be found in PC, legajos 110 and 188A, in the AGI.

103. See this tabulation dated Sept. 4, 1770, in PC, legajo 110, AGI.

104. See Fagot's license, signed by Lieutenant Louis Villars in Ste. Genevieve, July 27, 1770, in PC, legajo 188A, AGI.

105. On this subject, see *SRM*, 1:55.

106. License signed by Villars in Ste. Genevieve, July 23, 1770, in PC, legajo 188A, AGI.

107. See Vallé's license dated June 28, 1770, in PC, legajo 110, AGI.

108. See Arnold, *Colonial Arkansas,* 59–60.

109. Concerning Louis Villars and his role as Spanish military commandant of Ste. Genevieve, see Ekberg, *Colonial Ste. Genevieve.*

110. Villars's letter dated July 19, 1771, is in PC, legajo 188A, AGI.

111. See Fagot's license dated Feb. 27, 1772, in PC, legajo 111, AGI.

112. Bill of lading, Feb. 27, 1772, PC, legajo 111, AGI.

113. Deerskins were a large item of export from New Orleans during the eighteenth century. See Walker, "Commerce of the Mississippi," 180; Usner, *Frontier Exchange,* esp. 25–31, 244–49.

114. *SRM,* 1:57.

115. Ibid., 1:89.

116. Ibid., 1:95.

117. The account of this episode appears in depositions located in PC, legajo 107, AGI. I am indebted to U.S. appellate judge Morris S. Arnold of Little Rock, Ark., for having discovered, translated, and shared this document with me. The unusual mounting of a four-pound cannon on a commercial bateau was probably intended to ward off Chickasaw attacks. This incident occurred shortly after the American Revolution had ended, and the Chickasaws were British allies.

118. Data appended to census of 1796, Oct. 11, 1796, PC, legajo 2364, AGI.

119. *SRM,* 1: facing 414.

120. Nicolas de Finiels, *An Account of Upper Louisiana,* ed. and trans. Carl J. Ekberg and William E. Foley (Columbia: University of Missouri Press, 1989), 78.

121. Nov. 28, 1795, PC, 110, AGI. Trudeau's basic argument was reiterated in even more forceful terms in 1802 when Manuel Lisa and other members of the trading community in St. Louis wrote to Governor General Juan Manuel de Salcedo complaining that American flour from the Ohio River valley was being sold in St. Louis (Trudeau to Carondelet, May 27, 1794, in Abraham P. Nasatir, ed., *Before Lewis and Clark,* 2 vols. [St. Louis: St. Louis Historical Documents Foundation, 1952], 2:679).

122. Finiels, *Account,* 65.

123. Jefferson to Livingston, Apr. 18, 1802, in Thomas Jefferson, *The Works of Thomas Jefferson,* 9 vols., ed. H. A. Washington (New York: Townsend MacCoun, 1884), 4:432.

124. Hutchins, *Topographical Description,* 88–89.

125. Arthur P. Whitaker, *The Spanish-American Frontier, 1783–1795* (Boston: Houghton Mifflin, 1927), 7.

126. Thomas S. Berry, *Western Prices before 1861: A Study of the Cincinnati Market,* Harvard Economic Studies, vol. 74 (Cambridge, Mass.: Harvard University Press, 1943), 155.

127. Gayoso's "Report," in Abraham P. Nasatir, ed., *Spanish War Vessels on the Mississippi, 1792* (New Haven, Conn.: Yale University Press, 1968), 340.

128. Donald Zochert, "Illinois Water Mills, 1790–1818," *Journal of the Illinois State Historical Society* 65 (Summer 1972): 187.

129. Arthur Clinton Boggess, *The Settlement of Illinois, 1778–1830* (Chicago: Chicago Historical Society, 1908), 193.

130. Whitaker, *Spanish-American Frontier*, 176.

131. Walker, "Commerce of the Mississippi," 181.

132. Quoted in ibid., 182.

133. Ibid., 183.

134. John Reynolds, "The Agricultural Resources of Southern Illinois," in *Transactions of the Illinois State Historical Society for the Year 1917* (Springfield: Illinois State Historical Society, 1917), 151.

135. Early on this became the name for the broad swath of alluvial land lying on the east side of the Mississippi River and extending roughly one hundred miles from the mouth of the Kaskaskia River in the south to the mouth of the Illinois River in the north. See Lewis Caleb Beck, *A Gazetteer of the States of Illinois and Missouri* (Albany: C. R. and G. Webster, 1823; repr., New York: Arno, 1975), 13.

136. Christian Schultz, *Travels on an Inland Voyage . . . performed in the years 1807 and 1808* (New York: Isaac Riley, 1810), 2:38.

137. Berry, *Western Prices*, 158.

138. Ibid.

139. Schultz, *Travels on an Inland Voyage*, 2:100.

140. See Michael Allen (*Western Rivermen, 1763–1861* [Baton Rouge: Louisiana State University Press, 1990]) for a recent anecdotal study of river vessels, boatmen, and commerce in the greater Mississippi River watershed. Allen is weak for the pre–Louisiana Purchase era but is more authoritative for the nineteenth century.

141. On this issue, see the exhaustive study by Steven L. Kaplan, *Provisioning Paris: Merchants and Millers in the Grain and Flour Trade during the Eighteenth Century* (Ithaca, N.Y.: Cornell University Press, 1984).

142. See, for example, "État des fonds à remettre au port de Rochefort pour payement du fret des farines," Nov. 10, 1746 (ser. C13A, 30:215, ANC), where a shipment of 593 quarts of flour averaged 205 French pounds per quart; or another "État des fonds," Nov. 10, 1746 (ser. C13A, 30:219, ANC), where a shipment of 620 quarts averaged 212 pounds per quart.

143. Surrey, *Commerce of Louisiana*, 265.

144. Ser. B, 57:818, ANC.

145. Surrey, *Commerce of Louisiana*, 265.

146. Maurepas to intendant, Apr.26, 1739, Archives de Rochefort, 1E 129:273. The cost of shipping freight from Rochefort to New Orleans ran approximately 100 livres per ton, or 5 livres per quintal (see Maurepas to Charles de la Boische, marquis de Beauharnois [governor general of New France], ibid., 1E 117:79). French flour would therefore have been cheaper in New Orleans than that from Illinois, although this would not take into consideration substantial loss through spoilage during shipment from Rochefort.

147. Clark, *New Orleans*, 116.

148. Ibid.

149. Surrey, *Commerce of Louisiana*, 266.

150. Ibid.

151. Ibid.

152. *CP*, 187.

153. *NR*, 385.

154. *TP*, 348. Currency exchange rates in the eighteenth-century Mississippi Valley are difficult to reckon with any precision, but calculating twenty-five British pence per French livre (based on equivalencies in deerskins), 37 shillings, 6 pence, would have equaled 180 livres, which was indeed a "monstrous" price for a hundredweight of flour.

155. Quoted in Thomas M. Doerflinger, *A Vigorous Spirit of Enterprise: Merchants and Economic Development in Revolutionary Philadelphia* (Chapel Hill: University of North Carolina Press, 1986), 151.

156. *TP*, 558.

157. These prices come from Personalty, nos. 22 and 10, SGA; and from financial accounts of the Spanish lieutenant governor in St. Louis, François Cruzat, Nov. 30, 1782, PC, legajo 9, AGI.

158. Petition is PC, legajo 2362, AGI. It is not dated but seems to have been from circa 1794.

159. Berry, *Western Prices*, 158–59.

160. Whitaker, *Spanish-American Frontier*, 193.

161. Berry, *Western Prices*, 159.

CONCLUSION

1. This point is elaborated in David G. Allen, *In English Ways: The Movement of Societies and the Transferal of English Local Law and Custom to Massachusetts Bay in the Seventeenth Century* (Chapel Hill: University of North Carolina Press, 1981), 229–32.

2. See Philip J. Greven Jr., *Four Generations: Population, Land, and Family in Colonial Andover, Massachusetts* (Ithaca, N.Y.: Cornell University Press, 1970), 51–54, where he emphasizes the corrosive effect upon open-field agriculture of new immigrants who did not have communal agriculture engrained in their psyches.

3. Theodore Calvin Pease, ed., *The Laws of the Northwest Territory, 1788–1800* (Springfield: Illinois State Historical Library, 1925), xv–xvi.

4. Clarence E. Carter, ed., *The Territorial Papers of the United States*, 27 vols. (Washington, D.C.: U.S. Government Printing Office, 1934), 2:341.

5. Pease, *Laws of the Northwest Territory*, 498.

6. Greven, *Four Generations*, chap. 3.

7. *Vincennes Western Sun*, Aug. 22, 1807, p. 3.

8. William E. Foley, *The Genesis of Missouri: From Wilderness Outpost to Statehood* (Columbia: University of Missouri Press, 1989), 148–49.

9. The petition and Hamtramck's order are in the Porter Collection, folder 21, IHS.

10. Carter, *Territorial Papers*, 2:341.

11. "Minutes of the Board of Trustees for Vincennes University," ed. Robert Constantine, *Indiana Magazine of History* 14 (Dec. 1958): 355–59.

12. *Vincennes Western Sun*, Apr. 20, 1808, p. 3.

13. "Common Lands," Box no. 2, Vincennes University Regional History Collection, no. 116, Byron R. Lewis Historical Library, Vincennes, Ind.

14. Ibid., Box no. 1.

15. *The Vincennes Sun-Commercial,* Nov. 28, 1951, p. 1.

16. Cahokia Record Book B:423, ISA.

17. John Reynolds, *The Pioneer History of Illinois* (Chicago: Fergus, 1887), 211.

18. *Kaskaskia Republican Advocate,* no. 49, Feb. 3, 1824, p. 2.

19. Emil Joseph Verlie, *Illinois Constitutions,* Collections of the Illinois State Historical Library, vol. 13 (Springfield: Illinois State Historical Library, 1919), 85.

20. *Private Laws of the State of Illinois, First Session, General Assembly, 1851* (Springfield: Lanphier and Walker, 1851), 7–10.

21. Record book of the minutes for the Kaskaskia Commons, Document 363.1, ISA.

22. Ibid.

23. Ibid.

24. *SRM,* 2:249.

25. I wish to thank John A. Karel, director of Tower Grove Park, St. Louis, for information pertaining to Henry Shaw, the Prairie des Noyers, and Tower Grove Park. Shaw eventually donated to the city the land on which the public park is now located.

26. *Missouri Argus,* Jan. 29, 1836, p. 2.

27. *Missouri Republican,* Sept. 25, 1859, p. 3.

28. M. M. Yeakle, *The City of St. Louis Today* (St. Louis: n.p., 1889), 106.

29. Foley, *The Genesis of Missouri,* 14849.

30. The private law that created the "Big Field Corporation of Ste. Genevieve" was first enacted in 1822 (*Laws of the District of Louisiana, of the Territory of Louisiana, of the Territory of Missouri, and of the State of Missouri up to the Year 1824* [Jefferson City: W. Lusk and Son, 1842], 996–98); slightly amended in 1826 (*Laws of the State of Missouri, Passed between the Years 1824 & 1836* [Jefferson City: W. Lusk and Son, 1842], 110–11), and then reenacted with minor changes in 1855 (*Laws of the State of Missouri, Passed at the First Session of the Eighteenth General Assembly* [Jefferson City: James Lusk, 1855], 334–35).

31. With regard to the old French villages of the Illinois Country, F. Terry Norris has spent years tracing the archaeological remains of Cahokia, Kaskaskia, Prairie du Rocher, and the Old Town of Ste. Genevieve. See his "Where Did the Villages Go: Steamboats, Deforestation, and Archaeological Loss in the Mississippi Valley," in *Common Fields: An Environmental History of St. Louis,* ed. Andrew Hurley (St. Louis: Missouri Historical Society Press, 1997), 73–89.

32. J. H. Parry and Frank Thistlewaite, "The Development of the American Communities," chap. 21 of *The Old Regime, 1713–1763,* vol. 7 of *The New Cambridge Modern History,* ed. J. O. Lindsay (Cambridge: Cambridge University Press, 1966), 511. For a textbook version of French settlements in the Illinois Country as mere trading outposts, see Samuel Eliot Morison and Henry Steele Commager, *The Growth of the American Republic,* 2 vols., 5th ed., rev. (New York: Oxford University Press, 1962), 1:98, where Kaskaskia, Cahokia and Vincennes are characterized as mere "connecting links between Canada and Louisiana."

33. Jay Gitlin, "Empires of Trade, Hinterlands of Settlement," chap. 3 of *Oxford History of the American West,* ed. Clyde A. Milner II, Carol A. O'Connor, and Martha A. Sandweiss (New York: Oxford University Press, 1994), 108. This hyperbolic statement is

contradicted on the preceding page of this prestigious volume, where Gitlin acknowledges that "the Illinois country developed agricultural surpluses."

34. *Journal of the Illinois State Historical Society* 69 (May 1976): 107. In 1772 the British garrison abandoned Fort de Chartres, which was already being threatened by the meandering Mississippi River. From 1772 until 1776 the nominal British commandant in the Illinois Country was Captain Hugh Lord, and after he repaired to Detroit in 1776, the command fell to the curious adventurer Philippe Rastel de Rocheblave, who remained in Kaskaskia until he was captured by George Rogers Clark in July 1778. See Clarence Walworth Alvord, *Illinois Country, 1673–1818,* The Centennial History of Illinois, vol. 1 (Springfield: Illinois Centennial Commission, 1920), 317–24; James A. James, *The Life of George Rogers Clark* (Chicago: University of Chicago Press, 1928), chap. 6.

35. See the enumeration of 137 Americans at Kaskaskia in 1787 in *KR,* 421–23.

36. As previously explained, this process began with the Northwest Territory Law of 1799. See Pease, *Laws of the Northest Territory,* 498.

37. Greven, *Four Generation,* 51. Concerning open-field agriculture in seventeenth-century New England, see also Sumner Chilton Powell, *Puritan Village: The Formation of a New England Town* (Middletown, Conn.: Wesleyan University Press, 1963).

38. Ibid., 52.

39. Alvord, *The Illinois Country,* 397. Italics mine.

40. Concerning McCarty's life in the Illinois Country, see sporadic documents concerning him in *KR* and *CR,* passim. He seems to have arrived in the Illinois Country via French Canada, where he left a French Canadian wife and two children. See his final will and testament in *KR,* 230–31.

41. McCarty to Todd, Sept. 18, 1779, *CR,* 614–15.

42. McCarty to Montgomery, Sept. 19, 1779, ibid., 615–16.

43. Louise Dechêne, *Habitants et marchands de Montréal au XVIIᵉ siècle* (Paris: Plon, 1974), 313.

44. John Todd to Jefferson, January 24, 1781, printed in Edward G. Mason, ed., *Early Chicago and Illinois* (Chicago: Fergus, 1890), 335.

45. Henry S. Bartholomew, Joseph Greusel, Marie B. Ferrey, and Mary Agnes Burton, *Michigan Pioneer and Historical Collections,* 21 vols. (East Lansing: Michigan State Historical Society, 1900), 9:646. McCarty knew that traveling across country through Indian territory was dangerous, and he drafted his final will and testament before leaving the Illinois Country (printed in *KR,* 230–31).

46. *ASP, PL,* 2:194.

47. Amos Stoddard, *Sketches, Historical and Descriptive of Louisiana* (Philadelphia: Mathew Curey, 1812), 220. Italics mine.

48. Gayle Thornbrough, ed., *The Correspondence of John Badollet and Albert Gallatin, 1804–1836,* Indiana Historical Society Publications, vol. 22 (Indianapolis: Indiana Historical Society, 1963), 57.

49. Oscar Handlin, *The Uprooted* (New York: Grosset and Dunlap, 1951), 83.

50. Bela Hubbard, *Memorials of a Half-Century in Michigan and the Lake Region* (New York: G.P. Putnam's Sons, 1888), 117.

51. Alexis de Tocqueville, *Democracy in America,* trans. George Lawrence, ed. J. P. Mayer and Max Lerner (New York: Harper and Row, 1966), 744.

52. Reynolds, *Pioneer History,* 229.

53. Paul Wilhelm, duke of Württemberg, *Travels in North America, 1822–1824,* ed. Savoie Lottinville (Norman: University of Oklahoma Press, 1973), 408.

54. Quoted in Mason Wade, *The French Canadians,* 2 vols. (New York: St. Martin's, 1968), 1:185.

55. Jonathan Jennings, *Letters,* ed. Dorothy Riker (Indianapolis: Indiana Historical Society, 1932), 163.

56. Constantin-François Chasseboeuf, comte de Volney, *A View of the Soil and Climate of the United States of America,* trans. C. B. Brown (New York: Hafner, 1968 [1804]), 346–47.

57. Léopold Genicot, *Rural Communities in the Medieval West* (Baltimore: Johns Hopkins University Press, 1990), 45.

58. Richard C. Hoffman, "Medieval Origins of the Common Fields," in William N. Parker and Eric L. Jones, eds., *European Peasants and Their Markets* (Princeton, N.J.: Princeton University Press, 1975), 24.

59. Marc Bloch, *Les Caractères originaux de l'histoire rurale française,* 2 vols. (Paris: A. Colin, 1964), 1:46.

60. Ibid., 1:185.

61. Robert Mandrou, *Introduction à la France moderne* (Paris: Albin Michel, 1961), 125.

62. Richard Critchfield, *The Villagers* (New York: Anchor-Doubleday, 1994), 469.

63. Perrin Collection, 1785, ISA; John F. McDermott, ed., *Old Cahokia: A Narrative and Documents Illustrating the First Century of Its History* (St. Louis: St. Louis Historical Documents Foundation, 1952), 118–19.

64. Reynolds, *Pioneer History,* 126; John Reynolds, *My Own Times, embracing also the history of my life* (Chicago: Fergus, 1879), 51.

65. Ibid. Reynolds continued this passage by noting that the French habitants had had "a class of bataillers [*sic*], as the French called them, who prided themselves in single combat." Reynolds, who is the only source on these curious French creole *bateilleurs,* seems to be suggesting in this passage that interpersonal violence in French Illinois was institutionalized and confined to a small group of specialists; "pugilists," we would call them.

66. Thomas Marshall, *The Life and Papers of Frederick Bates,* 2 vols. (St. Louis: Missouri Historical Society, 1926), 1:133. Italics mine.

67. William E. Foley (*The Genesis of Missouri,* 284) quotes revealing passages from Bates in remarking on his anti-French biases.

68. Carter, *Territorial Papers,* 13:84.

69. William J. Eccles (personal communication, Montreal, May 1993) is unequivocal on this point.

70. KM 39:1:12:1.

71. William J. Eccles, *The Canadian Frontier, 1534–1760* (New York: Holt, Rinehart and Winston, 1969; repr., Albuquerque: University of New Mexico Press, 1983).

72. Marthe Faribault-Beauregard, ed., *La Population des forts francais d'Amérique,* 2 vols. (Montreal: Editions Bergeron, 1984), 2:94.

73. There was a flagrant case within the famous Vallé family. See SGA, Marriage Contracts, 138 a and b, SGA; Ekberg, *Colonial Ste. Genevieve,* 192–93.

74. Ekberg, *Colonial Ste. Genevieve,* 328–29.

75. Ibid., 373–74.

76. Foley (*The Genesis of Missouri,* 186) describes these cases.

77. Alvord, *Illinois Country,* 426.

78. Francis S. Philbrick, ed., *The Laws of the Territory of Illinois, 1801–1809,* Collections of the Illinois State Historical Library, vol. 25 (Springfield: Illinois State Historical Library, 1950), 36.

79. Bonnevie de Pogniat, "Mémoire sur la Louisiane," Dépôt des Fortifications des Colonies, Louisiane 26:30, Centre National des Archives d'Outre-Mer, Aix-en-Provence.

80. William Blane quoted in Milo Milton Quaife, ed., *Pictures of Illinois One Hundred Years Ago* (Chicago: R. R. Donnelly and Sons, 1918), 49–50.

81. James Flint, *Letters from America,* ed. Reuben G. Thwaites (Cleveland: Arthur Clark, 1904), 138.

82. Albert Bigelow Paine, *Mark Twain: A Biography* (New York: Harper and Brothers, 1912), 46–48.

83. Francis S. Philbrick, *The Rise of the West* (New York: Harper and Row, 1965), 356–66.

84. Elliott J. Gorn, "'Gouge and Bite, Pull Hair and Scratch': The Social Significance of Fighting in the Southern Backcountry," *American Historical Review* 90 (Feb. 1985): 18–43.

85. Ibid., 34.

86. Ibid., 36.

87. Reynolds, *My Own Times,* 40.

88. Parker, "From Northwest to Midwest: Social Basis of a Regional History," in *Geographic Perspectives on America's Past,* ed. David Ward (New York: Oxford University Press, 1979), 172. After making this interesting observation, however, Parker continues to comment, erroneously, that communal agriculture "was wholly unknown, undreamed of by the original rural population of the Middle West." This remark merely reveals the general ignorance, even within the scholarly community, of French colonial agricultural practices in the Illinois Country.

89. John Mack Faragher, *Daniel Boone: The Life and Legend of an American Pioneer* (New York: Henry Holt, 1992), 121.

90. For an introduction to frontier violence, see W. Eugene Hollon, *Frontier Violence: Another Look* (New York: Oxford University Press, 1974), and especially the article by Gorn cited in note 84.

91. This phrase (taken from Thomas C. Hubka, "Farm Family Mutuality: The Mid-Nineteenth-Century Maine Farm Neighborhood," in *The Farm,* ed. Peter Benes [Boston: Boston University Press, 1988], 13) was quoted by Naomi E. S. Griffiths (*Contexts of Acadian History* [Montreal: McGill-Queen's University Press, 1992], 57) to characterize what she saw as the profoundly cooperative ethos in traditional Acadian society.

92. Michael Zuckerman (*Peaceable Kingdoms: New England Towns in the Eighteenth Century* [New York: Knopf, 1970]) has analyzed the pacific quality of New England towns

after communal agriculture had been abandoned in that region; see especially chap. 2. Zuckerman suggests one reason for this was that "the very demography of the country predisposed its inhabitants toward peace, for men who live at such close quarters must 'get along'" (48). If purely physical circumstances of life have some relationship to a societal ethos of "getting along," Zuckerman's demographic explanation for the peaceful nature of colonial communities seems less persuasive than the more comprehensive structure of village life *and* communal agriculture explored in this study. Crowded living conditions, for example, have certainly not lowered the level of violence in our inner cities.

93. Thomas Jefferson, "Notes of a Tour into the Southern Parts of France, &c.," in *The Papers of Thomas Jefferson,* 11:415. Jefferson arrived in France in July 1784, replaced Benjamin Franklin as U.S. minister plenipotentiary in May 1785, and left for the United States in October 1789. His extended excursion through southern France and northern Italy in 1787 was not an official trip.

APPENDIX: GRISTMILLS AND RIVER VESSELS

1. Steven L. Kaplan, *Provisioning Paris: Merchants and Millers in the Grain and Flour Trade during the Eighteenth Century* (Ithaca, N.Y.: Cornell University Press, 1984), 221.

2. John Reynolds (*The Pioneer History of Illinois* [Chicago: Fergus, 1887], 176) described a hand mill used by the French whose stones were smaller than those used on horse mills and that was "propelled by man or woman power."

3. André Pénicaut, "Relation," in *Découvertes et Établissements des français dan le sud de l'Amérique Septentrionale (1614–1754),* vols., ed. Pierre Margry (Paris: Maisonneuve frères et Charles Leclerc, 1887; repr., New York: AMS, 1974), 5:490.

4. Diron d'Artaguiette, "Journal," in *Travels in the American Colonies,* ed. Newton D. Mereness (New York: Macmillan, 1916), 68.

5. John Reynolds claimed that "Jesuit missionaries were mostly responsible in procuring the erection of mills" (*Pioneer History,* 49).

6. Allan Greer, *Peasant, Lord, and Merchant* (Toronto: University of Toronto Press, 1985), 129–32; Richard C. Harris, *Seigneurial System in Early Canada, A Geographical Study* (Madison: University of Wisconsin Press, 1966), 72.

7. Ser. G1, 464, ANC.

8. Although there was some experimenting with horse mills in eighteenth-century France, horse-driven mills seem to have been little used. For a discussion of this issue, see Kaplan, *Provisioning Paris,* 240–42. Interestingly, Kaplan views horse mills as an alternative to water mills in France, whereas in the the Illinois Country it was just the opposite—water mills were the alternative to horse mills, which remained the principal mechanism for producing flour.

9. Lynn T. White, *Medieval Technology and Social Change* (New York: Oxford University Press, 1964), 80.

10. See, for examples, KM 27:9:30:1; 28:[?]:25:2; 31:8:23:1; 35:7:27:1.

11. KM 28:[?]:25:2.

12. Macarty to minister, May 20, 1753, ser. C13A, 37:190, ANC.

13. Public Sales, no. 108, Dec. 28, 1777, SGA.

14. Ekberg, *Colonial Ste. Genevieve,* 142–43.

15. Nicolas de Finiels, *An Account of Upper Louisiana,* ed. and trans. Carl J. Ekberg and William E. Foley (Columbia: University of Missouri Press, 1989), 56.

16. Charles E. Peterson (*Colonial St. Louis: Building a Creole Capital* [Tucson: Patrice, 1993], 33–34) provides some interesting details regarding horse mills in colonial St. Louis.

17. Map drawn by Frederic L. Billon and bound at the back of typescript of "Hunt's Minutes," MHS.

18. Arthur G. Draper, "Farming on the Missouri Frontier: Essays by Philander Draper," *Missouri Historical Review* 87 (Oct. 1992): 23.

19. White, *Medieval Technology,* 85–87.

20. D'Artaguiette, "Journal," 67.

21. KM 30:8:9:2.

22. This valuable map has been reproduced numerous times in various publications. The original print is in Thomas Hutchins, *A Topographical Description of Virginia, Pennsylvania, Maryland, and North Carolina,* ed. Frederick C. Hicks (Cleveland: Arthur H. Clark, 1904), facing p. 41.

23. Philip Pittman, *The Present State of the European Settlements on the Mississippi* (London, 1770; facsimile repr., ed. Robert Rea, Gainesville: University of Florida Press, 1973), 42.

24. *VOC,* K-225, 622–23.

25. Finiels, *Account,* 75.

26. Gratiot's deposition in "Hunt's Minutes," 1:199, MHS.

27. Peterson, *Colonial St. Louis,* 35; James B. Musick, *St. Louis as a Fortified Town* (St. Louis: R. F. Miller, 1941), 102.

28. Letter published in McDermott, *Old Cahokia,* 75–78.

29. White, *Medieval Technology,* 82.

30. Pittman, *European Settlements,* 48.

31. Donald Zochert, "Illinois Water Mills, 1790–1818," *Journal of the Illinois State Historical Society* 65 (Summer 1972): 185–86.

32. KM 37:5:23:1.

33. KM 37:7:11:1.

34. See GLO plat in *ASP, PL,* 2: following 182.

35. KM 37:9:15:1.

36. Vaudreuil to Macarty, Aug. 8, 1751, in Theodore C. Pease and Ernestine Jenison, eds., *Illinois on the Eve of the Seven Years' War,* Collections of the Illinois State Historical Library, vol. 29 (Springfield: Illinois State Historical Library, 1940), 306.

37. Pittman, *European Settlements,* 42.

38. *KR,* 417 n. 34.

39. Pittman, *European Settlements,* 85.

40. Reynolds, *Pioneer History,* 60.

41. See plat in *ASP, PL,* 2: following 182.

42. Zochert, "Water Mills," 187.

43. Reynolds, "Agricultural Resources," 152.

44. *NR,* 469.

45. Ibid., 470.

46. John D. Barnhart, ed., *Henry Hamilton and George Rogers Clark in the American Revolution* (Crawfordsville, Ind.: R. E. Banta, 1951), 161.

47. Cereal-grain production was never as large at Vincennes as at Kaskaskia (the 1767 British census discussed in chapter 5 indicated that Kaskaskia's was four times larger), but doubtless it was sometimes large enough to support agricultural commerce down the Wabash, Ohio, and Mississippi Rivers to New Orleans. In 1765 Captain Thomas Stirling remarked that Vincennes had the "most excellent soil and produces very good wheat and other grain, . . . The Capt of Militia [probably Drouet de Richardville] at this post has often had in his barns above a hundred-thousand livres of wheat" ("Stirling's Journal," in *Broadswords and Bayonets,* ed. Robert G. Carron [N.p.: Society of Colonial Wars in the State of Illinois, 1984], 68). No documentation exists, however, with which to compile any reliable data regarding flour shipments out of Vincennes during the colonial era. If during the French regime bateaux carried produce from Vincennes downriver, French officials in New Orleans did not differentiate these boats from the general mass of vessels that made up the Illinois Country convoys. The first solid documentation regarding agricultural commerce on the Wabash River seems to date from the 1820s (John G. Clark, *The Grain Trade in the Old Northwest* [Urbana: University of Illinois Press, 1966], 25).

48. Pittman, *European Settlements,* 50.

49. Ekberg, *Colonial Ste. Genevieve,* 143.

50. People of Ste. Genevieve to lieutenant governor De Leyba, Mar. 28, 1779, *SMV,* pt. 2, 1:335–36.

51. Trudeau to Carondelet, May 27, 1794, in Abraham P. Nasatir, ed., *Before Lewis and Clark,* 2 vols. (St. Louis: St. Louis Historical Documents Foundation, 1952), 1:214–15.

52. Frederic L. Billon, ed., *Annals of St. Louis in Its Early Days under the French and Spanish Dominations, 1776–1804* (St. Louis: F. L. Billon, 1886), 144.

53. This tract of real estate is still discernible in the street pattern of modern St. Louis, being circumscribed by Market, Jefferson, Branch, and Broadway; see chapter 2 on the physical layout of colonial St. Louis.

54. See especially the plan often attributed to General Victor Collot but probably drawn by Charles Warin, Collot's aide-de-camp, in 1795.

55. Finiels, *Account,* 59.

56. Trudeau to Carondelet, May 27, 1794, in Nasatir, *Before Lewis and Clark,* 1:215.

57. Trudeau to Governor General Carondelet, Nov. 14, 1795, PC, legajo 211, AGI.

58. White, *Medieval Technology,* 80–81. In his lengthy discussion of eighteenth-century mills in France, Kaplan (*Provisioning Paris,* 221–44) makes no mention of horizontally placed water wheels.

59. There is an ancient and primitive limestone buhrstone in the museum at Fort de Chartres State Historic Site outside Prairie du Rocher.

60. Kaplan, *Provisioning Paris,* 221–44.

61. An early granite millstone may be seen behind the Pierre Menard State Historic Site near Chester, Ill., but it is composed of one solid piece of stone.

62. See Manuel Gayoso de Lemos's report on his trip to Illinois, published in Abraham P. Nasatir, ed., *Spanish War Vessels on the Mississippi, 1792* (New Haven, Conn.: Yale University Press, 1968), 340.

63. For a biographical sketch of Tardiveau, see ibid., 40 n. 44.

64. *SRM*, 1:373.

65. Pierre-Charles Delassus de Luzières, "Observations sur le caractère, qualités, et professions des habitans blancs du District de la Nouvelle Bourbon," attached to the New Bourbon census of 1797, PC, legajo 2365, AGI.

66. *SRM*, 1:400.

67. Manuel Lisa, et al., to Salcedo, June 4, 1802, in Nasatir, ed., *Before Lewis and Clark*, 2:677–80.

68. See ibid, 688 n. 6.

69. Reynolds, *Pioneer History*, 315; see also Zochert, "Water Mills."

70. Nancy M. M. Surrey, *The Commerce of Louisiana during the French Regime, 1699–1763* (New York: Columbia University Press, 1916), 55–69. This volume remains the only full-scale study of this much neglected subject.

71. Indeed, bark canoes were only rarely used on the Missouri River. See Finiels (*Account*, 100) for a rare mention of these craft on the Missouri.

72. A detailed technical study of birchbark canoes is Edwin Tappan Adney and Howard I. Chapelle, *The Bark Canoes and Skin Boats of North America* (Washington, D.C.: Smithsonian Institution, 1964); see especially chap. 3.

73. "Morgan's Journal," in *NR*, 440.

74. Norman Walker, "Commerce of the Mississippi River from Memphis to the Gulf of Mexico," pt. 3 (136–389) of "The Commerce of the Mississippi and Ohio Rivers," in *The Executive Documents of the House of Representatives for the First Session of the Fiftieth Congress* (Washington, D.C.: U.S. Government Printing Office, 1889), 179. Walker's essay made up one section of a larger study, "Internal Commerce of the United States," that was commissioned by the U.S. House of Representatives in 1887.

75. Surrey, *Commerce of Louisiana*, 58. Surrey, however, vastly exaggerated the capacity of pirogues when she observed that they could carry up to "forty-five or fifty tons" (57).

76. Claude C. Robin, *Voyages dans l'intérieur de la Louisiane, de la Floride occidentale, et dans les isles de la Martinique et de Saint-Domingue . . .*, 3 vols. (Paris: F. Buisson, 1807), 2:208.

77. *VOC*, K-392, 872–73.

78. KM 26:8:12:1. Translation in *VOC*, K-410, 890, where *liar* (i.e., *liard*, cottonwood) is incorrectly translated as "black poplar wood."

79. "Records of the Superior Council," *Louisiana Historical Quarterly* 8 (Apr. 1925), 271.

80. *VOC*, K-360, 824.

81. KM 46:11:22:1.

82. Vaudreuil and Michel to Minister Rouillé, May 19, 1751, ser. C13A, 35:11, ANC.

83. Walker, "Commerce of the Mississippi," 179.

84. Adney and Chapelle claim that the French bateaux of the Great Lakes region were "sharp at both ends" (*Bark Canoes and Skin Boats,* 13). If this was indeed true, then it is apparent that the bateaux of Canada and those of Louisiana were vessels with very different configurations and that in eighteenth-century parlance, *bateau* was generic rather than specific in meaning.

85. Walker, "Commerce of the Mississippi," 59–60.

86. Ibid., 67.

87. See Commissaire-ordonnateur Salmon's dispatches to the minister, ser. C13A, 22:18–20, 176–79, ANC.

88. KM 37:12:16:1.

89. He was perhaps some kin to Jean-Baptiste Benoist de St. Claire, who served as interim commandant at Fort de Chartres on two occasions, 1740–42 and 1749–51 (see Pease and Jenison, *Illinois on the Eve of the Seven Years' War,* xxxviii n. 2).

90. Abstract of letter from Bienville to minister, Apr. 26, 1738, ser. C13A, 23:52, ANC.

91. KM 38:5:24:1. Original ms. in Chicago Historical Society.

92. KM 56:10:8:1.

93. Dumas to Macarty, Nov. 10, 1755, ser. C13A, 39:172–73, ANC.

94. *CP,* 531.

95. Ibid., 252–53.

96. See boat-building contracts in *NR,* 218–19, 328–29.

97. Ibid., 476–77.

98. Ibid., 476, 480.

99. Ibid., 383–85.

100. Concerning the business partnership of Winston and Kennedy, see *CR,* xxviii, lxxxv–lxxxvi.

101. KM 75:2:16:1.

102. KM 82:1:25:1.

103. Walker, "Commerce of the Mississippi," 184.

104. Bienville and Salmon to minister, May 11, 1737, ser. C13A, 22:18, ANC.

105. Walker, "Commerce of the Mississippi," 185.

106. Trudeau to Governor Carondelet, Nov. 14, 1795, PC, legajo 211, AGI.

107. De Luzières, "Observations," PC, legajo 2365, AGI.

108. Letter of Josef de la Peña, June 1, 1781, PC, legajo 13, AGI.

109. François Perrin du Lac, *Voyage dans les deux Louisianes et chez les nations sauvages dur Missouri* (Paris: Capelle and Renand, 1805), 166.

110. See Loyola to Ulloa, Dec. 17, 1766, PC, legajo 109, AGI.

111. Concerning endemic malaria in the Illinois Country, see Ekberg, *Colonial Ste. Genevieve,* 250–58.

112. KM 75:2:16:1.

113. Vaudreuil to minister, May 19, 1751, ser. C13A, 35:10, ANC.

114. See Surrey, *Commerce of Louisiana,* 74–75.

115. See "Records of the Superior Council," *Louisiana Historical Quarterly* 8 (July 1925): 490–91.

116. Ibid., 7 (July 1924): 520–21.

117. See, for example, KM 40:4:10:1. In this particular instance, the wages of the engagé, who was Jérôme *dit* Breton, were 225 livres, of which 150 were to be paid on arrival in New Orleans and 75 on the return to Kaskaskia. The employer was Jean-Baptiste Chauvin *dit* Charleville.

118. Militia roster for 1779, PC, legajo 213, AGI.

119. See Carpentier's letter of July 25, 1768, in PC, legajo 188-A, AGI.

120. *NR,* 384, 386, 447, 477, 584.

Index

CARL J. EKBERG is a professor of history at Illinois State University. His areas of special interest are Bourbon France and the colonial Mississippi River valley. His extensive publications include the award-winning book *Colonial Ste. Genevieve* and a translation of Nicolas de Finiels's *Account of Upper Louisiana.* He is working on a study of Indian slavery in the Illinois Country.